DIVA

To the illumined spirits of Hamet, the Priest and
Ingrid Lind, Lady Fraser

"Kein Musik is ya nicht auf Erden
die unsrer verglichen kan werden."

Des Knaben Wunderhorn

By the same author:

MAESTRO: Encounters with Conductors of Today (1982)
BRAVO: Today's Tenors, Baritones and Basses discuss their Roles (1986)

DIVA

Great Sopranos and Mezzos
Discuss their Art

Helena Matheopoulos

Northeastern Universtity Press

BOSTON

Northeastern University Press

Copyright 1991 by Helena Matheopoulos

First published in Great Britain in 1991 by
Victor Gollancz, Ltd., London.

First published in the United States of America in 1992 by
Northeastern University Press, by arrangement with Victor Gollancz, Ltd.

Library of Congress Cataloging-in-Publication Data

Matheopoulos, Helena.
Diva: great sopranos and mezzos discuss their art / Helena Matheopoulos.
p.   cm.
Includes index.
ISBN 1-55553-132-6 (alk. paper)
1. Women singers—Interviews.   2. Opera.   I. Title.
ML400.M359   1992
782.1'092'2—dc20
[B]   92-6653

MANUFACTURED IN GREAT BRITAIN

Music advisor to Northeastern University Press
GUNTHER SCHULLER

CONTENTS

ACKNOWLEDGEMENTS

First and foremost I should like to thank Livia Gollancz for her faith in the book, and Richard Wigmore for his stimulating and committed support.

Second, my friends Richard Byron, Sarah Granito di Belmonte, Alexandra Eversole, Oliver Gilmour, Willie Hancock, Peter Katona, Sir Emmanuel Kaye, Victor Sebek, Augustin von Paege, Sir Trevor Holdsworth, Count Spiro Flambouriari, James D'Albiac, Augustin Blanco, Lady Russell, Harriet Crawley, Giorgio del Fabbro, Docy Parigoris, Wilfred Davies, my cousin Nicky Broudo, and Daphne Voelin, for their vital support during those months of hard writing.

I would also like to thank the following:
Peter Adam; Peter Alward; Miss Isabel Caballé; John Davern; Colin Deane; Hugh von Dusen; Caroline Woodfield and Penelope Marland at John Coast Agency, for constant and extra-special help; Eve Edwards; Piero Faggioni; Carol Felton, formerly Press Officer, Philips Classics; Johanna Fiedler, formerly Press Officer, the Metropolitan Opera; Ubaldo Gardini; Susan Gould; Tom Graham of Harrison Parrot; Patricia Greenan; Jane Livingstone, Press Officer, English National Opera; Sir Peter Hall; Ron Hall; Frau Dina Hausjell, the Salzburg Festival Press Office; Dr Germinal Hilbert; Basil Horsefield; John Hunt, who helped steer so much helpful material my way.

Peter Jonas, Managing Director, English National Opera; Trevor Jones, House Manager, the Royal Opera House, Covent Garden; Tony Kaye; Dr Eddie Khambatta; Lothar Knessl, the Press Office of the Vienna State Opera; Mary Jo Little, Classic A & R Deutsche Grammophon; Sir Charles Mackerras; Leone Magiera; Yehuda Shapiro, International Press Officer, EMI International; Elijah Moshinsky; the Press Office of the Bavarian State Opera; Robert Rattray of Lies Askonas Ltd; Janine Reiss; Vera Rosza; John Schlesinger; Hilary Sheard of PolyGram.

Alan Sievewright, of whose knowledge and understanding of the voice I was the constant beneficiary; Nicholas Snowman, Artistic Administrator, the South Bank; Sir John Tooley, formerly General Director, the

Royal Opera House, Covent Garden, for being so generous with his time and thoughts over the past three years; Gloria Villardell; Edgar Vincent and Cynthia Robbins and Joe Reece of Edgar Vincent Associates, New York City; Nina Walker; Catherine Waltrafen, Press Officer, Paris Opéra; Dr Hans Widrich, Press Officer, the Salzburg Festival; Katharine Wilkinson, the late Opera Press Officer at Covent Garden whose friendship and support I will always miss greatly, Jackie Watson, Helen Anderson and Kate Hardy, Opera Press Officers, the Royal Opera House, Covent Garden; Serena Woolf, formerly Classical Press Officer, Decca Records and now with Nimbus Records.

Once again my thanks go to Herbert von Karajan and James Levine whose inspired remarks about the voice, singing, the present and future of opera in my previous book *Maestro: Encounters with Conductors of Today* I have made extensive use of in appropriate places.

FOREWORD

THIS BOOK WAS conceived as a companion to *BRAVO*, in which the major male opera singers of today discussed their repertoire and the art of singing. The aim of both books is essentially the same: asking the artists involved to analyse, both vocally and dramatically, some of the roles for which they are best known, trace their vocal development, comment on various aspects of operatic life and, where applicable, offer useful advice to young singers. Yet *DIVA* differs from *BRAVO* in one significant way: female singers attach far greater importance to their personal lives. Unlike their male counterparts, all artists in this book spontaneously brought up this factor, and consider personal stability and contentment to be a major contributing factor to the fulfilment of their artistic potential.

A book of this kind is not the place to delve into the psychological implications of such an attitude. What is certain, though, is that the peripatetic existence – from capital to festival and from hotel room to hotel room – is particularly lonely and depressing for female singers. As Josephine Barstow put it, 'I pity the single girls in this business.' Very few artists indeed – and they tend to be extremely powerful, confident personalities – have managed to reach the top without the presence and constant support of a partner.

The role of that often maligned breed – the diva-husband – should therefore not be underestimated. On the whole, he tends to emerge as committed, efficient in taking the tiresome, niggardly chores of everyday life off the diva's shoulders, and usually self-effacing. The ideal specimen manages to be all that without interfering in artistic decisions or assuming the role of manager for which he is seldom equipped. It's a lot to ask of a man. Yet most of the divas in this book seem to have found it in their second, if not their first, husbands. I suspect these gentlemen are the unsung heroes of this book.

As the chapters were written to be read individually as well as consecutively, some general points about operatic life today or the stylistic demands of specific composers may recur from time to time. The choice of artists is personal, though most of the artists included are obvious choices because of the distinction and importance of their careers. Notable omissions are: Marilyn Horne, who has written her own book and felt she has said all there is to say in that; Jessye Norman, who is writing her autobiography at present; and Margaret Price and Maria Ewing, neither of whom wished to be included. Shirley Verrett and Kathleen Battle are omitted because, despite several attempts, it proved impossible to arrange an appointment. Restrictions of space alone have prevented the inclusion of some first-class younger artists, such as Carol Vaness, Ann Sofie von Otter and Karita Mattila, who have emerged to full prominence in the past three years, after the space in the book was allocated.

Several other singers who have reached prominence in the last few years, such as Marie MacLaughlin and, more recently, Cecilia Bartoli, have also been omitted. The operatic profession is one in which it is all too easy to make hasty judgements. And only time will tell whether these singers have the staying power of the very finest.

GLOSSARY

appoggiatura: a term derived from the Italian verb 'appoggiare' (to lean or support). A grace note inserted before a note but to be sung equal length, to support or emphasize a melodic or harmonic progression

bel canto: literally 'beautiful singing'. A term associated with singing in the eighteenth and early nineteenth centuries when a beautiful vocal performance was more important than the dramatic. *Bel canto* composers most often referred to in this book include Bellini, Donizetti and Rossini

cabaletta: in nineteenth-century opera, the fast concluding section of an aria or ensemble. In the early part of that century, a separate aria in lively tempo

cantabile: literally 'songful' – denotes *legato*, expressive singing

da capo: return to the beginning

a cappella: unaccompanied singing

cavatina: technically a short aria but now used to describe widely differing types of song and therefore virtually meaningless

coloratura: elaborately embellished singing. The term later came to apply to singers specializing in roles needing great vocal agility

'covering' a note: singing it with a 'closed' throat, i.e., allowing the larynx to float downwards rather than upwards

fioritura: florid vocal embellishment

legato: from the Italian verb 'legare', meaning to bind or tie. Refers to the smooth passage from one note to another, as opposed to *staccato*

lirico-spinto: from the Italian verb 'spingere', meaning to push. Identifies a lyric voice leaning towards the dramatic

messa di voce: a crescendo and diminuendo on a phrase or note

mezza voce: literally 'half voice'. Denotes singing softly, but not as softly as piano. A special way of singing as if under the breath, referring not only to the amount of volume but to a different quality from that when singing full voice

passaggio: the notes E, F and G which lie between the head and the chest registers

piano: term applying to volume meaning soft; also

  pianissimo: very soft

  forte: loud

  fortissimo: very loud

portamento: from the Italian verb 'portare', meaning to carry. A practice by which singers slide from one note to another without a break

recitative: declamatory passages imitating speech which precede arias, duets and ensembles. Particularly common in eighteenth-century opera

register: a term used to denote a certain area or vocal range – 'chest', 'middle', 'head'

rubato: literally 'stolen time'. A way of performing without adhering strictly to musical time

solfège: an elementary method of teaching sight reading and ear training whereby the names of the notes (*do, re, mi* . . .) are pronounced while the notes are sung unaccompanied. The intervals have to be learned by ear. A common teaching method in France and Italy, known in English as 'tonic sol-fa'

tessitura: literally 'texture'. A term used to designate the average pitch of an aria or role. A part can be taxing despite the absence of especially high or low notes due to the prevailing range or *tessitura*

verismo: literally 'realism'. The opposite to *bel canto*, where drama is as important as beautiful singing. A term applied to the works of Italian composers after Verdi including Puccini, Mascagni, Leoncavallo, Zandonai and Giordano. Can also be used as an adjective, *veristic*, meaning realistic and applied to the way in which the works of these composers are sung – i.e. more freely and less precisely than those of composers such as Mozart

vocalize: exercise the voice. Can be a specifically composed wordless song or exercise

INTRODUCTION: OPERA TODAY

This section is reproduced, with modifications, from BRAVO.

Not since the days of Verdi, when it was the genuine, living theatre of the time, has opera been as popular as it is today. Opera houses are proliferating, new festivals – like Buxton, Santa Fe, Hohenems, Pesaro and Macerata, to name but a few – are springing up regularly in both Europe and America and recent years have seen an explosion of public interest in all things operatic. Films of opera, like Losey's *Don Giovanni*, Zeffirelli's *La traviata* and Rosi's *Carmen* have enjoyed, and some are still enjoying, long, profitable runs in the cinemas of most major cities. Sales of operatic recordings and videos are booming and opera is receiving considerable exposure on television, in the form of live transmissions, studio films and masterclasses conducted by famous singers. In the opera house itself, audiences are getting younger and include significant numbers of 'first timers'.

Several factors are responsible for this massive public interest: nostalgia for an art form now essentially dead – for few new operas have joined the general repertoire since the war; modern marketing techniques; and the efforts of megastars like Luciano Pavarotti and Placido Domingo to break away from the confines of the established operatic public through recitals and performances in venues like parks and stadiums with a 20,000–50,000 capacity. The result has been that millions of people whose geographical or other circumstances might preclude a visit to the theatre are now eager to experience the uniqueness, excitement and magic of opera. As Peter Jonas, Managing Director of English National Opera, points out, 'it is rare nowadays to encounter anyone who does not know what opera is, whereas twenty years ago it was perfectly possible to find people, both in Britain and America, who had never even heard of opera'.

But the main reason for today's operatic boom is the improved quality of the product itself. Opera would never have survived, let alone thrived, in this age of essentially cinematic criteria of dramatic credibility had it not undergone a thorough transformation in the fifties and early sixties: the Callas/Visconti/Wieland Wagner revolution that dispelled the notion that opera is 'just singing' in costume and against some crude naturalistic backdrop, turned it into believable theatre and invested it with the musical-dramatic unity essential to it as an art form. Maria Callas achieved this through performances of maximum dramatic intensity in which she experienced the characters body and soul, always using the music, the score, as her guide and inspiration; Luchino Visconti through the then unprecedented realism of his productions; and Wieland Wagner, the great composer's grandson, by 'smashing all the bombastic symbolisms and conventions of the nineteenth century at a stroke', in the words of Rolf Liebermann, former Intendant of the Hamburg State Opera and the Paris Opéra, and setting the works free to speak to our time – first, as usual, to scandalized derision and eventually to eulogies.

This is necessarily an over-simplification, because tomes could be written about this revolution and its perpetrators and also because, decades before Callas, opera had its first great singing-actor in the person of Feodor Chaliapin (1873–1938), the Russian bass whose performances apparently displayed the same dramatic credibility and searing intensity. But he was a solitary beacon of light in a dramatically primitive operatic age when audiences consisted mostly of canary-fanciers. (They're still around – mercifully on the decline!) What enabled the Callas/Visconti/ Wieland Wagner revolution to have such a profound and lasting impact on the development of opera was the fact that it happened simultaneously and at a time when other great artists were also thinking alike. These three geniuses were pivotal points in a wider movement that also included producers as inspired and influential as Günther Rennert and Walter Felsenstein and singing-actors of the calibre of Tito Gobbi, Hans Hotter and Boris Christoff, to name but a few, all of whom played a crucial role in spreading the new image of opera to all corners of the musical world.

The time was ripe. As Rolf Liebermann rightly points out, the German opera houses had been destroyed by bombing, their sets and costumes had been burnt and their audiences, stunned by their recent experiences, sat, wrapped up in mufflers, in draughty, unheated theatres. The collective unconscious was therefore more than receptive to the stark realism of the new productions and to the probing, psychological approach of the new producers. They and their much-maligned successors, the producers of today, have changed Everyman's concept of what opera is about. 'The great thing about a work of art is that it transcends its time and its fashion and speaks down the ages,' says Michael Geliot in *Opera*. 'Do we want Shakespeare to be performed in replica Globe theatres and spoken in the accents of the time? Do we want

Verdi to be fossilized in the nineteenth century, because we have among us critics who can research the "authentic" presentation styles? Do we want Mozart musicologically decorated according to prevailing eighteenth-century whim?'

I don't think so. We have reached a point where most of us would agree with Elijah Moshinsky's premise that 'the performance of opera must be drawn from some essential dramatic thread inside it. In order to make the work live for the audience, for the artists, for oneself, one must feel free to interpret: otherwise one would end up a dead repetition of tradition. When one looks at the D'Oyly Carte Company or the Berliner Ensemble, one sees the dangers. So, I resist the current tidal wave saying you merely have to reproduce the composer's instructions. That's not the point. What you have to do is to perform the opera! You can easily perform the instructions and miss the opera altogether. I derive great inspiration from a letter of Wieland Wagner's, where he wrote that, living in the age of Picasso and Matisse, he didn't feel compelled to adhere to the visual taste of his grandfather!'

Yet some, including Sir Peter Hall, then Director of the National Theatre and Artistic Director of Glyndebourne Festival Opera, feel there is a reverse side of the coin and that the giant dramatic strides opera has made in our day have resulted in too much dominance on the part of producers who often take unwarranted liberties and do not always express or follow the music closely enough: 'I am a militant classicist. I believe we have to journey to the words through the music and that the job of the producer and of the conductor is to try to reveal the piece to the audience. I don't think it's their job to publicize their own personal fantasies, induced in them by the music. There's a lot of that about and I don't like it. It doesn't hurt me but it bores and sometimes amuses me, because it's much easier to set opera in some jazzy new period and make it have some kind of historical resonance that never crossed the composer's or the librettist's mind, than it is to realize the piece. So, in this sense, the excessive dominance of the producer has resulted in a certain loss.' Since Sir Peter Hall spoke these words, in 1986, there have been signs of public fatigue with 'director gimmicks' and the tendency of many to resort to novelty for novelty's sake. The need is felt more and more for 'honest' productions which do not interfere with the works but do invest them with the insights of today.

Most of the singers in this book echo Sir Peter Hall's misgivings, although not always out of the purest motives. They tend to refer to our age as 'the scourge of the producer', to which phenomenon – along with the disappearance of the old-fashioned type of vastly experienced operatic conductors, like Tullio Serafin, Vittorio Gui and Antonino

Votto, who knew opera, understood the voice and had the patience, foresight and will to act as glorified coaches, nurture young singers and guide their vocal development to fruition – they attribute some of the responsibilty for the sad vocal decline that has accompanied, in inverse proportion, the dramatic advances made by opera in our time. The claim is unjustified. For although producers *are* sometimes guilty of violating the spirit of the works they interpret, they are certainly not guilty of causing the vocal decline we are witnessing. The only legitimate *vocal* complaint singers can hurl at producers is their suggestion that singers sometimes adopt positions not conducive to the best singing they're capable of. But this is a detail that can be, and usually is, resolved at rehearsals. 'What singers are *really* bitching about is the producers' preference for working with artists who do not just sing well, but also act well and look good,' says Peter Jonas.

'I think it is probably true that we live in the age of the producer, but I do not think it is necessarily a scourge,' he continues. 'It all depends very much on whether we are talking about opera as a whole. It goes back to what one really believes opera is. If you believe opera is theatre, if you believe the English National, or the Vienna State or the Metropolitan Opera is a theatre, a theatrical institution, then production is of paramount importance. To make the conductor God in opera is actually false from the musical-dramatic point of view and I think the composers would agree.* The composers – Mozart, Verdi and Puccini – were practical men of the theatre and quite commercially minded. Rather like the Jerome Kernses of their day, they were concerned with putting on a good show which people would want to go and see and which would make money. In fact the closest equivalent to the great composers of the past are not, I regret to say, the modern operatic composers but people like Stephen Sondheim and others writing new musical theatre. I think it's important for opera to have good conductors, great conductors, the best one can get. But if one is going to put on opera with any sense of honesty about what it is about – and not just mount a concert performance in costume – then obviously the producer of "the show" must be the most important person.'

Before going on to discuss the vocal decline plaguing opera today, it is worth dwelling for a moment on an important point brought up by Peter Jonas; the alienation of today's operatic composers from the mainstream of contemporary operatic life – a phenomenon unique in the history of

---

*Verdi certainly did, and in a letter dated 18 March 1899, shortly after the première of *Falstaff*, complained that 'When I began to shock the music world with my sins, there was the calamity of the primadonna. Now there is the tyranny of the conductor! Bad, bad, still less bad the former!' Plus ça change . . .

music theatre. The German tenor René Kollo is also deeply concerned about this dangerous trend and fears it may condemn opera to a slow death by atrophy. 'With very few exceptions, like Britten's *Peter Grimes* which is not all that recent, nobody is writing "real operas" any more, and especially not real *singers'* operas,' he laments. 'If this situation continues, combined with the rapid disappearance of sufficient great voices, it will result in the death of opera as an art form.'

Sir Peter Hall agrees, but is more optimistic about the eventual outcome: 'When you think of opera a hundred years ago, there was Wagner and there was Verdi, both of whom were absolutely modern and popular. Between the wars, there were Richard Strauss and Alban Berg. Since the war, few modern operas have really entered the repertoire. But I believe this will change. I think it should be possible to write modern operas about life as it is lived now. And when you consider the popularity of a great deal of music, I feel sure a way will be found to bring the two together. Of course, the real, basic problem is not so much to do with opera as with the crisis in modern music. In the past thirty to forty years most composers, when they sit down to write, almost re-invent music and the gulf between them and the public is enormous and unique. I am sure this cannot go on because no artist can exist without an audience.'

Personally, I feel convinced that some of the masterpieces among today's 'musicals' – like Bernstein's *West Side Story* and Gershwin's *Porgy and Bess* – are indeed contemporary operas which, within the space of a decade or so, will join the standard operatic repertoire. The fact that both the Metropolitan Opera and Glyndebourne Festival Opera mounted ambitious full-scale productions of *Porgy and Bess* within the past few years and Deutsche Grammophon recorded *West Side Story* with the best of operatic casts – José Carreras, Kiri Te Kanawa and Tatiana Troyanos – is a step in the right direction, indicating that these great works are finally being recognized for what they are. I am convinced that the future of opera lies, as Peter Hall mentioned, in bridging the gap between it and the popular music theatre.

Far more dangerous for the future of opera is the serious vocal decline we have witnessed in the past twenty years, and the tragic shortage of sufficient singers for some sections of the repertoire: Verdi baritones, Verdi mezzos and Heldentenors in particular are in such short supply that one has to make do with substitutes (i.e. Donizetti baritones taking on Verdi roles and lyric tenors tackling the Wagnerian repertoire), while top-flight tenors are also hard to come by. Placido Domingo's cancellation of his operatic engagements for six months following the Mexican earthquake, for instance, played havoc with the plans of every major international opera house. While, twenty years ago, one could think of at least a dozen top tenors for the Italian repertoire alone, the number has now dwindled to half – and half of *that* meagre figure consists of veteran singers now in their late fifties or early sixties! As Peter Katona, Artistic Administrator of the Royal Opera, observes, 'the vocal decline and shortage of sufficient singers seems to get more acute with each half-generation', while James Levine, Music and Artistic Director of the Metropolitan Opera, recently complained to the *New York Times* that 'whereas in the fifties a good performance of Puccini's *Madama Butterfly* could be taken for granted, today it would be the exception rather than the rule'.

The reasons for the vocal decline we have experienced in recent years are manifold: too much singing, too much travelling, too little time devoted to vocal training and consolidation, a dearth of good teachers, the disappearance of the old breed of knowledgeable operatic conductors already mentioned, and the need for operatic managements and the industry to exploit emerging talents beyond their capacities by asking them to sing the wrong roles or even the right roles at the wrong time. In short, the plague besetting opera today and endangering the vocal longevity of both young and established singers is due both to musical and to economic factors.

'The market for everything is different and, in order to live, these people have to lead different lives, as we all do', says Peter Jonas. 'We are required to earn a large living and to keep up, to a certain extent, with certain "de rigueur" things, all of which demands a certain turnover, and the need to keep going. The advent of the jet plane, the ease of travel, the popularity of opera, modern marketing techniques, modern theatre-going habits, modern theatre-going appetites and the way opera is consumed, have all resulted in a new breed of opera singer.' The eminent French coach and accompanist Janine Reiss concurs and explains that we have, perhaps, come to expect too much from our opera singers. 'Instead of letting them concentrate on their vocal development and the need to sing as beautifully and as perfectly as possible, we also demand that their acting is of a standard comparable to that of the Comédie Française or the Royal Shakespeare Company, that their dancing matches that of the starlets of *A Chorus Line*, and that their looks compare with those of matinée idols in other branches of show business. It's a lot, you know!'

The result, as Peter Jonas points out, is that conservatoires are no longer necessarily producing the right kind of operatic material we need, but tend to dish out 'people who are better actors than singers'. As a veteran operatic conductor who would rather remain anonymous recently remarked, 'the operatic stage is getting full of stage-struck strumpets who would be just as happy lifting a leg in a West End musical!'

Clearly, there is an acute need for this to be counterbalanced by a sufficient number of well-trained voices and of artists serious and dedicated enough to devote adequate time to the arduous, continuous hard work it takes to become a really great opera singer. Thank goodness such artists do emerge (like excellently trained, vocally dazzling and hard-working soprano June Anderson) – but not in sufficient numbers to service the needs of the relentlessly expanding operatic world.

While there is no shortage of beautiful voices, every artist I talked to in this book stressed that the problem lies in the fact that most of them are prematurely ruined. As Carlo Bergonzi and Graziella Sciutti – who now gives master-classes all over the world – observe, there are and there will always be plenty of good voices. But, as Sciutti explains, 'the problem is that these young people, some of whom are also well-prepared musically (especially in the United States and in Britain), are quickly taken up by theatres, managements and the recording industry and pushed into rapid stardom before they really know what it's all about and before their vocal chords have had time to settle down. Because the voice is a physical thing, part of one's anatomy, and singing is a bit like a sport: the muscles in question must be allowed time to grow and become elastic and resilient. This is why, when a promising young singer is immediately asked to sing roles that are too big and too taxing for his or her age, although the voice *itself* can do it, i.e. can sing the notes, the body doesn't yet have the necessary resilience to sustain such an effort. The voice thus loses its "bloom" and can also be permanently damaged. The misuse of the available material lies at the heart of the vocal problem besetting opera today.' The well-known coach and accompanist Nina Walker never tires of stressing this point too; and Bernd Weikl and Kurt Moll refer to the same problem in their chapters in *BRAVO*.

Those responsible for casting could therefore do a great deal to remedy the situation; in fact, as Nina Walker points out, the success or otherwise of any given production is already decided by the judiciousness or otherwise of the casting director or committee. But their task is not as simple as it might seem to outsiders. For while most managements do have endless discussions about individual singers and, in the case of ensemble theatres like the English National or the Welsh National Opera, try to map out a future for their young artists that takes into account both the latter's vocal development and the needs of the theatre, it is sometimes impossible to satisfy both. 'There are instances when managements are so hard-pressed economically and have such difficulties in making ends meet, especially in Britain, that we sometimes end up using young people too ruthlessly,' says Peter Jonas. 'But this is nothing new. If one reads the memoirs of Giulio Gatti-Cazazza, who ran the Met

at the beginning of the century, one comes across many instances where
he admits to exploiting singers beyond what he knew to be their natural
capacities. Managements then were, if anything, even more ruthless and
commercial than now. Singers were always asked to sing the wrong roles.
We just hear of those who survived, and there are plenty surviving now.
The problem is that we tend to look back on the whole period of 1900–40
as a single generation which, of course, it was not. If we look back on the
period 1945–85 in the same way, we will find just as many great singers,
especially up to the early sixties, when the jet plane began to influence
things adversely.'

Those in charge of the big international houses also bear in mind the
acuteness of this problem for the future of opera. According to Sir John
Tooley, former General Director of the Royal Opera House, Covent
Garden, 'we think a lot about this and take a great deal of care in our
casting and we *do* have sensible regard for the artists' development and
possible damage to their voices. But of course, as far as repertoire is
concerned, the choice is ultimately theirs. There are singers who have a
very clear idea of what to sing and what not to sing and who are not afraid
of saying "no" to managements. But there are others who are less sure of
themselves and terrified because they are worried that if they refuse to
sing a specific role, they might not be asked to sing at this particular house
again – which is essentially untrue, if they are talented! So, the reasons for
the very real vocal decline we have experienced and are still experiencing
are not just due to the jet plane but lie much nearer home: the
succumbing to economic pressures. Very few singers can afford *not* to
sing a great deal.'

The rewards are certainly substantial: more than twenty thousand
Swiss francs a performance for the top-flight singers (and more in some
Continental opera houses), lucrative recording, film and video contracts,
recitals in mass venues for which the most popular opera stars may
receive fees as high as fifty thousand dollars or more. But all this should
be viewed against the precarious background of insecure, short-lived
careers during which opera singers must more or less make provision for
the rest of their lives. So the pressures are great indeed.

Yet, despite these pressures and the temptations they are continuously
exposed to, the most dedicated artists do find it in them to say 'no', 'even
to Karajan', according to soprano Ileana Cotrubas, and to adhere to a
repertoire suitable to their voices. Among the great singers of the past
generation, for instance, Elisabeth Schwarzkopf, for one, is known to
have eschewed the role of Violetta in *La traviata* after she heard Maria
Callas singing it, while Mirella Freni has preserved her voice into her late
fifties by meticulously choosing her repertoire.

This increased awareness on the part of singers is one of several encouraging signs that we may be on the way to stalling, if not eliminating, today's vocal decline. Another hopeful development is the desire of most of the singers in this book to spend their retirement years teaching and coaching. This should go a long way towards alleviating the shortage of good teachers that all young singers complain about.

The third promising factor is the determination of conductors in charge of operatic institutions, like James Levine – who, according to the testimony of singers as distinguished and experienced as Sherrill Milnes, is fast becoming as knowledgeable about the voice as the Serafins, Guis and Vottos of yesterday – to spend as much time as possible in their theatres and devote considerable personal effort to the discovery and development of young voices. Levine is exceptionally conscientious in this way and is largely responsible for the careers of Kathleen Battle, Maria Ewing, Neil Shicoff and Catherine Malfitano. If Riccardo Muti, Artistic Director of La Scala and a renowned expert on the voice, and Claudio Abbado, the Music Director of the Vienna State Opera, decide to do the same – and both seem inclined to do so – this will be a giant leap forward in the battle to arrest declining vocal standards and ensure a better future for opera. James Levine sums up the situation as follows: 'Originally, we had a period when vocal development triumphed, but opera was often dramatically ridiculous. This was followed by a time when there were great dramatic strides, but opera was vocally inadequate. Now, the pendulum has begun to swing somewhere in the middle and this balance is essential for the future of opera.'

SOPRANOS

JUNE ANDERSON

'SOMETIMES I WISH I could take my voice out of my body and put it in a box so that it could be independent of me,' sighed June Anderson, the leading dramatic coloratura soprano of her generation. 'I envy other musicians whose instruments are not inside or dependent on their bodies. We singers have to take constant care of ourselves and control our emotional state in case it affects The Voice. In a way, I'm lucky to be a Capricorn because there is a serenity inside that keeps things in some sort of balance even when I'm nervous.'

The strain of this uneasy cohabitation, this interdependence between the voice and the singer's body and psyche, is part of the heavy toll extracted by an exhilarating but nervewracking profession, one that demands a degree of dedication arguably unequalled by any other in the Arts. In some cases (as, for many years, in Anderson's,) this dedication may exclude the possibility of any personal life. 'Speaking for myself, I'd say this has been the greatest sacrifice. It has taken me until recently to decide there might be something in life other than singing. But in a way I'm glad because this single-mindedness made me work so hard at my singing that I have now got to a point where I'm technically very secure and the career is going well. So I can finally take the blinders off. I don't think I put them on consciously, but I'm taking them off consciously.'

With characteristic candour and self-knowledge, American-born Anderson points out that her impressive self-control has something to do with the accusation that her singing is often too emotionally detached. So this process of opening herself up to life in general can only make her singing better. 'At any other time I would have considered this sort of attitude a direct threat to my career. I thought I should mention this because it's a very important part of my artistic growth. Of course my voice will develop and become bigger, fuller and more mature. But I think the big change in me as an artist is going to be on the emotional level. And I can't *wait*! Having acquired a sturdy technique – I had to, to protect my throat which seems made of glass – what I'm striving for now is interpretation.'

At the time of our conversations June Anderson had just returned from the first holiday of her life. Somehow, she had never had the time or the inclination for a vacation before. But that summer – after a packed and immensely successful 1985–86 season that had begun with Desdemona in Rossini's *Otello* at the Teatro La Fenice in Venice and included her débuts at La Scala as Amina in *La sonnambula*, and Covent Garden in the title role in *Semiramide* as well as her return to the Paris Opéra as Marie in *La Fille du régiment* – she had been a 'nervous and emotional wreck' and, after two bouts of tonsillitis, physically at the end of her tether. So her doctor recommended a holiday, 'and to my amazement I discovered I *liked* taking a holiday. I stayed in a villa two hours south of Amalfi on the Neapolitan coast. I *loved* going to the beach – I hadn't been on one for a decade because of my self-consciousness about not having the figure of a Vogue model – I *loved* the water . . . And I'm also glad to have some time off this summer to do up my new flat in London. Generally I don't like sitting around. But I'm enjoying choosing fabrics and knickknacks even though I feel I'd rather be earning some money while I'm spending it.'

She thinks her exaggerated seriousness and inability to be lazy (she invariably has to force herself to stop practising) have something to do with attitudes instilled in her by her mother, who made her take up singing lessons at the age of twelve. Before that she'd made her take ballet lessons, acrobatics lessons and even baton-twirling lessons. 'I was out every night of the week to some class or other. I never played. I don't know why I didn't resist. I guess I was interested in learning things.' When the need for surgery to her leg meant she couldn't dance any more, her mother thought of singing lessons instead. At the time June Anderson didn't like opera at all and was so embarrassed about taking singing lessons that she didn't tell anyone.

Fortunately she took a liking to her teacher in New Haven, Connecticut, where her family had moved from her native Boston. They started off with Italian songs and the first arias she ever sang were Musetta's Waltz from *La Bohème*, Gilda's 'Caro nome' from *Rigoletto* and Juliette's aria from *Roméo et Juliette*. She was the one to instil in her a deep love of all things Italian and, as they graduated to more difficult parts like Lucia and Amina, for *bel canto* especially. At the time, her teacher organized for her to sing at weddings, ladies' clubs and so on and again, 'I didn't want to do it but I did it.' Yet she never wanted to pursue a career as a singer. When it was time for College everyone thought she would go to Music School. But she chose Yale instead and majored in French literature.

It was at Yale that she first began to think seriously about becoming a singer, partly at the instigation of a friend who urged her to try 'or you'll never forgive yourself when you're 40,' she recalls. 'So I decided to go to New York and thought that if in two years' time I was not famous I would go to Law School. Well, at the end of about nine months I was *not* famous, I'd run out of all my money and it was at that point that I decided I would be a singer if it *killed* me. I suppose it must have been the challenge because nothing was easy any more. As a youngster and teenager, studying privately, everything had been easy and I was always being told I was wonderful. All of a sudden, nobody thought I was wonderful any more. So I thought, 'Damn it, I'll show them; I'll prove to them that I am!'

Luckily lots of 'little jobs' – singing concerts and operas in places like Duluth, Syracuse, small towns in Iowa – came her way so she could support herself. After *many* auditions, she was accepted as a company member and made her début as the Queen of the Night in *Die Zauberflöte* at the New York City Opera in 1978. 'At the time I didn't realize how difficult it was because when one is young, one has no fear. When I sang it again, three years later, I realized and decided never to sing it again. Once fear sets in, you simply can't.' Her début was followed by roles like the Queen of Shemakha in *Le Coq d'or*, Gilda and the four heroines in *Les Contes d'Hoffmann*. But all those performances were the last two or three in a run because she was always understudying someone else. So no critics, agents or managers ever got to hear her.

She first caught major public attention with a single performance as Cleopatra in *Giulio Cesare*, 'a wonderful role with extraordinary music expressing so many different facets of her personality: playfulness, coquetry, sensuality, ambition, pain, and vocally perfect for me because it sits around the middle and goes up from there. Her aria, "Se pietà di me non senti" is one of my favourites in all my repertoire, and I enjoy singing Baroque music because it is the natural precursor of *bel canto*.' A reviewer happened to be present and the audience reaction was good. He wrote enthusiastically about her and from then on the management began to pay more attention to her. Still, when she sang Elvira in *I Puritani* in 1981, again it was as somebody else's understudy 'which frustrated me so much that I decided to do something about it. It turned out to be something crucial for my future. I auditioned for an Italian agent who sent a tape to Francesco Siciliani at La Scala and eventually got me to sing for him. He also got me contracts for the Teatro Communale in Florence where I made my début as Lucia in 1983, the Teatro Massimo di Palermo (Rosina in *Il barbiere di Siviglia*) and the Geneva Opera again as Lucia. Since then I have come to think of the fact that things had gone so slowly in New York as a blessing in disguise. But if we had met at that time instead of now, you would have found me very bitter and wondering why it was all happening to everyone else and not to me . . . But once I came to Europe, I was surprised at how quickly things took off. When you think about it, in 1982 I was still an understudy at the New York City Opera, and by 1985–6 I had contracts with the best opera houses in the world.'

The fact that Anderson was ready to rise to the challenges presented by her international débuts in *bel canto* roles – which demand greater vocal prowess than almost any other – was largely due to the superb technique she had acquired from her New York-based teacher, Robert Lennard, with whom she has been studying since 1974. 'I'm not one of those singers who went teacher-hopping. There has to be consistency and trust between your teacher and yourself. After all, your throat is at stake. I don't happen to trust easily, I'm like a cat. When I was first introduced to this teacher by a coach I knew, I was dismayed: he looked like a hippie, he wore an earring and was scruffy. So I was very huffy and thought "I don't want to work with this man!" But my friend insisted that I have at least a trial lesson. I did and after discovering he loved cats which, to me, is a great recommendation, I also found out that, by the end of the lesson, I was singing better. So I thought, okay I'll try this a bit longer. And very soon I knew I could trust this man. He knew what he was talking about. I don't know whether he would be equally great for someone else, because the teacher-singer relationship is so personal, but he certainly knows *my* throat.'

Basically Lennard teaches the Garcia technique, developed by the famous Spanish nineteenth-century tenor, Manuel Garcia – the father of Maria Malibran – and set down in a book by his son, Manuel Garcia Jr. It contains the basis of his technique and exercises both for breathing and evenness of tone. Anderson states that he has been her secret weapon over the years. 'Without him I couldn't sing without getting a sore throat. I wasn't breathing correctly, I was putting too much pressure on the jaw and the throat. The result was that after singing a couple of arias, my throat got sore. Now, although I don't talk correctly, I sing correctly. If I have to speak in an opera, it still doesn't feel right, unless I think about it and use supported breath. As I said before, I have a very delicate throat, a throat of glass, and if I push two or three notes I'm already feeling hoarse. I suppose this is a great checking system because it means I don't push.'

Anderson's technique is praised by everyone in the operatic profession. 'She is a highly intelligent woman and a very intelligent *singer* with a technique that defies description . . . absolutely reminiscent of Joan Sutherland but, in my opinion, more interesting. What surprises me, though, is that she doesn't have a *real* trill. When a trill is called for, it doesn't come out as a true, proper trill – but with her superb technique she manufactures one and one hardly notices,' says laryngologist and voice expert Dr Eddie Khambatta. Peter Katona, Artistic Administrator at Covent Garden, feels that what is most remarkable about Anderson is that 'she is at her best where other voices stop. She has more high notes than anyone can expect. I don't think the timbre itself or the middle voice are exceptional. But her top notes are perfection, wonderful. Like someone who can jump higher than anybody else, she has a record-breaking talent up there.'

Anderson herself stresses that she 'always had the top. But my voice has expanded and filled out a lot. During the first half of 1986, for instance, I discovered a bottom to it that didn't exist before, which was very exciting because I'm a frustrated mezzo. I would love to be a cello, to make that kind of sound. But I've always been very careful, because when sopranos start pushing with the chest, they begin to lose their top. So, I've been prudent, too prudent, perhaps, but that can't hurt. Finding my way around the bottom without hurting my top came very slowly to me. But this way, I feel it is making the top better. Discovering that something suddenly works now whereas before it didn't is an incredible satisfaction.'

Anderson had the same feeling about the title role in *Semiramide* when she sang it in 1986 in a concert performance for her Covent Garden début. When she first sang it in 1982 at the Rome Opera she felt she wasn't ready for it even vocally, let alone dramatically. With typical frankness she attributes her success to the fact that 'so few people sing it that there could be no comparisons'. But by the time she sang it at Covent Garden, she was pleased with the progress she had made in the intervening four years and felt she was very much coming to terms with it vocally and, to some extent, dramatically.

In 1982, the most difficult things had been Semiramide's Act II duet with the bass, Assur. 'It is quite central and has to be a bit more "punched" because dramatically she is being so tough. In fact it is one of the moments when we find her at her hardest. This is very difficult to put across without pushing the voice especially when you consider what is going through her mind at the moment, all those threats she is hurling out. It is a fabulous duet and I enjoyed it much more this time than in 1982 when I didn't have as much voice at the centre.' The other bit she also found easier this time round was the beginning of Semiramide's famous Act I aria, 'Bel raggio lusinghier' which is all 'stop and start' as she puts it, alternating bits of recitative with bits of melody. 'I couldn't really make it work the first time round. It really did sort of start and stop. But by 1986 it had a definite shape, and although it remains a difficult piece of singing, I found it gratifying.'

She considers Semiramide an extraordinary role demanding a very wide vocal range, but finds the absence of any lyrical moments rather frustrating. 'I revel in legato line but it's totally missing from this role, the last that Rossini wrote for his wife, Isabella Colbran, in 1823. I was thinking about this the other day and came to the conclusion that it could be because, by then, she was past her vocal peak and had probably developed a bit of a "wobble". To detract attention from that, he wrote in a way that keeps the voice moving very fast. It is the only explanation because all the other roles he wrote for Colbran have a beautiful, lyrical, "Bellinian" line.'

The most taxing thing about this role – according to Marilyn Horne, 'the toughest you'll do until you get to Norma' – is the great length of Act I during which Semiramide is on stage most of the time, singing constantly – from 'bel raggio' right up to that huge finale – and very powerfully. 'She starts off with a quartet, which is good because it helps warm up the voice. But the cabaletta part of this quartet is very weird and strangely written, which is unusual for Rossini who understood the voice so well. But this cabaletta is most un-Rossinian: almost instrumental and expecting the voice to do certain things that are unnatural. I've read of instances of nineteenth-century prima donnas tripping over it and I must say, I find it awkward riding. I always get rather nervous about it because it doesn't give you time to breathe, and if the conductor takes it a bit too fast, I've had it. After this quartet, there is some respite before you get to "Bel raggio", which, apart from its start-and-stop beginning I mentioned a minute ago, is gorgeous and beautifully written; in fact a wonderful vocal exercise and everyone should sing it without necessarily going up to high E but purely as an exercise, to move the voice.

'In Act II, after Semiramide's duet with Assur, comes her big duet with Arsace; and once this is over, there is little more for her to sing except her prayer which I *adore* because it comes closest to being a lyrical moment, and, in case one had come to dislike Semiramide by then, restores a sort of balance by showing her other side as well. I myself don't dislike her *during* the opera, she doesn't do anything very terrible. It's what she did *before* the opera begins that I find a bit hard to come to terms with. She must have been an extremely passionate, sensuous woman who lived entirely through her passions and her senses – the total opposite of me! I'm wholly ruled by the head . . . Got to work on that and try to find a happy medium. I'm too controlled in every way, even in my singing. And although I've now come to terms with Semiramide musically, there is still something missing from the dramatic point of view. This something is what I feel I also lack for Norma, which I'm not ready for and will not go anywhere near. Norma is a complete woman and until *I've* become a complete woman I'm not going to sing it, even if my *voice* is ready for it – which as yet it is not. I have too much respect for Bellini and for the role's great interpreters before me. Of course I'm never going to do a Norma like Callas's. I'm a different singer and a different person. But hers was a Norma to be reckoned with and unless I feel that, with my own different resources, I can do justice to it, there would be little point in my attempting it.'

It is not to Maria Callas but to Joan Sutherland that June Anderson is always being compared. When Richard Bonynge introduced her to his wife in the latter's dressing room with the words 'meet June Anderson, she sings all your roles', Sutherland replied that she hoped her young colleague would get as much joy out of them as she had. Then, looking at Anderson in the mirror, she noticed the similarity of their wide jaws and added: 'I'm told the E flats are in that jaw!' 'And', smiles Anderson, 'it may be true.' She has once or twice borrowed variants and embellishments written by Bonynge for Sutherland, with their blessing – at the end of 'Bel raggio lusinghier' for instance. But almost always she writes her own. Alberto Zedda, who complained that her embellishments for Semiramide were 'un-Rossinian', sent her several of his own which she was looking forward to trying out in the future.

She would love to do a great stage production of *Semiramide* one day and laments the fact that so few good conductors and directors are interested in doing *bel canto* operas. 'Yet good conductors and directors are crucial to *bel canto* which can sound either deadly boring or the most exciting music imaginable. Singing those operas *has* to be more than simply making beautiful sounds. You have to deal with the words, the emotions and passions those characters are singing *about*. This is what attracts me to *bel canto* and this is where Callas was so marvellous. But, coupled to her own natural talent and dramatic instinct, she did have people like Serafin and Visconti working with her. And listen to the live performance of *Lucia* conducted by Karajan: it shows what two great artists working together can do for this music. A singer can't do it by herself just as a conductor can't do it by himself. But – apart from Riccardo Muti who has a wonderful feeling for Rossini and Bellini, and with whom I was lucky enough to sing Gulietta in *I Capuleti ed i Montecchi* at La Scala – most of the "big" conductors and directors are not interested in *bel canto*.'

She herself relished the experience of working with a great director when she sang Desdemona in a new production of Rossini's *Otello* at the Teatro La Fenice for the opening of the 1985–86 season. 'Although I'm always considered "difficult" because I ask a lot of questions, I got on very well and liked working with Ponnelle. I usually arrive at rehearsals very well prepared, having worked out all the whys and wherefores in my own head so that, in case nobody can give me any ideas, I can work out a

portrayal by myself. But Ponnelle's ideas, although very different from
my own, made sense and were logical. They always came out of the music
which made working with him wonderfully rewarding.'

Rossini's Desdemona was an extremely important role in her development. 'It tore me to bits, but I loved it. Basically Rossini's *Otello* is
Desdemona's opera and I feel he should have called it after her. In
Verdi's *Otello* Desdemona isn't as developed a character as she emerges
in Rossini's hands. Here it is Otello that is not all that well developed, and
neither are all the other characters, who tend to be rather cardboard. But
his Desdemona is one of the best things I have ever done and wonderful to
sing: a soprano role with a good middle and a lot of high Cs to sing, which
is a delight for me. To sing good high Cs you must be able to sing a D and
to sing an F you must be able to reach A flat.'

Another favourite part is the title role in Donizetti's *Lucia di
Lammermoor*, with which she made her Florence début in 1983 at the
Maggio Musicale Fiorentino. She has subsequently sung the role in most
major theatres, including the Chicago Lyric Opera in 1986, Covent
Garden in 1986–87, the Vienna State Opera for her début in 1987.
Florence is tuned higher than most theatres, but there she had her mentor
Alfredo Kraus – who has done a good deal to further her career by
spreading the word in earlier days and giving sound advice – as Edgardo,
which was a great help.

By now she feels so technically secure with Lucia that she can really
play with it (the way she can with Violetta in *La traviata*, which I have not
seen her in). 'In *Lucia* I feel I'm reciting the words, thinking about *what*
I'm singing rather than worrying about whether a high or a low note is
coming out right. I'm not afraid of this role any longer. I have a good
relationship with it and feel it's comfortably within my powers. There's
nothing in it that I can't deal with, either musically or dramatically –
unlike my Semiramide which still lacks a certain toughness. As a
character I feel closer to Lucia than to any of the roles I sing. She is very
romantic, very feminine, living in a fantasy world – she spends all her time
reading White Knight romances – and surrounded by violence. Her
whole family and environment are very violent. The only touch of
femininity was her mother, who has recently died. Then along comes
Edgardo – Errol Flynn! – and although he, too, is violent, there is
something romantic and passionately poetic about him that fascinates
her. At the same time, there is a bit of fear of him as well, which comes out
in their duet. But he is still her White Knight.

'Some people think Lucia is mad from the beginning. I don't think she
is. But she has an extremely fragile grasp of reality. She is "exaltée", as
the French would say. Then, all the events leading up to her marriage

push her over the brink. Her first aria, "Regnava nel silenzio" sets up this atmosphere of mystery and shows her fascination with the occult as well as her passion for Edgardo. It is the most difficult of all Lucia's music, both vocally and dramatically, because it is crucial to create this atmosphere of mystery from the moment you walk on stage. And there isn't much going on in the orchestra to help you, just the horns. Yet you must set the mood without overdoing it but by sort of letting it hover, the way Lucia herself hovers between sanity and madness. In the ensuing scenes, this "hovering" person is going to be pushed over the brink. It hasn't happened yet, but one glimpses it when Edgardo sings he's going to kill her brother. She calms him down and one gets the feeling this is not the first time she is having to do this. As I said before, one feels this violence in him frightens her, even if not aimed at her . . . I love the passion, sensuality and tenderness of their Farewell Scene, because it is the lack of him, of all of this, that will finally push her over the brink into madness.'

Contrary to what one might imagine, Anderson points out that the Mad Scene is not as difficult as Act I, *all* of which is very high. 'The Mad Scene just works. It's written to work and is not especially hard. The challenge here is interpretative, not vocal'. (Provided, of course, the singer has a dizzyingly easy top like hers.) 'What *is* hard is *getting* to the Mad Scene, and especially to the cadenza at the end, with a fresh voice. Basically even a lousy Lucia – and I have heard many – will still save the evening if she gets to the Mad Scene and sings a good cadenza, even if, dramatically, she has missed the point of the role.' Sad but true.

At the time of our conversations June Anderson's future plans included her return to the Paris Opera – where she had made her début in 1985 in Meyerbeer's *Robert le Diable* – with *I Puritani* in March 1987, and *La sonnambula* in early 1989, *I Capuleti ed i Montecchi* at La Scala, *Beatrice di Tenda* at La Fenice, and later at Carnegie Hall, *La traviata* in Hamburg, *Armida* in Aix en Provence and *Luisa Miller* in Lyons, *Maometto II* in San Francisco and her Metropolitan Opera début, as Gilda, in autumn 1989. She has a master plan for her career, from which she refuses to deviate. When the Met offered her Constanze in *Die Entführung aus dem Serail* some years ago she refused because "it's too high, it would strangle me. And although I like Mozart, I don't want to sing his music. I'm made for Italian *bel canto* – Maria Stuarda, *La straniera*, and later *Il pirata* and Anna Bolena – plus some more Verdi roles like Luisa Miller, Amelia in *Un ballo in maschera*, the *Trovatore*/ Leonora and possibly Elena in *I vespri siciliani* which has some really dramatic coloratura. So far I've been carefully choosing the roles for my débuts, and I don't really want to change my plan. I want to stick to the

way I have thought things out. Of course this gives me the reputation
of being very "difficult" because I turn down a lot of things. If I feel a role
is not right I won't do it, no matter *who* asks. People are always saying
that this or that singer was ruined because they had a bad agent or
manager and were pushed into doing the wrong things. But it's always the
singer's own fault. In fact it's easier to say "no" than "yes", which is a
longer word. And I've often found that, far from making people forget
about you, saying "no" tends to intrigue them.'

    Anderson has, so far, said 'yes' to singing some French opera:
Meyerbeer's *Robert le Diable* at the Paris Opéra and, on record for EMI,
Catherine Glover in Bizet's *La Jolie Fille de Perth* ('the most difficult
thing I've ever had to learn, full of coloratura but a coloratura which,
unlike any – Rosinian, Bellinian or Handelian – that I have sung before, is
frightfully badly written!'), and Madeleine in Adam's *Le Postillon de
Longjumeau*, 'a major breakthrough' because 'I feel less confident when
singing French roles and like to work with Janine Reiss, the best French
coach and one of the most astute musicians around. At first, I refused to
do the spoken dialogue in *Postillon*, but in the end, I did. It's a comic role
and the words were very important. The music is pretty and *bel canto*-ish
but the most vital thing was to get the character across. On the whole,
French music is more difficult, less dramatic and more contained than
Italian, in which I feel much more at home. I like the abandon, I like
being pushed off a cliff once in a while – which is what the Rossini
Desdemona did for me.'

    On the whole she prefers recording live performances or concerts – like
her recital with Alfredo Kraus at the Paris Opera – where the artists have
had time to rehearse together and create an authentic atmosphere. She
dislikes recording roles she has not yet performed on stage because 'they
can sound plastic and uninvolved. It doesn't mean one *is* uninvolved, or
that one is this kind of artist, but simply that this is the way of making
records today and it doesn't do justice either to the operas or to the
artists. It cannot because there is never enough time, despite the fact that
I come to the sessions very, very well prepared. For instance, when I
recorded Rossini's *Maometto II* for Philips, the producer in charge, Erik
Smith, was surprised that I knew it by heart [this was long before she sang
it on stage in autumn 1988 at the San Francisco Opera], as this is unusual
in recordings. But it's the only way for me to get hold of the music. If I'm
struggling with the book – and I can't *stand* singing with my glasses on – I
feel I'm just fighting the notes, full stop.'

    Anderson's extreme conscientiousness points to a person obsessed
with music. And music is, indirectly, her main hobby – collecting prints,
paintings and busts of famous singers of the past and any sort of antiques

connected with music, like the 1837 piano that used to stand in the entrance hall of her London flat. Her 'Malibran and Pasta fixation' has meant that she is now the possessor of many prints of Maria Malibran, Giulia Grisi and Adelina Patti as well as a beautiful painting of Madame Vestris, the contralto who sang Rossini's Otello to Malibran's Desdemona and also managed the King's and Lycaeum theatres. The painting was found at the Chenil Galleries in Chelsea and she hastened to add that she has now become friends with most print dealers in London, who ring her whenever something relevant comes in. At the time of our meeting, she was planning to take up horse-riding in Wimbledon, though her friends were teasing her because her beloved Maria Malibran had died after falling off a horse. Other interests include reading, the theatre and television, 'the single person's best friend. I always eat in front of the television and the first thing I do when I walk into a hotel room is switch the TV on.'

Since then, Anderson moved back to the States in early 1989 and cancelled all her operatic engagements except her Metropolitan Opera début in autumn 1989, a new *Lucia* in Chicago directed by Andrei Serban and designed by William Dudley, and a new production of *I Puritani* at Covent Garden in 1992. The reason has to do with disillusionment with the liberties taken by so many of the directors she has worked with during the past two years. (She hated her Lucias at the Vienna State Opera and at once cancelled her forthcoming performances in *La traviata*, and loathed the productions of *Luisa Miller* in Lyon and *Rigoletto* at Covent Garden). Henceforth she is determined to appear only in productions where she has more artistic control.

In any case she feels she will sing for 'less than twenty more years. Then I'll retire, get a cat and perhaps become an antique dealer. In general, I'm pleased with the way the master plan has worked out. But, as I said, I'm now beginning to think about who June Anderson really is. I know her as a singer, but I've always disregarded her as a person. The woman in me was always submerged in the artist. Now it's time to start looking for her.'

JOSEPHINE BARSTOW

'WHAT FASCINATES ME most about life as an opera singer is my contact with the mystery of the theatre – the whole process of communication between stage and audience and the subjectivity of it all', declares British-born Josephine Barstow, one of the most accomplished singing actresses on the operatic stage. 'While the audience are having what they *think* is a shared experience, in fact it is totally personal and individual, because the truth is perceived differently by each of its members. But a certain energy emanating from people gathered together and concentrated on the same thing creates its own impetus and makes them even more aware because they *think* they're sharing. This – plus the fact that no work is ever going to be the same in performances even by the same artists – lies at the heart of the mystery of the theatre and is what I love most about it. I've never been here for the applause. Some of the happiest moments of my working life are spent at the piano learning roles, or in rehearsal with a team of colleagues.'

In Britain, Barstow is best known for her work at English National Opera, where she made her name through a string of dramatically riveting portrayals of roles as varied as Violetta in *La traviata*, Elisabetta in *Don Carlos*, Leonora in *La forza del destino*, Emilia Marty in *The Makropoulos Affair*, Natasha in *War and Peace* and the title roles in *Salome* and *Lady Macbeth of Mstensk*. During 1989, a milestone in her international career, she sang the title role in *Tosca* at the Salzburg Easter Festival under Herbert von Karajan and recorded (for Deutsche Grammophon) Amelia in *Un ballo in maschera* under his baton. (Sadly Karajan died before she could perform the role with him on stage.) Karajan first fell under the spell of this highly individual, compelling artist – 'the best actress in Britain' according to director Jonathan Miller – when he heard her in the world première of Penderecki's *Die schwarze Maske* in which Barstow made her Salzburg début in 1986. In her view, visualizing her as Tosca and Amelia after seeing her in a contemporary work shows enormous imagination. For nearly a decade after making her professional début in 1964 as Mimi with Opera for All, for example,

Barstow was asked to sing very many twentieth-century works. 'Artists tend to get narrowly pigeon-holed', she explains ruefully. 'Karajan's kind of imagination is very rare, but then, he was a man of enormous instinct and extremely sensitive. I trusted him completely and felt utterly safe in his hands as an artist because he knew exactly what he was doing. The experience of working with him was the most rewarding of my career.

'As a director, he had an incredible eye for detail, missed nothing and was absolutely insistent about the way he wanted you to do certain movements. He asked you to listen to the orchestra all the time so that you felt like another instrument, very much part of the whole musical creation so that everything you did on stage became an extension of the music. He had a wonderful ability of making the music sound almost transparent, as if he were letting light into it and, metaphorically speaking, I felt he was letting light into me, too, as an artist. I found his serious, immensely profound way of making music both exciting and comforting – and I use the word "comforting" knowingly. Because sometimes one gets to feel, "goodness, this work of ours is just a job, after all". But working with Karajan wasn't just a job. It was something worth living for.'

Karajan's production of *Tosca* was, in Barstow's opinion, a totally honest, true-to-the-spirit-of-the-work production with a beautiful, realistic set: totally different from Jonathan Miller's controversial but gripping ENO production in which the action was transposed to Fascist Rome. Act II was simply brilliant theatre, with Scarpia emerging as a sado-masochistic Chief of Mussolini's secret police rather than an all-out sadist. By then, Barstow had become 'firm friends' with Tosca, whom she had not liked very much at first because she had thought her 'a rather stupid woman'. But by then she herself was more mature and 'no longer felt everyone *has* to be hugely intelligent. Tosca is a woman of instinct, very trusting and passionate. Therefore instead of trying to overlay her with what *I* thought she should be, I trusted in Puccini and did only what *he* indicated in the score. Although vocally it has its problems, it is also a very gratifying role to sing – especially under Karajan who, as I said, turned this dense score into the most transparent music. He wanted Act I to come across as very youthful, because at this stage Tosca and Cavaradossi's infatuation is just a youthful *coup de foudre*. This renders Act II – when we see this wonderfully, ecstatically happy woman placed in an impossible situation – even more brutal and makes it clear why in desperation she commits a murder in order to try and protect what she is losing.'

A few months after *Tosca*, Barstow and Karajan came together again for the new production of *Ballo*. She first knew he wanted her to sing Amelia in early 1988 when she was in Boston and suddenly he rang her up. 'So, of

course, I jumped at it. I love *Ballo* but it's a difficult piece and demands a
lot from the soprano, both vocally and dramatically. Essentially, it's a
very "black" piece and you have to put this across, but without being too
bland about it. From the dramatic point of view, the main difficulty is that
Amelia is always tragic. We never see her happy, we never see her not
weighed down by the situation. She is even *forced* by Gustavo' (Barstow
is talking about the Swedish setting of the opera, which is the version
recorded and performed by Karajan at Salzburg) 'to say she loves him. It
doesn't happen spontaneously, with *real* abandon. He drags it out of her,
more or less against her will. With most operatic heroines you get a
chance, at least, to show what they're like when they're happy. We don't
see Violetta happy for very long, but we do get a glimpse of what she's like
when she's in a state of bliss and this provides more aspects to build
around and project in the characterization. But we don't see Amelia in
anything like such a state and this makes her rather difficult to play. I shall
have to provide that out of my own imagination.'

Barstow felt that Amelia was bound to prove more difficult on stage
than in the recording studio. 'The main problem is that, from the
beginning of Act II to the middle of Act III, Amelia is on stage
continuously and has to go through a huge sweep of music, mostly
consisting of long, sustained lines. This requires immense concentration,
vocal stamina and flexibility. This is why, although Amelia lies basically
in the same part of the voice as Leonora in *Forza*, it is even more difficult.'

Barstow, who has scored big personal successes as Violetta and
Elisabetta at ENO, says she feels particularly fulfilled when singing Verdi
ladies. 'What I love most is the spiritual quality Verdi injects into his
heroines. With the exception of the heavy dramatic parts like Abigaille or
Lady Macbeth, most of his female characters – at least the sopranos –
have an inner spiritual life which you, the interpreter, get to know very
intimately. It's written into their music and I'm always very much aware
of it when singing a Verdi lady. Puccini heroines don't have this spiritual
dimension. They are much more limited and you have to bring artifice
into your interpretation because Puccini puts down everything very
precisely, in his score. He does it all for you. He was a master of the
theatre and if you do what he says and only what he says, it's perfect
theatre. If you do anything more, the interpretation becomes over the
top, vulgar and self-indulgent. Take Mimi, for instance. This role has to
be paced with utmost precision and restraint, like painting a miniature.
Every brush stroke has to be calculated and *right*. There can be no
improvisation, no broad strokes. What I'm trying to say is that Puccini
encapsulates his characters and defines them very precisely.

'Verdi is looser and leaves much more scope to you, the interpreter. He lets you know there is a spiritual quality to his characters but he doesn't sketch it out, he doesn't say "this is it". You have to find it for yourself. This is why it's not enough to sing Verdi merely with passion. You have to sing Verdi with *heart*. You have to bring your qualities as a human being to it because his characters are bigger. They are real people who are living real lives with hearts that are pumping. Whereas Puccini characters live only on the page and, if you do it right, on the stage, Verdi's are more "universal" in their motivations and concerns. They have this greatness about them and they have it because *Verdi* had it. What a man he must have been . . . '

Barstow's favourite Verdi role is Elisabetta in *Don Carlos*, which she first sang at Welsh National Opera, later abroad and then, in autumn 1985, at ENO, in a splendid production by David Pountney. 'She's the one I'm in love with because, although she's so delicate, she has incredible moral strength plus the spiritual quality I referred to earlier, which she expresses in the most sublime music. Her final duet with Don Carlos, "La su ci vedremo in un mondo miglior", is among the most beautiful moments in all opera. Vocally speaking, like most of Elisabetta's music, it's quite heavy. You have to sustain these long arches in her phrases and to do that, you need a resilient and reasonably mature voice and body. This is why it is inadvisable for very young sopranos to sing Elisabetta.'

She points out that singing this role in Italian for the first time, in a production directed by her second husband, Ande Anderson, was wonderful and much easier and nicer than singing it, or any Italian roles, in English, which she *hates*. 'The texture of the music is very much bound up with the structure of the language, and singing Italian opera in English is painful.' Yet in Britain at least, most of her Italian repertoire has had to be sung in English. This is because ENO is the theatre that gave her most of the big opportunities that turned out to be milestones in her career. As she told the *Guardian*, 'it has been a wonderful trial ground and I've always considered it my home company'.

She joined ENO as a company member in 1972, four years after joining Welsh National Opera and eight years after making her professional début as Mimi with Opera for All. During her time with this company, she also studied at the London Opera Centre, where she met her second husband, then resident producer at Covent Garden, where she made her début in 1969, as the second niece in Britten's *Peter Grimes*. She returned in 1970 for Denise in Tippett's *The Knot Garden*. And later, in 1976 for the Young Woman in Henze's *We Come to the River*, 'the most interesting contemporary work I had sung to date', and in 1977 for Gayle in Tippett's *The Ice Break*. At ENO she started off by making her name as

a distinguished interpreter of twentieth-century works, the first of which
was Natasha in Prokofiev's *War and Peace*. This was followed by Jeanne
in Penderecki's *The Devils of Loudun* in 1973, Marguerite in Crosse's *The
Story of Vasco*, Autonoe in Henze's *The Bassarids* in 1974, Emilia Marty
in *The Makropoulos Affair*, and the title role in Shostakovich's *Lady
Macbeth of Mtsensk*, in 1987, one of the towering achievements of her
career.

For the sake of this role, Barstow made an exception to her rule of
never singing in languages she doesn't understand. She was in the process
of learning Lady Macbeth in Russian at the time of our first meeting, for
performances in San Francisco in autumn 1988, and full of apprehension
about the magnitude of the task ahead. 'Singing in a language I don't
understand means I don't know how the sentences work. When I sing in a
language I can speak, even if I don't know each single word, I can just
look it up because I know how that language operates, how it makes its
points, and the vocal colours come to me automatically. But with
Russian, all this will be a closed book to me and the prospect is frightening
me a great deal.' (In the event, she coped magnificently and drew reviews
as enthusiastic as she had in London.)

Vocally she found Lady Macbeth a marvellous role to sing and not all
that difficult (the hardest of all her twentieth-century roles is undoubtedly
Renata in Prokofiev's *The Fiery Angel* which she sang at the 1987
Adelaide Festival). Her favourite bit is the aria in the first act 'Every
stallion desires to subdue his mare', when Lady Macbeth is sitting on her
bed, dangling her feet. 'God, it's beautifully written! The lines are
incredibly long, but fortunately I managed to sing them the way I wanted
to. What I was after were huge, long arcs of *thin* sound or rather, not
exactly thin, but delicate. Pulling it off made me very happy because it
was exactly what I was after and, in the beginning, I wasn't sure I could.'
From the dramatic viewpoint, learning Lady Macbeth was, she says, 'a
difficult birth. It took me ages to understand what this lady is all about.
Basically what she adds up to is a bored woman, always a dangerous
proposition. But that's no excuse for going about murdering people. I
couldn't understand why she *had* to do that. Then it dawned on me that
she is simply a "black" person, that there is this huge black area inside
her. What was wrong with my original approach was that I was trying to
find a sympathetic side to her – a normal human reaction among
performers, we always try to see the situation from the character's point
of view. But then I decided there was no excuse at all for Lady Macbeth's
behaviour. Her violence is entirely gratuitous, as is often the case with
violent criminals. Is there any *reason* why anyone should go battering old
ladies? No, these violent criminals are just "black". So is Lady Macbeth:

wholly black. So I began to play her very, very still – not *doing* anything, just *being* black – and suddenly, she began to fall into place.

'On the first night this state of blackness got hold of me to such an extent that I felt black about every member of the audience, I felt they were all expendable. And something extraordinary happened which I don't understand but can only attribute to the magic of the theatre: by not asking for it, by showing her motiveless malignity, I got sympathy from the audience. Many, many people told me they cried. Yet all I did was be very still. It was very hard for me not to dot the Is and cross the Ts, not to *explain* to the audience about this woman, but let her unfold before their eyes, trusting to the art of economy on stage.'

She first learnt this art from the Romanian director Andrei Serban whom she considers one of the most brilliant she has ever worked with and whose staging at WNO of *Eugene Onegin* in 1980, with Thomas Allen in the title role, remains one of the most unforgettable in recent years. What impressed her most about Serban was that he worked on a different wavelength with everyone, which is very clever, and also had a fascinating ability to perceive what each person had to offer and push them in a way that ensured they did offer it. He pushed Barstow further than any director in her career because what he asked her to do – be absolutely still on stage, for example – was very difficult for her. When Onegin came to stand behind her, her instinct was to tense her muscles because she felt herself *pulled* in his direction and wanted to indicate to the audience she knew he was there. 'But he said no, that would be far too simple. He was after a more subtle, invisible thing: a sort of emanation which, he explained, comes only through intense concentration and through the magnetic flow between performers on stage. He disciplined me tremendously and set me on the road that led to my portrayal of Lady Macbeth of Mtsensk.'

Discovering how this consummate singing actress arrives at her portrayals may come as a surprise to anyone who has experienced their searing intensity. For she doesn't follow the line of thought of certain colleagues who claim they *become* the characters they are interpreting. 'That's not how *I* work. I may enter the skin of a character occasionally, in rehearsal, to discover and understand what she is about. It's important to *have* such moments at rehearsals, because they are what you have to recreate, technically, at the performance, when you have to *manipulate* this identification so as to communicate it to the public. If you are not in a position to do that, you will fail to respond to the different vibes you are getting from them at each performance. Because every audience is different. It needs and pulls different things out of us. This is what makes every performance unique: these chemical components, which are never the same. Everyone in the audience, after a good or a bad day, brings their mood along with them. Mind you, a truly *great* performance can pull anyone out of any mood. But great performances don't just happen by miracle. They are created. And they are created by manipulators, i.e. us, the people on stage. We can't do it by presenting something to the audience which they just sit back and accept but by *drawing* them into it so that it can have a cathartic effect on them.

'This can only happen if we are in absolute technical control of the situation all the time. At least, that's what *I* try to do. Obviously I put commitment into it – in fact people think I'm totally committed to my roles and to a certain extent I am. But I'm *manipulating* the commitment all the time. This point is crucial because our job as interpreters is not to go splashing about, enjoying ourselves and "going on a trip". The audience, who have done us the honour to come and hear us, deserve the certainty that we know what we're doing. They actually *trust* that we know what we're doing and this great act of faith on their part is one of the most wonderful things about audiences, because it feeds us with confidence.'

Confidence is a quality Barstow says she acquired comparatively recently. For many years she was as relentlessly attacked by certain critics as she was praised by others. The sound of her voice is unusual, so individual that it has always aroused reactions either fanatically pro or anti. Hugh Canning summed it up well when he wrote in the *Guardian* that 'Barstow's unique sound can be veiled, smoky, limited in its range of timbres, occasionally harsh but always distinctive. No other leading singer, past or present, remotely resembles her and it is a sound you choose either to love or to hate. Very few remain indifferent to it.'

Barstow has always been aware of – and was, for a long time, dismayed by – the reactions she aroused. While realizing that most people come up against criticism at some point in their careers, she feels she has had rather more than most people because 'my voice doesn't easily fit into neat classifications and isn't, intrinsically, the most beautiful sound anyone has ever heard. It's a *characteristic* sound that belongs to me alone, and it has taken me a long time to accept this because I was always being told I was almost idiosyncratic. Thank God, it seems to have stopped now. But for a long time, every time I came to perform a new role the critics would say: "This isn't the right voice for Verdi or Strauss or Puccini *but* she makes a great success of it." It was devastating. It happened about almost everything I did – so often that I ended up thinking, "what the heck *am* I right for and why am I on the operatic stage at all?"'

These negative thoughts were unbelievably hard to live with and took a long time to disappear . . . But she is aware that everyone has their crises of confidence, and was fascinated to hear Lord Olivier talk about *his*. She stresses that 'confidence is the most important thing an artist can have' and has seen many colleagues go under because they were unable to resolve their crises of confidence. 'It's often painful, this profession of ours, and demands enormous sacrifices. First of all, we depend on our bodies. Perhaps you are right in saying you don't understand how most of us manage to stay reasonably sane and un-neurotic. In many ways, it's an awful life.'

As Barstow explains, this is why the most successful artists are those who also have a life away from the opera house. She and her second husband, Ande Anderson, – a former resident producer at Covent Garden who took early retirement – live on a 95–acre farm in Sussex where they breed Arab horses, for which Barstow has a real passion. It means she has to cope with *real* problems – such as delivering a foal or dealing with a colt that has got caught in a fence and strained its back – as opposed to the emotions of the theatre. Her involvement with her horses – 'creatures of tremendous integrity and very straight and honest in their reactions to stimuli; in fact sometimes on stage I find myself trying to imitate the immediacy of a horse's reaction' – has made her more distanced from her performing life. The fact that the farm and the horses are equally important has, she says, made her think more positively about her singing. 'It's no longer the only thing in my life and I don't spend all my time worrying about my voice. If it's there, it's there.'

The difference a stable personal life has made to her career makes her feel that 'the single girls in this profession are to be pitied – even on the most mundane level. Where, for instance, does a woman alone go to eat in a strange city? Hopefully, as her career progresses she will eventually acquire a caucus of friends in most major operatic capitals. But this takes time and the friends are seldom numerous or substantial enough to sustain her through a long rehearsal period. This often means eating alone in front of the television in some hotel room or rented flat.' (June Anderson, who is single, brought up precisely this point.)

But Barstow is quick to point out that the rewards of an operatic career are also immense. While it is practically impossible for entire performances to achieve perfection there are moments, sometimes whole scenes, that work and take off. 'At such moments you feel you have brought the audience up on stage with you, that they are part of the performance, understanding everything, and that all of you have come together and are one. This is very rare, but when it happens it's so wonderful that all the sacrifices you have made for the sake of your profession seem worthwhile. The act of singing itself is enormously uplifting in a three-dimensional way: spiritually because of the enrichment you get from your contact with each of the characters you perform;

emotionally because you can live out the full range of your own emotional
extremes and release your pent-up frustrations which seem to go out of
the window in a flash; and physically because, if you are doing it properly,
the act of singing is enormously sensual.'

One of the most sensual composers, in Barstow's view, is Richard
Strauss. 'One gets a gorgeous, sensuous feeling of sheer luxury from
singing it. Take that wonderful trio at the close of *Der Rosenkavalier*, for
instance. *Knowing* this is *your* line, that at this moment in time it belongs
to you, is a thoroughly satisfying experience. And his characters are
always interesting, especially the women. The Marschallin, for example,
is as many-faceted as a prism. Even if one were to sing her constantly, one
couldn't help finding new sides to her and one couldn't help loving her.
It's her the audience are thinking about as they leave the theatre. Even
when I sang Octavian in John Copley's 1974 ENO production, I was more
interested in her than in him, spoilt brat . . . ' Barstow eventually sang
the Marschallin in the same production and repeated the role in 1990, at
the Houston Opera.

She has also sung Arabella, in Jonathan Miller's 1977 ENO production, a character she didn't like very much at first because she thought her
too cold and unemotional. 'Everything is centred around herself and her
search for "the right one". She doesn't even *notice* that Zdenka is
miserable. But gradually I discovered that the secret of Arabella is that
she is a woman with an incredibly still centre. She is able to stand back
from life, including her own life, and look at it with dispassion. She is the
only one in her family able to do this. Both her mother and Zdenka are
completely emotional. But Arabella is a very clever woman with an
ability to organize her life, who concentrates on finding the perfect way,
for her, to live it. Actually this is very rare. Very few people are capable of
doing it. Most of us rush into crucial decisions "blind" so to speak. But
Arabella has the ability to *think* first. It's a selfish attitude, but an honest
one. It's important for her to live her life as she wants, to find the best way
for *her*. I myself am not at all that way, so having to investigate and
explore a character like hers was a good discipline for me.'

Barstow's most famous portrayal of a Strauss heroine is undoubtedly
the title role in *Salome* which she first sang at ENO in 1976, in a
production by the distinguished East German director Joachim Herz,
after which Philip Hope-Wallace wrote in the *Guardian* that this was the
most effective Salome he had seen since Ljuba Wellitch. The person
responsible for casting Barstow as Salome was Lord Harewood, then
Managing Director at ENO and the man behind some of the most
significant steps-forward in her career. Salome had, to date, been sung
mostly by huge voices like Nilsson's, so when Lord Harewood rang up

Barstow and suggested she might think about it, she thought he was mad. 'But he insisted I should listen to Caballé's recording before I made up my mind. I did and at once realized what he meant.'

Vocally Salome is an impossible role. The heroine is supposed to be sixteen, but the role requires the voice of a mature woman, 'a sixteen-year-old Princess with the voice of Isolde' according to her first interpreter, Marie Wittich, who protested to the composer that 'one does not write a thing like that, Herr Strauss: either one or the other!' It's true that if the conductor so chooses, he could drown even a Nilsson. There are the forces in the orchestra with which to do it. But there is way of conducting it the way Strauss wanted, as if it were chamber music and as if Salome really were a girl of sixteen. 'That's when it really works. But very, very few people do it. Instead of making it sound delicately nuanced, silvery, they make it come across loud and beefy.'

The first time Barstow sang the role in Herz's production, she followed his conception to the letter, which culminated in an orgiastic final scene with the kissing of the Baptist's severed head as its focal point. But by the time they revived it in 1987, Barstow had come to some very firm conclusions about what the piece was really about and the director was persuaded to change and modify his staging of the final scene. 'I had come to the conclusion that the kissing of the head at the finale is certainly *not* what this piece is about. It is about Salome's realization, quite early on in this scene, that what she was after was an unreality, something impossible to achieve, and that in getting the Baptist killed she destroyed her only hope of ever coming close to it. She realizes that although she has kissed his mouth, this is unimportant and irrelevant because it changes nothing.'

From the very beginning, in Barstow's view, Salome emerges as 'almost autistic, very closed-in on herself because she's unable to relate to all that's going on in the rotten world around her. She's drawn to and fascinated by purity, whiteness, the silvery moon. She knows there's something pure somewhere, but she cannot reach it. When the Baptist appears, instinctively she *knows* he has the key to whatever mystery there is beyond. But he doesn't turn the key in the lock. If he had not been so intransigent and preoccupied with his own vision, if he had seen the spiritual yearning and potential in her, if he had been a *real* Messiah instead of a mere prophet, he would have sensed that this woman could have been converted to a spiritual life.' (Behrens expresses similar views in her chapter.)

'But his lack of understanding leaves her no alternative but to react in the only way she has seen anyone react in the world she has grown up in: sensually. There is nothing sensual in her initial response to him. She doesn't begin to talk about his flesh and his hair and his mouth until after she's been rejected by him. That's what's so tragic. And the final scene is not about masturbating to his head but about the realization that her life has added up to absolutely nothing. She has been rejected and left alone and she disintegrates. That's how I see her and I would now find it very hard to discard this view if a director were to ask me.'

That is quite a statement from Josephine Barstow, who is noted for her respect for directors and the absence of diva-like inflexibility over interpretation. (After all, she has been married to two directors – her first husband was the Royal Shakespeare Company's Terry Hands, from whom she says she learnt a great deal.) But she stresses that 'one of the difficulties for a peripatetic singer – which nowadays most of us are – is that you may have performed a role in a particular production and then you have to pick up the strands and sing the same character on the other side of the Atlantic. This can be quite hard sometimes, because when a role has become part of you and you have decided how it works and how to do it, it is then very difficult to forget all that and do it the way someone else thinks it works. But it is a technique which, as an opera singer, I feel one *should* develop. One should be able to adapt. It would be totally wrong to travel from one place to another taking "an interpretation" with you.'

She confesses that she herself was once guilty of this cardinal sin. She had a beautiful set of veils in hand-painted silk from the Santa Fè production of *Salome*, and 'a dance' orientated to those veils; and she thought she would take the whole package with her everywhere and announce, 'this is how I do the dance and these are my veils and that's it'. Indeed she took them to Turin and Baltimore. 'But after these two occasions I decided it was really an impertinence and sheer artistic nonsense and have never done it since. I have the veils sitting in my wardrobe but never use them any more, because the thought process belonging to a particular production should also run through the dance. You can't bring a dance in designed for a different period or view of the work. You owe it to the audience who have come to see a particular production to give them a coherent conception, not bits and pieces from here, there and everywhere.'

Barstow, whose international career spans both sides of the Atlantic – she made her American début in 1978 at Miami and her Metropolitan Opera début immediately afterwards as Musetta and is a frequent visitor to the Chicago Lyric, the San Francisco and the Houston Opera – finally also sang Salome at Covent Garden, in 1980. Many people grumbled for years that she has not appeared more often at the Royal Opera. Barstow is not bothered about this – even though she does occasionally feel she is taken for granted – or about the fact that British singers are less lionized at home than abroad.

'This doesn't displease me because I love anonymity. I would *hate* to be public property and feel I have to look spick and span all the time. I often dress very badly. I like feeling smart [Barstow is one of the best clothes' horses on stage, always insists on meticulous costume fittings and, with her svelte figure and superb mane of red hair, invariably looks magnificent], but don't often bother because I'm lazy and end up wearing trousers and sweatshirts most of the time. My happiest moments as an artist are the ones spent in my own home, at the piano, entering the world of a new character. There is no pressure, nobody trying to influence me, no audience waiting for the finished product. Just my own instincts, brains and responses engaged on a wonderful process of discovery.'

HILDEGARD BEHRENS

HILDEGARD BEHRENS BECAME famous in a classic case of 'a star is born' after singing Salome under Herbert von Karajan at the 1977 Salzburg Festival. Her performance left critics, managements, fellow musicians and audience alike waxing lyrical. Here was not only a highly individual voice – ranging from a top register capable of exquisite lyrical sound to low, chesty tones that seemed to plumb the depths of the character's emotions – but also a rare musical intelligence combined with technical expertise and a magnetic stage presence.

Behrens attributes her Salzburg triumph to the fact that vocally she felt completely comfortable in this, as she does in most Strauss roles, 'because they tend to demand sopranos with a strong and easy upper register', and to her good fortune of being on the same wavelength as Karajan as far as Salome was concerned: 'We both felt she should be sung with utmost beauty and the innocence of a very young girl who is completely natural, direct and unscrupulous, and who finds it perfectly normal that any obstacle to her desires should be crushed. It would therefore be wrong to portray her as a viper or demon or perverted vamp, or even as *consciously* sexy, out to seduce the Baptist into submission. I don't think she is really aware of what she's doing or of "turning it on". She just wants something obsessively, with all the "innocence" of a very young but very intelligent girl with sensitive and sure instincts.' (Both Gwyneth Jones and Josephine Barstow express similar views.)

Behrens thinks the tragedy begins with Salome's initial reaction to hearing the Baptist's voice. From the very first, 'her soul rings'. She senses the presence of someone exceptional and responds to his spiritual power and integrity which could, she argues, also be called stubbornness. 'For I cannot help feeling that, had it been Jesus instead, he would have reacted very differently. He would have understood her need, helped and forgiven her, as he did Mary Magdalen. But the Baptist was no Jesus. We are still in the Old Testament with Old Testament rules and values. And this is the misery of it: that, spiritually speaking, they couldn't "meet". As she sings at the finale, which I find unbearably poignant, he never looked at her, he never saw her. He was so fixed in his own purpose that he couldn't sense or perceive her spiritual longing.'

Behrens was relieved that Karajan didn't try to feed her any specific dramatic concepts during rehearsal but simply let her get on with what she was doing and concentrated on refining the details of her vocal interpretation. For instance, he would stop her occasionally to suggest that, as in this passage there was little going on in the orchestra, she could afford to lighten and refine her sound even more, instead of making things harder for herself by giving out more voice than necessary. The result was a delicate, silvery, *shiny* sound – an accurate reflection of the references to Salome in the text as 'flowerlike' – with a wide, expressive range of colours. The critic of *The Times* summed it up as follows: 'Behrens's voice had a sweetness and purity which suggests Salome's youth; the sensuality in the timbre is that of someone who has just finished being a baby doll and is on the brink of maturity. The whole performance was immensely graceful and devoid of any hint of the overblown.'

After her Salzburg triumph, Behrens found herself in the enviable position of being able to choose what, where and with whom she sang. Luckily, she was well equipped for stardom. She had begun her singing career considerably later than most of her colleagues and was artistically and emotionally mature enough to cope with the demands of fame and to avoid its pitfalls. She had begun her musical studies at the age of 26, when already a third-year Law student at Freiburg. Coming from a musical family, she learnt to play the piano and the violin as a child. But her involvement with singing at the time was limited to local amateur choirs. When she arrived at Freiburg from her native Oldenburg to study, she came into contact with the professional music world through her brother, a Piano Professor at the Freiburg Conservatoire, who gradually immersed her in the city's musical activities. This stimulus deepened her love of music and prompted her to explore the possibilities of a professional singing career.

The first step was to find a suitable singing teacher and Behrens immediately came up against a problem facing many aspiring young singers: conflicting advice. While some teachers correctly classified her as a high soprano, others told her she was an alto! Luckily she listened to the right ones and began studying as a soprano. But, during her six-year period at the Conservatoire, she also finished her legal studies (and can now draw up her own contracts) with financial help from her father, who had never seen her as a lawyer anyway, and was probably happy to see her change. Behrens was later to explain in an interview with the *New York Times* that the main leitmotiv of her career has been 'a fantastic logic, even though at the time the logic of what was happening to me was not always obvious. But I never *planned* anything. The right roles seemed to come at the right time. And those years I spent at the Conservatoire helped me grow and develop as a musician. It was like playing out a role in my mind before actually singing it. To this day, I only have to *think* of a role, and my throat subconsciously assumes the correct positions without my having to sing out.'

After finishing her studies, Behrens joined the Opera Studio at the Deutsche Oper am Rhein in Düsseldorf for a year. Here she sang many comprimario parts before joining the company as a full member for six years, during which she also made frequent appearances at the Frankfurt Opera, and acquired a substantial repertoire. This included the Countess in *Le nozze di Figaro* (with which she made her professional début in a big role at the small North German town of Osnabrück during her first year at the Deutsche Oper am Rhein), Agathe in *Der Freischütz*, Elsa in *Lohengrin*, Elisabeth in *Tannhäuser*, Fiordiligi in *Cosi fan tutte*, Marie in *Wozzeck*, the title roles in *Katya Kabanová* and *Rusalka* (among her most enthralling portrayals to this day) and Leonore in *Fidelio*, in which she later made a memorable début at Covent Garden in 1976. This same year she also made her Metropolitan Opera début as Giorgetta in *Il tabarro*.

Shortly before her London and New York débuts came her discovery by Karajan and, not surprisingly, she remembers the occasion vividly. 'I was rehearsing the rather challenging role of Marie in *Wozzeck* in which my then ten-year-old son, Philip, was playing the part of my stage child. As this was the morning before the dress rehearsal I decided not to sing in full voice but concentrate on looking after what *he* was doing. Then, just before the Bible Scene, the tenor singing the Captain told me Karajan was in the stalls, so, of course, I started singing out in full voice at once! We were briefly introduced to Karajan at the end of the rehearsal and I went home with the distinct feeling something was about to happen. So I washed and curled my hair.'

Her instinct was right. The telephone soon rang, and Karajan's right-hand man at the time, Emil Jucker, conveyed the Maestro's congratulations and asked whether, as the latter had already left town, she could come and meet him (Jucker) that same afternoon. She went and he wanted to know what roles she had sung to date and what she would like to sing in the future. 'Salome,' she replied and this seemed to excite him. 'The Maestro has been looking for a Salome for years,' he enthused. 'Maybe he has found her.' That same winter of 1975–76 Behrens went to Berlin to make some test recordings of the final scene with Karajan. He liked them and invited her to come and work on the role with him in Salzburg throughout the coming summer. (As always with Karajan, a recording – for EMI – preceded the 1977 Salzburg Festival production.)

Behrens's next new part was the title role in *Ariadne auf Naxos* at the 1979 Salzburg Festival, Senta in *Der fliegende Holländer* and the Empress in *Die Frau ohne Schatten*, and, in summer 1980, her first Isolde. The sheer size, vocal range and length of this role – which, up to then, had usually been sung by huge voices like Birgit Nilsson's – make it one of the three most challenging parts of the soprano repertoire and apparently beyond Behrens's vocal capacity. Sensibly, she chose to sing it for the first time at the Zurich Opera, a small house with no acoustic problems, before tackling it at the National Theatre in Munich a month later. And, not surprisingly, her début in the role was awaited with bated breath by the musical establishment and with apprehension by her fans.

Her performance won high critical praise and remains to this day the most haunting portrayal of Isolde I have seen. 'Both in voice and movement this was a convincingly girlish, immensely dramatic Isolde,' wrote the *International Herald Tribune*. 'Her voice is not of the Flagstad/ Nilsson dimensions usually associated with this role. It is fundamentally lyric with an easy brilliance at the top, cutting through dense orchestral textures rather than riding over them, and ample power used selectively. The middle voice is solid and in Act I she sometimes shifted into a startlingly gutsy chest voice.' *The Times*, picking up the latter point, remarked that 'when she balances her hard chest register with the celestially poised upper voice, we will have an Isolde to challenge the greatest in the past'.

Behrens, whom I first met for a newspaper interview shortly after the Munich première in July 1980, stressed that her use of the chest voice in Act I was fully intentional. 'This opera demands a gradual process of vocal and emotional refinement from the suppressed anger and subsequent outburst in Act I to the transfiguration of Act III. In Act I, I go for acute dramatic impact: Isolde is in despair, seething with resentment at the wrong she has suffered at Tristan's hands, a wrong of which she has spoken to no one. And she hasn't slept, and she hasn't eaten, and she has tried and failed to reach Tristan at the other end of the boat, to look at him and make him look at her. Suddenly she realizes they are almost there, in Cornwall, so it's now or never. And her suppressed anger bursts out, first in her narration to Brangaene and then in her confrontation with Tristan himself.

'It's important to bear in mind that she never says she loves him. She tells Brangaene what happened before the beginning of the action and the key sentence is "er sah mir in die Augen, seines Elendes jammerte mich" ["he looked me in the eye and his wretchedness moved me to pity"]. She did not fall for Tristan in the usual "love-at-first-sight" way – he was, after all, the one who killed her fiancé, Morold – but felt an inexpressible sense of destiny, a certainty that the future would somehow bind her to him; and his deep longing for death so fascinated her that she was unable to kill him. Then, and to me this is the crux of Act I, she explains that she healed Morold's killer and is hurt and insulted by his behaviour now because "er schwur mit tausend Eiden mir ew'gen Dank und Treue" ("with a thousand oaths he swore eternal gratitude and loyalty"). It was not love he promised and it isn't love she expects from him but gratitude and respect. When instead, he carts her off as tribute to his uncle, King Marke of Cornwall, she naturally feels cheated and humiliated. So, during most of Act I, until they take the potion, Isolde is furious and hating, but always with this underlying instinct that she is destined for him. And it is because of this seething resentment buried deep down inside her that for Act I Wagner chose this low, chesty range, but with underlying lyrical overtones.'

Behrens explains that, of course, she works out all the details of her interpretation in her mind, during her period of study. But often, insights come to her suddenly, in a flash, at rehearsals or in performance, as a reflex reaction to a certain passage in the score. She then has to decide whether this spontaneous expressive point has a valid musical or dramatic reason for being incorporated into her portrayal. While rehearsing Act I of this opera, for instance, she was astonished that when she came to the passage where Isolde finally confronts Tristan with her sense of injury at his betrayal – 'Warum ich dich da nicht schlug?' ('why didn't I kill you then?') and 'Wer muss nun Tristan schlagen?' ('who must kill Tristan now?') – the words 'schlug' and 'schlagen' came out hardly in a singing voice, but in deep, chesty tones, almost a speaking voice. 'I thought about it afterwards and decided to retain the chesty sound for "schlug" which contains the deep, Gothic vowel "u", a visceral sound that fits in with her impulse suddenly to give vent to her bottled-up rage before eventually toning it down, so as not to show her feelings *too* much. You see, there is such genius in the works of very great composers that if you stay with them you cannot get lost but will find every clue for your interpretation right there, in the score . . . '

Act II is easier, in Behrens's view, because Tristan and Isolde find themselves in a dreamy, rapturous situation and the music is written for a more straightforward soprano range. But the problem here, she stresses, is that the voice has to sound pure and lyrical, unaffected by the extremely challenging, lower tessitura of the preceding act. Act III she sees as a gradual process of transfiguration. 'The singing in the Liebestod should be as ethereal and transcendent as it would be if it were all happening on the other side, and more and more so as it draws to its end. It's not a question of volume but of quality of *texture* of the sound and, of course, of the orchestral sound as well, which should also be extremely ecstatic but *un*physical, sort of dissolving out of matter into an oceanic, cosmic dimension . . . But this couldn't happen if you didn't prepare yourself technically in time, both vocally and dramatically, and if you didn't keep your emotions flexible enough to undergo this process of refining right up to the end. Technical control of this kind during performance is a vital part of a singer's artistic equipment and as automatic as the ear's spontaneous capacity to regulate intonation.'

A Greek laryngologist working in Munich, Dr Paris Alexander, had asked Behrens if, as a favour, she would allow him to examine her vocal cords on the morning after the première of *Tristan*. She readily agreed, and after the examination, he couldn't believe his eyes. Although a singer's vocal cords are usually red after a big sing, Behrens's seemed in pristine condition, as if she hadn't sung at all. She still cannot explain this phenomenon, but was naturally thrilled at the time because 'it proved I was right to take on Isolde when I felt ready for her'. The late Karl Böhm, who conducted her in a performance of *Fidelio* shortly after the Zurich première, told her that although he had had doubts himself about the wisdom of her singing Isolde, he was now sure she had not damaged her voice. 'Personally I never needed a test. I was never afraid of any role, or aware I was risking anything in taking it on. It was other people who felt the need to test me. I *knew* I wasn't going to harm my voice.'

She also knew Isolde is the kind of role an artist can go on refining for ever. By the time she sang it again, at the Metropolitan Opera in autumn 1983, the verdict of the *New York Times* was that 'the operatic world can now count on at least *one* Wagnerian soprano: Hildegard Behrens who although not possessed of the immense volume of tone and stentorian power of a Nilsson, sang the punishing role of Isolde with extraordinary intelligence and an expressive range Miss Nilsson never commanded in her greatest days'. Meanwhile, Behrens had also proved herself an outstanding interpreter of Brünnhilde during the previous summer's Bayreuth Centennial production of *Der Ring des Nibelungen*, conducted by Sir George Solti and directed by Sir Peter Hall, who feels that 'Behrens achieves exultation without embarrassment and has an extraordinary capacity for naïveté, which is at the heart of Brünnhilde. I loved working with her and never wish to see another [Brünnhilde]'. Unlike most colleagues who tend to learn Brünnhilde piecemeal, starting with either *Die Walküre* or *Siegfried* or, in rare cases, *Götterdämmerung*, Behrens learnt all three at once and this 'made it easier to show it is the development of the same spirit and, especially the same heart, beating through all the changes and transformations Brünnhilde undergoes in the course of the three operas.

'In Act I of *Die Walküre*, she is still a proud, carefree, high-spirited young Goddess in her element, a fish in water. She makes her entry with a jubilant "Hojotoho" but this is the only happy moment for a very long time. Soon after, things begin to go wrong: Wotan issues her with orders she cannot obey and even in her carefree first entrance it is important to show that, despite her youth, she is ready and able to follow her own conscience and take responsibility for her own actions. Like Leonore in *Fidelio* who also believes in the Universal Law above, Brünnhilde's total integrity is the only guideline for her actions. She is also a very warm, emotionally responsive nature with an enormous capacity for love, which is what prompts her, at each instance, to act as she does. She *knows* Wotan loves Siegmund and Sieglinde, even though he feels compelled to reject them and, in her dramatic confrontation with him in Act II, one senses from her answers that she doesn't agree with him but has her own views on justice. And when confronted by the love between Siegmund and Sieglinde, her heart responds at once: she gets emotionally involved and defies Wotan's orders.'

In Brünnhilde's Farewell Scene with Wotan at the finale of Act III, Behrens feels it's crucial to have her start off shy, restrained – frightened and almost resigned – yet still a strong personality whose perception of truth never falters. And when she hears Wotan condemn her to a fate worse than death – losing her godly status to become an ordinary mortal and experience the extremes of human existence, from ecstasy to humiliation – it is important, in order to bring out her true heroic quality, to show her overcoming her own fear and growing beyond her own limitations. 'For her kind of moral strength and courage doesn't just happen by itself. It is earnt the hard way, after one has outgrown one's doubts and fears.'

Behrens stresses that the role's tessitura is part of a complex structure – comprising words, dynamics, orchestration, leitmotivs, etc. – which mirrors the dramatic situation. In *Die Walküre*, the highest tessitura is to be found in the joyful 'Hojotohos' of the opening scene. In *Siegfried*, Brünnhilde's awakening to human existence, the tessitura is generally high, bright and light, because 'it heralds a new beginning, Brünnhilde is greeting the light, being *in* the light and not aware, at first, that she is no longer a Goddess. When she realizes she is now a woman, a mere mortal, at first she is desperately afraid. By the end, when she is ecstatic in her love for Siegfried, the tessitura is at its highest, and her voice blends with his in a way that reminds me of the waters of a fountain, shooting upwards . . . '

At the prelude to *Götterdämmerung* the tessitura is altogether different. In Behrens's words, 'the colours are slightly muted, burnished, autumnal rather than silvery because this is a Farewell and Siegfried is off on his journey. Unlike the preceding two operas, the highest tessitura in *Götterdämmerung* is to be found in moments of deepest despair, as, for example, in "falscher Gunter" in Act II, where Brünnhilde finds herself in an inferno of humiliation and you have high outbursts alternating with low, chesty notes. In the *Todesverkündigung* scene at the end of Act II, the tempo is very slow, and at this point I go for a shiny, yet almost unreal sound, like a shimmer of light on a distant horizon: serene, godlike and *un*physical yet at the same time very definite because Brünnhilde is taking part in a solemn ritual.'

During her first Bayreuth cycle, in 1983, some critics had remarked that Behrens's 'bottom register sometimes had the tendency to disappear in the orchestra' (*The Times*). In the following winter, she did a lot of work on her lower register, so that by next summer, she could easily produce 'a shiny blend of colours' in the *Todesverkündigung*. In the preceding outbursts in Act II, she says she 'just smashed in without giving a damn if some tones sounded a bit harsh because, like Isolde's in Act I when she is raging against Tristan, they come right out of her animal centre.'

For Behrens, *Götterdämmerung* is the most rewarding of all *Ring* operas because it's the most complex, it's where the whole *Ring* comes together. At the end, she feels she has undergone 'a catharsis' and come to terms with the world of the *Ring* – whereas at the end of the previous two operas she is always conscious of more to come. And although vocally this is the longest and most taxing of all for Brünnhilde, at the end of the Immolation scene she feels fresh and ready to produce the right shades of vocal colours – 'unlike Act II with all that complaining and smashing about'. And the reason is that here Brünnhilde finds the serenity and detachment to look at everything that has happened objectively and clear-sightedly, and take responsibility for the destruction of the world, so that it can begin afresh.

'She understands why, despite following Wotan's inner wishes rather than his word, she had to pay for it and she is prepared to make her peace with him. She sings "Ruhe, Ruhe du Gott" ("peace, peace, you God"), and the word "Gott" should resonate with everything she has understood about Wotan. It should also be reminiscent of the way *he* sang it during the Farewell Scene in the finale of *Die Walküre*, "freier als ich, der Gott" ("freer than I, the God"), and resonant of her realization that he, who seems all-powerful, is the weakest of all, the one whose actions triggered off all this misery. But now she understands why and is prepared to help him rest in peace. I find this moment the most poignant in the entire *Ring*, and feel a deep affinity and love for Brünnhilde.'

Heroic roles like this one never seem to wear her out – on the contrary, she finds they carry her with them. But if she cannot make an imaginative link with a character, 'if it is contrived or spiritually destructive, then I turn it down. Because I don't want to *play* characters. I want to, and I do, *become* them,' trusting her superb technique to see her through any vocal problems. Since leaving the Conservatoire, she has never had a teacher, but feels grateful to a former colleague in Düsseldorf, an American tenor called Jerry Lo Monaco who 'broke the taboo of the chest voice' and convinced her to use her chest register more. In four or five sessions, he taught her how 'to manipulate the voice like a juggler'. Now, when vocalizing, she takes the chest voice as high as possible and the head voice as low as possible, 'which enables you to blend those registers and make the transition from one to the other smoothly. It also gives you greater control over your voice, especially in performance, when you can count on it doing what it should as if it were second nature. This way, it becomes easier to control that tricky area, the passaggio (the notes E, F and G) which most sopranos and tenors hate. But if you are not in total control of this area, you tend to *squeeze* the voice into the head register, which is *the end*. Apart from not sounding right, it forces you to take very short breaths, so your throat gets tighter and tighter and you more and more exhausted.'

She insists that, apart from acquiring as secure a vocal technique as possible, the best guideline for vocal health and longevity is rationing the big, dramatic roles and scheduling them between lighter, lyric ones. 'If you overload your repertoire with the heavy roles, you would unbalance it at the expense of everything else, especially at the expense of Mozart roles.' Yet in order to prove that 'you can sing Mozart after singing Wagner' she chose to sing Donna Anna at the Met almost immediately after her New York Isoldes. She greatly enjoys the discipline imposed by Mozart, who demands total purity of sound, precise, consistent phrasing and the need to express extreme emotions in a very 'discreet' form.

'This discretion, which nevertheless contains all feelings, all conflicts, all failures – in fact, all human emotions – is something I relish in Mozart.' Yet in rare instances, as, for example, Fiordiligi who tends to over-react to everything, Behrens is not averse to using the chest register, despite the fact that this is Mozart. Classical discipline should not, in her view, be confused with vocal anaemia and she finds the 'over-rarefied' way of singing Mozart 'anathema'. As the explained to *Opera News* some years ago, 'the trouble is that nowadays there is a lot of puritanism in music. People listen to all those voices with no hormones and think this kind of singing is so cultivated. But I think it's fishy – in *any* opera but especially in Mozart, a man whose life was far from carefree and who had his own, private inferno to live through. Yet people *will* think of him and his era as powdered wigs and perfume.' Apart from the Countess, which she has not sung since the early seventies, Fiordiligi and Donna Anna, Behrens's other major Mozart role is Elettra in *Idomeneo* which she sang both at the Metropolitan Opera and the Salzburg Festival in 1983.

Before her Donna Anna at the Met proved 'you can sing Wagner before Mozart', Behrens had already proved you can sing Wagner before *any* classical composer when she sang Leonore in *Fidelio* under the late Karl Böhm (as already mentioned) only days after her first Isolde at the Zurich Opera. She singled out this occasion particularly because it had marked a landmark in the development of her vocal technique: 'It was incredible. It was as if singing Isolde had tapped an unknown potential in my voice. Suddenly, I could do more with it than ever before. I discovered I could speak on the scale and this – speaking in whatever register you are in – gives you a wonderful sense of freedom, because it means you can bring unlimited expression to the lines. You no longer have to worry about sound production. Your technique is so developed that you can totally rely on and forget about it. I can only liken this sensation to taking a walk in a place you know so well that you don't need to watch your steps for fear of tripping over and falling into a hole. You are free to look at the sky and admire the view . . . '

Behrens's masterly technique, coupled with her acute musical intelligence and self-appraisal, explains why she managed to make such a successful transition into the Wagnerian repertoire. In 1989, she filmed the Bavarian State Opera's production of the *Ring* for television, and in spring 1990 she started filming the Met's production*. New parts since then have included the title roles in *Tosca* and *Elektra* and Emilia Marty in *The Makropoulos Affair*, which she first sang in 1989 in German at the Bavarian State Opera and will do so again in Czech at the Houston, the Chicago Lyric Opera and Covent Garden.

Her portrayal of Tosca, which she first sang in 1983–84 at the Metropolitan Opera, proved controversial, basically because of an innate lack of 'Italianità', both vocal and temperamental. Yet this consummate artist managed to carry one away regardless, with a sensitively sung and dramatically thrilling portrayal. Her 'Vissi d'arte' had a peculiarly ethereal, gossamer sound which reflects her view of the situation: 'Although "Vissi d'arte" is an extremely beautiful aria, it shouldn't be sung only for beauty, because it's a prayer, out of the deepest recesses of her soul. It shouldn't sound a *bit* sentimental or melodramatic but very introspective, in a way, because she has just been stunned by a stark blow: the intrusion of reality, in the shape of the brutal world of politics, into

*Both *Ring* cycles were seen on British television.

her artistic world of ideals. For the first time in her life she realizes she has been living in a dream world: her art and her love for Mario who, incidentally, is flattered by her jealousy. But confronted by Evil, in the person of Scarpia, she asks herself: "Where did I live until now? It was a dream world and here I am, in hell, and there is no one to help . . . "'

Behrens's next new role, Strauss's Elektra, was to prove one of her greatest interpretations. She first sang it in 1987 at the Paris Opéra, in a production directed by her husband, the American film-director Seth Schneidman. Since then, she has also sung it in semi-staged concert performances in Boston and London under Seiji Ozawa – to enthusiastic public and critical response – and at the Bavarian State Opera in autumn 1989. Her reason for waiting so long before taking on Elektra was fear lest it unbalance her repertoire *too* much in favour of the heavy, dramatic parts. Does she then consider this a heavier role than Isolde or Brünnhilde?

'No, but it is a more excessive, more relentless, high-voltage role that goes from confrontation to confrontation. It is fantastically well-written but larger-than-life – a hundred-minute nightmare. The action takes place in a single day and it's a bit like the day before an earthquake: all the lizards come out. On this day, Klytemnestra decides to seek out Elektra in the courtyard, something she hasn't done for a long time. This is the first big confrontation. Then comes Elektra's confrontation with Chrysothemis whom she tries to hypnotize out of her true nature so that she may go along with her plan for revenge.

'Because all these years, Elektra has been living only for revenge. Her daily ritual has been to mourn at her father's grave and then focus her mind on vengeance, which she hopes will take place after Orestes returns. But when he is presumed dead, she finds herself at point zero and, in her brother's absence, decides to assume the role of a man and do it herself. As she indicates during her reminiscing after the recognition scene with Orestes – another big confrontation – if she had not found herself in this situation, she might have developed quite differently.

'But I feel she would always have been a very strong personality with a masculine, i.e. a logical rather than an emotional, mind. We catch a glimpse of this during her confrontation with Chrysothemis, whom she is trying to manipulate for her own designs. I always feel that Elektra's is only one view of this family tragedy, and a very partial one. Everyone has their reasons for feeling and reacting as they do, and she knows only one side of the story. Obviously she must have been her father's favourite and never very close to her mother, which is why, perhaps, she is so subjective, direct and immovable, like marble. Only in the recognition scene with Orestes does her other side, the tenderness her father would have known, come out. Here Elektra gets totally phased out. She forgets to give him the axes and plunges into her reminiscences – all the things she's had to deny herself during those years. It's important to remember that this passage sounds more noble if sung soberly and not sentimentally . . . Then comes the finale, where at the sound of the axe falling, Elektra screams like a demon with exhilaration and exultation, and from then on, it's as if the heavens are ringing for her. She is burnt out. She tries to participate in the general rejoicing, but she's so over-charged that the machine runs out. She has fulfilled her mission and, like a burnt-out torch, she is sucked into herself and collapses.'

Vocally, the hardest part is Elektra's monologue, which Behrens thinks should be poised somewhere between passion and restraint because Elektra is performing a solemn ritual: first she invokes Agamemnon so that she can work herself up into that mood of obsessive ecstasy which is what keeps her alive. 'So you have to set this big frame, and from then on the role flows by itself. But you have to bring every kind of colour into the voice: strident for nailing her mother, sensuous for mollifying her sister, maternal for Orestes. The tempi are usually those of a dance. In fact the whole work is written in dance rhythm, and is like a suite of dances: first, there is Elektra dancing on Agamemnon's grave, and then her dancing herself to death.' Behrens, who relishes this role both vocally and dramatically, with its strong and gutsy libretto by Hoffmannstahl, sang it again in autumn 1990, at the Vienna State Opera under Claudio Abbado.

Another new role, albeit only on disc, is the Dyer's Wife in *Die Frau ohne Schatten* under Sir Georg Solti. Behrens found this part more interesting than the Empress – which she sang for the first time at the Paris Opéra in 1980 – because 'it's more real, more earthy and full of passion, anger, frustration and disappointment. Her conflict with Barak is so true to life. The Empress, on the other hand, is a little artefact, even though she does get a bit more substantial towards the end. But I always felt as "hungry" after singing her as I did after the title role in *Ariadne auf Naxos*.'

An unconventional Aquarian, Behrens is one of the few singers who are as compelling off-stage as on: magnetic, courageous, independent, an instantly likeable individualist and very much a woman of today. For many years she was the unmarried mother of a son who is now in his early twenties and who was always a great companion, travelling with her everywhere – never shrinking from the truth about that night's performance! If there were no appropriate schools for him to attend, she drew from her own experience and gave him lessons herself – and made them such fun and so interesting that he actually enjoyed learning. Now she and her American film director husband have a daughter; the family live in New York and spend summers in Europe.

Behrens feels that her resilience, independence and emotional security stem from her very happy childhood. Both her parents were doctors and she was the youngest of six brothers and sisters who loved to pamper and mother her. But before long, she began to surprise them by inventing her own rules at games and having opinions of her own, 'right or wrong'. And this, as she once explained to *Opera News*, has always given her a wonderful sense of freedom. As 'an Aquarian and a free spirit' she has never felt shy in any company, embarrassed at not having seen the latest play or read the latest book or impressed by either money or titles. She respects 'truthful, genuine people' and the quality she most admires is integrity. 'Thank God I have my family and wonderful friends and a lot of colleagues I respect.' It is as much for her remarkable personality as for her artistry that she is held in such esteem by the musical profession, where her aim has always been to earn trust and the freedom to choose when, where and with whom to sing. 'This is my greatest luxury. Singing is the most wonderful experience imaginable and I wouldn't want to change my life with anybody's.'

MONTSERRAT CABALLÉ

'I WAS BORN with a voice. But this isn't enough to make me a singer, let alone a musician,' declared Montserrat Caballé, the renowned Catalan-born soprano whose career spans four decades and who has done more than any other singer since Callas to put little-known operas on the map. 'A singer's vocal cords are not that different from a normal person's. So the music cannot come from them alone. It must therefore come from somewhere else, or rather, everywhere else, inside. I also believe that music, sound waves, are everywhere *around* us. Why don't we hear them? Because we are not yet ready to. We are still too deeply immersed in matter and have as yet developed only a tiny part of our mind potential. By the time we develop half, we will understand each other's thoughts automatic-ally and communicate without needing to talk. When we evolve even further, we will become aware of the state of union that binds us to everything in creation and be able to hear, to be inside and part of the music around us without having to "make" it.

'I know this may sound strange to many people. An example of what I mean are those extra-special moments that occur from time to time in every artist's career: moments when you no longer feel you're on a stage making music, but in a different dimension, *inside*, at one with music, and no longer aware of the act of singing or conscious of yourself and your body. The body is a concrete thing, made up of physical matter. But when you are in this stage of fusion with music you are totally unaware of it. You feel light, weightless, and afterwards, boom, you feel so heavy again . . .'

Sometimes, during performances, Caballé is aware of colleagues and conductors experiencing the same sensation, 'this sort of trance when all of us feel we are not wholly here. Then suddenly, it's over in a flash. We look into each other's eyes and know we have just woken up and are no longer in another world but down here, on a stage, making theatre. I don't know why this happens or how to explain it but I know that it does and that audiences feel it, too. One of the worst things that can happen at such moments, when you are suspended in a dimension beyond, out of, time and space, is applause.'

Like many colleagues who have had to cope with frequent or prolonged periods of ill health, Caballé attributes in part to the therapeutic powers of music her miraculous recovery from a string of illnesses and seven operations, including one on her knees in 1969, one for cancer in 1974, two on her kidneys in 1976 and 1982, and her second heart attack backstage in Vienna in 1983, from which she made a swift and thorough recovery. In 1985, she collapsed with a brain tumour for which she had to undergo intensive treatment with laser, at the end of which, not knowing yet whether she was completely cured, she had to make a crucial decision: whether to continue singing or not. 'I thought, come what may, I want to go on with my music and the doctors agreed to make me try.'

She was due to sing Gluck's *Armide* at the Teatro de la Zarzuela in Madrid and was scared stiff. But as sooner or later she had to find out if she was cured or not, she couldn't think of a better way of doing so than on stage, singing. Everyone who knew the situation – her family, a few close friends, the people in the theatre – rallied around her and she went on stage thinking: 'This is a crucial night for me and I must be careful not to push too much vibration into the brain or do a number of other things, either. I knew the score minutely – not just my own part but everybody else's, including every pause – so I reckoned I could pace myself. But an extraordinary thing happened: I forgot myself completely. I abandoned myself to the music and felt as if new life were coming back to me. I sang the entire performance in this state and it was a big emotion for me, the family and the people in the theatre. I had the feeling of being reborn, or newly born.'

Afterwards she underwent tests and check-ups with scanners to see if any damage had been done to the brain by the sound vibrations, but there was none. All was well and the experience of being in contact with music again after so long made her – like Herbert von Karajan who also underwent a number of painful illnesses and operations – savour life more fully: 'I am a big woman, I weigh 103 kilos – terrible but true – yet I feel wonderful. The prospect of never singing again made me realize and appreciate more intensely things I used to take for granted. Every day, every performance now seems like a gift, a reward. My husband Bernabé says "Good, because you always had it too easy!" *Easy*, I exclaim. "Well, finally you appreciate what you were born with". And I think he is right.'

Caballé – an intelligent, warm-hearted and coquettish woman with an impish sense of humour and much given to giggles and peals of laughter – was talking in Madrid in spring 1987, between performances of Marguerite in Boito's *Mefistofele* at the Teatro de la Zarzuela. At the age of fifty-four, she had displayed the qualities for which she is renowned: fabulous, floated pianissimi and seamless, soaring lyric phrasing. She is the first to admit she is not, and never has been, a singing-actress in the contemporary mould. 'As an actress, I cannot make impressive gestures. But the few I make are sincere and the public realize it.' As with the great Italian tenor Carlo Bergonzi, with whom artistically she has a great deal in common, her characterization is done entirely through *vocal* acting: expressive phrasing, subtle colouring and dynamic shading.

Her musicality is such as to astound even old hands such as the eminent Italian coach Ubaldo Gardini who, through his work at Covent Garden, the Metropolitan Opera and the recording studio, has coached most singers of the past 30 years. Gardini says that throughout his career he has never felt envious of the musicality of a conductor but has, on occasion, been totally taken aback by the instinctive musicality of certain singers, of whom a prime example is Caballé: 'I found myself thinking this was sheer perfection. She often arrives at rehearsals not knowing her scores, [indeed a German colleague was flabbergasted to discover that when Caballé came to rehearse her first Isolde at the Teatre de Liceu in Barcelona in 1989, she didn't know her lines. "I admired her guts!"], but by the end, when she does, the result is perfection: the tempi are perfect, the phrasing out of this world and you are left breathless. Her musicality is extraordinary, unbelievable – which is why, on stage, she tends to go more for beauty of sound than dramatic impact; the diametrical opposite of a Renata Scotto, who sometimes goes for an ugly sound – but an ugly sound that means so much you instantly accept it.'

Yet Caballé passionately believes in the revolution, begun by Callas, which has turned opera into believable theatre. But again, like Bergonzi, she feels her physical limitations would render attempts at graphic acting ridiculous. Instead she has concentrated on a vocal artistry based on profound musicianship, a superb technique and an overwhelming love of music, evident in everything she says and does. She is one of the most versatile sopranos of her calibre, past or present, with a repertoire of about 125 roles ranging from Gluck and Mozart ('over 400 performances of Donna Elvira under my belt, but very few people know this'), and *bel canto* to Verdi and verismo, and from the French repertoire to Strauss and Wagner. Her versatility has allowed her to express the extreme beauty of her voice to the full. Like most Spanish voices, it has a gutsy timbre that makes it seem laced with a drop of alcohol. (So many Spanish voices, male or female, when compared to Italian voices, display this specific quality.) She is a lirico-spinto soprano with some coloratura – a combination rare enough to enable her to alternate roles such as Strauss's Ariadne or Wagner's Sieglinde with Rossini's Semiramide, sometimes within a fortnight! She admits that, like most people, she did many wrong things in her youth because 'youth gives you the strength to believe you can do anything! But if I didn't have a good technique I would have been out of business within a decade. I believe it is essential to know all there is to know about sound emission and projection. And the only way is through a sound, solid breathing technique.'

Caballé became aware of her gift early on. Coming from a musical family she learnt to play the piano at the age of eight. By the time she was thirteen she already knew she wanted to study singing. But no one under seventeen was admissible to the singing classes of the Barcelona Conservatoire. Her mother lied about her age to the authorities, pretending she was fifteen. But she told the truth to the singing teacher, Hungarian-born Eugenia Kemmeny, who turned a blind eye to this white lie because she knew that, in compliance with her method of teaching, her young pupil would do no singing whatsoever throughout her first year in class. 'She said that, because it is a sacred privilege to be born with "a sound", she had no intention of ruining my instrument. On the contrary, one should treat it like a growing tree, giving it water, support and anything else needed in order to develop healthily.'

Caballé and the rest of her class spent their entire first year at the Conservatoire learning how to breathe. Kemmeny devoted the whole time to breathing exercises or 'respiratory gymnastics', as she called them. She based her technique on the theory that singers must build the support necessary for guiding and controlling the passage of air through the body to the larynx. Her breathing exercises were aimed at building 'a big, solid wall around the diaphragm by using and controlling all those muscles under and behind the abdomen which support the diaphragm and the back. She wanted to strengthen them to the point where the diaphragm doesn't need to *work* but only to support the breath. The actual work of pushing up the air is done by the abdominal muscles.'

Kemmeny, who had been a champion runner in her native Hungary, also stressed that singers should always conserve their maximum strength for the finale, 'the last 150 metres'. She had a chronometer at hand to measure how long her pupils could manage to hold their breath and how slowly they could dose out and release the air they exhaled. She explained that if they succeeded in developing a firm, solid wall around the diaphragm, this would protect and allow it maximum expansion, like that of underwater swimmers, and also enable them to regulate the air intake without any contraction in the throat.* She never talked about voice placement because she believed that if the throat stayed relaxed and untensed, the sound would automatically be placed correctly.

Unlike some of her classmates, who thought Kemmeny crazy and

*Joan Sutherland also states that if she feels *any* sensation in her throat, this means she is singing badly or singing the wrong role.

complained to the authorities that her lessons were more like a gymnastics than a singing class, Caballé found her theory interesting, and says her whole career is based on it. Gradually, others, too, began to realize that this revolution in the teaching of singing had a lot going for it and to flock to Kemmeny's classes, which became over-subscribed. Kemmeny promised that her method was guaranteed to prolong a career by at least a decade and prevent a wobble which, she explained, has nothing to do with the vocal cords but with muscles becoming loose.

A healthy way of breathing – the basis of yoga – is also extremely helpful in preserving and restoring bodily health in general, and Caballé, who has discussed this with several doctors, is convinced it has something to do with the fact that, after so many illnesses and operations, she is 'still able to do what I'm doing'. Again like Bergonzi, she does breathing exercises for 30 or 40 minutes every single morning of her life. 'As well as keeping my abdominal muscles firm, it also helps keep the bloodstream clean.' These are followed by a further ten minutes of holding then releasing her breath rhythmically, 'a good principle for spiritual health as well, because come rain or shine, you begin your day in a positive, optimistic way'.

When asked by the late Editor of *Opera News*, Robert Jacobson, whether she always had the capacity for those famous, sustained pianissimi, she replied 'No.' This was something she learnt from her father's collection of records of the great Spanish tenor Miguel Fleta who had 'this incredible pianissimo which was never a falsetto. I thought, a woman can do this, too, and it became my obsession. I tried, but I couldn't do it. I asked my teacher and she said: "Of course you can do it. It's a question of practising with your breath – how to project not the sound but the *breath*. The voice must never sit, but always *float* on the breath." So you see I have it because I learnt it.'

During her second year at the Conservatoire, Caballé began proper singing lessons and, while continuing to work on technique with Kemmeny, she also started studying repertoire with Napoleone Annovazzi. The first parts they worked on were Fiordiligi, Susanna, the Queen of the Night and Lucia. 'When I went to him I could hit a top F. But he assured me I was not a coloratura, but a lyric soprano with a bit of agility and if I continued singing pure coloratura roles such as the Queen of the Night I would ruin my voice. [Yet it is this bit of agility that enables Caballé to sing so much *bel canto*.] Within a year, he had taught me how never to force the voice but produce a steady stream of sound seemingly naturally.'

Caballé graduated from the Conservatoire in 1954 and was awarded the Gold Medal of the Liceu. Shortly afterwards she made her professional début in the small town of Reus near Barcelona; this was soon followed by the soprano part in Beethoven's Ninth in Valencia. In 1956 she signed a three-year contract with the Basle Opera in Switzerland where she made her début as the First Lady in *Die Zauberflöte*, followed by a small part in Prokofiev's *The Fiery Angel*. Her first major role was Mimi in *La Bohème*, when she stood in for an indisposed soprano on 17 November 1956.

Yet it was a mostly German repertoire that Caballé acquired during her three years in Basle: Wagner parts such as Elsa in *Lohengrin*, Elisabeth in *Tannhäuser* and Eva in *Die Meistersinger von Nürnberg*, Strauss parts such as Chrysothemis in *Elektra* and the title role in *Arabella*, and many Mozart ladies such as the Countess, Pamina, Fiordiligi and Donna Elvira. Italian parts were few and far between: Tosca, Aida and Nedda in *I Pagliacci*, and her one excursion into the French repertoire was to sing all three ladies in *Les Contes d'Hoffmann* in one evening. At the time she saw herself primarily as a Mozart and Strauss singer. In 1959 she made an immensely successful début at the Vienna State Opera as Salome, for which she was awarded the House's Gold Medal for the best Strauss singing of the season. She admits that, to this day, Strauss remains her favourite composer. 'He was the last of the romantics and I love him very much. His music has great delicacy and fragility, but there is always this grandiose, oceanic element in his orchestrations. It always makes me think of the sea because of the way it flows, swells and ebbs. One moment it's dark, next moment it's light; the voice alternates between floating on the surface and submerging itself in the sound. Ever since my days in Basle, I have loved Strauss, and made some important débuts in Strauss operas.' (As well as the VSO début as Salome, she made her Barcelona début in 1962 as Arabella and her Glyndebourne début in 1965 as the Marschallin.)

After three years in Basle, Caballé moved to Bremen in 1959 and added more new parts to her repertoire: Violetta in *La traviata*, Tatyana in *Eugene Onegin* and the title roles in Dvořák's *Armida* and *Rusalka*. During her time in Basle and Bremen, she always tried to save as much money as possible to travel all over Austria and Germany in order to hear her favourite singers: Elisabeth Grümmer, her idol in Mozart, whose Donna Anna she caught in Berlin, Lisa della Casa as Arabella in Munich, Elisabeth Schwarzkopf as the Marschallin in Vienna. 'It was a terrible time for the body and the mind – but for the soul it was something special,' she told *Opera News*.

These were lean, depressing years indeed. Her career in Germany was not progressing as fast as she had hoped. A tape of that first Mimi in Basle reveals a voice in superb condition, with exquisite beauty of phrasing and a secure technique. But nobody seemed to take any notice. Even her very successful Vienna début as Salome, followed in 1960 by her début at La

Scala as a Flower Maiden in *Parsifal*, had not led to further major invitations. Life was at a low ebb. On top of which, she missed Spain and her family desperately. Her parents came to stay with her for a while and when they left she felt so despondent that they returned. She was putting up with being away from her roots and working like a beaver for very little money – and for what, she kept asking herself. 'I was an idealistic enthusiastic girl, music was embracing me all the time, I wanted to do something, through music, and when these aspirations didn't look as if they were going to be realized, I felt deceived and disappointed in myself. At that point, I was ready to quit my career.'

It was her brother Carlos, aged nineteen, who changed her mind and proved instrumental in changing the course of her career. 'Give me a year and if by the end of it you are not satisfied, you can pack it up and come home,' he reasoned. A year later, his sister was singing in Lisbon, Mexico City, the Lucerne Festival, with all gloomy thoughts banished from her mind; and after making her début at the Teatre de Liceu in her native Barcelona in 1962, she was able to make her home town her base. 'Suddenly, I felt free.' Since that highly successful début as Arabella, Caballé has sung all her new roles at the Liceu, staying close to her roots and gathering her entire family under one roof.

In 1964 she married tenor Bernabé Marti, whom she met when he sang Pinkerton to her Butterfly at the Liceu. They married at the top of a mountain called Montserrat, and have a grown-up son and daughter. Caballé deeply treasures her family life and has always been unwilling to consider her career to be the be all and end all of her existence. In return, her family have been enormously supportive. 'I have found in my family a support many singers lack – which is why they don't feel as confident as I do. Confidence has nothing to do with prestige, money, success or fame and everything to do with human relationships.' Caballé is convinced of that and has taken care to nurture her personal life, never allowing it to assume second place in her life. Indeed, when she received a great offer for a ten-year contract from the Metropolitan Opera in 1971, she turned it down because it would have meant uprooting her entire family. Instead, she made regular annual guest appearances at the Met which, along with her other international engagements, allowed her to return home at short, regular intervals. After her kidney operation in 1976, the intervals became even shorter: she asked her brother to ensure she returns home at least every six weeks, even for a few days, because she felt a biting need to spend as much time as possible with her children. 'We have a wonderful home in Barcelona and a farm 100 kilometres outside. Our children live there [while her parents were still alive they, too, lived with her], my brother has his office in Barcelona and *his* family is there, so for me going to live in another part of the world would have meant cutting off part of myself. I never considered it,' she told *Opera News*.

Her decision, which cemented the close association with the Liceu already referred to, was to have far reaching consequences for the general direction of her career. When she arrived at the Liceu to make her début there as Arabella, she still thought of herself primarily as a German singer. But an important contact there, with conductor Carlo Felice Cillario, persuaded her to take a different direction. Despite her protestations, Cillario insisted that she include a *bel canto* aria – the final scene from Donizetti's *Anna Bolena* – in her first recording, which he conducted. Reluctantly, she agreed. Soon she was to discover how right and prophetic was Cillario's insistence that she make contact with *bel canto*. During a run of performances in the title role of *Manon Lescaut* under his baton, shortly after that recording, Caballé received a telegram from the American Opera Society, asking her to replace Marilyn Horne, who was expecting a baby, at a concert performance of *Lucrezia Borgia* at Carnegie Hall in April 1965. She showed the cable to Cillario who exclaimed: 'Yes, this is the right role for you!' But she had never sung any *bel canto* apart from that single aria of Anna Bolena's and however much he tried to persuade her she was born for it, she refused to believe him. Her disbelief became even more vociferous when she looked at the score. 'How can I possibly sing that?' she asked him in dismay. 'Very easily,' he replied, 'the way you sing *Così fan tutte*.' 'So I put Fiordiligi into my Lucrezia and it worked. By which I don't mean that it sounded Mozartian. What Cillario had meant was that Lucrezia must be sung in exactly the same vocal position as Fiordiligi. The tessitura is the same. But of course the style is different and one has to approach it in a different way *musically*.'

Her Carnegie Hall début literally took New York by storm and bowled over the critics who unanimously hailed her as a born *bel canto* singer. The American Opera Society immediately invited her back to sing two more *bel canto* operas – Donizetti's *Roberto Devereux* and Bellini's *La straniera* – during the next 1965–66 season, during which she also made her Metropolitan Opera début (in December 1965) as Marguerite in *Faust*. It had taken seven years of study and nine struggling in small theatres, but now her international career was launched and all doors were open: London, where she made her début in autumn 1968 as Lucrezia Borgia in a concert performance organized by the enterprising impresario team of Denny Davies and Alan Sievewright; La Scala, where she sang the same role in 1969; the Chicago Lyric Opera in 1970 as Violetta, the role in which she also made her Covent Garden début in 1972. Although she would never renounce her German repertoire, she would hitherto be known primarily as an Italian singer.

Caballé's vast repertoire has always reflected her intense desire to alternate standard repertory works with rarities which, apart from being interesting, also constitute 'an integral part of a particular composer's development and the continuity of operatic history, like links in a chain binding us to our musical heritage. To learn a new opera is to have a new life. I prefer constantly to renew myself through new roles rather than only repeat what I have done before, only to sing some of it less well than I have done in the past. I want to know where the voice is *now*, not where it has been before. So I organize myself.' These rarities have included Gluck's *Armide, Telemacco* and *Paride ed Elena*; Salieri's *Les Danaïdes* and *Axur, Re d'Ormus*, Rossini's *Ermione, Adelaïde di Borgogna* and *Elisabetta, Regina d'Inghilterra*; Spontini's *Olympie* and *Agnes von Hohenstaufen*, as well as *La vestale*, one of Maria Callas's great roles; Massenet's *Hérodiade* and Respighi's *La fiamma*. Her standard repertoire includes Wagner's Sieglinde and Isolde, the Strauss and Mozart roles already mentioned, almost all Verdi's lyric and lirico-spinto parts, much of Bellini and Donizetti, and a smattering of verismo.

She is convinced that, as long as it is based on a rock-solid technique, a soprano voice can and should, sing everything within its natural range and extension – and nothing that 'God and nature never intended' – because each composer improves and takes the voice a stage further. 'Provided they have a good knowledge of every composer's stylistic requirements, most sopranos can have a repertoire that defies classification. What *can* damage the voice is to sing certain composers such as Strauss without knowing their style. While vocal technique is one and the same for all music, the style of each composer is different and demands a different kind of support in projecting the sound. You cannot sing Wagner the way you sing Mozart. As far as Mozart and especially *Le nozze di Figaro* and *Così fan tutte* are concerned, you need exactly the same projection as you need for Verdi's *La traviata* and *Rigoletto*. Dramatic roles such as Rossini's Semiramide, on the other hand, require the same sort of support as Strauss's Salome. I know this sounds surprising because one is an Italian coloratura and the other a German lyric/dramatic part, but despite their stylistic differences, the two roles have the same tessitura and require the same kind of support for the sound projection. These are the sort of things young singers should pay attention to and know before they can expand their repertoire safely.'

Caballé's preferred time for studying new roles is the early morning, because then the mind is 'quiet and relaxed'; she likes to devote two hours to music, two to voice, an hour to memorizing and an hour to anything else that might need repetition. If she is dealing with a score such as *Telemacco*, which she had never heard before, she starts off by playing it on the piano, 'badly, but at least I can do it', just to hear what the music sounds like. 'The first time I played this particular score I thought, my God, what wonderful music. Then I played it through once more to discover what feelings lay behind this sound-world. You see, I *need* the music to speak to me in order to discover what a new work is like. I cannot begin my approach from the libretto, through the words. Of course poetry speaks to me, too, but in a different, more limited way. It has to do with words, specifics, whereas music goes beyond that and deals with feelings, with the Infinite. I form my impressions of a new work not according to what the libretto tells me, but according to what the music, the sound, the composer's line, tells me.'

But what about the crucial importance attached to the words by composers such as Verdi? He is known to have exhorted the original protagonists of *Macbeth* to 'serve the poet rather than the composer'. But Caballé remains adamant. 'Verdi could afford to say this because he was himself the composer, and maybe composers find that words stimulate their imagination. I, a mere interpreter, a tool in the realization of a masterpiece, *must* be inspired by the music if I am to serve it well, and not divert attention to myself. When a singer truly feels and experiences what the music is all about, the words will *automatically* ring true – it's logical because the meaning of the words is there, in the music, and Maria always said so, too.'

While this is certainly true, Maria Callas also maintained that once a singer understood the meaning of the words, the music would automatic-ally sound right – a statement confirmed by most singing-actresses in this book. Basically, it boils down to different kinds of artistic imagination: some are stimulated by and veer towards the dramatic, while others respond primarily to the musical side of opera. This fundamental contrast of priorities underlines today's different conceptions of what opera is really about and divides operatic interpreters into two categories: singers pure and simple versus singing actors and actresses.

Nevertheless, one cannot help but be struck by Caballé's frequent references to, and admiration and affection for Callas, or forget the genuineness of her grief at her great colleague's death (as seen in the documentary on Callas screened on the tenth anniversary of her death). She wishes she had kept tapes of their many conversations over the years, which never consisted of gossip or reminiscences but always centred on music, composers and the art of interpretation. On occasion, Callas also gave Caballé valuable advice. On hearing the latter had just been offered the part of Abigaille in *Nabucco*, which she didn't know (and for which she was studying Callas's recording), Callas exclaimed: 'What? Your voice in *that*? It's like putting Baccarat glass in a very shaky box. It will break!' 'So I said that if she didn't think it right for me I wouldn't do it. And she added, "Remember, it is not right for your voice, not only today – *always!*"' For similar reasons Caballé has always refused to sing Lady Macbeth, a role she feels particularly drawn to. 'But it needs a fierce kind of voice. Mine is too sweet, it cannot serve this music well.' (*It cannot serve this music well.* One wishes these words, expressing the sincere artistic humility of one of the great singers of the century, could be pinned over the bedstead of every aspiring young singer.)

Never content to rest on her laurels, in 1989 Caballé confronted the ultimate challenge: she sang Isolde, first at the Liceu and later in Madrid, in a co-production between the two Theatres. James Levine, Music Director of the Metropolitan Opera, had long been trying to persuade her to 'put Isolde in the calendar', even if it meant losing her Verdi roles. But she always hesitated and kept putting it off. Even after singing Ariadne and Sieglinde, which convinced her she was up to Isolde vocally, she preferred to wait until after she had sung *Telemacco*, Piccinni's *Saffo*, *Ermione* and *Hérodiade*, which would 'go out of the window after Isolde'.

To the question of why she considers Ariadne and Sieglinde good preparation for Isolde, she replied that 'Isolde needs a certain body, a certain weight in the middle, underlying and supporting the sound, and especially the top. Sieglinde, which has a lower tessitura, helped me develop just the right kind of weight in the middle that I needed for Isolde. The heaviest voice I used in Sieglinde is the right basis for supporting the higher tessitura of Isolde. Yet the actual texture of the sound should never be heavy. If you listen to Flagstad's recording of *Tristan und Isolde*, conducted by Furtwängler, one hears a big, but not a dark, sound. Flagstad is considered the ideal Isolde and while I would never dare to compare myself with her, I nevertheless agree with her approach. I don't want a "heavy" Isolde, either. I may weigh over 100 kilos but the voice should be light and have a youthful lyric/dramatic sound. Now I think I have the necessary vocal resources with which to produce it. I am now 54 [Caballé was talking in early 1987], and it would be nice if Isolde were to be my last role.'*

I did not see Caballé's Isolde, but from reading the international reviews, the overall verdict seems to be that although this was a valid and at times musically thrilling interpretation, it is not as Isolde that Caballé will be best remembered. Her place in operatic history has already been assured by her immense achievements in the area of *bel canto* where she admits that she has been 'useful'. Indeed this is how

*Indefatigable as ever, Caballé followed Isolde with Silvana in Respighi's *La fiamma* in 1990.

she, herself, views her artistic life, as she confided several years ago to Robert Jacobson:

'All my life I have wanted to be a great artist. I am not one. I am a singer with a beautiful voice. But I have always done my best, wherever I have found myself, to serve my country, my career, my music, in order to feel proud and walk through life feeling clean . . . With all the operations, all the difficulties, many enemies but also with millions of friends. And the greatest friend is the music.'

There can be no doubt that when this great lady eventually retires from the operatic stage, something unique and quite irreplaceable will have been lost from the art of singing. Nothing could have expressed the universal esteem in which she is held better than the Gala Tribute organized in her honour by the Liceu for the 25th anniversary of her début in that House on 14 December 1986. At the end of a recital accompanied by the orchestra and chorus of the Liceu conducted by her old friend Carlo Felice Cillario, thousands of leaflets were released from the Gallery, on which was written: 'Congratulations Montse [An affectionate abbreviation of her name in Catalan]: 25 Years – January 7, '62 – January 7, '87,' and 'We are with you, Montse.' In her words, it was 'the most moving tribute my city could give me'.

GHENA DIMITROVA

IN 1970, BULGARIAN-BORN Ghena Dimitrova, whom Italian voice-expert Rodolfo Celletti rightly names as 'one of the most interesting and electrifying voices of today', won First Prize at the Sofia International Singing Competition for her interpretation of the gruelling role of Abigaille in *Nabucco*. Yet, to the lasting shame of most of the world's major operatic managements, this important dramatic soprano did not begin to receive the recognition she deserved until 1978, when she made her Vienna début; then, after another five years, came La Scala in 1983, Covent Garden in 1984 and the Metropolitan Opera in 1987. Meanwhile, opera had to make do with smaller voices trying to cope with the dramatic and lirico-spinto repertoire that more often than not severely overtaxed them, as Dimitrova, equipped with exactly the right voice for these roles, was waiting in the wings, singing in theatres like the Colon in Buenos Aires, the Regio in Parma, and on occasion, the Liceu in Barcelona. With average voices now hyped out of all proportion to their real merit, how could such a major talent have been ignored for so long?

In Dimitrova's view, one of the reasons may be that 'today, big dramatic voices are very, very rare. There is Eva Marton and there is me. So people are unused to our sort of sound. In recent years, they have got accustomed to hearing our repertoire – which includes most early Verdi roles like Abigaille in *Nabucco*, Odabella in *Attila*, Elvira in *Ernani* and Lady Macbeth plus some middle Verdi and most of verismo – sung by lyric voices, despite the fact that it requires a much more robust sound. Consequently, when dramatic voices do emerge, people, especially conductors, don't know how to react to them.'

Another reason is that the recording industry, capable of amplifying smaller lyric voices beyond their natural capacity, has played a part in conditioning public taste and influencing the casting in major opera houses – sometimes disastrously. But Dimitrova also places part of the blame for her slow ascent squarely on her own shoulders: 'I was naïve enough to believe that if you sing well, it doesn't matter what theatre you do it in because people are bound to hear about it. But today public relations and commercial considerations play a major part in carving a career in opera. I realize now that I should have fought and pushed much harder at the beginning of my career and sought to audition for all the important conductors. Instead, I relied solely on good reviews, thinking agents and managements would read them and come and hear for themselves. I did some wonderful work, some of the best work in my career, in South America in the mid-seventies. But nobody came and the years went by . . . '

Dimitrova was never after a diva's life – jetting from place to place in a blaze of publicity – but she did feel sad at times, especially when attending performances by famous singers in great theatres only to discover they sang less well than she. Obviously, she thought, being a success today involves more than being a good singer. But after changing her agent, her luck turned. 'Finally, my moment to sing in big theatres did come and I hope I proved – and will continue to prove – myself worthy of it.'

For the Italian dramatic repertoire Dimitrova has indeed proved herself unbeatable. As laryngologist and connoisseur Dr Eddie Khambatta explains, her vocal technique and approach to breathing go back, through her teachers Margherita Carosio and Gina Cigna, to Ester Mazzoleni, one of the great dramatic sopranos of the first two decades of the century. 'There is the same amplitude to her vibrato (and I'm not talking about a wobble, I'm talking about a true vibrato of strength within the voice, not like the one Callas unfortunately developed) that one comes across in some of Ester Mazzoleni's recordings and in Gina Cigna's live performances from the Met, especially her *Norma* and *Aida*. Yet her commercial recordings do not display quite the same phenomenal breadth of phrasing and breath-span, because, like Ghena's, her voice didn't record as thrillingly as it sounded in the opera house. This is true of all large Italianate voices with a wide vibrato. Ghena once told me that her voice records *really* well when she is not in good health. Obviously this is because the amplitude of the vibration of her vibrato is reduced to a size more easily picked up by the machines. Whereas, like Cigna's, the full amplitude of her vibrato cannot be fully captured on record.' (The critic of New York's *Village Voice* also stressed this when reviewing Dimitrova's performance of Abigaille in concert at Carnegie Hall. 'Voices of this size and quality come along once a generation, if that often. Not even recordings can suggest the amplitude and cutting power of this thrilling instrument when hurled into the spaces of a large hall.')

In Britain and America, it was the critics and the opera-loving public who, aided by a couple of adventurous and far-seeing concert managements, discovered Dimitrova and compelled the major theatres to sit up and do something about this exceptional voice. It happened in the early eighties when, after a string of triumphant appearances at the Verona Arena in 1980 (as Aida and Gioconda), 1981 (as Abigaille) and 1982 (as Lady Macbeth) which were televised worldwide, she made two memorable débuts in the concert hall: London's Barbican Hall in April 1983 in *La Gioconda* (organized by the ever-enterprising impresarios Alan Sievewright and Denny Dayviss), and New York's Carnegie Hall in *Nabucco* in May 1984. After the former, *The Times* wrote that 'Dimitrova's London début proved that although the dramatic soprano is an endangered species, it is not yet an extinct breed. She has fire in her voice, stamina and a magnificent lower register,' while the *Sunday Times* added that 'we hope to hear much more of this grandly dramatic soprano'. Duly impressed by the public and critical acclaim, Covent Garden invited Dimitrova to make her début the following year, as Turandot.

Similarly, the impact of her Abigaille in New York, under the auspices of Eve Queler's Concert Opera Orchestra, was such that it had the critics slaying the management of the Metropolitan Opera for having so far ignored Dimitrova. 'Why the Met has been slow in engaging Miss Dimitrova could not have been obvious to anyone in this hall tonight,' wrote the *New York Times*, while the *Village Voice* added that 'Dimitrova is indeed a major voice, a commodity woefully scarce at the Met too often in recent years . . . The immediate point is that Dimitrova, who was 46 when she made her Met debut in 1987, should have begun her Met career in her 30s.'

Dimitrova is acutely aware that her slow ascent to fame allowed her time to mature naturally and to acquire a solid vocal technique – vital for all singers but a matter of life-and-death for dramatic sopranos whose special, more forceful way of using the diaphragm could otherwise prove catastrophic. 'I envy no one who made it before me because many of those who start early also finish early.' (The early demise of the sensational young Greek dramatic soprano Elena Suliotis, who in the late sixties seemed earmarked for a great career, is a sad but eloquent example.) Yet no amount of blessings in disguise can obscure the fact that, for Dimitrova, the road to recognition was long, arduous, and often downright discouraging.

She was born into a peasant family in a small village in northern Bulgaria which had no theatre and no music school. But it did have three good choirs – always an essential feature of Slav community life – a cinema and an exceptionally good school, with a knowledgeable music master and a biology mistress who was an opera fanatic. As soon as Dimitrova's voice began to stand out in the choir, both teachers did their utmost to encourage and steer her towards a professional singing career.

The local cinema, which at the time screened all the Italian and Russian films of the lives of great composers, also played a part in firing her enthusiasm. Her family had set their hearts on her studying medicine, one of the most 'secure' professions in Eastern Bloc countries, but had no objection to her attending the Sofia Conservatoire at the same time.

But, apart from singing in her village choirs, Dimitrova had no musical education to speak of, could barely read music and had, so far, never vocalized. As soon as she arrived in Sofia, aged eighteen, she discovered that her lack of formal training barred her from the Conservatoire's stringent entrance exams for the time being. At least a year's preparation was needed before she could qualify. So she began studying with Bulgaria's most distinguished teacher, Christo Brumbarov, who had also taught Nicolai Ghiaurov. Brumbarov thought she would have a better chance of being admitted if he began training her as a mezzo, because the Conservatoire's criteria were less exacting for the mezzo than for the soprano section. (Dame Joan Sutherland and Dame Gwyneth Jones, who also began their training as mezzos, have interesting things to say in their chapters about the importance, for dramatic sopranos, of a solid middle voice on which their top can rest.) During her second year, Dimitrova was recognized as a dramatic soprano, with already a range of three-and-a-half octaves. Christo Brumbarov – with whom she continued studying right up to her departure for Italy five years later – told her that the more she enlarged her voice the more agile it would become, and she always followed his advice. Except once.

After graduating from the Conservatoire in 1966, she was employed by the Sofia State Opera, along with nine other top pupils, on a sort of 'working scholarship' basis. During the first season, they were only allowed to sing small parts, to get used to being on stage and gain experience. But the following season they were permitted to choose a couple of major roles and Dimitrova's choices were Leonora in *Il trovatore* and Amelia in *Un ballo in maschera*. In the event, she was destined to make her début in a different, far more arduous and challenging role: Abigaille in *Nabucco*, so far considered the property of the theatre's three principal divas (all over 40 to Dimitrova's 26). During rehearsals, the diva chosen to sing Abigaille withdrew and the management cast their eyes around: would Miss Dimitrova be prepared to learn the role? Against her teacher's advice she did, in nine days, and scored a big success at the première.

Dimitrova, who has now been singing Abigaille for over twenty years, is adamant that no singer under 35 should ever attempt it. She herself was lucky to survive and did so only because the management allowed her to sing it only once a month. 'That saved me because, like most early Verdi roles, Abigaille has a *murderous* tessitura – stratospheric high notes and two-octave leaps up and down – that could easily damage a young singer's vocal cords. Verdi was very young at the time he composed *Nabucco* and although his genius is apparent throughout, so is his inexperience as far as vocal writing is concerned.

'Abigaille is written for a dramatic soprano with coloratura and a rather metallic timbre. Yet a "hard" voice is not enough because the role also has lyrical moments and is full of nuance; so flexibility is essential.' (Anyone familiar with Dimitrova's performance on stage or disc for Deutsche Grammophon cannot fail to notice her sharp switch from a harsh, metallic sound in the Act I recitative 'Prode guerrier' to melting, caressing tones for the phrase 'Io t' amava' that immediately follows.)

In Act I, on top of the vocal difficulties stemming from Verdi's inexperience, the singer is also faced by the dramatic challenge of interpreting a very aggressive character, a warrior-woman full of fury. 'And if you are not on top of any technical problems and free to interpret the character, you would miss the point altogether.' Act II begins with the exciting yet enormously demanding aria 'Anch'io dischiuso', preceded by an even more difficult recitative, 'Ben io t'invenni, o fatal scritto', which is full of two-octave leaps from low notes to high and vice versa. 'If you don't guide your voice very carefully indeed, those leaps could ruin your vocal cords once and for all. Because an impaired larynx can never be restored to full health.

'The aria itself is high and lyrical and needs very substantial, sustained support from the diaphragm. But the hardest moment in Act II is undoubtedly the cabaletta "Salgo gia del trono aurato" which needs great agility. But nothing I have said so far compares with the difficulties in Abigaille's Act III duet with Nabucco, which is full of "picchiettati", and springs up and dives down again. The choice at this point is to make either the top, or the low, F sharp audible above the full orchestra. If you go for both, you've had it.'

Dimitrova was fortunate in having had first-rate teachers throughout her developing years. Part of the prize of the Sofia Singing Competition she won in 1970 was a two-year scholarship to La Scala's famous 'finishing school' for singers, the Scuola di Perfezionamento, where, building on the foundations already laid in Bulgaria by Christo Brumbarov, she studied repertoire with Renato Pastorino, Gina Cigna who passed on her performing experience of all her great roles, and Margherita Carosio. These were crucial years for her artistic development and she feels forever indebted to her inspired teachers.

'This is where I learnt to eliminate the heavy vibrato of Slav voices – which has nothing to do and should not be confused with the *good*, wide vibrato of dramatic and lirico-spinto voices of all nationalities – focus my voice and learn how to sing on the breath and on the word and, most important, how to *interpret*. I learnt my roles note by note with Renato Pastorino who made me understand the true meaning of style. He explained that while notes, and even written indications like "with passion", are the same in all scores, the passion of Norma, for instance, is different from the passion of Santuzza or Gioconda, because the roles are *written* differently. As Brumbarov had also tried to make me understand earlier, indications like piano and pianissimo do not apply only to dynamic but to inner tension and to colour. One must always look for the colour. And the person who did this more than anybody was Maria Callas, who stands unique, a lesson to us all.'

She learnt a great deal from listening to Callas's recordings – 'but without ever trying to imitate her because if I had, like so many other singers nowadays attempt to, it would have cost me my voice' – and to those of Renata Tebaldi, Montserrat Caballé and Mirella Freni, from all of whom she learnt a great deal about lyric phrasing and refining her sound. One regret is that she never studied with Antonino Votto. 'With maestri like him who were prepared to coach and teach young singers, one hardly needed professional coaches. Nowadays conductors like their singers to arrive fully prepared and expect to make only minor adjustments to their interpretation. But who is there around capable of preparing them properly?' (The answer is that apart from coaches like Ubaldo Gardini, Janine Reiss and Roberto Benaglio, there is hardly anyone.)

By 1972, at the end of her two years in Milan, Dimitrova won the 1972 Treviso Singing Competition with Amelia in *Un ballo in maschera* and was immediately engaged to sing this role at the Teatro Regio in Parma. Her partner was an unknown young tenor also making his Italian début, José Carreras. The 'loggionisti' of this theatre, considered among the world's most demanding publics, were enthusiastic, but it took seven years, until 1979, before Dimitrova was invited back (for *Nabucco*). Similarly, her first appearance at La Scala – the last of a run of performances of *Ballo* with Domingo and Cappuccilli – went unnoticed. Instead, she toured the French provincial cities with an Italian cast and sang her first Turandot at Treviso in 1974. (A critic remarked this was the first time since Dame Eva Turner that someone was *singing* the role instead of screaming.) In 1975 she made her Spanish début in Zaragoza as Maddalena in *Andrea Chénier*, which led to an invitation to make her début the following year in Barcelona's famous Teatre Liceu, in *Ballo* and the title role in *Manon Lescaut*.

Around the mid-seventies, she also began her series of very successful appearances in South America – Caracas, Mexico City, Rio de Janeiro and the Teatro Colon in Buenos Aires, where she spent six very fruitful seasons, sang many of her famous roles for the first time and became a big local star. Yet she wouldn't advise young singers to establish themselves so far from the big European centres. She did, of course, return to Europe every year – and to her native country where she was named a People's Artist. In 1978 she made her début at the Vienna State Opera as Tosca and Santuzza (in repertory performances) and at a string of important German theatres like the Bavarian and the Hamburg State Opera and the Deutsche Oper am Rhein. After 1980, when her annual appearances at the Verona Arena began to be televised worldwide, her career took a sharp turn upwards; Giuseppe Sinopoli invited her to sing Amelia in *Simon Boccanegra* at the Teatro La Fenice in Venice and later she sang Abigaille in his recording of *Nabucco* (with Cappuccilli, Domingo and Valentini Terrani) for Deutsche Grammophon. At about the same time, December 1982, he also conducted Dimitrova's Minnie in *La Fanciulla del West* at the Deutsche Oper in Berlin. This performance was attended by the artistic director of La Scala who was finally impressed enough to invite Dimitrova to make her début at La Scala, as Turandot in Franco Zeffirelli's new production for the opening of the 1983–84 season, conducted by Lorin Maazel.

Turandot had always been 'a natural' for Dimitrova. After her performances at the Teatro Colon in 1977 (which were soon followed by another production in Rio), *Opera* wrote that 'Dimitrova must surely be the reigning Turandot of the day: she has the right steely voice for the role, with absolute freedom at the top'. Indeed, after this production Dimitrova had been inundated with offers to sing nothing *but* Turandot. So she took a deep breath and vowed not to sing it again for five years, losing a great deal of money in the process. But the alternative was losing her voice, because 'although Turandot is a short role, amounting to about 25 minutes' singing, the way it is written forces you to sustain the voice at high tension all the time, which on a regular basis would prove extremely damaging. Renouncing it for the time being was not an easy decision to make back in the seventies. But it had to be made.'

She rightly points out that Turandot should always be sung by an authentic dramatic voice and 'not by a lyric voice looking for work. For, like Abigaille, it is the sort of role where you stand or you fall by your voice. The difficulties in it are purely vocal.' Dimitrova sails through them seemingly effortlessly. 'She sings a Turandot which in terms of sheer power, attack and fearless handling of tessitura goes back to Nilsson in her prime,' wrote *The Times* after the 1983 première at La Scala.

'Only at the end of the opera, when Turandot tells Calaf how she felt when she first saw him, does she melt and become a woman. And only then should the icy, metallic sound the role requires become softer and mellower.' As always, the clues for Dimitrova's dramatic interpretation are found in the score. 'Puccini tells you exactly what he wants. Before the final scene, one can hear the softening of a woman in the orchestration which, for Turandot's theme, changes from the brass to the celli. Dramatically, just as Abigaille always reminds me of Amneris – both women are Princesses scorned in love for the sake of a slave and full of fury – so Turandot reminds me of Lady Macbeth, who is also cold and bloodthirsty, and needs a cold, metallic voice with a cutting edge to it. At first glance, Lady Macbeth might seem more fierce, but that is not really so. Turandot has already ordered twelve young heads to be cut off – and enjoyed doing so. Yet the similarity between the roles ends there. They may need the same sort of timbre, but vocally and musically they are entirely different.'

Dimitrova first sang Lady Macbeth at Marseilles in 1979, and has since done so with great success at the Teatro Regio in Parma (1981), the Verona Arena (1982), the Salzburg Festival (for her debut in 1984 and again in 1985), the Vienna State Opera and Covent Garden (1985, in a production also taken to the Athens Festival). She considers this role every bit as difficult as Abigaille but for different reasons: 'Lady Macbeth demands considerable *artistic* maturity. And if you manage to put her across well, it is a role in which you can make a very big impact. In Abigaille, the vocal aspect is overwhelmingly important. Basically, you win or lose by your voice. But in Lady Macbeth the dramatic aspect is equally vital because she is the motor of the whole plot. Without a really strong, substantial Lady Macbeth the opera fails to gel. Therefore you have to have solved all your vocal problems and be free to interpret the character.

'I was lucky I sang it comparatively late in my career because vocally it is quite tricky: full of passages marked "sotto voce", plus a lot of hissing, whispering sort of sounds. And if you don't know how to recite and how to declaim, you are bound to flounder. You also need considerable vocal versatility because each of her arias demands a different expression. In her first aria, "Vieni, t'affretta", she is still a young, ambitious woman with aspirations to the throne. The moment she reads Macbeth's letter telling her of the witches' prophecies – the first of which has already been fulfilled – all her ambitions come together. She tastes blood, so to speak, and becomes quite unstoppable, coaxing and goading her more reluctant husband to be bold, to dare.

'In her second aria, "La luce langue", which is vocally quite low, she is even more ferocious. It's a very "gloaty" aria because she has blood on the brain and realizes that, although they now have the Crown, they will have to commit even more murders in order to keep it. Then comes her drinking song, the Brindisi, in which we see her false, double-faced, hypocritical side, acting the gracious hostess in order to cover up her husband's weakness. The important thing here is to make a sharp distinction between the two verses. The first verse is light-hearted and brilliant, reminiscent of the Brindisi in *La traviata*, but the second verse is more anguished – with sighs and gasps between the words – and more emphatic, because she is trying to *impose* gaiety and make the guests forget the spectacle Macbeth has made of himself after seeing Banquo's ghost.' (Indeed when Dimitrova sang Lady Macbeth at Covent Garden, *The Times* commented on 'the subtlety of inflexion with which she bends the banquet's drinking song in all its absurdity'.)

'And by the time we come to their last duet, when she urges Macbeth to be strong again, their hands are so steeped in blood that she realizes there is no going back: the time has come either for vengeance or for death. The interesting point here is the contrast between her state of mind when awake and when asleep. Awake, she still appears to be the stronger of the two. But in reality, her mind is already sick. In her sleepwalking scene, "Una macchia", which you have to study word for word, she is an old, sick woman who has crumbled under the weight of her guilt. She hears bells and all sorts of ill omens and wonders if it was worth while to have spent all their lives murdering and killing, just in order to get and keep the throne. The aria ends in a thrilling "fil di voce"* culminating in D flat and reducing to nothing.'

The experience of hearing a huge voice like Dimitrova's gradually reduced, through an arc of sound, to that magical thread, was truly thrilling. (A perfectly spun 'fil di voce', such as Dimitrova also produced in Norma's aria 'Teneri figli' at the Teatro San Carlo, is, to my mind, every bit as exciting as an effortless high C.) 'Dimitrova's voice is, as Verdi wanted, the voice of the Devil,' wrote *The Times* after her Covent Garden performances.

Dimitrova's exemplary portrayals of Abigaille and Lady Macbeth won her the Verdi Prize awarded by the city of Bussetto in 1987, and she also received the Puccini Prize at Torre del Lago (November 1989). So she is well equipped to comment on the comparative difficulties and demands facing interpreters of these two composers. 'There is a saying in Italy,' she remarks, 'that Verdi carries you on his shoulders but Puccini you have to carry on yours. And it's true. Verismo operas are the most difficult of all. Even roles like Tosca and Minnie – to say nothing of Turandot – can be quite dangerous. Yet nowadays inexperienced young sopranos, even inexperienced young *lyric* sopranos, have a go at Tosca,

*Literally a 'thread of sound'.

which can be very harmful indeed to a lyric voice. An experienced lyric soprano *could* sing Tosca at 40. But if she values her vocal health, she should not attempt it before.'

Puccini's verismo, however, is very different from the even heavier verismo of composers like Mascagni, Leoncavallo, Giordano and Ponchielli. Indeed she considers the title role in Ponchielli's *La Gioconda* – which she first sang in 1978 in Nice, and subsequently at the Arena di Verona – as *the* most difficult of all her parts. 'Yes, even more difficult than Norma, because Bellini is pure *bel canto*. You could sing a whole page of his almost with one breath. But *La Gioconda* is written in a totally different expressive style and makes greater demands on the singer because it needs a different sort of breathing and use of the diaphragm. Even her lyrical moments tend to be dark in colour because they occur in love-hate duets that swing from one emotional extreme to another. And her aria "Suicidio", when she is contemplating suicide, must sound *really* desperate – but with power in reserve.'

As Dimitrova explained in *Opera News* some years ago, she disagrees with the current vogue of 'cleaning up verismo' too much. 'If a scream is written into the score, it should be done – but well done, not overdone – because it constitutes good theatre, and theatre is what verismo is all about. I also disapprove of the contemporary fashion of substituting pianissimo high notes for forte high notes because in situations like Gioconda's suicide scene, you cannot hold back the onrush of emotion. The singer must *flood* the theatre with sound and no amount of acting can compensate for the sound of Gioconda's anguish. In fact such extreme emotion is best conveyed with minimal movement.' ('She had fire in her voice . . . a Gioconda with all the passions Ponchielli wanted,' wrote *The Times* after her concert performance at the Barbican Hall.)

She advocates the same 'no holds barred' approach to the role of Santuzza in Mascagni's *Cavalleria rusticana*, which she first sang in 1976 at Caracas and in July 1989 at Covent Garden, though this approach has been modified over the years. 'When I was young, I used to throw myself into it quite unthinkingly until I felt that, had the composer written but one more note, I probably wouldn't manage to get it out. But fortunately, youth is oblivious to difficulties and can take more strain. As one grows older, one needs more space between performances, especially of roles such as Turandot, Gioconda and Santuzza, to recover one's breath.' As far as the latter is concerned, the most important thing from the dramatic point of view is not to portray her as a vulgar woman. 'On the contrary, her tragedy lies in the fact that she is a very *respectable* woman who happened to make one big mistake and in this sense, she epitomizes how life was, and maybe still is, for Sicilian women.

'Santuzza's desperate situation is reflected in Mascagni's vocal writing and should be expressed in your singing. The sound – and the breathing – should come out of her guts, the roots of her being. Her weeping is *real* weeping, her scream a *real* scream. I'm not saying you should scream relentlessly from start to finish. The sound should, of course, be measured. But it should never be *smooth*, as in other roles, because Santuzza is a very sanguine character with blood written *into* the part, so to speak. At times I feel I haven't got *enough* resources to give to this role. I'm not saying this to defend myself but to defend the *composer*, *his* conception, as reflected in the vocal writing. As I keep explaining to the students who come to study this role with me, when singing Santuzza they should move *only* the diaphragm. This is what verismo is all about. *This* sort of breathing. You cannot sing verismo with the same sort of breathing you use in *bel canto*. You should sing it the way you do Azucena in *Il trovatore*, and for the same dramatic reasons. And when critics say this kind of sound is like screaming they are wrong, wrong, WRONG! But sadly, the nonsense they sometimes write is read by many people whose judgement is thus influenced and misled.'

In an effort to redress the damage caused by such misguided opinions and inadequate teaching, Dimitrova has already started giving master-classes in Italy and Bulgaria and eventually plans to devote herself to teaching full-time. Yet she stresses that having been a singer herself does not automatically qualify her to be a teacher because 'my personal career and experience consist only of trying to master my own instrument. But as a teacher I will be faced with, and have to be able to help, all types of voice.' She is already trying to devise a teaching method and busy translating French and Spanish books on *bel canto* and Italian books about expression in opera which, in her opinion, should change completely: *all* singing, whether of Italian, French or German music, should get closer to *bel canto*. And Placido Domingo's superb performances of Lohengrin at the Vienna State Opera in 1985, pure *bel canto* in their style of delivery, were a perfect example of what Dimitrova means.

Dimitrova is one of the most honest, conscientious and self-critical singers around. Indeed, for a long time, she suffered a good deal from being over-humble and *hyper*-critical. Instead of going for the hard sell, she always said what she thought of her own performances and recordings. But she admits to being proud of the fact that she stuck to the right repertoire and never tried to be anyone but herself. 'When I was younger and had to sing some of the lyric roles, I was, perhaps, looking for something that was not innate or natural to my voice. But gradually I limited myself to the dramatic and lirico-spinto roles and my aim was always to do my best so that the audience felt they had seen a great Abigaille, Lady Macbeth, Gioconda and Turandot.

'The voice is a very volatile instrument and changes colour according to the day, the season of the year, the hormonal flow in the body. The hormones regulating the female voice, which start at puberty and end with the menopause, affect the larynx in exactly the same way that they do one's facial complexion, by dehydrating the mucous membrane that resonates the sound. There are days when you can barely manage to sing at all and others when you feel almost reborn.' Yet she is wholly against trying to adjust this hormonal imbalance, 'from outside', through Hormone Replacement Treatment. 'Today everyone is trying to help women through the menopause. But I feel this is wrong because unless you go *through* this phase, you are bound to crumble eventually. It's best to wait for it to pass, and for the next phase to arrive, the way God meant it to. If the voice disappears in the process, so be it. If it returns, so much the better. I read in a book on oriental philosophy that the soul passes through three compartments of the body. And through the three different stages in life – youth, maturity and old age – the soul should succeed in inhabiting all three. I mean to try.'

Dimitrova is not afraid of that day when she will finally bid farewell to the stage and is not sure whether she will miss her life as a performing artist. 'We singers are slaves to our voice. We live in a perpetual state of nervous tension and our life is full of sacrifices and psychological problems. Especially the realization that while we were concentrating on our art and carving a career, life passed us by without our living it. We have to look after our health so diligently – ensuring we get enough rest and so on – that there is no way we can enjoy and savour the pleasures of life like normal people. Here we are, my husband (whom she married in 1968 two days after meeting him, 'a real *coup de foudre*') and I, childless, constantly on the move, unable to enjoy our home. When I retire I shall look back on my life until then with the knowledge that I never really *lived*. But there is no going back. I suppose it was all worth it . . . '

MIRELLA FRENI

MIRELLA FRENI'S EXEMPLARY, 35-year career, which began in 1955 at her native Modena, should serve as a model for present and future singers. Like Leontyne Price's, it has always been managed with acute self-appraisal and guided by an instinctive musicianship which, to the mystification of more academically 'sophisticated' but less intuitive or perspicacious artists, has never let her down. In June 1989, after singing the title role in Cilea's *Adriana Lecouvreur* at La Scala, her vocal lustre not merely intact but enhanced by that richness that comes with age to singers who have taken care of their voices, *The Times* wrote that 'Freni has clearly discovered the secret of eternal youthfulness'. How does she do it?

'I have a shrewd head on my shoulders and a sound instinct which I always obeyed. Right from the beginning, I felt deep love for my vocal instrument and determined to treat it with respect and protect it jealously. So, I tried not to let myself be influenced by the wrong advice and to stay one step behind what I could do. This way, I avoided straining the voice, allowing it time to develop slowly and naturally. Then, when I felt it had grown sufficiently resilient and my technique was secure enough, I gradually expanded my repertoire to include some of the heavier, more demanding lyric, and eventually lirico-spinto, roles – usually at the rate of one new role per year.'

Gradually is the keyword. For over a decade, Freni's repertoire consisted of a cluster of lighter lyric roles like Micaela in *Carmen*, Marguerite in *Faust*, Liù in *Turandot*, Susanna in *Le nozze di Figaro*, Zerlina in *Don Giovanni*, Nanetta in *Falstaff*, Adina in *L'elisir d'amore*, Elvira in *I Puritani*, Violetta in *La traviata*, Mimi in *La Bohème* and, on occasion, Marie in *La Fille du régiment*. Then, the success she made of the very demanding title role in Bellini's *Beatrice di Tenda* convinced her she was ready to go a stage further, to some of the easier Verdi roles like Amelia in *Simon Boccanegra* and also to the soprano part in the *Requiem* which 'require more dramatic expressive colours and certain notes I had not needed up to then'. By the mid-to-late seventies, she moved to more substantial Verdi parts like Elisabeth de Valois in *Don Carlos*, Desdemona and Aida. By the early eighties she felt sufficiently secure for certain verismo parts such as Manon Lescaut and Adriana Lecouvreur and heavy lyric roles such as Tatyana in *Eugene Onegin*.

There have been only two notable mistakes in her long career, and she is the first to admit them. The first was taking on Violetta in 1964, at La Scala under Karajan. Although a lot of the fracas in the theatre was orchestrated by organized claques, Freni admits it was too early for her to sing Violetta. (A pirate recording exists of one of the performances and makes interesting listening.) 'And if one makes a mistake, it's important to recognize the fact. And I did.' Three years later, she sang Violetta again, far more successfully, at Covent Garden under Giulini.

The second role she considers was wrong for her was Elvira in *Ernani* which she sang under Muti at La Scala and recorded on both disc and video film. The result, in her words, was 'okay but not brilliant'. After a few performances, she withdrew from the production because she realized Elvira could prove dangerous for her voice. 'It demands a special, more abrupt way of using the diaphragm, and this could affect its elasticity. And if it did it would be impossible for me to sing anything other than dramatic roles like this. So I paused and asked myself: What is Mirella Freni's speciality, what is she best known for? And the answer is long, lyric, *bel canto* lines. If I lost those, I'd no longer be myself. I decided I'd rather lose Elvira. Because a lyric soprano relies entirely on expression. This is what differentiates it from other kinds of soprano voices, such as coloraturas, who have high notes and agility, or dramatic sopranos, who have big voices used with a special sort of thrust. But a lyric soprano is the most "normal" of female voices and can only convince with vocal beauty and purity: soft, even singing in the high notes, and tender expression.'

On top of these vocal qualities, Freni possesses natural charm and an earthy spark that adds extra spice to soubrette parts like Susanna and Zerlina plus 'an enchanting, obviously Italianate personality', according to James Lockhart, formerly Music Director of the Welsh National Opera and now Music Director of the Koblenz State Theatre. 'Without being beautiful, she is very attractive – an open, outgoing soul with a *beautiful* voice – and a very musical singer, very quick to absorb tuition. She can well afford to select a small slice of repertoire and sing it to perfection.'

Freni, always an appealing presence on stage, firmly believes that acting is now an essential part of an opera singer's equipment. Her fruitful collaboration with distinguished stage directors such as Zeffirelli and Konshalovsky has enhanced her innate theatrical instinct and prevented her interpretations from ever becoming routine, 'Good directors manage to reveal more layers, new nuances and details, thus keeping me constantly interested in heroines I may have portrayed dozens of times.' After her umpteenth performance as Mimi at the Bavarian State Opera, the German critic of *Opera* remarked: 'The fact that the incomparable Mirella Freni, in the twenty-odd years she has sung this part, has never allowed Mimi to become a matter of routine in the slightest detail, that every note, every gesture seemed to arise out of the immediacy of the moment, is a great tribute to her art and discipline.'

'The most important point to remember when singing Mimi,' according to Freni, 'is that she should never be "overdone" but sung very simply and naturally, without affectation. Your singing should reflect the fact that she is not a typical operatic character, but almost a real person, simple and very human. Vocally, it's quite difficult. You need the right kind of voice for Mimi. A cold, metallic sound would be quite wrong in a character for whom humanity is the keyword; and this is brought out most poignantly in Act IV, where she is dying but finds time to console and say a good word to everyone. Act IV is the key to her character, and this is where I began my study of Mimi. (And it is this act Karajan wanted to hear when I auditioned for him at La Scala.) In Act I Mimi is flirtatious, but in Act III she undergoes a big change: all her drama and despair come out – a typical Puccini formula. Most of his heroines – Tosca, Butterfly, Manon Lescaut – start off gay and insouciant and end up tragic. Yet all of them possess immense willpower and strength of character. I always enjoy singing Mimi. But as I said, it's far from easy. "Mi chiamanno Mimi", for example, is pure, lyric singing and has to sound extremely beautiful. But it happens to be written around some of the most difficult zones of the soprano register.'

Mimi has been the key role in Freni's career: she sang it under Karajan in 1963 at La Scala, and later at the Vienna State Opera and Salzburg, and for her début at the Metropolitan Opera in 1965. 'Whenever I sing it, I go on stage secure in the knowledge that it can never harm my voice. In fact, if a role *ever* causes me the slightest vocal discomfort or requires any sort of special effort – as did Elvira in *Ernani* – I drop it. This has always been my salvation.'

Born in Modena in 1935, Freni discovered she had a voice at a very early age, thanks to an opera-loving uncle who noticed she always sang along with his recording of *Lucia di Lammermoor*. He convinced her father to watch and encourage his daughter's gift and the family were more than gratified when, at the age of thirteen, Mirella won a National Singing Competition with 'Un bel di vedremo' from *Madama Butterfly*. Fortunately, they followed the advice of Beniamino Gigli, the world-famous tenor who happened to sit on the jury, who cautioned against her straining her voice at such a young age, and advised her to wait a few years before training seriously. Freni started learning the basics of singing from a local teacher, Maestro Bertatoni, and his nephew, who were relatives of her future husband's, and went on to study with Ettore Campogalliani, Pavarotti's teacher, in nearby Mantua. (Pavarotti and Freni are not only both natives of Modena but also exact contemporaries.) Like Pavarotti, Freni cannot read music and learns her roles by ear. The two share the same astounding innate musicality. In fact, both Freni's teacher and her first husband, the coach Leone Magiera, toyed with the idea of her learning to play the piano. But they decided against it, in case it interfered with her instinctive ability to follow the line and colour musical phrases.

In 1955, Freni was ready for her professional début: Micaela, in her native Modena. A year later, after her marriage to Magiera she had her first child, a daughter christened Micaela, and gave up her career for a while. She resumed her professional life in 1958, at the instigation of her husband (and after winning the Vercelli Competition the previous year), singing Mimi, Liù and Marguerite at various Italian provincial houses and, in 1959–60, at the Netherlands Opera in Amsterdam. She made her British début at the 1960 Glyndebourne Festival as Zerlina, and returned the following year for Susanna and Adina. In 1961 came her Covent Garden début as Nanetta, and in 1962 her Wexford Festival début as Elvira (*I Puritani*) and her début at La Scala as Nanetta. Of her early repertoire, her favourite heroine is definitely Susanna, which also happens to be the longest of *all* her roles, because 'she is a real, a complete woman who has everything and who understands everything. In all her reactions – from her expressions of affection to her flashes of anger – she is the eternal, quintessential female. Zerlina was also very enjoyable and easier to sing, as long as one remembered to put her across naturally and not as too much of a Viennese soubrette.'

Freni sang both these roles under Karajan, who – after auditioning and casting her as Mimi in his historic 1963 La Scala production directed by Zeffirelli – became her mentor and she one of his very favourite singers. 'There was a very strong rapport between us. We understood each other perfectly and seemed to be on the same wavelength. He was always sweet to me and our collaboration enriched me tremendously as an artist – as did, many years later, my work with Carlos Kleiber [under whose baton Freni has sung Mimi and Desdemona in Munich and La Scala].'

Freni had begun her move to the important Verdi roles in 1973, when she first sang Desdemona under Karajan in Salzburg and on film. But she had to be convinced not only about its vocal, but also its dramatic suitability. 'I had to be persuaded that she is not stupid, as I had always thought, but so pure and good that she is incapable of seeing evil in anyone. There are people like this, such as Don Quixote. It is important to stress this aspect of total goodness when portraying Desdemona, and also to inject her with something from your own personality. Otherwise she risks coming across as rather vapid. The role's not easy, but it's lovely to sing, and demands great sweetness of tone.' One of the most memorable productions of *Otello* in Freni's career was Zeffirelli's for the opening of the 1976–77 season at La Scala, under Carlos Kleiber, of which the première was televised live. It proved that whatever Freni's original misgivings about the character 'the impression was one of warmth, tenderness, femininity yet also pride and anger' (*Opera*).

Her next new Verdi role had been Elisabeth de Valois, which she first sang in Karajan's Salzburg production of *Don Carlos* in 1975 and has since performed at La Scala and the Vienna State Opera under Claudio Abbado in productions by Luca Ronconi and Pier Luigi Pizzi. At the beginning of her career, she explains, this role would have seemed out of the question. 'My voice then was a much lighter lyric and I never dreamt I would, one day, be able to sustain these heavier lyric roles.' But, right from the start, she sang Elisabeth without trace of discomfort, 'without forcing her tone or altering the quality of her voice' (*Time*), while the critic of *Opera* found her 'an excellent, wounded, elegiac Elisabeth'. Freni particularly likes and identifies with this heroine who starts off, in the first two acts, restrained but begins to really show her character in her Act IV confrontation with King Philip II, 'answering him back with considerable force. And her last act duet with Carlos is fabulous for its humanity.'

In 1979, again at Karajan's prompting, Freni took on Aida, potentially a bigger risk than either Desdemona or Elisabeth de Valois. Aida is usually sung by lyric voices heavier than hers, but Karajan insisted he wanted a 'very soft, very lyrical Aida, not the screaming kind' and convinced her she could sing the line he wanted. Indeed, he scaled down the orchestra to his protagonists (Radames was sung by José Carreras, for the first time in his career) and produced exquisitely nuanced, subtle sound. After the dress rehearsal, he went up to Freni and exclaimed, 'Mirella, if I had a voice, I would sing just like you.' Still, all of us present on the opening night of that production felt – on that first season, at least – that something was missing from this Aida, both in terms of volume and vocal intensity. It was more intimate than heroic, especially in the first three acts. In Act IV, which for the soprano and tenor consists of pure lyrical singing, Freni was in her element and delivered the final duet in a most moving, transcendent way.

When we discussed the role she confided that, for her, the most difficult part of this opera is Act III, which is very long, and especially 'O patria mia'. What made it extra difficult was singing it in Salzburg, with the

Vienna Philharmonic in the pit. 'They have a wonderful, brilliant sound, excellent for concerts but more problematic for opera because their pitch is a trifle higher. This means the high Cs become even higher, so that by the end of the evening, one feels very tired indeed.' (Placido Domingo made the same point when discussing the prospect of singing Riccardo in *Un ballo in maschera* at the 1989 Salzburg Festival, and when I mentioned it to Abbado who as Music Director of the Vienna State Opera regularly conducts the Vienna Philharmonic, he replied that the orchestra are aware of this being a problem for many singers and have taken steps to change it.) But the more Freni got into the part, the more at home she felt. By the following summer, 1980, she was perfectly comfortable. It showed, and she has since sung Aida again at the Houston Opera in 1987.

From the dramatic viewpoint, the greatest help in shaping her portrayal was Shirley Verrett. 'I went to see her extraordinary perform-ance as Lady Macbeth at La Scala and for the first time I noticed how differently black people move. I studied Shirley's bodily movements and reactions over several performances and this helped me learn how to react in some of Aida's duets.' She agrees with Leontyne Price that the most important thing to remember about Aida is that although she is a very human, intimate character, she is also a Princess. 'This is what gives her her amazing self-control and makes her sadness quite unlike Mimi's or even Elisabetta's. It's a *prouder* sadness.'

She finds singing Verdi excellent for the voice. 'You have to sing "correctly", with a clean, even line – much more even than in Puccini where you can swell and enlarge the sound here and there. But Puccini can be dangerous for the voice. For example, it is very hard to sing Mozart after singing Puccini, because in Mozart you must be able to use your voice as an instrument. Every note must be in place, whereas in Puccini and, to a lesser extent, in Verdi, the odd portamento can pass off as "expression". Yet from time to time I did sing Mozart after Puccini precisely in order to clean up the voice.'

Freni's first Puccini role, Mimi, was followed, in the mid-seventies, by the title role in Madama Butterfly, on disc, under Karajan, and in the superb film by Jean-Pierre Ponnelle with Placido Domingo as Pinkerton. Yet she rightly judged this role too dramatic for her to sing on stage. By the eighties, though, she felt ready for another major Puccini heroine: Manon Lescaut. 'You always *know* when you are ready for a new role, you feel it, instinctively, under your skin. But, as with all roles that vocally constituted a new departure for me, I agreed to sing it with one proviso: a clause in the contract stipulating that if, during the orchestral rehearsals, I didn't feel vocally at ease, I would withdraw from the production. This way I could relax and work better because I knew that, if things didn't work out, I could always leave. Theatres have had to accept this option.' In the event *Manon Lescaut*, which she first sang at the San Francisco Opera during the 1983–84 season, proved one of the biggest successes of her career, and she has since sung it in Vienna, Munich and Japan.

The reason why Freni had been so afraid of Manon was because it contains very dramatic phrases and accents that demand all the technique and experience a singer can muster. 'If you are not sure of your technical possibilities, you will fall flat on your face. So, it's better to wait until you *are* sure.' Her first hand experience of the role proved she had been right to wait so long. Acts II and IV in particular are very demanding indeed. 'In Act II Manon is on stage almost continuously. First there is the famous aria, "In quelle trine morbide", then the duet with the baritone and at the end, her very dramatic duet with the tenor, beginning with passages that involve speaking on the notes. The breathing becomes quite heavy at this stage and if you haven't got enough experience to control when and how much you give out, Manon Lescaut could become very dangerous indeed.'

Yet, to her surprise, Freni felt totally at ease. Everything happened spontaneously, without her having to *think* about it – a sure sign that the singer and the role are right for each other. But although at ease vocally, she found Manon – undoubtedly one of the most interesting, many-faceted heroines she has ever portrayed – dramatically draining. Her view of her is that 'she is not really bad – just a high-spirited, frivolous, capricious young girl who wants to *live* and savour all the good things of life. All that glitters draws her like a magnet, and although she really loves Des Grieux, she wants all the rest, too. It's vital to put all this across instinctively, without contrivance or thinking about it too much. It should just be suggested by your whole demeanour. Yet despite Manon's extreme youth, the role requires a mature artist who has lived and knows what life's about, yet with the physique of a young girl. Otherwise the whole thing would be ridiculous. The same, by the way, is true of Adriana and Tatyana.'

She points out that, as usual in Puccini, the big change in Manon occurs in Act III when she realizes she has ruined this young man's life and, because she's not really bad inside, she is shattered. 'And Act IV, where the two are alone, fugitives in the desert, is stupendous. In the face of disaster, they reach the highest, truest and most passionate climax of their love story. Even at their first encounter, the music makes it clear there is an immense magnetic attraction between them and grips you at once. Now, in the finale, Manon understands this side of their relationship and, in a wonderful aria into which she pours everything, she thinks back to their first meeting, realizes how much she has hurt him and curses her beauty. It's incredible how well Puccini understands women. Some things in *Manon Lescaut* are absolutely modern. And of course he is a man of the theatre and knows exactly how to strike the right atmospheric and emotional chord. His music is very expressive and beautifully blended with the words. But this, like all Puccini operas, demands good taste from its interpreters. Many people have given verismo a bad name because of their bad taste and tendency to go over the top. Puccini has written *everything* down minutely in the score. [Josephine Barstow makes the same point.] But of course, this is more difficult because it's always harder to have enough confidence to offer the public nothing but simplicity and class. But if you do, you make a greater impact than those who rely on cheap effects, because class equals class in everything, including singing.'

The success of her first Manon Lescaut encouraged Freni to tackle another, even heavier and potentially more dangerous verismo part: the title role in *Adriana Lecouvreur*, which she sang a year after Manon, in 1984–85 also in San Francisco. (It is noteworthy that the San Francisco Opera, along with the Chicago Lyric, the Teatro Liceu and Covent Garden, is a firm favourite with a good many singers and has given artists like Freni, Thomas Allen and Leontyne Price the opportunity of trying out new roles.) It proved even more successful than Manon and has since become one of her most popular, sought-after portrayals. Her performances at the Bavarian State Opera, La Scala and the Teatro Liceu were considered a personal triumph, all the more satisfying in view of the role's difficulty.

'Vocally, Adriana is extremely taxing for a lyric voice, because in addition to a lot of sustained singing, it also contains plenty of recitatives and declamatory passages.' Apart from purely vocal considerations, her chief concern was how to put this character across as naturally and spontaneously as possible. She had seen too many phoney, 'actressy' productions. Yet when she read up the life of the real Adrienne Lecouvreur, about whom she had previously known next to nothing, she discovered this lady had been one of the first actresses to bring realism and simplicity to the French stage and to clean up all sorts of bad habits and traditions. 'She was a very simple person in real life. When I came to study the score, I realized there are only two instances in the whole opera where she is "acting": at the beginning, where we see her rehearsing and saying this is not good enough – which is pure declamation – and in Act III, where she recites *Phèdre*. In the first instance, immediately after the rehearsal, she begins the aria "Ecco respiro . . . io son l'umile ancella del genio creator". And the fact that she doesn't feel self-important is the key to her whole personality. So I told myself one shouldn't ham or play the actress all the time. One should make a sharp distinction between the moments when she is really acting or reciting, and the moments when she is herself, living her own life, her own drama – which is no comedy – racked by jealousy for her man. In moments like this she has to behave naturally and totally differently from the way she does on stage. As with Manon, instinct has a lot to do with getting this part right.'

'Mirella Freni breathes dramatic nuance into the slightest phrases and commands Cilea's very mixed idiom with such naturalness that some of the phrases that seem most intractable on paper work most effectively in performance . . . "Poveri fiori" was a moment of pure catharsis, a tragic lament for the transience of happiness that would have wrung tears from even the crustiest critic.' So wrote *The Times* after the performance at La Scala.

Freni once explained in *Ritmo* that singers should feel the drama and the meaning of the words they're singing with every fibre of their being. This is as important a part of operatic interpretation as the purely vocal aspect. She went on to add that this dimension of 'vibrant participation' in the drama is lacking in most of today's young singers, even in these post-Callas days. 'A famous colleague once told me that today's singers, like the times we live in, can be summed up in one word: nylon. And I must say I agree with him. You cannot sing on stage the way you do in the Conservatoire. You have to do it with all your heart, you have to feel the meaning of the words, and experience the dramatic truth at every moment; you have to know how to listen to the music coming out of the pit and how to blend your sound with the orchestra's. Operatic singing is not an academic act, it is an *artistic* act. And, when the time comes eventually for me to retire I would like to try and help young singers by teaching them something about the art of interpretation.'

Anyone familiar with Freni's interpretation of her most recent new role, Tatyana in *Eugene Onegin*, which she first sang in 1985 at the Chicago Lyric Opera, can only hope the day of her retirement lies in the very distant future. Her portrayal was stylistically impeccable, and heart-rending in its passionate intensity. Freni feels forever indebted to the Soviet film director Andrei Konshalovsky who directed the production of *Onegin* she sang at La Scala and who was responsible for transmitting to her the essence of nineteenth-century Russian life and culture. 'He made me understand how those girls, Olga and Tatyana – who were not nobility but country gentry – would have lived, and also explained all about the nanny who was married at thirteen. At the beginning of the opera, Tatyana is very sensitive and emotional. She is a more profound person than her sister Olga, who is a mere butterfly – in fact Tatyana and Lensky are the deep ones in this story – and feels strange and isolated in her surroundings. She spends her days reading these romantic novels which have conditioned her into a state where she is ready for love. And a girl who is ready for love is bound to get ignited by the first suitable male who comes her way. In her case it's Onegin, who is a blasé, corrupt aristocrat, perpetually bored. But, as Konshalovsky pointed out, even when bored, Onegin remains very "classy".'

The centrepiece of the opera is undoubtedly the Letter Scene, which also happens to be the most difficult vocally. 'It's important to bring out all the contrasting feelings Tatyana is experiencing: doubt and fear simultaneously mixed with the bold, rash impetus to ask this man to marry her. When one thinks about it, it really seems an incredible thing for a nineteenth-century girl to do, especially for Tatyana, who is outwardly very controlled. But inside she is very fiery and her passionate nature comes out in this letter written when she is all alone, in the middle of the night. Then, looking for an excuse to tell someone what she's experiencing, she questions her nanny about her life, while waiting for the right moment to pour out her own feelings. In a way, it reminded me of my daughter who, at the age of eight, fell in love with a boy at school. She longed to tell me about it but wanted *me* to drag it out of her. So, when we sat chatting after she went to bed, she said, "Mummy, please ask me something . . . " That memory, which flashed through my mind when rehearsing Tatyana, helped me very much in that scene.'

Konchalovsky also pointed out that at the moment when Onegin hands Tatyana's letter back to her, she learns a very painful lesson. Out goes the innocent young girl and in comes the woman. The two discussed the opera for two whole days before beginning rehearsals and everything became 'clearer and sort of mellower', according to Freni. She understood that this opera is really the story of a woman's life, and Tatyana a character who develops enormously during the course of the action. Through the intense emotional pain she experiences, the gauche, dreamy girl becomes a mature woman who finds the strength to make something positive out of this pain. 'In the finale it is *she* who gives Onegin a lesson in honour and integrity. She tells him how much she learnt from him, from the things he had told her in a manner so brutal it still makes her blood curdle to think about it, and makes him understand what a cad he is.'

Vocally, she considers Tatyana one of her most difficult roles: very wide-ranging and frequently moving from low to high passages very abruptly, as well as containing dramatic declamatory sections that have to pass suddenly into piano singing. There is also the problem of the language. Freni first started learning Tatyana with a coach in San Francisco and later studied Russian pronunciation and enunciation with a teacher at home. She also had the benefit of her (second) husband's advice. He is the world-famous bass Nicolai Ghiaurov, who was always at hand to 'show me all sorts of tricks about singing Russian idiomatically'.*

Freni's partnership with Ghiaurov began ten years ago in 1979 and after she got her divorce, they were married. Partners, she feels, are important in anybody's life but especially so in a singer's. 'It's important to decide whom you are going to have at your side and I am happy to say that, in my case, both my husbands have been men of music, capable of understanding the pressures of this ultra-demanding profession. I don't know what life would have been like if I'd had, say, a banker at my side. In any case, combining an operatic career with a satisfactory home life, and especially motherhood, requires great sacrifices.' After resuming her career when her daughter was two, Freni tried to ensure that whenever the child needed her, she was always there, participating as fully as possible in the everyday problems of life at home. While her daughter was growing up – from the mid-sixties to the mid-seventies – she concentrated her career on Europe so that she could easily go home between assignments. And when she changed schools – which coincided with a busy rehearsal period at La Scala followed by the run of performances – for two months Freni took the train back to Modena every single night, getting there at about three in the morning so that she would be home for breakfast and see her off to school. Then, in the afternoon, it was back to Milan by train.

'It was important for her to know that although my work is terribly important to me and although I love it to death, *she* always came first. My career always took second place to *her* needs. And she knew it.' The rewards of this extremely close mother-daughter bond, based on mutual respect and sincerity, have been enormous. It is her daughter whom Freni – now a grandmother of two but looking barely 40 – has charged with telling her when the moment will have come for her to retire: that will be 'when singing is no longer a joy but a worry caused by vocal problems. And such problems are bound to appear eventually. When that happens I hope I'll have the strength and willpower to recognize the fact and retire with good grace. If not, my daughter has promised: "Don't worry, mamma, I'll tell you".'

*Her next new role will be another Tchaikovsky heroine, Lisa in *The Queen of Spades*.

EDITA GRUBEROVA

EDITA GRUBEROVA IS the world's Number One coloratura soprano and, in the words of Peter Katona, Artistic Administrator of the Royal Opera, one of the few singers who really have full command of their voice. 'Hers is a fully trained, perfectly educated vocal instrument and, like a pianist who can accomplish any physically feasible feat, she has total vocal flexibility at any tempo or dynamic range from pianissimo to fortissimo. Although this is obviously the desired ideal, very few singers nowadays have such a choice of possibilities.

'If, like Gruberova, you do have this choice, you can decide to sing a phrase or passage in a certain way because you feel it is the *right* way. But if, as most singers are forced to do, you sing it a certain way because it is the *only* way you can manage to get these notes out, there is little merit to your interpretation because it springs from necessity. Some, though by no means all, of the floated pianissimi for which a certain soprano is famous, strike me as belonging to the latter category; and I can't help contrasting them with the singing of Jussi Bjoerling in his two recordings of *Faust*: in one of them he sings the famous high C piano and in the other forte. But you never get the feeling he is doing it because he cannot manage it any other way!'

One *has* to begin a chapter on Gruberova by drawing attention to her almost superhuman technique which enables her to deliver some of the most difficult arias in the soprano repertoire, such as Zerbinetta's in *Ariadne auf Naxos*, with apparent ease, and no hint of nerves. Yet technique is by no means the whole story. Her voice is not limited to the hard-edged, monochromatic brilliance characteristic of coloraturas but, as rightly described by voice expert John Steane, possesses 'a pure, exhilarating sound, capable of warmth and softness'. Most important, it has a sparkle that communicates an infectious joy in singing. Gruberova's most famous parts are the Queen of the Night, Zerbinetta and the title role in *Lucia di Lammermoor*. Her own favourites, though, are Zerbinetta and Marie in *La Fille du régiment* because she enjoys herself and feels herself at her best as a comedienne, 'a clown'.

So far, Gruberova has remained faithful to the coloratura repertoire which consists of a handful of roles such as, apart from those already mentioned, Blonde and Konstanze in *Die Entführung aus dem Serail*, Olympia in *Les Contes d'Hoffmann*, Cleopatra in Handel's *Giulio Cesare* and the title role in his *Alcina*, Amina in Bellini's *La sonnambula* and Elvira in *I Puritani*, the title role in Rossini's *Semiramide*, the Queen of Shemakha in Rimsky-Korsakov's *Le Coq d'or*, Gilda in *Rigoletto*, Violetta in *La traviata*, plus the title roles in seldom performed operas such as Delibes's *Lakmé* and Massenet's *Esclarmonde*. The fact that Gruberova has resisted expanding into lyric roles explains why, after twenty-one years of singing the excruciatingly difficult coloratura repertoire, her voice remains in superb condition. 'I would much rather confine myself to a handful of roles and be the best for those than try to expand into the lyric and lirico-spinto repertoire which is much wider, yet harmful for my kind of voice.'

Gruberova's rise to the top was slow and painful. She spent six frustrating years at the Vienna State Opera, where she moved to from her native Bratislava in 1970, under-employed and unappreciated, before striking gold in 1976 with a production of *Ariadne auf Naxos* directed by Filippo Sanjust and conducted by Karl Böhm. Although she did not come from a musical family – her father was a workman and her mother took in other people's washing – she discovered her voice early, through a schoolteacher, who assured her she should not waste such a gift as hers. She sang in several school and local choirs, and after studying for four years at the Bratislava Conservatoire made her début at the local opera house in 1967, aged 21, as Rosina in *Il barbiere di Siviglia*. On the strength of this performance, she was engaged by a small provincial Slovak theatre, where she remained for two years and sang a variety of roles ranging from Eliza in *My Fair Lady* to the three heroines in *Les Contes d'Hoffmann* and Violetta in *La traviata*. She was then engaged by the Vienna State Opera (on a two-year contract which has always been renewed) where she made her début in 1970 as the Queen of the Night. 'The Queen of the Night is either there from the beginning, or it never will be. It's so high that either you can do it immediately or you never will. There is no point in working on it for ten years, because by then you may not have any top notes left!'

This was followed by Olympia but although this, like the Queen, was a success, she was not particularly liked by the Director, and given no further big roles. Apart from a monthly performance as Olympia and the Queen, she spent the next six years singing Flora in *La traviata*, Kate Pinkerton in *Madama Butterfly* and an assortment of 'maids and servants' such as Barbarina in *Le nozze di Figaro*. Yet this may have been a blessing in disguise, for all the while she was studying with Ruthilde Boesch – her teacher to this day – learning from famous colleagues and perfecting her technique. Very few singers today have the benefit of such in-depth study and preparation.

One of the roles Gruberova had set her sights on and spent two full years learning with her teacher was Zerbinetta. She had never studied any Strauss at the Bratislava Conservatoire because they tended to concentrate on Mozart, Schubert and Czech composers. 'Every single day for two years I worked on Zerbinetta at the piano, to the point where I dreamt of it at night. When I first looked at the score I gasped in disbelief. It didn't merely look difficult – it looked impossible! I couldn't imagine how anyone could sing those millions of stratospheric notes.' But slowly, with her characteristic Capricornian patience and persistence, she learnt it and asked the Management if she could try it on stage. No, they replied, young singers don't perform roles such as this in Vienna without first trying them out in some small provincial theatre. So she asked her agent to find her a place but he drew a blank. Apparently *Ariadne auf Naxos* is not put on very often, and when it is it tends to be in big theatres and with famous casts. All that hard work for nothing, she thought forlornly. No one wanted to know about her Zerbinetta. Except one man: Professor Josef Witt, a former singer, then a coach at the Opera Studio.

One day, Gruberova decided to try singing Zerbinetta in his class. He was impressed enough to start explaining the whole opera and analysing all its parts – what goes on in the introduction, the meaning of this opera-within-an-opera, what Zerbinetta is actually saying in her famous aria and so on. Gruberova was lapping it all up and he seemed pleased. She must absolutely sing this part on stage, he urged. *And* he was prepared to back his judgement by barging in on the Director, despite the fact that he knew he did not like Gruberova, and announcing he could vouch on his head that she would score a big success in this role. So, he gave her five performances during the following season, 1974–75, which made people sit up and realize that 'this Gruberova really can sing'.

For a time she was very happy. Karajan had invited her to make her début at the Salzburg Festival, in 1974, as the Queen of the Night. But as far as the Vienna State Opera was concerned, she felt she was back to square one. No performance of *Ariadne auf Naxos* was planned for the following season, and she wasn't offered any new roles, either. The only ray of hope on the horizon was the present Director's impending departure and his replacement by Egon Seefelner, who was planning a new production of *Ariadne auf Naxos*, to be conducted by Karl Böhm. Gruberova arranged to audition for Böhm and impressed him enough for him to promise they would 'do this opera together'. It was the lucky break she had been waiting for. Once Böhm accepted her, the management had no choice but to comply. (As mezzo Lucia Valentini Terrani rightly states in her chapter, in many, if not most cases, it is not only the public but also the important conductors who propel singers to international fame.) Even though, as he confessed to her later, the new Director didn't much care for her either, he had to do what Böhm wanted.

Böhm could be a tartar on occasion but was invariably sweet to Gruberova throughout the rehearsals, which went extremely well. 'I could tell everyone was excited and impressed by my singing. I was expecting the première to go well, but it was such a big occasion and so important for my future, that I really had to get a grip on my nerves in order to keep my cool and stop myself from getting tense. But everything went well.' Her performance aroused tumultuous applause and she became the talk of the town. After this, all doors were open: La Scala, the Metropolitan Opera, Hamburg, Munich, Berlin – all opera houses were suddenly interested. 'This was the breakthrough I had been waiting for. It got me where I had only dreamt of getting. Sometimes I had to nudge myself to see if it was all real.'

Since then, Gruberova has sung Zerbinetta all over the world. But her favourite production remains Dieter Dorn's for the 1979 Salzburg Festival, also conducted by Böhm. In preparation for my first book, *Maestro*, which included a chapter on Böhm, I happened to be present at the last few rehearsals – the first time I heard Gruberova sing – and shall never forget the frisson experienced throughout her aria, which poured forth seemingly without the slightest effort, faultlessly executed. The stagehands downed whatever they were carrying and, like those attending the rehearsal, burst into clamorous applause; and the subsequent première brought the Kleines Festspielhaus down.

The secret of Gruberova's success in this role is, she thinks, the fact that she always sings it with immense joy and not a trace of nerves. 'The only time I ever felt nervous about Zerbinetta was that time in Vienna when I first sang it with Böhm – and then not because I wasn't sure I could sing it well, but because making a big success of it mattered so much. Since then, I have always felt sure of myself and enjoyed the fun of it all. I like Zerbinetta, her effervescence and down-to-earth philosophy. Do I agree with what she says? Basically yes. It's not the end of the world if a man leaves you or you haven't found the right partner. It doesn't mean life is over. There will always be another man. This is true for all of us, including Ariadne, who is spending her days weeping. But when the next man comes along she is as ready as anybody else to be swept off her feet!'

The quality of Gruberova's singing as Zerbinetta leaves one convinced it wouldn't matter if one never heard this role again because one has

already heard it sung to perfection. 'One can hardly conceive a
performance more brilliant than her Zerbinetta, and yet the most
acrobatic feats are accomplished with a smiling security in the spirit of
comedy (which Zerbinetta embodies), almost as though they were
something slightly comical in themselves,' wrote John Steane in *Opera
Now*. Indeed, Gruberova's next role at the Vienna State Opera after her
triumph as Zerbinetta, was in another comedy, Norina in Donizetti's
Don Pasquale, in German, in a production which toured the provinces
with great success.

Now she could ask the Management to mount any production she
liked; and she asked for *Lucia di Lammermoor*. The production, a very
poetic and beautifully designed one by Boleslaw Barlog, which opened in
1978, proved the perfect vehicle for her and she scored as big a personal
success as with Zerbinetta. Lucia was soon to become her second
warhorse and, along with Zerbinetta, remains the role she has performed
most often all over the world: Berlin, Covent Garden, La Scala, the
Metropolitan Opera, bringing the house down and collecting eulogistic
reviews along the way. ('Gruberova scored a triumph with a Lucia based
on extraordinary vocal technique and real interpretative depth', wrote
Opera after her performances at La Scala.)

'Lucia was my first big Italian role. I had wanted to sing it since my
student days at the Bratislava Conservatoire. I always thought it would
suit my voice and a couple of performances in Graz at the very beginning
of my career had convinced me I was right. But I had to wait until 1978 to
prove it to the world,' she says, not without a hint of bitterness, 'just as I
had to wait so long for my chance to show what I could do with
Zerbinetta.' She finds Lucia 'gorgeous to sing and a "complete" role in
the sense that the music, the voice and the feelings expressed all come
together to produce a very moving and haunting character. Vocally
speaking, at least as far as I'm concerned, the most challenging moment is
not the Mad Scene but her duet with her brother which demands an awful
lot of strength – not just vocal power and physical stamina but also
emotional power in order to make this confrontation believable. To
achieve this, a lot also depends on your partner – the two of you have to
feed each other – and on the director.'

She singles out a recent production of *Lucia* at the Zurich Opera by
Robert Carson – 'rather modern but very, very interesting' – as the best
she has sung to date and deeply regrets the fact that very few good stage
directors are interested in doing productions of *bel canto* operas. 'The
same is true of conductors. Apart from Muti [and the late Herbert von
Karajan who conducted a memorable production of *Lucia* with Callas, of
which a live recording is available], few top-class conductors are

interested in *bel canto*. In a way, I understand them because the orchestration is rather basic and I don't suppose they feel they have enough to do. They consider *bel canto* works to be "singer's operas" full stop. But they shouldn't be just that. They should be much more of a team effort. The problem is that the Grade Two conductors who usually deign to busy themselves with this repertoire just haven't got what it takes to make these operas really live.'

Gruberova's point is very important. Karajan, one of the few great conductors who did not consider it beneath him to conduct *Lucia*, told me à propos of *bel canto* operas that it took no less a man than Toscanini to convince him of the intrinsic worth of operas such as *Lucia* which, with typical conducting-student arrogance, he used to look down at. When Toscanini came to Vienna with La Scala to conduct this opera, he and his fellow students wondered why on earth he chose to waste his talents on such a banal work. 'But it took two minutes of the overture, as conducted by Toscanini, to convince us we were wrong. It was indeed the same score my fellow students and I had studied; but it was played by him with the same devotion and meticulousness he might lavish on *Parsifal*. And this completely changed my attitude: *no* music is vulgar or trivial unless played in a way that makes it seem so or implies that one expects it to be different.' He went on to say that it could be transformed into something trivial by conductors, often but not always foreign, who approach it with an attitude of contempt.

Apart from Norina and Lucia, Gruberova's Donizetti repertoire also includes the title role in *Maria Stuarda*, which she has recorded for Philips, in *Roberto Devereux*, one of her more recent parts, which she sang in Barcelona in 1990, and Marie in *La Fille du régiment*, which she first sang in early 1991 at the Zurich Opera in a very good production by Giancarlo del Monaco. Marie immediately became a firm favourite. 'The piece is an enchanting little comedy which the public seemed to enjoy greatly and I found the part a joy to sing and fun to play. Apart from Rosina, Norina and Zerbinetta, I haven't done very much comedy, so Marie was very special for me. It was also special in a musical sense. She has lots to sing, most of it lively, ebullient music consisting of almost Verdian melodies. In *Roberto Devereux* as well, I felt Donizetti leaning forward towards Verdi: you have those long arches, beautiful to sing, but the orchestration of course is not as heavy as in Verdi. This is why, as far as Italian singing is concerned, I have to stay mostly with Donizetti and Bellini.'

Bellini is 'the sweeter of the two. His music has a very special, instantly recognizable melodic line and harmonic structure and emotionally he is a gentler, softer and more melancholy nature.' Gruberova's first Bellini role was Giulietta in *I Capuleti ed I Montecchi* which she first sang in Florence in 1983 under Riccardo Muti with Agnes Baltsa as Romeo. When the production came to Covent Garden in 1984, Gruberova won the Olivier Award for her part in it. 'Miss Gruberova possesses a much larger voice than most coloratura sopranos and she uses it with taste. Her ability to fine down the tone to almost a whisper resulted in the house hanging on to her every note. When at full volume above the stave the voice sometimes hardened, and perhaps she could have coloured it more; none the less her Juliet was a real flesh and blood figure and she looked and moved well.' Gruberova's second Bellini role, Elvira in *I Puritani*, which she first sang in 1990 at the Metropolitan Opera, is heavier than Giulietta. 'The tessitura is middle-to-high, it hovers around the passaggio and then leaps upwards with lots of high notes. But it's beautiful and very expressive music, with long, melodic phrases requiring long breath. As with Donizetti's *Roberto Devereux*, one almost feels Verdi around the corner.'

Verdi, whose orchestration is much more dense and substantial than that of *bel canto* composers, makes altogether heavier demands on the singer and as Gruberova admits somewhat ruefully, 'there isn't much Verdi I could sing'. Her only Verdi roles are Gilda and Violetta, which take her to the limits of her vocal possibilites. Gilda she first sang in Vienna, in the controversial (and ultimately boring) original version, minus all high notes not actually written in the score. Gruberova is rightly ambivalent about this trend: 'In a sense Muti is right. These operas *should* be cleaned up from more than a century's accumulated débris in the form of other singers' additional high notes. But if you do them without *any* high notes, just as they were written, you have another problem: acute lack of excitement. The composer didn't write any high notes because he expected his singers to add some, according to their particular abilities. In the original version, I thought that Gilda's duets both with the duke and Rigoletto were very flat; they didn't carry you away at all. Half the visceral excitement so typical of Verdi was gone and everyone, except a few academic purists, was bored.' (To succeed in making *Rigoletto*, of all operas, seem dull is, one would have thought, an eloquent enough argument against such purist excesses. Which is not to say one is in favour of the opposite kind of excess: riotous ornamentation licence of the kind practised by Beverly Sills and, on occasion, Joan Sutherland.)

Gruberova has also sung Gilda in Zurich and in Lliubimov's controversial production in Florence. It lies very comfortably for her voice and is, 'much easier than Violetta in *La traviata*' (which she first sang at the Bavarian State Opera in Munich in a production conducted by Carlos Kleiber in 1986 and later, also under his baton, at the Metropolitan

Opera). 'Gilda is a girl and consequently one-dimensional, with very light, "youthful" music to sing, whereas Violetta is a woman. More than that, she is a woman in the process of transformation, experiencing a wide gamut of emotions and dramatic situations: from a courtesan's forced gaiety to overwhelming passion, happiness in love, self-sacrifice, abuse at the hands of her former lover and finally reconciliation before death. Dramatically she is a deeply rewarding character to portray.

'Vocally, she represents the limits of my possibilities. Further than that I cannot go and remain a true coloratura. There aren't any other Verdi parts for me because I don't have a "Verdi voice". My timbre is too light and my voice couldn't survive his orchestrations. I can manage Violetta because the very fact that he wrote Act I the way he did, with lots of coloratura music, means that he obviously didn't want the remaining acts to be sung in *too* heavy or over-dramatic a way. Certainly they should be sung in a very *expressive* way because the music is emotion-packed – in fact the density of the music amazes me, how he manages to pack so much emotion into a relatively simple musical structure. But if he had wanted a heavy, lirico-spinto sound in the last three acts, he wouldn't have written the kind of first act he did. Obviously he wanted a voice that could sing all four acts and depict in vocal terms, through a variety of colours, Violetta's emotional development. So I sang it with *my* natural voice, without trying to be anything I'm not. This is important for all singers to remember: to sing with *their* natural voice and never strive to reproduce another's sound.' (Lucia Popp also stresses this important point.)

The Munich *La traviata* with Kleiber joins *Ariadne auf Naxos* at the Vienna State Opera under Böhm and Ponnelle's production of *Die Zauberflöte* in the truly magical setting of the Felsenreitschule in Salzburg as the highest points in Gruberova's career. 'Everything in this *Traviata* was so simple because everything *is* simple with a genius at your side! The mere fact that Kleiber chose and accepted me to work with him was an honour equivalent to being awarded a medal.' Parts such as Violetta have filled out Gruberova's voice, making it rounder and a tiny bit darker, even though from the start it possessed more volume and amplitude than the average coloratura's. In early recordings – and recordings don't do full justice to the sparkle and excitement of her singing – the voice naturally sounded lighter. 'But roles such as Violetta and Manon require a different kind of focussing than the Queen of the Night, Konstanze or Zerbinetta. Yet as I already said, I don't want to expand any further but stay well within my natural limitations and possibilities.'

Massenet's *Manon* fits the bill admirably. Gruberova loves the French language with those nasal sounds, and the French style of composition seems to suit her voice; 'French music is no less emotional than Italian but there is a greater lightness of touch about it and this is reflected in the orchestrations which are different and much less heavy than Verdi's. Otherwise, in dramatic terms, Manon has a lot in common with Violetta, and undergoes an even wider gamut of emotions – from the light-hearted, carefree volatility of youth, to the experience of a great passion, then the famous Gavotte Scene in the park, the very dramatic Cloister Scene and finally death. All this is reflected in a myriad musical and vocal shades of colour. French, which I had studied privately for two years, is, after Italian, undoubtedly the most beautiful language to sing. I love all those nasal sounds, although Italian is much easier. Having enjoyed Marie and Manon so much, I was discussing possible further roles the other day with Dame Joan Sutherland. She suggested Lakmé, Thaïs and Esclarmonde but I must say I find them excruciatingly dull. [Gruberova has a strong point here!] I have also been asked to do Lucrezia Borgia, Anna Bolena and Semiramide but so far I have accepted only Semiramide. But I can't say I'm in love with the part. It is a bit too dramatic for me [indeed, it requires more "metal" in the sound], and the most exciting singing belongs to Assur. So, on the whole, I will remain within my present repertoire and do some more Mozart.'

Recently Gruberova, already a famous Queen of the Night and Konstanze, added two new Mozart parts to her repertoire: Giunia in *Lucio Silla* which she first sang in Zurich in 1991, and Donna Anna in *Don Giovanni*. Giunia she considers the most difficult of all her Mozart parts. 'It makes considerable technical demands, especially her second aria, which is pure fireworks with some really *excruciatingly* difficult coloratura.' (For Gruberova to use this word, which she hasn't for any of her other roles, this aria must be a fiend.) The Mozart of *Lucio Silla* was much less experienced and emotionally mature than the Mozart of *Entführung*, and this is why Giunia is not only vocally more difficult but emotionally less *clear* than Konstanze.

Konstanze, which Gruberova first sang in Vienna in the 1970s and later in 1980 in Munich under Böhm, is one of, but definitely not *the* hardest of her Mozart roles. (She performed Konstanze for Presidents Carter and Brezhnev at the 1979 Vienna summit.) 'Dramatically she is very straightforward. She is in love with Belmonte and that is that. I don't think there is anything ambiguous or enigmatic in her attitude to the Pasha Selim. The only problem in this context is that Selim, which is, of course, a speaking part, is usually played by some gorgeous, tall, slim and virile actor, who utters these noble sentiments in a dark, sonorous voice. Then in comes Belmonte, usually sung by a small podgy tenor, and in the circumstances, the soprano singing Konstanze can't be blamed for having difficulty in producing an equal amount of enthusiasm for *him!*' She stresses that when she talks about Konstanze not being especially difficult she means this relatively, because 'it goes without saying that Mozart is the most difficult of *all* composers. Everything about his musical writing is pure, precise and crystalline and so should your singing be. There is nothing to hide behind, whereas in Strauss or Puccini you have more leeway, you can hide behind a light portamento.' To the comment that she has managed to preserve her voice intact after 23 years on stage singing some of the most difficult roles in the repertoire, she replies that she owes this to two factors: 'The first is unremitting hard work. Ever since my young days, I was stubborn and refused to give in to any technical difficulties I might encounter in my roles, accept defeat or make do with approximations. I just worked on and on until I got it right, with the help of my teachers – Maria Medvecka in Bratislava and Ruthilde Boesch in Vienna, with whom I have studied all my new roles and who still comes to all my premières. Even if this hard work did not produce immediate results I am convinced it was necessary. As my teacher used to say, "keep on working and your time will come".' The fact that Gruberova's apprenticeship, the period before she rose to the top of the profession, lasted eight years plus four in the Conservatoire is, perhaps, an eloquent reason for her undiminished vocal virtuosity. The second reason is that 'I never wander too far from this focus of roles we've discussed, otherwise I'd get lost. First of all I would lose my Mozart and if I lost Mozart I'd lose everything. Every singer should sing a little Mozart, no matter what kind of voice they have. It need not be on stage and it need not be a whole operatic role. But anything by him, a concert aria, for instance, would greatly improve their vocal health.'

One of Gruberova's most interesting Mozart parts, even though she says she *likes* it less than Konstanze, is Donna Anna, which she first sang in Giorgio Strehler's production at La Scala in 1987, conducted by Riccardo Muti. When it was announced that she would sing it 'people stupidly said I was changing my repertoire, which was nonsense because Donna Anna is very similar to the Queen of the Night. Naturally it needs more volume [and, as John Steane points out, like Joan Sutherland, Gruberova has "a good house-filling strength as well as dazzling agility"], but otherwise anyone who sings the Queen of the Night could also sing Donna Anna. Her first aria, "Or sai chi l'onore", is very similar to the Queen's *second* aria, while her second, "Non mi dir", is similar to the Queen's first, minus the highest top notes, of course.

'Dramatically, while it is extremely interesting, it is also a deeply frustrating part, because Anna's very real bond with Don Giovanni is never consummated. The two circle around each other but the thing doesn't gel, they don't manage to make real contact. It is clear that through this contact with Giovanni, Anna has experienced something extremely powerful, which runs through the piece. There is this terrific energy between them, or hovering around them if you like, but there is also great tension. Anna's very tense first recitative is an expression of this stressful link. She lives through this experience musically, and expresses the energy of this encounter which may be the reason why she responds to Ottavio in such an anaemic way.'

Future new roles include the Countess in *Le nozze di Figaro* on record, Gounod's *Roméo et Juliette* ('a real lyric part') in concert and, as already mentioned, Semiramide at the Metropolitan Opera, where in spring 1991 she again sang Elvira in *I Puritani*. Gruberova also gives a great many Lieder recitals. She had just returned from a recital tour in Japan at the time of our last meeting in 1990, and was flushed because it had turned out to be a major triumph, gaining her the 5,000,000–Yen award for the best Japanese concert of the season. She has always been deeply drawn to the more intimate and introspective world of Lied, and plans to devote much more time to Lieder – especially those of Richard Strauss – in the future. She would advise all singers to start training themselves in this genre early on in their career and not wait until their voice begins to go because by then 'it is too late, you cannot master the nuance and subtlety of the style quickly, you have to work on and perfect it over the years.'

Gruberova, now in her prime as a singer, also strikes one as a balanced and contented woman despite a life touched by deep tragedy. For the past few years she has been living in Zurich with her two teenage daughters whom, since her husband's suicide in the early eighties, she has had to bring up alone – and *that* while coping with a career as demanding as hers. But she is not given to complaining. Her elder daughter plays the piano and the younger, aged fifteen, is very gifted for dance, especially jazz dancing, for which she does her own choreographies. But neither girl would contemplate a career in singing because 'they don't like this peripatetic and very demanding life of ours, so much of which is spent away from home and often alone in hotel rooms.' Twelve years ago, when the children were pre-school age, she had confided to *Opera News* that 'every singer who has children will know what I mean when I say that wherever one is, no matter what one is doing on stage, one's mind is always at home with the children wondering what they're doing, whether they are all right and why am I here and not with them? They need me and I need them. This is the harsh reality of my profession.'

The compensations, if any? 'Having a voice, experiencing the physical sensation of singing in your body, and feeling the spiritual rapport with the public: all this is a great blessing.'

DAME GWYNETH JONES

'SOMETIMES I FEEL like a big chest of drawers,' mused Dame Gwyneth Jones, whose outstanding international career as one of the best-loved British divas is as remarkable for its longevity as for the vocal power and wholehearted dramatic involvement of her portrayals. 'In each drawer lurks a different character with new sensations, new emotions and new movements. The last is absolutely vital. Regal characters like Elisabeth de Valois, for instance, should move quite differently from Aida, whose movements, although dignified, are always watchful, or from Salome who creeps about the stage like a cat.'

Gwyneth Jones does a lot of research in order to find the right movements for every role. When preparing Salome for the first time she studied with a belly dancer as well as a ballet dancer to get 'a flavour of the Orient' into her movements, and before first singing Madama Butterfly, she went to the Kabuki Theatre in Japan to watch the actors move 'on bended knees all night so that the whole body seems to be dancing' and study the way their special wigs make them carry their head. Yet even so, she explains that sometimes it takes her quite a long time to 'find' a character. 'Then suddenly, I feel I've got it. And once I do, I never lose it. It's stocked in one of those drawers for ever.'

This wholehearted commitment to her roles, along with the immense power of her dramatic soprano voice, is her salient characteristic as an artist. She literally throws herself into them with total abandon. According to director Elijah Moshinsky, 'she submits herself to them almost masochistically. In fact, she enjoys *over*submitting herself and parading her personal responses and emotions in a way that is absolutely right for Wagnerian characters. In fact she is almost *too* right for Wagnerian characters and makes these awful, neurotic, oversexed* and masochistic women like Elisabeth in *Tannhäuser* come across as more sympathetic than perhaps they should.'

This, of course, is a personal opinion and very much a minority point of view. Most people find Dame Gwyneth's very human portrayals of

*Gwyneth Jones disagrees strongly on this point!

Wagnerian heroines (she has sung Senta, both Venus and Elisabeth, Eva, Kundry, Isolde, Sieglinde and Brünnhilde) deeply affecting. The distinguished accompanist Geoffrey Parsons considers her 'one of the most generous personalities I know. And this is what comes out in her performances, her fabulous Brünnhilde to whom she brought this wonderful human tenderness – so unlike Nilsson's, for instance, who always remained too heroic and remote – and her fabulous Turandot.'

What is equally remarkable about Gwyneth Jones is the fact that she retains such vocal power after a twenty-five-year career of singing mainly the heavy dramatic repertoire. She made her début at Covent Garden in 1963 (singing Wellgunde in *Götterdämmerung*), and the summers of 1987 and 1988 respectively found her delivering portrayals of the gruelling roles of the Dyer's Wife in Strauss's *Die Frau ohne Schatten* and the title role in *Elektra* that were quite sensational. As Peter Katona, Artistic Administrator of the Royal Opera House, Covent Garden, puts it, 'it is no less than amazing to find someone capable of doing this after such a long and distinguished career in this repertoire. Her vocal stamina is simply extraordinary. She is also a performer who is intensely emotionally committed to her roles, which makes her a very strong and individual artist.'

'I try to *live* the characters I play and relate the emotions of each character to personal experience, to something in my own life and nature,' she explains. The role that brought this home to her more than any other was Isolde – it means 'the White One' in old Gaelic which, coincidentally, is exactly what Gwyneth means in Welsh – a very special role for her, *the* role she feels she became a singer for. She first sang it in San Francisco on her birthday, 7 November 1978, in weird circumstances which she interprets as a special omen: for a start, she had caught bronchitis from the conductor, her chest was aching, her throat felt as if a knife were cutting through it and she was afraid she would end up having to cancel the première. But her rented apartment was in Jones Street and the street around the corner that led to the Opera House was called Eddy Street. The two street names together added up to that of her late father, Eddy Jones, whom she loved passionately. So she felt everything was under his wing and her first Isolde was *meant* to be on her birthday, never mind her cold.

Afterwards she felt as if everything she had done before – 'all the experience, all the studying, all the *living*' – was a preparation for this role, so that she could understand its meaning which is 'three-dimensional'. The experience which above all helped her do that was her father's death, at which she was present. Having lost her mother at the age of three, her relationship with her father had been particularly warm.

She was only eighteen when he died, and his death hit her very hard. It happened only one hour before she received a letter from the Royal College of Music announcing she had been accepted as a student there. This, she explains, makes Isolde's cry of 'nur eine Stunde' so moving and meaningful. 'Having experienced death at close quarters, I remembered the delirium my father went through for three days and nights when he was conscious of "a presence" which he referred to as "sleep come to fetch me" at the foot of his bed. Then, on the fourth night, his expression changed to one of utter bliss, as if seeing someone special with whom he was being reunited. I feel sure it was my mother and it was wonderful to witness his absolute joy. I *knew* he was all right and this helped me a lot.'

Still, life was very hard. She was in London for the first time, with practically no money, alone in the world, distraught, unable to eat and walking about in a daze, as she put it. Nevertheless, she felt comforted because her father was freed of his suffering. This whole experience came back to her during the first Isolde. 'I understood the true meaning of the Liebestod, one of the most difficult scenes to interpret. It is perfection because Isolde, or rather her soul, is joining Tristan. Although not yet clinically dead, she is nevertheless out of her body, in a state of the fourth dimension. She can see him and he can see her, they *are* together in a transfigured state where they can experience eternity, surrounded by stars and clouds. Although physically present, she is no longer incarnate. It is vital to convey on stage the impression that you're floating, not solidly on earth any more. I think that my experience of my father's death has given me a deep understanding of this.'

Her close relationship to her father was also a help in understanding Brünnhilde, which she first sang at the Bayreuth Festival in 1974 and subsequently also in both Covent Garden Götz Friedrich productions and the 1976 Bayreuth Centenary production conducted by Pierre Boulez and directed by Patrice Chereau, which was televised worldwide. She particularly enjoyed working in this production which was 'wonderful teamwork'. Conductor, producer and cast all worked very closely with one another and developed their interpretation further every year. Obviously the first year was not as satisfactory, musically or dramatically, as the last.

Jones responded particularly strongly to Chereau's concept of Brünnhilde starting off almost as a child, but a very wise child because she had inherited the wisdom of her mother, Erda. 'At the beginning, she is a warrior-maiden who worships and is very close to her father. But soon she undergoes a series of transformations. She witnesses the love of Siegmund and Sieglinde, her first contact with human love, or any form of love other than that for her father. It awakens and moves her enough for her to disobey Wotan's orders and help the unfortunate pair. Yet because she is Wotan's second self, she intuitively knows that in so doing she is also fulfilling his own secret wish. The finale of Act III, when Wotan banishes her from Valhalla and puts her to sleep on a rock, is so overwhelmingly moving and beautiful that, really, it is a privilege to sing it. My own tremendous closeness to my father always makes it very special for me.'

Brünnhilde's second contact with human love is, of course, her awakening to life as a mortal by Siegfried in the finale of Act III of *Siegfried*, where she begins to experience a new gamut of emotions: 'Being a virgin, the fire and excitement of desire terrifies her. The ecstatic love scene between them is out of this world . . . In the last year of the Chereau production I felt as if time were standing still.'

When we next come across Brünnhilde at the beginning of *Götterdämmerung*, she is already wise enough to know that, in order to keep Siegfried's love, she must give him freedom. She must set him free so that he may always return to her of his own free will, without feeling *bound*. She sings 'Zu neuen Taten' and this scene is, in her view, dramatically difficult because 'she is sending away the one person she wants *not* to go away! Although she knows she has to do it, it is still very hard to bear.' But the scene she relishes most is Brünnhilde's confrontation with Siegfried (who because of Hagen's drug has no recollection of her), where she experiences betrayal in love, torment and humiliation.

'It makes me feel ten feet high, with flames blazing from my eyes and about to set the stage alight with rage and fury! Yet this is also a moment where experience and technical control are essential so that one can save something for the big scenes ahead. This, believe me, is very hard. For, as Brünnhilde, you are experiencing and having to emit those outsize emotions with the utmost power and conviction. Yet you, the artist, must be in complete technical control not only of your voice, but of every movement and every muscle on your face and body. A part of you must always be detached, watching and controlling what you're doing . . . It's elating to feel the electricity in the air and sense the emotions created in the audience. The other thing to watch for is not to get carried away by the fantastic, incredible orchestral sound which makes me feel I could fly. It takes very great stamina and physical strength to sustain the voice so that it soars effortlessly over the orchestra, in one of the most exciting scenes not just in the *Ring* but in my whole repertoire.'

Jones stresses that it is absolutely *essential* for singers to know what they're doing, to be in good health and to have reached a stage of sufficient maturity before tackling those big Wagnerian roles. This is precisely why Wagner is considered so dangerous for young voices. First, because of the sheer physical stamina required which takes many years to build up; second, because of the experience needed before they can pace them properly so that the voice stays fresh until the end. This is why, even if young singers can sing all the *notes* in these roles, they should first familiarize themselves with Wagner through small parts – like Rhinemaidens, Norns and Valkyries – before they plunge into the deep. The two most taxing of all Wagnerian roles, Isolde and Brünnhilde (in *Götterdämmerung*), present a further problem. After the very long and dramatic first two acts, there is a long hour-and-a-half's rest before the Liebestod and the Immolation scene. This is very dangerous because 'after singing for so many hours your vocal cords are very warmed up, then, all of a sudden, there is nothing for over an hour. It is therefore crucial not only to rest completely after those demanding first two acts so that you regain your strength, but also to warm up the voice thoroughly again, as if for a new performance. This way it will be ready to respond immediately and cope with the very strenuous final scenes.'

For all these reasons she vowed to herself at the beginning of her career not to tackle the heavy Wagnerian roles until she had had at least ten years' experience. After singing Rhinemaidens, Valkyries and Norns, she eased herself into the bigger roles with Sieglinde and Senta (in 1965 and 1966 respectively). She still sometimes sings Sieglinde, which she relishes both musically and dramatically. Although its tessitura is a notch lower than Brünnhilde's, the same singer can sing both roles. 'Dramatically, Sieglinde differs from Brünnhilde in that she is completely human; a mortal woman who experiences this rapturous love for Siegmund. Theirs is much more than a normal man/woman love, though, because they are twins. This blood bond makes their love all the more compulsive. They have both suffered terribly from being separated, so their reunion is all the more ecstatic – and their love duet is quite wonderful to sing.'

Like most Wagner sopranos, she is more cautious about Senta in *Der fliegende Holländer*, which has a tricky tessitura, hovering largely on the passaggio (the notes F and G) and climbing up to B from there. Wagner was still young and relatively inexperienced when he composed this opera and this probably explains why Senta is not as well written as some of his later heroines. 'Her big aria, "Wie aus der Ferne", for instance, lets you sit on the passaggio for so long that it saps away a tremendous amount of your energy. This is why even seasoned Wagnerian sopranos shy away from it.'

One of the main reasons why Gwyneth Jones has managed to sustain such a long career in this heavy repertoire is the fact that her vocal development was gradual and rests on very secure foundations. It probably also explains why she has managed to surmount a vocal crisis

Left: JUNE ANDERSON as Elvira in
Andrei Serban's production of
I Puritani: 'Good conductors and
directors are essential for *bel canto*,
which can sound either deadly boring
or the most exciting music imaginable.'
(*Daniel Cande*)

Right: JOSEPHINE BARSTOW as Elisabeth
de Valois in *Don Carlos*, her favourite
role: 'Verdi heroines have an inner
spiritual life which is written into their
music and which you, the interpreter,
get to know very intimately. This is why
it is not enough to sing Verdi with
passion. You have to sing Verdi with
heart.' (*David Scheinmann*)

HILDEGARD BEHRENS as *Salome*, the role that propelled her to international prominence, and which she feels 'should be sung with utmost beauty and the innocence of a very young girl who is completely natural, direct and unscrupulous.' *(Siegfried Lauterwasser)*

Left: MONTSERRAT CABALLÉ. After undergoing laser treatment for a brain tumour that threatened to end her singing career in 1985, the Spanish soprano returned to the stage in Madrid in Gluck's *Armide*. 'I feel as if new life is coming back to me,' she said. 'I am a big woman, I weigh 103 kilos – terrible but true – yet I feel wonderful. The prospect of never singing again made me realize and appreciate more intensely things I used to take for granted. Now every, every day, every performance, seems like a gift.' *(Courtesy of Montserrat Caballé)*

Below: GHENA DIMITROVA as Lady Macbeth (with Renato Bruson as Macbeth), a role which she feels demands considerable *artistic* maturity. 'She is the motor of the whole plot. Without a really strong, substantial Lady Macbeth, the opera fails to gel. Therefore you have to have solved all your vocal problems and be free to concentrate on the drama.' *(Christina Burton)*

MIRELLA FRENI, who from the start 'felt a deep love for my vocal instrument and a determination to treat it with respect and protect it jealously', and who has preserved her voice in excellent condition well into her fifties. She is pictured here as Tatyana in *Eugene Onegin*. *(Donald Cooper)*

EDITA GRUBEROVA in the role that brought her fame, Zerbinetta in *Ariadne auf Naxos*. 'The secret of my success in this role is that I always sing it with immense joy. I like Zerbinetta, her effervescence and down-to-earth philosophy. I feel sure of myself in the part and enjoy the fun of it all.' *(Donald Cooper)*

Left: DAME GWYNETH JONES as the Marschallin in *Der Rosenkavalier*, an opera which after *Salome* and *Elektra* feels 'like a different world, almost like singing the music of another composer. The orchestration is lighter, too, because we are in an altogether gentler world . . . And singing it under Carlos Kleiber in Munich was as if he had a feather duster that took all the cobwebs away. He made it sound as if it had just been created – sparkling, exciting and new, like a breath of spring.' *(Christina Burton)*

Opposite: EVA MARTON as the Empress in *Die Frau ohne Schatten*, an 'allegorical opera that opened doors for me'. When she sang it at the Metropolitan Opera, with Birgit Nilsson as the Dyer's Wife, the latter autographed her score. 'I knew exactly who had sung the role before.' (Leonie Rysanek.) 'I knew exactly that my time had come. I knew I had to grab this chance. I knew what I know and what I can do. What I didn't know was how the public would accept me.' *(Gert von Bassewitz)*

Right: DAME KIRI TE KANAWA as Arabella, a role with which she immediately identified because 'there is a lot of me in her. I, too, can detach myself from emotional situations and look at things fairly coolly.' And, as always, it was the music that provided the real clues to the character. 'If you listen to the music as Arabella is walking down the stairs at the finale, you can hear the softening of a woman. And a woman is wonderful when she is softened up and made to feel feminine and is giving in to a man.' *(Christina Burton)*

Left: ROSALIND PLOWRIGHT as Donna Anna in *Don Giovanni.* She tries to conquer her natural nervousness by remembering Carlo Maria Giulini's words: 'You must not be nervous, Rosalind. God has given you a great gift. Now please go on stage and give it back to him.' *(Christina Burton)*

Right: LUCIA POPP as Eva in *Die Meistersinger von Nürnberg* at Covent Garden, her first Wagnerian role which, to her surprise, she found she could sing 'with my natural Lucia Popp voice . . . By the end I found myself wishing it could go on longer, and that I could sing more Wagner.' *(Christina Burton)*

and emerge triumphant in recent years with performances in roles like Turandot, Elektra and the Dyer's Wife. Born in Pontnewynydd, Wales, she sang in various choirs as a contralto. Indeed, it was as a mezzo that she was accepted at the Royal College of Music, where she studied from 1956 to 1960 with Arnold Smith and Ruth Packer. She points out that, for a dramatic soprano, starting off as a mezzo is not as unusual as it may seem. 'When you listen to Flagstad you can hear this very warm middle voice which sounds very much like a mezzo at the bottom and then opens up at the top. In a way, it's *good* not to start using the top voice until later because this way you minimize the danger of strain and start building a very solid foundation on which the top can rest. [Dame Joan Sutherland makes this point, too.] If the middle and the bottom of the voice are healthy, then you have no problems at the top. It's a bit like building a house that rests on solid rock. But if you build it on sand, the whole edifice will soon crumble.'

Still, the natural placement of her voice began to move upward while still at the Royal College. When she went on to study at Herbert Graf's International Opera Studio in Zurich with Maria Carpi, a former soprano, the latter immediately sensed that her new pupil was really a soprano. So they started taking the voice up, albeit very cautiously. It was the pupil who stubbornly refused to believe her. Then, whilst working on the role of Fidès in Meyerbeer's *Le Prophète*, which is a very high mezzo, Maria Carpi gently pointed out that without realizing it, she was singing it the way a dramatic soprano would. 'Whereas one would have expected a mezzo to have some difficulty with the very high coloratura, I was storming away merrily and relishing every minute of it,' she recalls. It was only after hearing the role performed by a mezzo at the Zurich Opera that she herself realized just how differently *she* had been singing it.

During this time, 1962, she made her operatic début in Zurich in mezzo roles like Orfeo in Gluck's *Orfeo ed Euridice* and the Third Lady in *Die Zauberflöte*. At the same time, she was preparing some really heavy mezzo roles like Azucena in *Il trovatore* and Ulrica in *Un ballo in maschera*. But she never got round to singing them. Conductor Nello Santi, Music Director of the Zurich Opera, heard her singing Czipra in *Der Zigeunerbaron* and noted how she was helping Adele Leigh, who had a cold, by singing her top lines in the ensembles. Next day Santi dragged her into his office and made her sing some really high soprano music. She recalls that it was easy to impress him because she coped effortlessly. At the end, Santi slammed the lid on his piano and exclaimed 'Basta così. You will never sing in this opera house again as a mezzo because you are a soprano.' So instead of singing Ulrica in the forthcoming production of *Un ballo in maschera*, she sang Amelia.

Meanwhile she had auditioned for Solti, then Music Director of the Royal Opera House, with Eboli's aria 'O don fatale' from Verdi's *Don Carlos*, and been hired to sing this part as well as Amneris in *Aida*. But after the production of *Ballo* in Zurich she wrote to him saying that she had become a soprano. Therefore, she would prefer not to sing Amneris and Eboli, but would be quite prepared to try small soprano roles such as Rhinemaidens rather than present herself to the public in a way in which she didn't mean to go on. So all she sang during her first season as a full company member at Covent Garden was Rhinemaidens, Valkyries and Norns, and it was only on tour in Manchester and Coventry that she got a chance of something more substantial: Octavian in *Der Rosenkavalier* and Lady Macbeth.

She acknowledges a huge debt to Covent Garden, and especially to Solti, for the superb training she was given there and the great personal interest he took in her career. During her second season, 1964–65, he gave her a chance to sing a performance of Leonore in *Fidelio*, in place of Régine Crespin, and, more importantly, to replace an indisposed Leontyne Price in the Visconti production of *Il trovatore*, conducted by Carlo Maria Giulini. He also offered her Santuzza in *Cavalleria rusticana*. When the possibility arose to be the second cast to the great Leontyne Price, the then Artistic Administrator, Joan Ingpen, pointed out that she would have to audition for Giulini. He accepted her on condition that she study the role with the famous coach Maestro Luigi Ricci in Rome. On the last day of her studies there, Ricci took her to Giulini's home to sing the role through for him. The next day she returned to London and received a telephone call from Sir David Webster informing her that Leontyne Price had withdrawn from the production because of illness and that Giulini was happy for her to sing the première. She treasures the memory of those performances, 'of those wonderful long fingers of his almost reaching up to me on stage and carrying me through the evening. With Giulini you always feel this gentle love coming up to you from the pit.'

From Giulini and Ricci she learnt a great deal about Italian singing in general and Verdi in particular. She agrees with the view that Verdi is very good for the voice because 'he demands a beautiful line, purity and roundness of sound, a gentle soaring in the pianissimi and, occasionally, brilliant coloratura. It is also important when singing Verdi to project a certain serenity through your facial expression as if, through the face, your whole soul were being projected, along with the sound.' Interestingly, one of the things that had struck me most when I heard her first Leonora in *Il trovatore* (while I was still a student) was the amazing candour and feeling she projected through her eyes which looked enormous and, somehow, instantly put one on her side. Her repertoire of Verdi heroines expanded to include Elisabeth de Valois in *Don Carlos*, Desdemona in *Otello* and the title role in *Aida*, all performed with distinction.

For the vocal reasons she explained, Gwyneth Jones would like to continue singing Italian opera as long as possible, and adds that those long legato phrases and gentle pianissimi have also helped her enormously in her singing of German opera. Despite the sheer volume of orchestral sound, she says she is now less inclined to push her voice, and tries to sing piano as often as possible (for instance in 'War es so schmählich' in Act III of *Die Walküre*). Of all her Italian roles her finest is the title role in Puccini's *Turandot*, which she first sang at the Los Angeles Opera during the Olympic Festival in 1984 and soon afterwards at Covent Garden. It was a towering achievement. She had studied the role with Dame Eva Turner, one of its most famous interpreters, and the result was that all her former vocal problems (like a disturbing wobble which had tended to make some of her performances erratic) seemed to have disappeared. She had not sounded as secure vocally for several years, unleashed wave upon wave of glorious sound and says she enjoyed the experience enormously.

'I just *adore* the feeling of singing high notes. They give me such a thrill! There is only one thing more exciting than singing high Cs and that is singing them with a gorgeous tenor! You can't *believe* the sensation when soaring up there in the stratosphere with a tenor like Placido Domingo. I could never imagine feeling scared of high notes. The day I do I would have to give up singing.'

As always, she tried to look for the more sympathetic side of this steely heroine's character. For although at the beginning Turandot is very much the Ice Princess, underneath it all she is a very feminine and full-blooded woman. 'I think she knows this, which is why she tried to erect this wall of ice around her in the first place. In fact, one of the riddles she has set asks precisely that: "What is ice outside but burning inside?" So she is aware of this incredible fire in her but also frightened of it and trying to conceal it.'

The only drawback about a lot of Italian opera in Jones's view is the rudimentary nature of the libretti. A good case in point is *Il trovatore*. For years she searched in vain for some hidden meaning but eventually gave up. 'It's just very basic and very static, and this puts you in a kind of straitjacket; despite the actual beauty of the words, of the Italian language, you just have to accept that everything hinges on beautiful singing.' (Herbert von Karajan, who had a special affection for this, as indeed for most, Italian opera, agreed with her about the plot which he, too, found 'incomprehensible, complete nonsense. There is simply projection by the music of basic human emotions: love, hate, jealousy,

revenge and so on – a little bit like eating a hamburger. Very
wholesome!')

Does that mean that Dame Gwyneth, who describes herself as 'a text
fanatic', finds singing German opera more fulfilling? She hesitated. 'It's
simply a question of concentrating on different priorities. It is true,
though, that in German opera in general, and Strauss in particular, the
texts do tend to be more interesting.' And a case in point is Hugo von
Hofmannsthal's translation of Oscar Wilde's *Salome*. She first sang
Salome in 1970, at the Hamburg State Opera, in a production directed by
August Everding and conducted by Karl Böhm. From the very start, its
combination of singing, dance and sublime poetry made her feel
'complete as an artist'. It is also very exciting to sing because it starts off
innocently and then gets more and more feverish and crazed towards the
finale. This, in turn, demands a wide variety of vocal colours. As always,
she feels that clues about vocal interpretation are to be found not only in
the score, but in the text as well. 'In this case, every reference to Salome
in the text alludes to her whiteness and purity. I feel that, at the
beginning, she is just a very spoilt child and a virgin who hates the
sordidness, decadence and orgies going on at the palace. The combination of her virginity, naïveté and capriciousness attracts every male in
sight. They all lust after her precisely *because* she is so different from
everybody else – pure and white and flower-like. This is why Narraboth is
prepared to kill himself for her and why Herod is prepared to grant half
his kingdom just to see her dance.

'But she is oblivious to all this and, as yet, only a spoilt child used to
having her every whim granted. What fascinates her about the Baptist is
that he is the first man ever to deny her something she wants. Like the
forbidden fruit, she finds this irresistible. And, because she hates all the
goings on at the palace, she is also drawn to his mysterious aura and finds
it thrilling and fascinating. I don't think that at the beginning she really
knows what she wants from him. She is curious, she wants to touch him,
stroke his hair, kiss his mouth, quite innocently. I don't think there is any
sexual desire as yet. But his rejection makes her adrenalin rise and she
experiences real anger.

'What awakens and changes her completely is the Dance of the Seven
Veils, which for this reason should always be performed by the singer and
not by a dancer. It starts off softly and naïvely, as a folk dance which she is
used to performing before the court. But something seems to be calling
her, drawing her towards the Baptist's cistern – there is a particular
passage in the orchestra that sounds like a bird, a death bird, you can
almost hear the fluttering of its wings. She responds to this calling which
gets stronger and stronger and draws her away from Herod, she becomes

more and more oblivious of him and increasingly lured toward the
Baptist, until she works herself into such a frenzy that, in her mind, she
loses her virginity and gives herself wholly to him.

'After the dance, Salome is a changed person. She has experienced
such longings, such sexual lust and ecstasy that when the dance is
finished, she has driven herself practically to distraction, to the point
where she is mentally unhinged. So that when the severed head comes
out, she has only one thing in mind: her desire to kiss his mouth which is
so obsessional that she doesn't understand why the severed head doesn't
answer back. And in her final ecstasy, Salome goes through an experience similar to Isolde! I mean that, by the time the soldiers come to
crush her with their shields, Salome is already in another dimension.
And I'm convinced that, unbeknown to her, it was a subconscious
longing for this kind of "religious" experience, this fusion – even though
it came about only in and through death – that drew her to the Baptist in
the first place.'

Salome is not among her best portrayals, but her performances of the
Dyer's Wife in *Die Frau ohne Schatten* in summer 1987 and the title role in
Elektra in summer 1988 must be counted among the finest achievements
in her career: vocally glorious and dramatically gripping. It was therefore
not surprising to hear that before she sang Elektra for the first time, at the
Cologne Opera in 1984, she visited Mycenae, where it all happened, and
found the experience revealing.

'Climbing that hill and standing in that bathroom where Agamemnon
was murdered, seeing this weather-beaten place with its extremes of heat
and wind made me understand what kind of people were moulded out of
that landscape. It told me tales about how Elektra lived, how she walked,
the type of woman she *could* have been, about all that hate but also about
all that love inside her. [Again, it is love for her father that we are dealing
with.] As I said à propos of Turandot, I always look for, and have to find,
the love in every character. Without this, I cannot make the imaginative
link with them.'

When she first saw *Elektra* many years ago at the Geneva Opera, it hit
her under the belt. She sat in the front row of the stalls, barely able to
breathe and thinking she was going to be physically sick. Afterwards she
felt ill for days and her reaction was that she never wanted to see, or sing,
or have anything to do with this opera, *ever*. Shortly afterwards she was
singing the Fourth Maiden and later Chrysothemis at Covent Garden, to
Nilsson's Elektra, so that by the time she came to sing the title role herself
she was well acquainted with the work as a whole (just as she felt familiar
with the world of *Die Walküre* when she first sang Brünnhilde). 'Being
familiar with the work helped with both Brünnhilde and Elektra, because

I had been hearing the music constantly and watching my colleagues from
the wings.'

Even so, she had felt her Elektra would be very different from
Nilsson's. The critic of *The Times* rightly noted that 'quite unlike the
Elektra of her own Chrysothemis performances, Jones presents a woman
who never gloats, is never gleeful in her taunting of Clytemnestra.' Jones
felt that, in the *Oresteia*, there are clues that speak mountains about
Elektra's character: that she was a woman full of love but now made
desolate and grieving and hurt. But because she is a King's daughter, she
is very proud and has great strength of character. This strength (because
of her tremendous love for her father and horror at the great wrong that
has been perpetrated) forces her to sacrifice everything in order to
achieve her aim: revenge. 'I feel that *if* her father hadn't been killed, she
would have made the most loving wife and mother to somebody because
she has so much love and tenderness to give. This is evident from her
attitude towards Orestes, for whom she has been waiting for years. But
meanwhile, she has shrivelled up and become dismally arid as a woman.
Her only raison d'être is her burning hate – which was nevertheless
inspired by love – driving her to her revenge. Her wonderful cry of
"Orest" says everything about her, as do the phrases that follow it, which
should be sung with great warmth and beauty. (Again, I have found my
singing of Italian opera very helpful here.) The text is very poetic, she is
remembering how beautiful her hair used to be and uses such sensitive
language that we are offered a glimpse of the sort of woman she *could*
have been. It is important to show that what has driven her to this state of
being almost like a wild animal was her grief and revulsion at her beloved
father's murder and the treatment she received at the hands of her
mother. I find her moving beyond words to perform.'

Vocally, the role is ideal for her. 'Everything in Jones's voice equips
her exactly for this performance,' wrote *The Times*, 'but especially those
high fortissimos that are perfectly controlled to scald the ear like burning
ice: at once fiercely impassioned and dead cold; her ability to go on
flinging out these yells of the id while always radiantly singing and not
shrieking, is something of Elektra's own superhumanity. Power, though,
is not her only weapon. There is also the dark principal language of her
interpretation, at once threatening and threatened; there is also a weird,
moonlit sensuality and an uneasy repose: a performance that fires
everyone else on stage.'

Yet Jones is quick to point out that Elektra is, nevertheless, a
dangerous role, for the simple reason that she never stops. She starts off
with a monologue and goes on ceaselessly until the end, with a lot of
running around at the same time. 'It's a very modern piece. Maybe

Strauss felt that with this work he was reaching the frontiers of sanity.' One knows that this is just what he did feel.

Does the Marschallin in *Der Rosenkavalier* (which she first performed in 1972 at the Bavarian State Opera under Carlos Kleiber and returned to year after year for well over a decade) feel part of the same composer's world? After all, it is hard to imagine a contrast more stark than that between the gut-splitting emotions of *Elektra* and the faintly decadent sensuality and sentimentality of rococo Vienna. 'No, it's almost like singing music by another composer. There is an enormous difference in the orchestration as well. It seems lighter, somehow, because we are in an altogether gentler world. In this sense I feel that *Die Frau ohne Schatten*, is much closer to the world of *Salome* and *Elektra*, which is to say, to Strauss's youth, than his "drawing-room" operas like *Der Rosenkavalier*, *Arabella*, *Ariadne auf Naxos*, *Capriccio* and *Intermezzo*.' She was quite terrified before singing her first Marschallin – she recalls that her daughter was in a carry cot at the time – because she knew how exacting Kleiber is: immensely interested in detail, not only as far as the score and singing are concerned, but also dramatic detail like facial and body movements. 'He is a perfectionist, and it is vital to him that you do it exactly as he wants. If he asks you to accentuate a little dot, it is well worth trying your utmost to do it, if you can, because you can see from his eyes that he is waiting for it. And if it comes out right, you get a look of pure bliss in his face.' Jones learnt a great deal from Kleiber and appreciated the fact that every time they came to rehearse this production in Munich it seemed as if they were doing it for the first time (Lucia Popp and Brigitte Fassbaender, who sang Sophie and Octavian, make the same point about working with Kleiber.) 'It was as if he had a feather duster that took all the cobwebs away and made the piece sound as if it had just been created: sparkling, exciting and new, like a breath of spring. He also managed to make every performance feel like an opening night, a gala, by creating a very special atmosphere of excitement.' (Kleiber is known to detest routine and will go to extraordinary lengths to ensure it never rears its ugly head. For example, after every performance he sends singers and orchestral musicians alike little notes, known in the music world as 'Kleibergrams', in which he indicates details he would like done differently at the next performance.)

At the time, he explained to Jones that the most important thing about the Marschallin is never to be too sad – *ever*. In his view it is crucial that the ending should be 'with one eye wet and the other dry' because the Marschallin is a very feminine woman and there will be a 'next one' for her. But it is obvious that she and Octavian really enjoyed their fling and his kissing of her hand at the finale 'tells just about all'. Act I, on the other hand, should come across as 'one of those mornings' where she just got out of the wrong side of bed: the fright of her husband's arrival interrupts a cosy breakfast *à deux*; after that, everything gets on her nerves: the levée, Ochs, the way her hair looks. There is this sense of destructiveness that springs from a bad mood.'

As we're talking about moods, it seemed the right moment to ask Gwyneth Jones how her appealing, expansive personality copes with the pressures of such a high-powered international career. She replied that the most important thing of all is having a fulfilled personal life. This she has achieved with her Swiss husband, Till Haberfeld, and their teenage daughter, on whom she dotes. (She tries to schedule her international engagements so that they can be together during school holidays.) The family live in a quiet village outside Zurich where she spends as much time as possible, replenishing the well and recuperating from the strain of operatic life: a life spent travelling, interpreting characters who take her into different spheres, experiencing strange and extreme emotions and living a very unreal life on stage. It amounts to giving and receiving so much in turn that she, like most singers, feels she needs something very solid in her life, to keep her feet on the ground.

'You have to have the warmth of your family, your loved ones, and you need to have built as normal and as peaceful a life as possible. Obviously in operatic life most of the time you find yourself in hotels and airports. So you *have* to be able to go back to your roots, to normality, as often as possible and be a mother and housewife, cooking, doing flowers and growing plants. (I can't imagine a life without the beauty of plants and flowers.) And, of course, being a mother has been a crucial experience for me, both as a woman and as an artist: because you have to *know* the feelings you are portraying on stage. It helps make your interpretations richer if you've lived and have personal knowledge of those emotions. Someone who hasn't known love cannot convey it convincingly. Maybe that's not the way others feel – but it's how *I* feel.'

Gwyneth Jones – who was made a CBE in 1976, a Dame of the British Empire in 1986 and awarded the Shakespeare Prize for services to European Art in 1987 – has every reason to feel satisfied with her life and achievement. There is no mistaking the enormous hard work or the enormous amount of love she has poured into it over the years. She rightly feels that artists must always continue to grow. They must work constantly on perfecting their technique and refining their interpretations. And as her comments make abundantly clear, she considers the psychological preparation to be as important as the physical.

'Obviously one is very dedicated and conscious that this is what one was born *for*, that this is one's mission in life. At the same time, I feel very privileged because I think singing is one of the most wonderful things that can happen to a human being: being able to give joy to other people and to oneself through the beauty that is in music – in great works like Wagner's, Strauss's, Verdi's, Mozart's or Puccini's – is truly a unique privilege.'

EVA MARTON

In an age when big female voices have almost vanished from the operatic stage, Hungarian-born Eva Marton is the possessor of a huge, gleaming dramatic soprano voice ranging from a clear, powerful top to a gutsy, expressive chest register. But, aware that huge voices can easily become relentlessly loud or monochromatic, she has taken care to colour it with a subtle palette of nuances and dynamic shadings that bring out the humanity of the characters she interprets – something that sometimes eluded even Birgit Nilsson until after she was past her vocal peak.

Marton's acclaimed appearances as Turandot at Covent Garden in summer 1987 illustrated this quality to perfection. Seldom had the redoubtable Ice Princess appeared as vulnerable and, through this crack in her panoply, as lovable as she did in Marton's portrayal: it was as if we, too, were seeing Turandot through Calaf's eyes and perceiving the woman behind the mask. 'There is a radiance to her singing that hangs on in there even when she is at her loudest and highest: at last, a Turandot of commanding beauty and believable youth,' wrote *The Times*.

Turandot is the role that turned Marton into a star. She first sang it in 1983 at the Vienna State Opera in a new production featuring José Carreras as Calaf, conducted by its then Music Director, Lorin Maazel, directed by Hollywood's Sam Wanamaker, televised live throughout Europe and subsequently recorded by CBS. 'After this production, the public began to treat me as a star, the new sensation,' she recalls. 'It was very interesting. I had worked well and at a high level for several years and had made my Salzburg début in the previous summer as Leonore in *Fidelio*. Yet it was after those Vienna Turandots that I began to emerge as a favourite even with the Salzburg public. It's always the public and, to a lesser extent, the Press and the recording industry, who create new stars.'

Although those Vienna performances were dazzling because of the sheer size and brilliance of Marton's voice, they had not been as moving or as dramatically interesting as those in the later Covent Garden run. Marton, who has since sung the role all over the world and who is an acute perfectionist and knows herself and her voice well, had meanwhile set out to polish and deepen her portrayal. 'After I had sung my second production of Turandot, I made up my mind that, while remaining true to my essential view of the character, my interpretation must, nevertheless, be constantly renewed and perfected. I see Turandot as a very simple, very normal girl. What makes her different is her power. We are in China and she ranks second only to the Emperor. As a symbol of power she is the object of constant public adulation. It is therefore natural she shouldn't want to offer herself to any willing Tom, Dick and Harry, regardless of their princely lineage. She will only yield to someone special, exceptional. That's all. Far from being afraid of love, she is secretly longing for it. What she *is* afraid of is losing her power and status.'

She points out that although the role is short – about twenty-five minutes' singing – it is still very difficult. 'It is the equivalent of only a 400-metre race [Marton is a keen sportswoman who was once a member of the Hungarian National Volleyball team]. But every performance is an Olympiad! The tessitura is very high, very dramatic, and one can never be sure one will hit all those high notes spot on . . . Maybe now, but only now, after so many performances behind me, can I begin to trust myself and feel relatively confident. In fact, I'm now beginning to feel this way about most of my repertoire.'

Marton's self-confidence is justified. Since her emergence to 'big-time' stardom in 1983 she has gone from strength to strength. In autumn 1984 she stopped the show in a Metropolitan Opera production of *Lohengrin*, featuring Placido Domingo in the title role, with a riveting performance of Ortrud; during the 1985–86 season she sang her first Brünnhilde in a new production of *Siegfried* by Nikolaus Lehnhoff at the San Francisco Opera; and this was followed, in 1986–87, by a *Götterdämmerung* in which she was hailed as a new great Brünnhilde. 'Soon this Brünnhilde who, like all her colleagues, was new to her role, proceeded to give us one of the most noble, reposeful, *evolving* Immolation Scenes in Wagnerian annals,' wrote the veteran critic Arthur Bloomfield in *Opera*. Marton is to sing Brünnhilde again in a new production of *The Ring* at the Chicago Lyric Opera in 1992, conducted by Zubin Mehta.

At the moment, Brünnhilde is Marton's favourite role. Indeed, she declares that after her first *Götterdämmerung* she felt completely fulfilled, 'both as a human being and as a woman', and she experiences the character very intensely. 'When we first encounter Brünnhilde in *Die Walküre*, she is like a white page. With time, she will gather experience and fill the white page. But when she gathers too much, she breaks. She begins her human existence in *Siegfried*, and by the time we reach *Götterdämmerung* the page is filled to overflowing and her life on earth is over because she can no longer bear the burden of human existence, she is not strong enough for it.'

Despite the formidable difficulties of this role which, along with Isolde and Norma, is considered one of the three sacred monsters of the soprano repertoire, she explains that 'when one feels and experiences the emotion of a role deeply, one can do anything one wants with the voice and find all the right colours, tones and dynamic shadings.' But she admits that what a singer needs, above all, for Brünnhilde is 'stamina and plenty of stage experience. The *Götterdämmerung* Brünnhilde is five-and-a-half hours long and no inexperienced twenty-five-year-old could cope with it! I had the choice of starting my San Francisco *Ring* cycle either with *Die Walküre* or with *Siegfried*. I thought it best to do so with *Siegfried*. First because it is the shortest – twenty-seven minutes' singing – and also because it is the beginning of Brünnhilde's human existence. Going straight from *Die Walküre* to *Götterdämmerung* without going through *Siegfried* would have meant travelling too great a distance, from the dramatic point of view. For it is in *Siegfried* that Brünnhilde understands the meaning of death and rebirth and learns what it feels like suddenly to rejoice in the sun, in Light. As a human being, she begins to savour everything she had taken for granted in *Die Walküre* where as an Amazon and demi-Goddess, she had had the best horse, the best looks, eternal youth, eternal beauty, and no need to look at herself in the mirror because she knew it was all there, for ever. She had no interest in men, either, except the dead heroes she escorted to Valhalla. Then, through her experiences with Siegfried, she becomes a woman. So I didn't feel I could make the imaginative link with her in *Götterdämmerung* without first going through *Siegfried*.

'Like Turandot, the *Siegfried* Brünnhilde is very short and very high. But the main problem is that it must be sung at eleven o'clock at night! In San Francisco, for instance, the curtain went up at seven in the evening, and I was still at home at nine, waiting, and so nervous I couldn't do anything except watch basketball on television. Eventually I would drive to the theatre and leave my car a few blocks away so I could steady my nerves by walking. Once inside the theatre, there was more waiting until Brünnhilde wakes up, at the finale of Act III. You cannot imagine how daunting it is to wake up in the morning knowing the climax of the day won't happen until eleven o'clock at night, when you have to get dressed, put on your make up and go on stage and sing for a twenty-seven-minute sing! This interminable waiting is the only problem with *Siegfried*.'

Vocally, the hardest of the *Ring* operas for Brünnhilde is *Götter-*

dämmerung, which Marton compares to a Marathon race. 'But it's so indescribably beautiful it makes every day I sing it seem like a feast day. The first time I sang it, the entire audience stood up and cheered me, me alone, the greatest compliment for a performing artist, and an experience for which I am deeply grateful. In fact my whole contact with Brünnhilde has been unique because through it I have, I think, become a better person. And if I were to die tomorrow, or whenever it is my time will come, I'll be ready!'

Marton's previous experience of Wagnerian roles consisted of Eva in *Die Meistersinger von Nürnberg*, in which she had made a respectable but not outstanding Metropolitan Opera début in 1976, Elisabeth and Venus in Götz Friedrich's Bayreuth production of *Tannhäuser* in 1977 and '78, and both Elsa and Ortrud in *Lohengrin*, the latter her first major international Wagnerian success. She explains that although the tessitura of both these roles is almost the same, Ortrud's is higher and more dramatic. 'She is also a much more interesting character. For my personality, fiery, temperamental roles are always easier, and although Ortrud is a shorter role than Elsa, as a highly dramatic part it is automatically more interesting than a young, lyric-dramatic, virginal role like Elsa. It is almost German verismo and I played her in a way that made it hard to decide which of the two roles is the positive and which the negative, because even negative people are convinced they have right on their side and feel justified in whatever they are doing. So, I thought myself into the part and absolutely believed in her.'

The results were electrifying: *Time* reported that, 'Domingo notwithstanding, the Met's *Lohengrin* was far from a one-man show. Marton, a dazzling Wagnerian soprano who is equally adept at setting off such potent Italian fireworks as *Turandot*, made a gloriously fiercesome opponent as the evil sorceress. Her blazing fury as she confronts her weak husband Telramund near the start of Act II won a spontaneous ovation that stopped the show.' Marton says that after this sort of experience, which 'jolts me out of the role', she needs at least a quarter of an hour before she can calm down and immerse herself fully back into the drama.

'I sometimes think the public needs the applause almost more than we do, as a release of tension and excitement. Of course, one feels grateful and happy to have given such pleasure. But I must say, I don't like streams of people pouring into my dressing room afterwards. I like going home as quickly as possible and being alone with my husband. We sit up, have a drink and go over the performance in detail. After the première of *Lohengrin*, for instance, we sat up till five in the morning, drinking champagne and relishing the whole experience again. It was impossible to sleep. In fact I learnt later that many of the people who had been to that performance couldn't sleep either, and this is good. Because the true aim and function of theatre is to shake people up.'

Marton is an outgoing, tough and attractive woman with plenty of temperament and Hungarian fire ('a tiger', laughs her husband Zoltan). She has achieved a seemingly perfect balance between her professional and her personal life. ('I try, but inevitably there are times when the scales tip more in one or the other direction. Still, I see to it that the family seldom get short-changed'). She balances an absorption in her art with an earthy, joyful capacity to savour the pleasures of everyday life and the fruits of her fame to the full, without becoming blasé. 'I have worked hard and honestly for many years to earn such acclaim as I now have. I said to myself during this high excitement, "remain calm, stay as you were". And so I continue to work,' she told *Opera News*. 'With more than forty roles in my repertoire in four languages, I sometimes think, "enough". But then came Fedora, a wonderful role, and La Gioconda and now Brünnhilde. I should also start giving recitals, but when do I have time to learn that repertoire . . . ? Such is the life of an operatic artist – a short life and one cannot do too much during its span, so all of us hope it won't be forgotten.'

Marton was born Eva Heinrich to parents who were not musical and who, like most Hungarians, were having a difficult time during the post-war years. She didn't even get to see an opera until she was about fifteen. Her musical life began as a piano student with a 'wonderful woman' teacher who had been a pupil of Bartók's. She continued taking piano lessons for three years but confesses she had 'neither the patience, talent or nerves to make the piano my career.' But her teacher told her she had a marvellous voice so, at the age of fourteen, she changed her studies to singing and sang folk songs, little operas for schoolchildren and in the Budapest Radio Chorus for two years, 'only in one octave, neither higher nor lower'. When she was older, she entered the Liszt Academy where as well as singing she studied music history, folk music, some philosophy and political theory and the Russian and Italian languages. (German came later, after she moved to Germany with her husband and baby son, in 1972.) While still a student, she met and married Dr Zoltan Marton, now a surgeon in Hamburg, had her first child and decided to pursue her career under her husband's name. ('What if there were a divorce?' protested her mother. 'Never!!!' was her determined daughter's reply.) 'Of course it is difficult to mix career and family but in my case it's not so terrible! I'm lucky to have a husband who takes a great interest in my work and career and two beautiful children who have always travelled with me as much as possible and seen places I only knew from books at their age. When they were younger, both read a lot and I am proud of

them. They are so well-behaved I can take them into any society,' she told
Opera News. The family live in a large house outside Hamburg, equipped
with sauna and swimming pool because as well as being a sports fanatic by
nature, Marton believes fitness is especially crucial for opera singers.
When at home, she loves wallowing in domesticity, cooking, gardening
and going for walks or bicycle rides in the country with the family, all of
which helps restore the right perspective on things and recharge her
batteries.

Marton made her professional début in the coloratura role of the
Queen of Shemakha in Rimsky-Korsakov's *Le Coq d'or* at the Budapest
Opera in 1968 and spent the next three years as a company member but
felt increasingly frustrated that she was stagnating because of lack of
opportunities. All the plum parts seemed to go to older colleagues.
Luckily, Peter Katona, then Artistic Administrator of the Frankfurt
Opera (and now at Covent Garden), who saw her as Freia in *Das
Rheingold*, was impressed enough to invite her to sing Alice Ford in a new
production of *Falstaff*, following which he and Music Director Christoph
von Dohnányi offered her a three-year contract in Frankfurt and
arranged for her exit visa from Hungary. The Martons arrived in the West
with two large suitcases weighing about a hundred kilos each and little
else. Her first salary was DM2,400 a month, and they started life in a
furnished flat before moving into another, which they had to decorate
themselves – Marton made all the curtains – while spending virtually all
their free time learning German. Before long, Dr Marton found a post in
a local hospital and life became more settled.

Marton's five fruitful years in Frankfurt were crucial for her artistic
development. This is where she perfected her technique and learnt most
of her repertoire. During one insane year, for instance, she learnt eight
new roles including Aida, Amelia in *Un ballo in maschera*, Leonora in *La
forza del destino* and Eva in *Die Meistersinger von Nürnberg*, all in the
original language. She also made her first international guest appearances
during this time: her Vienna State Opera début as Tosca in 1973, her
Bavarian State (1974) and Metropolitan Opera (1976) débuts, as well as
appearances in Berlin, Zurich, Geneva and Marseilles (worth
mentioning because it was where she experienced her first real ovation,
after Tosca). In 1977 she followed Dohnányi and Peter Katona to the
Hamburg State Opera, with a contract that stipulated a certain number of
performances but left her free to travel.

The coming years established her international reputation. But, after
ten years' apprenticeship as a company member in Budapest and
Frankfurt, her career rested on solid foundations. 'My vocal development had begun with Mozart – literally dozens and dozens of Donna

Annas and Countesses – followed by lyric roles and then a slow, gradual progression to dramatic parts. As long as my voice retained its elasticity, I avoided Wagner and Strauss as far as possible. Then, when the time was ripe, I began to sing them. It's vital to know one's own limitations, and never go beyond them. If anything, it's better to do less than one could rather than more, because once the voice is damaged, there is no way out', she told *Opernwelt*. So she was well prepared for the string of important international débuts: Bayreuth in 1977, La Scala in 1978 as Leonora in a production of *Il trovatore* conducted by Zubin Mehta, closely followed by the first La Scala production in Hungarian of Bartók's *Duke Bluebeard's Castle*. Her first Maddalena in *Andrea Chénier* at the Chicago Lyric Opera in 1979 was followed by *Tosca* at La Scala with Pavarotti and a televised production there of *Andrea Chénier*, with Carreras in the title role. And there were further personal triumphs as the Empress in *Die Frau ohne Schatten* at the Teatro Colon in Buenos Aires and the Metropolitan Opera, in 1981. In fact the Empress and Tosca are the roles 'that opened doors for me'.

Marton, who has now sung Tosca all over the world, feels a strong personal identification with the character, 'as an artist, as a human being and as a woman'. She first sang it in Hungarian at the Budapest Opera and for the first time in Italian at the Vienna State Opera in 1973. She modelled it, as she does many of her verismo roles, on Anna Magnani, whose films she admired. 'She has always been an example for me, and I wanted to bring to my Tosca the same fire, temperament and vitality she brings to all her film roles. I wanted to show that there is an alternative way of portraying Tosca to Callas's. Callas, who began the operatic revolution that has turned opera into believable theatre, was unique and inimitable. What is the point of trying to ape her? I, and every other singer, should sing Tosca with our own colours and personality.'

Marton was therefore particularly amazed and overjoyed to discover that Jonathan Miller, who directed her in a controversial 1986 Florence production of *Tosca* (with the opera set in 1944, during the last days of Fascist rule in Rome) had based his conception on Roberto Rosselini's film, *Roma, Citta Aperta*, which starred Magnani! Although she had initially been apprehensive about this approach, Marton found it the most stimulating production of *Tosca* she has ever sung in. 'Never, in all the years that I have been singing Tosca, have I felt as scared of Scarpia as I did in this production.' And although she hates a 'lot of these vulgarities' one sees on stage these days, from Jonathan Miller she would accept anything. Along with Götz Friedrich and Nikolaus Lehnhoff, he is the director from whom she has learnt most.

Marton greatly enjoys singing verismo. 'When I sing Wagner, Strauss or Verdi, I am the ship on the waves. But when I sing verismo, I *am* the waves! Yet verismo can be very dangerous if you don't use your body and your voice properly. What it requires, above all, is a strong, solid middle voice because this is what takes most of the brunt.' Another key verismo role in her career is the title role in Ponchielli's *La Gioconda*, which she first sang in 1982 in a Metropolitan Opera production that also featured Placido Domingo as Enzo. She considers La Gioconda one of the most difficult roles in her repertoire. 'It is a really high, dramatic role, yet with a very wide tessitura ranging from low, chesty notes – especially in the famous aria, "Suicidio" – to coloratura passages in the finale. This is why it is seldom sung by singers who sing roles like Brünnhilde, Turandot or Ortrud. The plot is rather stupid and far-fetched. It is no secret that Arrigo Boito, who wrote the libretto, based on a story by Victor Hugo, under a pseudonym, thought so himself. However, as an artist who has to interpret this character, I must find a way of identifying with, and being convinced by, the work before I can in turn convince the audience and my colleagues. I see *La Gioconda* as a story about loving a man more than he loves you. (I'm not speaking from personal experience. My husband Zoltan and I are still very much in love, and have been from the beginning!) Gioconda is pretty and sexy and Enzo did love her once, up to a point. But she is not good enough for him, a Grimaldo. She is a street singer, and this is a very important thing to remember, both vocally and dramatically, because it is what distinguishes her from Tosca, who is an opera singer. And although this difference is hard to portray – because women who are in love are very similar – it is nevertheless real and must be brought out. Tosca's anguish is expressed in a beautiful, artful song, "Vissi d'arte", but Gioconda's song is all instinct, it comes out of her guts and calls for a "coarser" sound for all her outbursts, which are more expressive and temperamental than Tosca's.

'Act IV begins with Gioconda alone, brooding. Then her friends, the actors, arrive and she asks them to look after her blind mother, whom she doesn't want to abandon unprotected. Then Laura's drugged body is brought in. [Gioconda has given Laura a sleeping draught that makes her appear dead, to save her from her jealous husband's revenge, in gratitude for her having saved Gioconda's mother from the hands of the Inquisition.] Then she sees the carafe and the poison and conceives the idea of killing herself. She proceeds to work herself up into a frenzied, distraught state because it is only by doing this that she can commit suicide. I don't believe anyone can kill themselves in cold blood. You have to work yourself into a state where it seems like the only logical solution, the only way out.'

Having now recorded La Gioconda and almost all her verismo roles – Fedora, Turandot and Maddalena in *Andrea Chénier* – for CBS, Marton is convinced they should be recorded in a manner that conveys a feel of the

way she experienced them on stage. 'No one expects just beautiful sounds
from me. They expect a bit more. Therefore I feel I can allow myself to
take an audible breath or make a gasp here or there, if this helps make the
whole thing more real. On record one needs more tension, more colours,
and, above all, the courage to reveal the emotion of the work rather than
just sing beautifully.'

Shortly before recording *La Gioconda* in summer 1987, Marton had
been busy in the studio with a role that particularly excites her: Judith in
Bartók's *Duke Bluebeard's Castle*, which she had sung for her graduation
examination at the Liszt Academy and had also been the first to sing at La
Scala in Hungarian. Judith is particularly close to her heart because
during her student years she had 'a very special relationship to Béla
Bartók, whose portrait used to hang on my walls because I love his face.
It's a wonderful, *clean* sort of face with clear, piercing, yet deeply
unhappy blue eyes, into which I would gaze whenever I felt dispirited. He
was an unhappy man, because after he left Hungary to settle in America,
he never really found himself again and lived in very poor circumstances,
in an awful, tiny flat in New York which I visited as a sort of
pilgrimage . . . Anyway, I used to have these silent dialogues with his
portrait in my student days, and singing his music is something that means
a great deal to me.'

While preparing the role of Judith for her graduation examinations,
Marton studied it with a professor who had in turn learnt it with Bartók
himself. Judith, now considered a classic of the twentieth-century
repertoire, is very difficult, both vocally and dramatically. 'The text is
very important and very personal: like Elsa in *Lohengrin*, Judith is the
eternal curious, questioning female who wants to know everything. Yet
unlike Elsa, who is naïve and virginal, Judith comes across as quite
experienced and sophisticated. The Duke is given no first name. He is just
'Duke Bluebeard', a symbolic, allegorical character that could be
Everyman. Because everyone has their own personality and inner
sanctum, a secret garden they wish to keep private even from those they
love – one is what one is and one doesn't want everybody to know
everything about one. Yet when Bluebeard opens the doors to his soul
and his past but wants to keep one door shut, Judith cannot take it. And I
find it deeply disturbing that this woman wants to know and to invade
everything. This dramatic, allegorical part of the work interests me a
great deal.

'The music is very Hungarian. It's pentatonic (five-tone) music and
Bartók manages to give the opening of each door a different pitch. When
one door opens on to those beautiful cornfields and Judith rejoices, we
are in a different sound world from the one that greets us after the door

that opens on to a storm . . . Then, all of a sudden, Judith begins to have doubts and to be afraid of this man. Her insecurities surface and she wonders whether she is good enough for such a rich man – rich in every sense of the word. And through her insistence that he open the very last door, through her failure to trust, she destroys everything. Exactly like Elsa in *Lohengrin*, and the message seems to be the same: that fear and doubt always, invariably, destroy love.'

In 1989 Marton sang her first *Elektra* at the Vienna State Opera, in a new production conducted by Claudio Abbado and directed by Harry Kupfer. Then, in 1990, she scored a major triumph in the role at Covent Garden with Solti. Marton is 'absolutely mad about Strauss', and her number one favourites among his operas are *Ariadne auf Naxos* and *Die Frau ohne Schatten*, both allegorical works. She first sang Ariadne at the Bavarian State Opera under Sawallisch with great success but has since become 'too expensive to be hired just for a one-act opera'. Yet she has a very personal and special conception of the role and the opera as a whole which she is eager to try out. 'I would like to sing both the Composer and Ariadne, thus highlighting the inner link between them. I sing the Composer and I throw the Prima donna, who is an extraneous character, aside because she cannot read my notes. Then, as the Composer, I step forward and sing the role of Ariadne in the opera-within-the opera. When a director comes along who thinks this idea is fabulous, I'll be ready.'

Two other Strauss roles Marton has sung are the Countess in *Capriccio* and the Marschallin in *Der Rosenkavalier*; but she doesn't think she is ideally suited to the latter. 'It just doesn't seem like *my* role. I'm too temperamental for it, too fiery to play a poised Viennese lady. One always knows when one has taken on the wrong role. One fights and fights, valiantly and against all odds, like Don Quixote, but one knows it's a losing battle. I had this feeling twice in my career: with Leonore in *Fidelio* [which, despite fifteen invitations after her Salzburg début, she decided was not for her] and the title role in Strauss's *Die aegyptische Helena* which I sang in Munich and which, despite its beautiful music, I found very hard to make something of, because of its stupid, far-fetched libretto.'

One of her very favourite Strauss roles, one which, as we have seen, also played a vital part in furthering her career, is the Empress in *Die Frau ohne Schatten*, in which she scored major triumphs at the Teatro Colon and the Metropolitan Opera. Both productions featured Birgit Nilsson as the Dyer's Wife* and, after the second occasion, she autographed Marton's score. The Empress had been superbly sung for many years by Leonie Rysanek who, Marton knew, was a hard act to follow. 'But I knew

*Marton will sing her first Dyer's Wife at the 1992 Salzburg Festival, under Solti.

that my time had come. I knew I had to grab this chance. I knew exactly what I know and what I can do. What I didn't know was how the public would accept me,' she told *Opera News*. The production proved that not only was Rysanek's successor at hand but also Nilsson's. For it was during the last performance of this run that Nilsson passed the mantle of Turandot to Marton.

'Just before the curtain went up on Act II, when we were all in position and at Birgit's feet, she suddenly said: "You know, I've been thinking about what would be a good part for you." (Imagine! The great Birgit Nilsson thinking about what would be good for *me*.) "Which one?" I asked. "Turandot" she replied. "I made my career with that one." "Thank you very much, Birgit, but do you think I can sing it?" "Sure," she answered as the curtain went up. And I find it beautiful that when one artist is about to relinquish a role there is someone else there, prepared to assume the mantle and carry on the tradition. It doesn't happen very often, it's just chance – that's why it's so wonderful when it does.'

ROSALIND PLOWRIGHT

ROSALIND PLOWRIGHT'S LARGE, dark-hued, Italianate voice – ideal for Verdi and *bel canto* – is among the most exciting, dramatically expressive soprano sounds around, while her tall, striking good looks make for a compelling stage presence. Much to her consternation, she has often been compared to Maria Callas, whom she admires immensely. Understandably, though, she would rather be known as 'the first Plowright' than 'the second anyone'. Every voice is unique – the blueprint of the artist in whose body it lodges – and the comparison of singers a futile pastime. However, it is true to say that, at her best, Rosalind Plowright displays some of the best characteristics of both Callas and the equally unforgettable Leontyne Price, one of the greatest Verdi sopranos in living memory. Plowright's portrayal of Elena in *I vespri siciliani* at English National Opera in spring 1984 provided some of the most thrilling Verdi singing since Price, while her Norma performances in Montpellier, Pittsburgh, Lyons and Paris proved that here, at last, was the first one-hundred-per-cent plausible Norma since Callas.

At the time of our first conversation, Plowright felt she had not yet reached her vocal peak. Five years later, with sixteen performances of Norma under her belt, she believed it was now in sight. Both then and now, her aim has been to concentrate on roles like Norma because 'they give me confidence and show me off at my best. Elena and Norma are strong characters and I find that when I have to be dramatically strong I can sing some of the higher, more difficult phrases easily.' The exception to the rule is Desdemona, a purely lyric role in which she scored a big success when she first sang it at ENO in 1981 and which 'really suits my voice. I don't have a nerve in my body when I sing it. There is nothing really difficult in it. All you have to do is just sing very beautifully.' Verdi himself wrote to his librettist Arrigo Boito: 'Desdemona is a role in which the line, the melodic thread, is never broken from first note to last. I repeat, Desdemona *sings* from her first notes, which are a melodic phrase, right up to the last "Otello non

uccidermi", which is another melodic phrase. Just as Iago should only
declaim and sneer, so Desdemona must always sing, sing, sing . . .'.

Desdemona is a 'B natural role' and B natural happens to be one of
Plowright's best notes. Indeed, she was dubbed 'Queen B' by Placido
Domingo at the recording of *Il trovatore*.

On the whole though she tends to prefer the more dramatic roles, 'those
that give me something to get hold of and be myself in'. This was one of the
reasons why singing Elena in *Vespri* was one of the greatest experiences of
her career. She is longing for a chance to sing it again, but only in Italian.
'Singing it in English was awful – much, much harder because the
consonants aren't as clear and the vowels aren't as open as in Italian. But
the main difficulty of this role is its immense length, spread over five acts.
In the ENO production, there was no interval between Acts IV and V. This
meant I was on stage continuously, which was *murder*. The other difficulty
was the different mood of these two acts. Act IV is strongly dramatic and
after so much dramatic singing it is very hard to switch moods, lighten the
voice – especially at the end of such a long evening when one is already
exhausted – and sing the "Bolero" in Act V.'

Yet Plowright sailed through this and all other challenges of this
demanding role seemingly without effort, and her performance drew
enthusiastic reviews. 'Her phrasing in the great Act IV quartet was the
crown of the evening but she capped it with a dazzling account of the
Sicilienne,' wrote the *Sunday Times*. *The Times* headed its review with the
title 'Rosalind Plowright: Thrilling Throughout a Taxing Evening', and
went on to remark: 'She had been serving notice for some time now that she
is the most exciting of the British sopranos and this performance endorses
it.'

When singing this kind of role, Plowright explains, getting enough rest is
essential. Ideally there should be three days between performances,
because 'the harder the role, the more crucial it is to be well rested'. She
made sure she had plenty of time for rest and preparation before singing
her first Norma – a semi-staged performance at an open-air theatre in
Montpellier in July, 1985. 'I knew I would need six months to prepare
Norma and I had six months. My preparation was so thorough that it is
hardly surprising the performance was such a success. I had learnt by then
that you can't go about throwing roles together, that you need time to delve
into and master them properly. Never again will I make the mistake of
rushing through a role. Apart from being unfair to the music, it's silly
because only after a long period of study do I feel confident and secure.'

The first step was a special course in Italian at a school in Florence; then
came a week in Milan with the veteran coach Roberto Benaglio who had
proved enormously helpful when coaching her for the Deutsche

Grammophon recording of *Il trovatore*, conducted by Giulini. These sessions were followed by a visit to England by the conductor of the Montpellier production to work with her. Her leisurely preparation meant that 'amazingly enough, I was quite relaxed at the performance and felt wonderful – rested and very healthy. I hit the top Cs at the end of the cabaletta "A bello a me ritorna" spot on and although there were a couple that could have sounded better, on the whole the performance went very well.' The French press hailed her as 'a revelation' and Peter Katona, Artistic Administrator at Covent Garden, was so impressed that he immediately set plans afoot for a revival of *Norma* just for her. 'You see,' she sighs, 'it takes something like this to show people what you can do.' (In the event, though, the revival was replaced by a production of *Medea*.)

As several artists in this book stress, Norma is one of the most taxing and difficult roles in the soprano repertoire because of its length, range and the stamina it demands. 'You can go into the performance with a fresh voice but it takes a lot of technique and a lot of experience for it to remain fresh. Because the *real* Norma begins after the duet with Adalgisa – that's the bit I love and where I let it all hang out. The beginning is quite contained, except for that fiery bit "No, non tremare". This is why I always feel that, to sing Norma, you have to use an almost Mozartian discipline. You can't do what you do in Puccini. You must control and pace yourself very carefully. For a big voice like mine this demands immense technical skill. But after a year of doing Norma I feel I have developed a new approach that allows me to use less energy and less voice, though the sound is actually more focused.'

Plowright was speaking six months after the birth of her first child, Daniel Robert: and she recalled that 'to begin with, everything seemed a huge effort. I sang *Alceste* at La Scala six weeks after giving birth, which was a bit sooner than I would have liked. A month later would have been perfect. But having to sing so soon after childbirth made me work very hard on my diaphragm, getting my energy back and the voice in shape. Luckily I had a maternity nurse, so I could get some sleep; one feels like jelly after having a baby. But being able to rest set me free to get the voice back to normal, the way I do after a holiday break; and by the time I sang my next Normas in June I felt the voice had never been in better condition. I seemed to have become more technically secure in the meantime – around April – because I had begun to realize what I was doing wrong before: I was singing loud all the time and had lost the ability to shade my voice. By going right back to the basics, I think I managed to adjust everything and felt in total command.'

Our previous meeting had been shortly before her son's birth, and at the time she had been excited and curious about being a mother, for both personal and professional reasons. 'In so many of my roles, like Norma and

Medea, I am being a mother, so it will be interesting to find out what it
really feels like . . . and lovely to sing Norma one day with my own two
children. [Her second child, a daughter, born on Christmas Day 1988,
makes this a concrete possibility.] I particularly love that scene where
Norma is torn between maternal love and the urge to avenge Pollione's
betrayal by killing their children. But, and this is the difference between
the two women, she doesn't kill them, whereas Medea does. But then,
Medea is a psychopath – a wild, unhinged, witch-like creature, full of
vengeance. She has been separated from her children who live with their
father, Jason, while Norma lives with hers; her love for them is thus
nurtured by constant contact. She is also a more loving person, full stop.
Medea has very sudden changes of mood. First she sings a deeply moving
aria, full of compassion for her children. But then she looks into their eyes
and in them sees their father, whom she hates. So she pushes them away
and asks Neris to get them out of her sight. Then she works herself into a
state where she is in a wild fury, ready to kill.'

Plowright first sang Medea at the 1984 Buxton Festival, and later in
Lyons in 1985, in the French version with spoken dialogue, *Médée*,
incorporating Cherubini's own cuts only. She relished the fact that she
was required to perform a sort of ritual with a sacrificial knife and says
that 'once again, the drama came to my aid and helped me lose myself in
the character'. This was picked out by the critic of the *Observer* who
wrote that 'Plowright responded with a performance of vibrant intensity'.
The next time she came to perform the role it was in the Italian, Callas
version. After singing the role of Alceste in Italian, rather than in the
more frequently performed French version, at La Scala, she remarked
wryly that she was fast becoming a reluctant exponent of operas in
different editions!

Singing Medea in the Italian version, and coping with the extensive cuts
made by Callas, seemed like a totally new experience. 'Much though I
admire Callas, I sometimes wish she had never existed! Not only because
of the endless comparisons, but also because, having brought these roles
back into the repertory, everybody treats everything she did as the Bible,
which is frustrating and at times infuriating. Take all those cuts she made
to the Italian version of *Medea*. I suppose she did it because she wanted to
include all Lachner's recitatives, which are quite interesting, very
dramatic and rather beautiful. Otherwise I cannot imagine how anyone
could go through a score as beautiful as the original French version and
cut it! But once you incorporate all those recitatives of Lachner's, then
you do have to make extensive cuts, otherwise the opera would become
very long. Take the aria "Dei tuoi figli la madre", for instance, which
Callas shortened considerably. The truth is that, after performing the

recitatives, which are in turn gentle and fiery, there is no way anyone could sing the full aria. I restored four pages of music at the finale and felt quite tired afterwards. Which is why, if one wants to sing the Italian version, one has to have the cuts. But it's a great pity because Cherubini's music, with those duets and arias and repetitions, is dramatic enough. It doesn't need Lachner's recitatives. It builds up the manic, obsessive side of Medea and I feel this is lost in the Italian edition, which almost hindered the interpretation I had built up after singing it in French at Buxton. Can you imagine, they even wanted to cut that wild bit at the end? Fortunately I dissuaded them. But in future I will only sing the French version.' When she did so, at Covent Garden in autumn 1989, the critical and public response to the production was – through no fault of hers – lukewarm.

Plowright has now largely overcome the nerves and insecurity that used to torment her in earlier years, and her considerable portrayals of both Norma and Medea prove that she is right in feeling she is approaching her prime. But she is quick to add that this self-confidence is comparatively recent. Plowright was first recognized as an unusually promising talent at the 1979 Sofia International Singing Competition, where she won First Prize. This major breakthrough came after a harrowingly difficult, uncertain decade during which she was nearly destroyed by conflicting vocal advice and lack of opportunities. The fact that she found herself and triumphed over such fraught circumstances is a tribute to her courage, tenacity and dedication. It is worth dwelling on what happened to her on her way up so as to show what can go wrong with even the most promising young artists if they are not lucky enough to find the right teachers straight away; also in order to dispel the illusion that life for top opera singers is from the outset all stardust glitter.

The man who 'started the whole thing' and pointed Plowright towards a musical career was her father, who played the double bass in jazz orchestras and musicals and whose mother had had an excellent singing voice. When Rosalind was twelve, he took her to see a performance of *The Mikado* and that, apparently, did it. She became stage-struck and kept imitating Katisha on their way home in the car, using a dark, plummy voice, quite unlike the one she used for singing songs and musicals. Her father was impressed and asked her to concentrate on producing this kind of sound.

At that point the family moved from their native town of Warsop in Nottinghamshire to Wigan, where the local school boasted an excellent music department. As she had learnt to play the violin at the age of ten, she joined the school orchestra and soon became its leader; she also sang in the school choir where, with her already powerful voice, she 'drowned everybody else out' and soon became noticed. Before long, she was given several solos to sing and her voice became more important to her than violin-playing, which she gave up at around the age of seventeen. The voice kept growing and she began to perform at local amateur operatic societies.

Her parents, anxious to know if it really had professional potential, asked her music teacher to arrange an audition with Frederick Cox, the Principal of the Royal Northern College of Music. 'He wrote back saying it would be a tragedy if I didn't train properly because I had the possibility of becoming an international opera singer! Of course, I got very excited and immediately began attending Singing and Movement classes at the RNCM, before starting my official course there. So, by the time I enrolled as a full-time student, I was a bit more advanced than the rest and, of course, it was considered a great honour to have Frederick Cox as your teacher because he was the Principal and because he had also taught Annie Howells and Ryland Davies, who were all the talk at the time.'

Cox had prophesied that it would be years before the large Plowright instrument was ready, because large voices are more difficult to control. He concentrated on voice placement, and Plowright remembers him trying to teach her how to get her voice into the head resonators. 'It was terribly plummy and terribly down-in-the-throat because I have this strong, natural middle voice which I had discovered while imitating Katisha and used to revel in. I also had a layer at the top which was much thinner – and nothing in-between. I couldn't link my middle voice to my top and always seemed to quiver around the passaggio. I also occasionally cracked a top note – but at least I had a top. I could sing arias like "Vissi d'arte" from *Tosca* and roles like Frasquita, Fiordiligi and Elsa – in fact, I had won the Peter Stuyvesant scholarship with Elsa's dream – and soar up to a top C.' On completing her course at the RNCM in 1973, she joined the soprano section of the Chorus at the Glyndebourne Festival Opera, where she also understudied the Countess in *Le nozze di Figaro* for the Touring Company.

But her winning the Peter Stuyvesant Scholarship to study at the now defunct London Opera Centre nearly proved her undoing and 'set me back five years'. For this 'extraordinary institution' wrote that it was in her best interests to join the mezzo section. 'I think they did this for their own good because they had an abundance of sopranos but very few decent mezzos. So obviously they wanted anyone who sounded even vaguely like a mezzo – which I, with my strong middle voice and dark timbre, did – to take on mezzo roles. Their decision had nothing to do with concern for me. I was quite upset but, being young and inexperienced, I thought it best not to contradict them. Freddie Cox, whom I consulted, said he didn't think this would do me any harm!

'Well, it did. The first role I was given was the mother in *Louise*, a real contralto part that made me use mostly chest and push the middle voice. It felt utterly wrong and, not knowing what was what, I went to see the Principal, James Robertson, to ask if I could be given some higher roles. He got very upset, shouted at me and told me I should be grateful for anything I got and that he didn't think I was a soprano anyway. In fact, I feel very bitter about the Opera Centre. Everything in me was destroyed there: my voice, my confidence, my immediate professional prospects. My top notes absolutely disappeared, my hair began to fall out – alopecia was diagnosed as a result of stress. I was desperately unhappy, living in the East End of London – a horrible place – because the Centre was there, lonely, miserable, and totally misunderstood.'

It is interesting to point out at this juncture that the Opera Centre had also classified Kiri Te Kanawa as a mezzo when she arrived from New Zealand to study there, despite her first teacher's assessment that she was a 'heavy lyric' soprano, and she, too, had been thoroughly miserable there. In Plowright's case it was not her coaches at the Centre but a music-loving friend who had heard her sing in a competition who correctly assessed her voice by pointing out she could 'hear Bellini and Donizetti in it'. The only other person was pianist Roger Vignoles, who urged her to 'get out all those Verdi roles' and who remained sympathetic and encouraging even though he could see she had problems with them.

After winning a Peter Moores Scholarship for her second year at the Centre, which was not quite as harrowing as the first, she was glad to turn her back on it in summer 1975 and escape to Glyndebourne again, where she was given Agathe in *Der Freischütz* to understudy. She got a chance to sing a performance when Linda Esther Gray became ill and she acquitted herself well. As a reward, she was offered twelve performances of the Countess in *Figaro* with the Touring Company. 'The role was very good for me because Mozart is always very good discipline. They were aware of my vocal problems – I sometimes cracked on A natural in "Dove sono" and seldom had enough energy left for "ingrato cor" – but they were pleased enough with my Countess [which also got her some good reviews] to offer me Elvira in *Don Giovanni* for the 1977 season in Peter Hall's new production with Thomas Allen in the title role.'

Elvira is a much more demanding role than the Countess and exposed her weaknesses acutely. 'I had the notes. I also had problems. I wasn't asked to sing at Glyndebourne again – the first of many doors that were to shut in my face during the next year or so because of my lack of a sound technique . . .'

The only work she still had at the time was with Kent Opera, where she sang small roles like the Second Lady in *Die Zauberflöte* and the

Messenger in Orfeo – 'at the time I would do *anything* to earn a living as a singer' – but eventually this, too, fizzled out. Meanwhile, she had married her first husband, who was still a university student, and they lived in Liverpool. She was offered some work at the Welsh National Opera – Helena in *A Midsummer Night's Dream*. But they, too, could hear the problems in her voice, and she wasn't asked back, there, either. 'Nobody was interested in me any more. I was out on a limb. Fortunately my husband had a good grant, and we struggled on. At least I had my marriage to keep me happy while my career was slipping into the background. I even thought maybe I should forget about being a singer altogether and settle for being a wife and mother. But my husband wouldn't hear of it. He was keen I should make something of myself and, having heard me at Glyndebourne, was convinced I had it in me to succeed. So I felt I had to carry on singing otherwise he'd leave me. (In fact, this is when problems with my first marriage began.) So, I would get on the bus from Liverpool to London once a week to study with Erich Vietheer.'

The late Erich Vietheer remembered hearing from her 'out of the blue', on somebody's recommendation. They made an appointment and her first question was: 'Do you think I am a soprano?' 'And I, having heard her Elvira at Glyndebourne and remembering my fascination at the beauty of her voice and consternation at her lack of technique at the time, replied "of course you are!" So that's how we started off. She used to spend all day on a bus from Liverpool and arrive towards the end of the afternoon for her lesson, and then get on the bus back. And she did that for two years. In fact I've seldom known a singer have a tougher time on their way up. She deserves every ounce of recognition she is now getting.'

Vietheer was the first to teach her the rudiments of breath support, 'deep low, abdominal breathing. She had never done this before, she used to breathe from the chest up, which left her no reserves for top notes. And I remember the first afternoon when she sang her first, properly supported top C. It was intoxicating. Before long, I had surreptitiously slipped a D flat in a cadenza from *Il trovatore* and she managed that, too.' Plowright recalls how 'Erich would do extraordinary things like punch me in the stomach to get me to breathe as low and deep as possible, which was all new to me. After five years as a student at the RNCM and two at the Opera Centre, nobody had shown me how to support my top. I was also going at it too full-throated and never "covered" the passaggio notes. But the more I got the hang of it, the better everything began to sound. It was very exciting. As well as giving me back my top, Erich also gave me a tremendous amount of confidence and hope and boosted my morale even when I wasn't singing particularly

well. He also provided a contact with the world of opera at a time when I
had no work at all.'

For six full months, she had no work except study, study and more
study, in a freezing, unheated room kindly put at her disposal by the
owners of a rambling mansion where she and her husband rented a flat.
(She often practised in layers of sweaters and woollen gloves.) The
catalyst that finally got the ball rolling was her friend Peter Knapp, who
one day rang up out of the blue and announced he was starting his own
opera company and would she consider singing Fiordiligi in his
forthcoming production of *Cosi fan tutte* at the Riverside Studios,
Hammersmith, in 1978? He stressed that he couldn't as yet afford to pay
her. 'But after so many months with no work I was so demoralized that all
I wanted to do was sing! It was also a good opportunity to try out the new
technique I was learning with Erich.' The production, which sported a
small orchestra and no chorus, got good reviews and she enjoyed her part
in it even though she says she hadn't got it all together yet and 'cheated my
way through' the role. 'The top was coming but I still hadn't conquered it.
I still occasionally cracked on a B flat. Then, one night, he gave me some
exercises which put the voice securely in the mask, and suddenly my B
flats were totally secure.' The performance of *Cosi* that night was a
revelation. 'I felt as if I'd been given a new toy. Finally, I was beginning to
have a technique and to be in control of my voice. Maybe Freddie Cox,
who always said my voice wouldn't settle until I was thirty, was right after
all . . .'

Peter Knapp also suggested she audition for the prestigious Sofia
International Singing Competition, for which she would have to apply six
months in advance. His opinion was reinforced by Tom Hammond at
English National Opera, one of her former coaches at the Opera Centre
and himself an ex-member of the jury at this competition. He had
auditioned Plowright recently, confirmed she was now definitely a
soprano and offered her the Countess in *Le nozze di Figaro* in September
1978, replacing Valerie Masterson. 'It was nerve-racking to step in at
such short notice but I was well rested after a cycling holiday in Scotland
and I had Erich Vietheer there to support me – a very warm, caring
person, utterly committed to his students – and actually sang quite well.'

To her surprise, Tom Hammond suggested she prepare Elvira's
aria 'Ernani involami' from *Ernani* and the *Trovatore* Leonora, which
'flabbergasted' her because this role is full of top Cs. But, to her
amazement, the top Cs appeared during her lessons with Vietheer and
her coaching sessions with Hammond. This happened two months before
she went to Sofia. The result was that she won First Prize in Sofia. This
was the turning point in her career. (It was also in Sofia she met her

second husband and manager, Tony Kaye.) As a result she received her first invitations to sing abroad, the title role in *Manon Lescaut* in Puccini's home town of Torre del Lago, Abigaille in *Nabucco* and Leonora in *Il trovatore* in Sofia the following year. Back home, the English National Opera engaged her for their new production of Britten's *Turn of the Screw* as Miss Jessel, for which she won the Society of West End Theatres award. A successful series of auditions led to three offers from Switzerland, where she accepted a year's engagement at the Bern Opera for the 1980–81 season. She valued the chance to work with Gustav Kuhn, the music director, because 'he taught me to soften and shade my voluminous voice'. In Bern she scored big successes in the title roles in Strauss's *Ariadne auf Naxos* and Gluck's *Alceste*, and offers began to pour in from Frankfurt, Hamburg, Munich, Berlin for roles like Aida, Ariadne, Amelia in *Un ballo in maschera*, Donna Anna and the *Trovatore* Leonora.

After those successes on the Continent came her first major British breakthrough: Jonathan Miller's 1981 production of *Otello* at ENO, where Plowright had already made a mark as Queen Elizabeth in a special production of *Maria Stuarda* with Dame Janet Baker in the title role, to mark the latter's final ENO appearance. After *Otello* she made her American début in Philadelphia in 1982 in a concert performance of Act II of *Un ballo in maschera* conducted by Riccardo Muti; this was followed by Medora in *Il corsaro* and the title role in Chabrier's *Gwendolen* in San Diego. In 1983 she made her début at the San Francisco Opera in the title role in *Ariadne auf Naxos* and her Carnegie Hall début in the title role in *Die Liebe der Danae*. She also sang Elsa in a concert performance of *Lohengrin* at the Edinburgh Festival under Claudio Abbado and made her débuts at La Scala in the title role in *Suor Angelica* and at Covent Garden as Donna Anna. A year later she returned to the Royal Opera House for Maddalena in a new production of *Andrea Chénier* with José Carreras in the title role and made her début at the Munich Festival as Vitellia in *La clemenza di Tito*.

During the same year, 1984, she made her first major studio recording: *Il trovatore*, Carlo Maria Giulini's first operatic recording in over a decade, for Deutsche Grammophon. She had already sung Leonora on stage at Sofia and Frankfurt – and since then at the Verona Arena and Covent Garden – but was only given the recording after rigorous training in Milan with Roberto Benaglio. She still considers it among the most difficult roles in her repertoire: 'Leonora is a "stand-up-and-sing" role, something I always find hellishly difficult to cope with. Her first aria, "Tacea la notte", has to be almost as pure, ethereal and controlled as a Mozart aria and ends in a top C. Her second aria, "D' amor' sull' ali rosee", is another beautiful sing; I never know what to do on stage with arias like that, and nobody has ever shown me. They demand sheer vocalism, full stop. This particular aria has a great many high notes which have to be sung piano and which are also very exposed, with very little going on in the orchestra. I like the support of a big orchestra, of a lot of sound around and underneath me, and when it's lacking, I feel very exposed. After this aria, the rest of Leonora's music is easy and very "singable". No, the coloratura in "Vivrà" isn't very difficult and doesn't frighten me.' Plowright sang Leonora again, in a new production by Piero Faggioni at Covent Garden in June 1989 to very mixed reviews both for herself and the production.

She greatly enjoys singing Verdi, even though it is almost as exposed as singing Mozart. 'He demands great purity, keeps you on your toes and disciplines the voice, whereas Puccini is less exacting in this sense. But in *his* operas, the drama is so strong and the music so passionate, that singing it becomes more strenuous and uses up twice as much voice. And while you are not as exposed as you are in Verdi, the problem here is that you have to compete against a very loud and dense orchestration.' Dramatically, she finds Puccini heroines generally more interesting than Verdi's because 'they tend to be real, flesh-and-blood women rather than victims of fate. But I don't intend to sing much Puccini. The longer I can keep my voice contained, the longer it will last.'

She intends to concentrate largely on Verdi and *bel canto*: Norma, Medea, Elena, Abigaille in *Nabucco*, Violetta, the two Leonoras (in *Il trovatore* and *La forza del destino*), Elisabetta in *Don Carlos*, Odabella in *Attila* and later on, *Lady Macbeth*. Erich Vietheer agreed with this choice but added two youthful-lyric Wagnerian roles: Elsa in *Lohengrin* and Elisabeth in *Tannhäuser*. 'Can you imagine how beautiful "Dich teure Halle" would sound with Rosalind's voice? That lovely, rich, deeply feminine, juicy voice? It would be mind-boggling . . . ' Plowright herself is not keen on exploring the German repertoire. She doesn't feel Senta in *Der fliegende Holländer*, which she sang at Covent Garden in 1986, was quite right for her, and of the Strauss heroines in her repertoire she enjoyed Danae but found Ariadne boring. 'Because I have a big voice, everybody asks why I don't sing Wagner. But the moment I start singing Wagner I'll no longer be able to sing my Verdi and *bel canto* repertoire, which I want to stick to for at least ten years. If, when I am 50, I have maintained a youthful appearance, I might sing Isolde!' Until then she will follow the late Harold Rosenthal's advice. After praising her performance of Maddalena in *Andrea Chénier*, a verismo opera, he had added that Plowright 'is by nature a Verdi and *bel canto* singer and that should be her chosen repertoire'.

The success of Plowright's début recital at the Queen Elizabeth Hall whetted her appetite for more in the future. She enjoys the intimacy and immediate contact with the public and the different sort of challenge recitals represent: 'I can put across my own personality. Of course, I have to "act" out each song. But between songs, people see me as I am. I think it's good for the public to see and get to know us as we really are and not merely as child-stabbing operatic characters – and lovely to get a packed house and know one can sell out the 1,100-seat Queen Elizabeth Hall!'

She has had to discipline herself considerably in order to cope with the mounting pressures of a big international career. She vocalizes and tries to get some physical exercise, too, every day 'crucial for singers' – and abstains from alcohol for a week before a performance because it tends to dehydrate her throat. 'On the actual day, though, a glass of port is in order because it helps relax me.' She is fully aware that the better known she becomes and the bigger the career, the greater the pressures and the more 'everyone will come to expect a marvellous sound every time I open my mouth. I have to live like a nun on the day of a performance and on the day before, and be very relaxed and do my exercises . . . I try to remember something Giulini told me when he saw how nervous I was at the recording of *Il trovatore*. He was totally taken over by the music from the moment he heard the sound of those strings, whereas I couldn't lose myself completely because of my nerves. So he said to me: "You must not be nervous, Rosalind. God has given you a great gift. Now please, go on to the platform and give it back to Him."'

LUCIA POPP

THE SINGLE WORD that best describes Lucia Popp as artist, singer and personality is 'natural'. She seems to sing as naturally as she breathes; her charm both on and off stage is as natural as the unaffected way she slips into the characters she portrays, making the process look as simple as changing a dress. And her exemplary career has been a natural progression from the coloratura repertoire of her early years to lighter and eventually heavier lyric parts, chosen so judiciously that they appear to fit her like a glove.

As everybody knows, the appearance, or illusion, of naturalness is the most difficult thing to achieve in art. And this is even more true of an art as dependent on craftsmanship as singing, where technical control is crucial, not only in order to master the roles, but also to balance the artist's urge, during performances, to abandon him or herself to the music. And Lucia Popp is nothing if not a meticulous, conscientious craftsman, passionately dedicated to the patient, analytical, detailed work that goes into refining what was a natural gift. But the end result always appears effortless: the craftsmanship is cloaked in a miraculous spontaneity that wins the audience's heart and puts it on the side of the characters she is portraying.

Popp's ability to conceal the craft in her art implies acute self-knowledge. And no trace of self-indulgence or delusion has ever obscured the clear-sighted critical faculties of this warm-hearted Czech, at once sophisticated and earthy, whose openness and sensitivity to people, spiced with an impish sense of humour, win friends easily. Her accurate appraisal of her artistic equipment, coupled with her lovely voice – clear as a bell and still with a trace of the silvery, brilliant timbre that bespeaks a former coloratura – has helped her stay consistently at the top of her profession for nearly 30 years.

Popp's career began in 1963, when she was engaged by the Vienna State Opera. She remained as a full member until 1967, when she moved to Cologne, having meanwhile made a string of successful international débuts. Throughout the sixties, she concentrated almost exclusively on the coloratura repertoire; the seventies were devoted to lighter lyric roles (mostly Mozart parts, some Rossini and Sophie in *Der Rosenkavalier*), and the early eighties saw a transition to heavier lyric parts, in which she has acquitted herself with distinction. Throughout her career, she has also sung operetta, a genre reflecting her own *joie de vivre*, and delivered delicious portrayals of Hanna Glawari in *Die lustige Witwe* and both Adele and Rosalinde in *Die Fledermaus*. (She can be heard as Adele in a vintage Deutsche Grammophon recording, and has also recorded an album of operetta arias for EMI.)

Popp discovered her voice in the most natural way possible, by singing at home. Her mother was an ardent opera fan with a lovely voice, and she taught her young daughter various tenor parts from the standard repertoire so that they could sing love duets together. During her schooldays in her native Bratislava, Popp sang and travelled widely with a variety of local choirs. After graduating from school she studied medicine for two semesters before deciding science was definitely not for her. She yearned for something more extrovert and amusing like the stage and, indirectly, this was to lead to her singing career. She was hired by a small local company to play Nicole in Molière's *Le Bourgeois Gentilhomme*, and the part required her to sing a 'pastorale'. An Austrian-born singing teacher, Anna Hrušovska-Prosenkovà, who chanced to be in the audience and had herself been a high coloratura soprano, went up to her at the end and asked her if she would care to develop her lovely voice and become a singer. Delighted with this suggestion, Popp began to study with her right away and continued to work on new roles with her through the years. She is convinced that 'luck plays a great part in finding the right teacher and I thank my lucky stars that I fell into such good hands. But you must believe in your teachers and do what they say. Although I don't think every singer can be a teacher, I think it would be difficult for someone who hasn't done any singing to teach others to do so. One of the first and most important things my teacher taught me was to develop a strong visual imagination of sound, and get a mental picture of it from the score, before I open my mouth to sing.'

She still follows this method when studying new roles. One of the first tasks is to banish all recordings from her sight as well as her mind, lest she be tempted to listen and perchance to copy. 'You *cannot* reproduce the sound of another, it doesn't ring true and however much you might wish to repeat something a much-admired colleague has done, it never works because each voice is individual, unique. Your ideas should come from the printed page, not from the recorded sound. So first of all I read the score through, not just my own part but the whole thing, like a book, because it helps to know what the others are saying! (Don't laugh, this is not as usual as you might think!) Then I start picking out my part. As I have a good visual memory, I learn easily and can even remember which part of the page contains my lines. After that I go to the piano and, either alone or usually with a coach, I begin the detailed work of looking for the right vocal colours and balancing the intonation – I have relatively good but not absolute pitch – the rhythm, then mastering the words and finally the melody. After that it's a question of constant repetition until finally I know it.'

In accordance with her teacher's instructions, Popp never starts to sing out in full voice until she knows exactly where the sound should be placed because (pointing at her throat), 'this apparatus here, the vocal cords, are so intimately connected with the brain that the moment you *think* of a certain note everything down there, in the throat, is automatically geared up to produce it. Therefore if you don't already know the part or feel sure that the sound is correctly placed in your mind, it's stupid to try to reproduce it. I feel sorry for singers who were inadequately taught and have had to find this out for themselves, because it can harm or even ruin their voices. But I was taught first to prepare, then focus and go!'

She likens the kind of preparation she has just described to 'working with clay', because 'I cannot produce pots without clay, by which I mean that no artist can produce art without first working on the craft. The next stage involves building up the phrases and finding the right places to breathe – even though the breathing may later have to be adjusted when you are on stage and singing with the full orchestra.' She tries to start preparing new roles early so that she can read the part through in a leisurely fashion, absorbing it in depth as she goes along, and doesn't believe in being forced to learn it by heart right away, 'like a parrot'. Memorization should happen naturally, almost by itself: 'One day, it's all there, I know it. Of course, things don't always work out in such an ideal way because nowadays time is such a luxury in our profession.'

Once she knows it, she likes putting the part aside for a while, perhaps for a few months, even. 'Then, when I return to it again, you can't believe how familiar it feels! The muscles seem to be doing the right thing automatically. The same thing happens with songs for a recital. The physical difference you feel in your muscles when you come to a song you already know well and have sung before is unbelievable. You go through it seemingly like a knife through butter, you can do anything with it, whereas with new songs you have to be careful. Fortunately though, sooner or later every new song becomes an old song. This "muscle memory" factor is an additional reason for taking time to learn things correctly and for not taking on too many things at once.' She explains that these are things young singers can learn from a teacher. The rest – such as the question of vocalization on which no two singers seem to agree, because what suits one voice may not suit another – they have to learn for themselves. Popp does not vocalize every day because my voice 'is quickly and easily warmed up, and easily tired. Some people, especially those with big voices, have to work hard on warming up and keeping the voice well oiled. Mine is easily summoned: all it takes is a few scales and it's there.'

After absorbing all this through four years of study in Bratislava, during which she also made her professional début at the local opera house as the Queen of the Night in *Die Zauberflöte*, Popp went to visit relatives in Vienna. Her aunt, a great opera buff, volunteered the information that the State Opera was always looking for coloratura sopranos. What Popp didn't realize at the time, as she explained in *Opera*, was that anyone in Vienna could walk in and ask for an audition. Naturally, they would not sing for Karajan, then Artistic Director of the VSO, right away. But if, as in Popp's case, the material was considered promising enough, they would eventually get to Karajan. Popp did and was promptly engaged. But she made her Vienna début at the Theater an der Wien as Barbarina in 1963, before her State Opera début as the Queen of the Night the same year.

The Queen of the Night is more of a stereotype than a real character – the sort of role that hinges entirely on vocal pyrotechnics. Singers can keep it in their repertoire for a relatively short time because it is only briefly that the voice can be in a condition to sing both the arias in a satisfyingly spectacular fashion, because the opening of the first aria is rather low while the second is consistently very high. At the beginning of her career Popp had 'all those giddyingly high notes and consequently no problems with the second aria. It went like fireworks! But the first aria, which is much lower, gave me the feeling that I *just* managed it. Then, as the voice began to get lower with the years, the position was reversed: the first aria became easier and the second more difficult. For a brief, blissful moment things sort of evened out! The voice was perfectly poised for both and I felt really on top of the role.'

As long as singers retain the Queen of the Night as their main warhorse, everything, their whole life, depends on those high notes which must not be harmed at any cost. Provided this need is recognized and the rest of the repertoire restricted to a handful of light, lyric parts that cannot disturb the high notes – like Norina in *Don Pasquale*, Rosina in *Il barbiere di Siviglia*, Blonde and Konstanze in *Die Entführung aus dem Serail* and Oscar in *Un ballo in maschera* (with which she made her Covent Garden début in 1966) – sopranos can keep the Queen in their repertoire for a few years. It would have been very difficult to expand further without 'disturbing the Queen'.

But perhaps the biggest sacrifice singers have to put up with while singing the Queen of the Night is the toll on their nerves. Popp confides she 'had terrible nerves every time I came to sing it and it is very hard to survive this kind of tension on a long-term basis. Singing the Queen is not like walking on a tightrope, it's like *dancing* on a tightrope. I suppose this is why the operatic world is full of singers who can do this part at the dress rehearsal but not on the night itself. I really admire anyone who can keep it in their repertoire longer than ten years.' In 1971, after a particularly successful broadcast performance at the Metropolitan Opera (where she had made her début in 1967 in this role), Popp decided there and then to give up the Queen of the Night. 'This way people will remember me at my best.'

The moment she made that decision, she realized that the entire Mozart lyric repertoire was now open to her, as well as parts such as Gilda in *Rigoletto*, Zdenka in *Arabella* and Sophie in *Der Rosenkavalier*. She had left the Vienna State Opera (although she has continued to sing there regularly throughout her career) for Cologne in 1967, and this is where she tackled most of her best-known Mozart roles for the first time (with the exception of Despina, which she first sang at Covent Garden in 1968): Pamina, Zerlina and Susanna, all of which she later performed in Ponnelle's famous Mozart cycle in 1977–78. Although her Pamina is one of the most moving in living memory, her favourite, and perhaps most-famous, Mozart role is definitely Susanna, which she sang all over the world – including Vienna, Salzburg, Munich, London – until the early eighties.

'Susanna is a very complex and interesting character. I would hate it if anyone were to ask me to portray her as a frivolous chambermaid, lightweight and rococo, as used to be the fashion. She is the one pulling all the strings because she is the only one who really knows everything that's going on, the whole plot. This should be made very clear from the start, when she tries to alert Figaro to the imminent danger at hand. It should also be made very clear that Figaro is the only one she cares about. There should be no ambiguity in her attitude to the Count (which is very difficult when he is played by Thomas Allen!). As far as the Count is concerned, Susanna is just another prospective feather in his cap. What needles and prompts him to go in such hot pursuit is the fact that, unlike most other girls, she resists him.'

In order to make the last act believable, both musically and dramatically, it is important for Susanna and the Countess to be physically and vocally somewhat similar. 'I don't like a Susanna with too thin and a Countess with too creamy a voice. Nor should they vary too sharply in size and shape if the finale is to be really comic. Vocally, the role is extremely demanding on your concentration and very, very long, one of the longest in the soprano repertoire – longer than Butterfly, for instance. In addition, Susanna is almost constantly on stage, with barely enough time to recover breath in the wings before she has to leap into

action again. I never entered my dressing-room at all until the long
interval when I sang Susanna, a role as demanding on your memory as it is
on your stamina. But it is one of the most rewarding parts. Every page is a
miracle! Like all Mozart roles, it is very exposed. There is nothing to hide
behind, so any idiot will notice if you make a slip. This is why people
rightly say that if you can sing Mozart you can sing anything. But I
wouldn't say Mozart can never harm your voice. He can if you sing his
music wrong [Placido Domingo expressed the same view in *Bravo*], but
not if you sing it right. Basically, nothing can harm you if you sing it right.

'Generally speaking, Mozart, Bach and Schubert are very good for
vocal hygiene. Theirs is the purest vocal craft, like a brushing away of all
bad habits and, because the emotions they express are of the purest kind,
also quite cleansing for the soul.' Popp has sung a lot of Bach – the *St
Matthew Passion* and the *Mass in B Minor* as well as recording an album
of Cantatas. 'Bach's music is very special. First it has to be taken apart,
analysed, and then put back together again, bit by bit. The rhythms are so
balanced that your singing has to reflect this economy, like a necklace of
perfectly graduated pearls. You cannot rush any bar too much, as this
would disturb the whole rhythm, the balance of the piece. Any increase of
speed from bar to bar has to be very, very gradual and almost
infinitesimal.'

According to Sir Charles Mackerras, the essential vocal qualities for
singing Bach, Handel and Mozart with distinction are 'vocal clarity and
the ability to sing with expression but with a brilliant edge to the voice so
that, however expressive it becomes, it still has that clarion-like
brilliance. To my mind, Lucia Popp is an ideal Bach and Mozart singer,
whose Queen of the Night, Pamina and Susanna are unforgettable.' It
was with regret that, in the early eighties, Popp decided to give up
Susanna (exchanging it for the Countess), along with Pamina and another
of her earlier favourite roles, Sophie in *Der Rosenkavalier*, which no one
since has portrayed to such perfection.

She first sang the role in Linz, in 1964, sent by the Vienna State Opera
to try it out before singing it in the full public glare of Vienna. 'I wish
young singers today could be nurtured in such solicitous fashion! When I
first looked at the score of *Der Rosenkavalier*, I was appalled and thought
I could never master it, not least because of the language. My German
was not good at the time, because although my mother was born in
Vienna, since the war my parents had decided not to speak German. (The
German in Mozart operas is far, far simpler than Hofmannsthal's texts.)
Fortunately Karajan had brought a special coach to Vienna from
Hannover, where the purest German is spoken, and he helped me with
Sophie. He also sent me to a special language coach in Hannover, who

worked extensively with me, perfecting the sound of each vowel and diphthong. For hours on end we did nothing but repeat the vowels "e", "ä", "u" and "ü". Sadly, nobody seems to care for such minute, perfectionist detail any longer. But I think that, in your effort to understand what the composer imagined, and to interpret it on stage, you need as much technical knowledge as possible. It's hard work, and it never stops.'

Technically, Sophie is an easy role to underestimate because, text apart, on paper it looks vocally quite easy. 'But in fact it is very demanding. It has long, flowing lines culminating in ringing top notes. Act III is very long and you need stamina to go through with it. Then, in the finale, the line keeps going up and up, higher and higher, above the Marschallin's and up to a high D, to the point where you feel almost on the edge of a precipice. You feel that if it went on for one minute longer, your voice would break. But I took to it from the moment I first sang it. I didn't have to *act* Sophie, I *was* Sophie, I was so inside her that I could sing it without any tension, at any tempo. Like Susanna, it is a part with infinite possibilities. Each time I sang it I found something new to do and, again like Susanna, I felt very possessive of it. I felt it was *my* role in *my* opera, that it belonged to *me*. But there came a time when I thought this was it. I couldn't do it any better. I had been singing it for twenty years all over the world but most notably in Otto Schenk's production at the Bavarian State Opera in Munich, which was the ultimate as far as this opera is concerned. Nobody would improve on or surpass it. Being part of something so perfect was an incomparable joy.' (All the protagonists in this production, such as Dame Gwyneth Jones, Brigitte Fassbaender – and, in *Bravo*, Kurt Moll – express the same view.)

Popp is aware that technically she could have gone on singing Sophie and Susanna until she was 60. 'But who wants to see a 60-year-old Sophie or Susanna? By the beginning of the eighties I was beginning to feel out of place portraying a fifteen-year-old just out of a convent. As you grow and mature as a woman, you start to seek new challenges, new, interesting roles to sing. The early eighties were an important time for me in this respect. My voice was changing and *I* was changing. So I decided it was time to change my repertoire, shed some of the old parts and see how far I could stretch myself. Because if you don't stretch yourself you don't grow as an artist. I had waited a long time before taking on Eva, Arabella, the Marschallin, the Countess in *Capriccio* and Elsa. But I thought it was time, at last, to take the plunge. I thought, who cares if I still have a fresh voice at 70. Certainly I don't want to ruin my voice. But I *do* want to use it.'

In retrospect, she feels she ought to have taken a sabbatical at the time, just to learn the new parts. She didn't, so for a while she found herself singing all the old parts whilst learning the new ones and already performing some of them. The first was Eva, which she first sang at Covent Garden in 1983. Until then she had never sung any Wagner and was not terribly keen on his operas. 'I never sought to attend performances or listen to recordings of Wagner operas, either. But once I did, I couldn't tear myself away from it. It was like a drug, I felt I could almost become addicted to it. Wagner takes hold of and occupies your mind so much that I prefer not to listen to it too often. For instance, I had neither seen nor heard a complete *Tristan und Isolde* until Kleiber's recording was released, and then I found myself listening to it twice within a single afternoon.' By the time she had sung Eva on stage, though, she was yearning for more Wagner roles.

She was afraid Eva might make unnatural demands on her voice and prove to be a 'very rigid, unchanging role. But it didn't. *Meistersinger* is a beautiful, very moving and human piece and, despite its musical complexity and the fact that it contains several conversational passages, I found I could sing Eva with my natural Lucia Popp voice. My biggest fear had been the aria, "O Sachs, nein Freund", which several sopranos had warned me could be very difficult. But then, they don't come from the coloratura repertoire, which is stratospherically high. Eva's aria is not that high, although you have to give out more volume. Naturally I could only give out the amount of volume I have and no more, otherwise the sound would be forced and ugly. By the end, when Sachs realizes he loves Eva and she realizes how fond she is of him, I found himself wishing it could go on longer, or that I could sing more Wagner.' She was to fulfil her wish in 1989, when she sang Elsa at the Bavarian State Opera.

After Eva, Popp's next new role was Arabella, which she first sang in Munich in 1983, with Wolfgang Sawallisch conducting. In purely dramatic terms, she finds Zdenka, which she first sang in the seventies, more interesting, because she develops a good deal through the course of the opera, whereas 'Arabella is more static, her character is already formed before the action begins. In fact I wish Hofmannsthal had called the opera "Zdenka", as the prose piece on which he based it was called *Lucibor*. Having said that, musically Arabella is undoubtedly the star. Her music is much more beautiful and demanding, consisting of fabulous soaring lyric phrases. Although she is a very young woman, the role is quite "heavily" written, with the orchestration assuming almost dramatic proportions.' Her performance was enthusiastically greeted, both in Munich and in London, where she sang it in 1986. 'The overwhelming applause at the end greeted a great and enchantingly unaffected artistic achievement. With her warm, round voice, without a hint of trouble on the high notes, Popp combined the artfulness and

warmth of her Susanna with the caprice of her Rosalinde,' wrote *Opera*
after the revival of the Munich production.

Arabella is one of several operas in which Popp has effected a
transposition of roles. The first was *Die Entführung aus dem Serail,* in
which she sang Konstanze after singing Blonde, then, as already
mentioned, *Le nozze di Figaro* when, after years of singing Susanna, she
assumed the role of the Countess for the first time in 1981 in Vienna (and
for a while says she got some of the lines mixed up), then *Don Giovanni*,
in which, after singing Zerlina in the sixties, she took on Donna Elvira, so
far in concert and on record only; then there was Adele and Rosalinde in
Die Fledermaus and finally Sophie and the Marschallin in *Der Rosenkavalier*.

'This sort of transposition of roles is an enormously rewarding
experience that has to do with your own development, with the passing of
time, and having your repertoire catch up with you, bringing it in line with
your personality, so to speak. Now, when I sing the Marschallin, the most
fulfilling of all my roles [which she first sang in Munich in 1985 and later
also at Covent Garden], I can't think why I used to love Sophie so much, I
find her silly and uninteresting! But the Marschallin is a complete woman,
and singing it now is pure bliss. It amazes me how much Hofmannsthal
knew about women . . . The other day I, too, found myself looking into
the mirror and thinking: "I have changed so much; but I'm still the
same!"

'Technically it is not a difficult role. Musically everything hinges on
interpretation, on really putting across the words, the fact that you *know
what* you are singing. It's almost an acting part, in fact, but with a
beautiful line, composed exactly the way you have to say it: the melody of
the language emerges from the musical line and every page contains a
new dramatic insight. There are a few spots in those parlando passages
though, where you must be careful because the orchestra is very strong.
But the only *real* singing comes in the final trio.' Having sung Sophie next
to so many distinguished Marschallins helped Popp form a definite idea of
the way she wanted this character to be. She retained this or that detail
from various of her Marschallins, mixed them up with her own views and
insights, and out of this mixture grew her own impressive portrayal. She
had described her début to German critic Beate Kayser as 'work in
progress', stressing that it can take years to develop a role such as the
Marschallin.

But, as the same critic reported both in the German press and *Opera*,
the début was 'a triumphant success. What she had announced as the
beginnings of a début already emerged on stage as a well-rounded and
many-faceted human portrait . . . There is nothing but praise for her

singing: the progressive darkening of her voice over the years suits the Marschallin. The timbre remains light, but the volume is adequate to carry over the orchestra.'

In 1987, Popp took on another Strauss role, the Countess in *Capriccio*, at the Salzburg Festival and, the following year, for the 1988 Bavarian State Opera's Strauss Festival. On record and in concert performances in Geneva, she also sang the title role in *Daphne* (Strauss's wife's favourite among all his works), which she finds similar to *Salome* because 'the beginning and the end are lyrical but the middle part is very dramatic'. Recently she was asked to record Salome but refused as she doesn't really like recording parts she has not performed on stage, 'because I don't know what the characters are really like. I did it with Elisabeth in EMI's recording of *Tannhäuser* and with *Daphne*, but at the time of our recording, no opera house had a production of the latter. In any case it is hard to stage [the BSO subsequently did, but not with Popp], and really better off in concert.'

Her last major new role to date was Elsa in 1989, which came about by chance. Her second husband, tenor Peter Seiffert, whom she married in 1986, was due to sing his first Lohengrin in Munich (where the couple also make their home), and the soprano billed as Elsa, Gabriella Benackova, withdrew from the production. Popp was asked if she would consider replacing her and, 'if only for the joy of singing on stage with my husband again, I agreed to try. But it was very funny because for a long while he was not satisfied with my interpretation. In fact we had such rows in the Wedding Scene that August Everding [the director] was chewing his tie in the stalls and I thought that after this *Lohengrin* we would get divorced! But in the end all was well. I must say, I had never imagined I could sing Elsa. But it turned out to be a totally, absolutely lyrical part. There are very few moments where you have to sing out in full voice against the full orchestra. The rest of the time, as in the "Dream", for instance, the sound should be soft, floaty and faraway. One thing I learnt from Karajan was the art of singing softly. If you want to be heard, he always said, sing softly. "Never compete with the orchestra, you'll lose, you can't possibly win against 120 people!" But to do that, of course, you need first-class conductors and orchestras. The best operatic orchestra is the Vienna Philharmonic who are so sensitive that they immediately reduce their volume the moment you do. Generally I have never understood why, in our day, Wagner is linked to so much noise. It's never like that in Bayreuth. You have to have climaxes, of course, but a great deal of it, such as Act II of *Tristan* in Kleiber's hands and *Parsifal* in Karajan's, is almost chamber music.'

Popp describes herself as a 'theatre cat, not an academic singer', which is probably why, in addition to her effervescent personality, she has always enjoyed singing operetta. 'I love comedy and those operettas are wonderful bits of escapism with *gorgeous* music which is at least as difficult as opera. Rosalinde in *Die Fledermaus* [which Popp first sang in Munich and later in Vienna in a production with fabulous costumes by Milena Canonero, who designed films like *Barry Lyndon* and *Out of Africa*] is vocally more difficult than Violetta and also very demanding physically: you have to dance and speak as well as sing.' Popp's portrayal of Hanna Glawari in *Die lustige Witwe*, which she found 'terrific fun and not very demanding', epitomizes the charm, artfulness and lightness of touch that sums up the genre. She first sang it at the Volksoper, where her Danilo was the famous and dashing baritone Eberhard Wächter, now Director of the Volksoper and Director-Elect of the State Opera as from 1992. 'Lehár is the Hungarian Puccini. I love Hanna and always sing the "Vilja Song" as an encore in recitals.'

Looking back on her career with justified satisfaction, Popp says she has now sung virtually everything she wanted to sing. Her only remaining wish is to sing Donna Elvira (which she has already sung in concert) on stage and the title role in *Ariadne auf Naxos*, 'which is not too long, requires the kind of solid middle voice I now have and, because she is an allegorical figure, doesn't have to be too young! Then I would have sung everything I *could* sing.'

Popp is also passionately involved in art in Czechoslovakia now that it is once again a democracy, and active in the organization, with Vaclav Havel's patronage, of a 'Mozart and Dvořák' Festival in Prague in September 1992, which will include a visit by the Vienna State Opera. Otherwise, she is enjoying being happily married. 'All I really want to do is cook. But as you see, I'm still singing!'

LEONTYNE PRICE

Leontyne Price retired from the operatic stage in 1985. However, as she happens to be one of the greatest Verdi sopranos of all time, and my number one favourite soprano in her repertoire – the one who gave and, through recordings, still gives me the most intense pleasure and excitement – it was inconceivable to write a book about female singers and not include her.

'THERE IS NOTHING in the world more embarrassing or pathetic than the artist who can no longer give his or her best,' declared Leontyne Price. To ensure this would never happen to the greatest Verdi soprano of our day, and one of the greatest of the century, Price retired from the operatic stage in January 1985, a month before her 58th birthday, with a thrilling performance at the Metropolitan Opera of her most famous role: Aida, the part with which she had made operatic history back in 1958 with a string of international débuts at the Vienna State Opera (under her mentor Herbert von Karajan), La Scala and Covent Garden.

After Aida's Act III aria, 'O patria mia', the Met audience stopped the performance and gave her a four-minute ovation. The *International Herald Tribune* reported at the time that, although Price remained in character, her lips trembled and she bowed her head. When she raised it, her eyes were glistening . . . For it must be an unbearably poignant feeling for an artist to *know* they are singing those phrases (which no one in living memory has sung better) for the last time. But rather than wait until she had become a shadow of her former self, Leontyne Price, as befits a true diva, opted for the dignity, pride and intense pain of parting from her beloved roles while she could still do them justice. This way, she will always remain a legend. 'I am trying to exhibit good taste. I prefer to leave standing up, like a well-mannered guest at a party,' she said at the time. 'And it's thrilling to be asked why I'm retiring rather than why I'm not.'

One wouldn't expect anything less than impeccable taste from an artist whose hallmark, throughout her 32-year, barrier-breaking career, was Quality with a capital Q. First and foremost, there was the quality of her voice: supple, shining, breathtaking in its beauty and expressive range, 'the most beautiful Verdi soprano I have ever heard, whose power and sensuousness were phenomenal', according to Placido Domingo, while *Time* aptly described it as 'capable of effortlessly soaring from a smoky mezzo to the pure soprano gold of a perfectly spun high C'.

Concern for quality was also the sole criterion in her choice of repertoire, which centred on four composers: Mozart, Verdi, Puccini and Strauss, 'who writes exquisitely for my type of voice and certain parts of it which I call "nosebleed country" or the "high-heel" area that I enjoy most because this is the *real* soprano *Fach*, the reason why you are you. If you don't enjoy that area, you can't grow, for without a top a soprano is a hybrid, as is a tenor. They might just as well be mezzos or baritones . . . I came to Strauss at a mature stage in my career, when I sang *Ariadne auf Naxos* at the Met and the San Francisco Opera, and was extremely excited by the contact. She's some woman, Ariadne. She went on a banana trip for a man who came, swept her totally off her feet and then took off. And she's been moaning and groaning ever since, totally involved in what happened to her. This is the gist of it and it should be sung this way. There should be a kind of sensuality running through it because Strauss is one of the most sensual composers of them all. To me the most sensual composers are Strauss and Puccini. They totally *kill* you because they're so in love with the heroines they create that you really have to be on top of it, in total control, not to *die* while you're singing them . . . or, as with Tosca, for instance, not to kill Scarpia in earnest.'

But she recognizes that the composer to whom her vocal apparatus was best geared to was Giuseppe Verdi, whose roles made up the bulk of her repertoire, 'both in terms of substance and enjoyment'. It wasn't intentional, it just happened that way, she explains, as is often the case between some composers and some interpreters. The most important milestones in Leontyne Price's career always seemed to be associated with Verdi heroines. 'As far as repertoire was concerned, I was never a gambler. I liked the luxury of winning too much. I *adored* to win and make a go of everything I tackled. I got my thrill that way.'

This is why she never sang Elena in *I vespri siciliani* or Abigaille in *Nabucco* and why she dropped Lady Macbeth after singing it once. 'These roles are all too dramatic and would have been a waste of a beautiful lyric voice . . . This is why I also said "no" to Karajan in 1961, when he asked me to sing Salome. Although I have since sung it in concert with Zubin Mehta, it would have been quite wrong for me to sing it on stage at that point. So I had to decline, I had to look into those eyes and say "no", which was *very* difficult. But you have to say "no" sometimes, you have to look after your vocal instrument, and no one can do that but you. I often said "no" to conductors even though no one likes to win more than a conductor. But once in the pit, I never argued with them about tempi. If they wanted it slower or more *rapido*, I always adapted. I never antagonized conductors, and I never had a bad one.'

Price, an immensely elegant, fashion-conscious woman, was described by French writer and film-maker Marguerite Duras as follows: 'not heavy but *opulent* . . . this body was needed in order to *enfold* this voice and, like some good and generous earth, to nourish it so that it could achieve such depth, such a miraculous velvet'. She likes to compare the operatic repertoire to fashion and her best roles, especially her favourite Verdi heroines, to couture dresses that fit her supremely well. 'If something is fashionable but not suitable to your figure, looks and personality, why wear it? Think by how much more bravura your entrances and exits, or simply your presence and the exuberance of your personality, would be enhanced if you wore a dress that suits you to a T. My couturier and friend Chuck Howard (another native of Mississippi) and I have developed certain designs that suit my figure and personality. We vary the colours and fabrics, but we always stick to certain patterns so that I'm always at ease because I know they fit, that I'm absolutely at my best and not laden down by something unbecoming.

'I felt the same way about everything I sang. If I didn't love a role or song, if I didn't feel it was something I could express with great joy, I simply wouldn't touch it. Because to me singing was undiluted joy. As it says in Doretta's song in *La rondine*, of what importance are riches, glory and all the material things of this world if you don't find happiness? And the thing that made *me* happiest was singing. When I sang, I felt totally beautiful, I felt luxurious, at ease and fulfilled, I felt like I was out of myself and at the same time that I *was* myself.'

To Price, singing was an outgoing not an introverted thing, and certainly never a *labour*. She solved all technical problems in the studio and got the details and pacing figured out so that she could be totally at ease. Again, she compares this process to fashion: 'Choosing, from your wardrobe, the accessories best suited to the dress at hand. This needn't imply you have a wardrobe full of garments and accessories. I deal in quality rather than quantity. And vocally this saved me. It also kept me excited, young, never bored and selective to the point of total distress for some operatic managements who began to understand my reasons only towards the end of my career. It never disturbed me in the least that I didn't sing every day. I don't think you can deliver quality if you sing every day. As in love affairs, or any kind of relations between people, mystery is always the trump card. You don't have to be the most beautiful woman on earth, but the way you package yourself can make you more alluring, easier to be with, and make someone want to see you more often than someone else who is a clinger, a great beauty, perhaps, but also a colossal bore . . . A performing career, a love affair with an audience, is something even more special and you have to be even *more* careful. I suppose this was even more true in a case like mine because – shall I be blunt? – I was a pioneer, a barrier-breaker, a black pioneer in grand opera, for my country, and also here in Salzburg.' Price's operatic career did indeed begin with a big, barrier-breaking bang in 1955, when she became the first black opera singer to appear on American television: NBC's production of *Tosca*, after which she was promptly re-engaged for two more productions thus opening up the media to her black successors.

'How can I put it? If you're the person that's given that space to express something that constitutes some kind of breakthrough, you find yourself in a position similar to an athlete's. You've been chosen by your country to run, so you train and you run, with all your might, to *get* that gold medal. It probably has something to do with the timing of your life. I don't want to sound like a chocolate Joan of Arc, because it could easily have been someone else. But if that moment of truth comes to *you*, you grab it and you do everything you can to make it possible for it to mean something for those who come after you. As a person who breaks tradition, you have this extra responsibility. You *must* speak for more than just yourself. If you fail, more than just you fails: certain elements or sections of people fail. I never lost sight of that aspect. It's what kept the juices flowing – the reason why being a pioneer was not a liability but a challenge that brought out the best in me. In the end, the joy of breaking tradition became like an addiction . . . And with an awful lot of luck I struck gold.'

Luck would have it that 1955, the year of Price's sensational success as Tosca on NBC-TV, was also the year when Herbert von Karajan came to America on his first tour as Music Director of the Berlin Philharmonic. Price – who before this Tosca had had a triumph on Broadway as Bess in *Porgy and Bess* in 1952 and given a series of concerts and recitals, mostly of contemporary American music,* nationwide – had been signed up by the influential Columbia Artists Management whose director, André Mertens, wanted her to audition for Herbert von Karajan, then Music Director designate of the Vienna State Opera (parallel to his job as Music Director of the BPO).

*By Virgil Thomson, Samuel Barber, Lou Harrison, William Killmayer and John La Montaine.

'So he took me by the hand and into Carnegie Hall where this salt-and-pepper haired man was sitting in the stalls munching a sandwich at the interval of his rehearsal. Mertens asked if he would listen to this promising young soprano. He mumbled something to the effect of "if I must, I must", so I walked up to the platform with my accompanist and began singing "Vissi d'arte" from *Tosca* and "Pace, pace mio Dio" from *La forza del destino*. Halfway through the latter, Karajan threw away his sandwich, leapt up to the platform, waved my pianist aside and sat down at the piano himself. At the end he announced I would be one of the first artists he would invite to Vienna. And he kept his word.'

Before going to Vienna, Price made her début at the San Francisco Opera in 1957 in Poulenc's *Les Dialogues des Carmélites* and shortly after that she was asked to replace an indisposed Antonietta Stella 'who, bless her, had to have an appendectomy', as Aida. The reception was tremendous and since then, 'it was boom, boom, boom'. Her Vienna State Opera début under Karajan, also as Aida, was in 1958 and she was hailed by the press as 'a phenomenon' and promptly re-engaged for the following two seasons. Her débuts at La Scala (where a critic wrote that 'our great Verdi would have found her an ideal Aida') and Covent Garden quickly followed, also in 1958.

In 1959 she made her début at the Salzburg Festival under Karajan in Beethoven's *Missa Solemnis*. She returned the following year for her stage début as Donna Anna in a historic, star-studded production of *Don Giovanni* conducted by Karajan and featuring Eberhard Wächter in the title role, Elisabeth Schwarzkopf as Donna Elvira, Graziella Sciutti as Zerlina, Cesare Valletti as Ottavio and Walter Berry as Leporello (a live recording exists of this production). In 1961, she made her Metropolitan Opera début as Leonora in *Il trovatore* – to a 42–minute ovation, the longest in that house over the past 25 years!

It was a long way from Laurel, Mississippi, where Leontyne Price was born on 10 February 1927, the daughter of a sawmill worker and a midwife who both sang in church choirs in this segregated town, and the granddaughter of Methodist ministers (the foundation, perhaps, of her own deep-seated, all-permeating faith without which 'I could do nothing'). She herself sang in local church choirs with her parents, to whom she remained extremely close until their death in the seventies and from whom she drew much strength. After school she went to the predominantly black Central State College at Wilberforce, Ohio, where, through singing at various glee clubs, the quality of her voice was first recognized and she was encouraged to pursue serious musical studies. She won a scholarship to Manhattan's Juilliard School, which she was able to accept through the generosity of a Laurel-based white couple, Mr and Mrs Alexander Chisholm, who ensured her maintenance in New York. (Their daughter attended Price's farewell performance at the Met as her guest.)

Price struck gold in her teacher, as in so much else. Florence Page Kimball laid the foundations for her vocal development by pointing out that she should always sing with her interest and not with her capital. 'In other words, if you have the mental capacity for it, the technical things will straighten themselves out and, as you grow into a career, which takes a bit of doing, the experience itself becomes part of your equipment and poise. You sing the same way, with your roots, but you also develop a wide palette of colours to draw from. I was fortunate enough – and I hope this doesn't sound arrogant – to possess a voice like an impressionistic painting. I could tap a colour here or a colour there at will, and this is a quality abundant in lyric sopranos.' She stressed that although she has often been classified as a lirico-spinto, she 'and my friend who is my voice' think of it as a lyric. 'I talk like that because my voice is my best friend. Otherwise we wouldn't have survived.'

Throughout her career, Price stuck to her teacher's advice, which ensured her voice's remarkable longevity and preserved its quality and lustrous sheen unto the end. But she vividly recalls what happened on one occasion when she felt cocky enough to deviate from it. It was in 1977, when Karajan invited her to Salzburg again for a revival of their 1961 production of *Il trovatore* (a commercial recording is available of the 1977 revival, from EMI, and a superb pirate recording of the 1961 production). 'In fact, he was asking me, at the age of 50, to be in competition with the younger version of myself at 32. I was thrilled to be back on the same stage, the same ambience and the same production, and during the rehearsals before the Dress I was having a lovely time showing off – I'm a terrible show-off, an egomaniac really. I was singing not with my interest but with my capital, and it was fun. But Karajan, who had been in at the developing stages of this voice, was unimpressed. Everyone was falling over their seats, and quietly I noticed that the one person whose approval I would like to have more than *anything* was totally bored.

'And next morning, he presented me with the reason why. He sent me into a room alone with some tapes of our 1961 performances so that, in his words, "I could get acquainted with this wonderful, fresh young lyric soprano from America." And, listening to the tapes, I had to laugh. Because he was right. *She* was terrific. What I'd been doing at these last rehearsals certainly hadn't sounded like her. As he put it, "*this* person I'm not sure I know and positive I don't like". (Of *course* he said that to my face! How else do you grow?) So I promptly gave up trying to sound like Brünnhilde and fell back to singing with my interest. The première went very well and afterwards he took my face in his hands, kissed it and said only one word: "sublime". It was enough. All he had done was underline the philosophy I had been given by my teacher. Afterwards he asked me to promise not to let the bad habits, which I had now cleaned up, creep back. This is what being a real mentor is all about: knowing when you're off the rails, showing off, and refusing to fall into the trap of thinking you're the greatest regardless.' (She and Karajan remained close friends, and she would sometimes ring him when she knew he was depressed or off-colour and sing 'O Karajan, O Karajan' to the tune of 'O Tannenbaum'.)

Price, who made her milestone débuts singing either Mozart or Verdi heroines, insists that she uses the same vocal approach for both and points out that 'Mozart isn't more demanding than Verdi. He's merely more *exposed*. The *vocal delivery* is more exposed and the orchestra and period he was composing in have a lot to do with it. So, while my approach to singing Mozart is a pure, open-throat, *bel canto* delivery, it is a little bit more *contained* than it is for Verdi because in Mozart we are dealing with a more chamber-operatic dimension. We are also dealing with a Central European, who is by definition more restrained than an Italian. Mozart loved Italy and had a flavour of it, but his terra firma was Austria, and vocally this is very evident to me. I don't mean he's stiff – Central Europeans are among the most deeply emotional, sentimental people imaginable, but they are taught to control and contain their emotions more. This is the way I feel about Mozart. His is a very warm, but contained way of singing. It expands a bit in the magnificence of *Don Giovanni*, but generally speaking his are chamber and especially *ensemble* operas.

'So are Verdi's, in the sense that the ensembles express the delivery-pattern of the characters *together*. And these two composers are un-surpassable in their genius for painting on a totally open canvas, with a palette of absolutely unbelievable character-colours. When performing, or learning how to be, a Mozart or a Verdi character, you feel completely overwhelmed, because each character is so beautifully painted into the collage of the whole opera that you know exactly where you fit and your work is already done for you. In purely vocal terms, though, I would say that in Verdi, because there is a certain bravura in the orchestration, you may press – and I mean press, *not* push – the pedal a little and open up the vocal channel a bit more. The kind of vocal delivery best suited to each composer – which constitutes the essence of what is normally called his "style" – is, as I said, a natural result of the period and the area in which he was composing.'

She explains that the area in which *operatic characters* are placed also plays a crucial part in determining the way they should be interpreted. As an example, she chose the difference between singing Aida and singing one of the Spanish court ladies like Leonora in *Il trovatore* and Leonora in *La forza del destino*, both of whom were brought up in the strict Spanish Catholic tradition – as indeed was Donna Anna in *Don Giovanni* – which demands that they try to suppress their passions and emotions. 'But smouldering emotions are sometimes even more potent', and one of the reasons why she thinks she always made a success of these roles was that she wasn't afraid to portray them 'as wonderful, full-blooded women with *beautiful* music to sing who are also very *brave* to behave the way they do despite their upbringing. Aida is a totally different kettle of fish. She is a royal princess, but the ambience she finds herself in is totally different. And ambience is what determines how a character should be delivered.'

If she had to choose one role as her favourite it would definitely be Aida. 'She was my warrior-part, my heart-beat. She helped me feel even more *beautifully* black, if you know what I mean. I'll tell you why. As a black soprano, it was the only time I got to sing a black character. Normally, being black is of no artistic significance whatsoever. But in this case it was and it still is. Because this very minute, Aida says things about where I am as a woman and as a human being, about *my* life and the progress, or lack of, of millions of people at home in the States – things I could not have said as eloquently in other ways. Very simplistically, she exhibits the conflicts not only within myself, but also racial conflicts, turmoil, duties and obediences, all these very profound things.'

Price explains that when she first sang the role in 1958 in San Francisco, Vienna, Milan and London, her Aida was in more of a turmoil. Later on her interpretation changed to something totally different. 'It came full circle, to the pure spirit of Aida, who was by then out of the turmoil, very pure and *much* more royal. I think that sometimes the notion that Aida is truly a princess has been lost sight of. But I feel that Aida should not be subservient in *any* way. This is why she is so disturbing to Amneris who senses that something about this slave is wrong. And it irritates her to death. I feel that one of the reasons why I was always considered a good Aida was that I never crawled on the floor begging Amneris for pity, *or* had my head down, *or* was submissive, *ever*. Even though I was captured and found myself in the position of a slave, I'm to the manor born, as she is. This is why I didn't hesitate to accept Radames's attraction and advances to me. Why shouldn't I? I'm the same *class* as he is. And even when fear forces me to try and be humble, I can only go so far, because I *am* royalty . . .'

The role of Aida is, in her view, as much an expression of her as it is of America as a whole. 'Because one of the great things about America – and although I have great respect for many countries I am disgustingly, chauvinistically American – is that we have only one difficulty: getting things done *once*. After that, they are accepted and all the former difficulties forgotten. Of course, many martyrs have given their lives for this freedom to exist. But it's in the soil of my country.'

Leontyne Price is the only operatic artist ever to have been honoured with America's highest civilian award: the Medal of Freedom. Her country has been well aware that in this great lady – the only opera star to be featured in *Life* magazine's Bicentennial Issue, 'Remarkable American Women' – it has one of its best representatives. Miss Price was invited to the White House to celebrate the signing of the Egypt-Israel Peace Treaty, to sing at the welcoming ceremony for Pope John Paul II, and also to dinner with the Queen and Prince Philip on the *Britannia* in New York Harbour.

Just recognition for the proud, brave pioneer and incomparable artist who can look back on a career of consummate distinction secure in the knowledge that 'I did something right. I took care of the most extraordinary thing I have: my voice. And [laughing], I think I've had one of the most beautiful lyric soprano voices I've ever heard. I'm *mad* about my voice. It was *gorgeous*. I loved it so much that from time to time I used to take out one of my best crystal glasses, sip a little champagne and toast it. I also think it was a soul instrument. You know how the Eastern Orthodox Churches allow no musical instruments in their Mass because they believe the only instrument worthy of praising God is the human voice? I think I understand why. There is a darkness about Russian voices that seems to emerge out of the guts and at the same time out of the deepest recesses of the soul and which reminds me of a sort of undercurrent also present in black voices.

'I'm bringing this up because it leads to a very important point: that singers should train, but never try to get rid of, the baggage of natural attributes that constitutes their individuality. If that is lost, they end up sounding like hybrids. Because your voice is the most personal thing you have. This is why singing is the most popular and sought-after emotional and artistic experience by the public, and this is what gives us, singers, an edge over the instrumentalists of this world. However, it also brings us an abundance of problems. Because your vocal apparatus is *you*, an expression of your personality, it's with you at all times. It's with you when you feel bad, it's with you when you feel good, it goes through all the emotional and psychological processes *you* go through. The first thing you have to learn as part of growing up is how to control it and not let it control you.'

Even so, the voice always manages to control the *life* of the artists it dwells in, demanding total dedication and often great personal sacrifices. In Leontyne Price's case, after an early marriage and rapid divorce in her

Broadway days, it has meant life alone, with no children – sacrifices which, although she has not been 'bereft of love', can't have been easy to make. But having made them, she felt serene – 'and by that I don't wish to imply stagnancy' – in the knowledge that 'no one can give you what an entire audience can give you. That's why I never married again, or let myself get totally involved in anything but my singing. And although I've been lonesome at times, I've not felt lonely. I've been a happy, fulfilled woman. Because no single human being could have given me what my audiences, those groups of two or five thousand people, gave me.'

KATIA RICCIARELLI

WHEN KATIA RICCIARELLI was a child of seven or eight, she used to climb up trees and sing to the birds. Afraid someone might hear her, she always made for the highest branches; as soon as she reached them, she burst into song – usually her favourite tune, 'Un bel di vedremo' from *Madama Butterfly*. A shy, solitary child, Ricciarelli was deeply marked by the death of her father when she was two, and by that of her three brothers and her sister soon afterwards. She grew up very close to her mother, who was a custodian in the local school at their native Rovigo in the Veneto. They were poor, and it was after working for three years in a factory assembling portable phonographs that she had saved enough money to study singing with Iris Adami-Corradetti at the Benedetto Marcello Conservatoire in Venice.

She stresses that being a singer requires not only a voice and artistic talent, but also the necessary strength to cope with any obstacles that might stand in their way. 'There are people who are born for singing and people who are not. I *am*, I think, because I am very strong. From the beginning I had a voice. But after that, you need many things. You must have the will, the character, the ambition to succeed. If you don't have ambition, you cannot have a career,' she told *Ovation* magazine some years ago.

The grit that enabled Ricciarelli to reach the top and withstand the pressures of her big international career – she is not a Capricorn for nothing – goes hand in hand with an appealing, feminine vulnerability. Even when she is at her most carefree, there is a sense of hurt somewhere, not far beneath the skin. This vulnerability is reflected in her voice and, projected into the heroines she interprets, it makes for very affecting portrayals. No one on stage today, for example, can better Ricciarelli's Desdemona or, in earlier years, Luisa Miller. While several sopranos can *sing* them well, there is no one with a combination of physical, vocal, dramatic and emotional qualities – the lachrymose colours she can inject into her radiant lyric sound, the fragility of her blond looks and the unaffected simplicity of her acting – that results in such perfect fusion between artist and role.

Ricciarelli's repertoire is rooted in *bel canto*. She has most Rossini operas under her belt, is a moving Giulietta in Bellini's *I Capuleti ed i Montecchi* and considers Donizetti's three Queens – the title roles in *Anna Bolena* and *Maria Stuarda*, and Elisabetta in *Roberto Devereux* – among her most satisfying achievements, though she wouldn't put them on *quite* the same level as her Desdemona and Luisa Miller. Nevertheless there have been some mistakes in her choice of roles, notably a 1980 Lucia di Lammermoor in the original, higher version, Aida in 1984 at Covent Garden and Turandot on disc with Karajan, for all of which she was vocally wrong. Fortunately, she realized the inadvisability of these roles and gave them up immediately. These aberrations occurred mostly in the early eighties, a time when she was in two minds about the future direction of her career: whether to stick to her *bel canto* and lyric Verdi roles or expand into the heavier, lirico-spinto repertoire, including some verismo.

'Katia went through a period of singing a lot of Puccini and her voice got bigger,' says Nina Walker, formerly Italian Language Coach and Assistant Chorus Master at Covent Garden, and now a recording executive. 'But she also ran into problems: her voice began to sound quite strained, which is what happens when singers take on the wrong roles. Then she spent a long time studying and preparing Anna Bolena and this seemed to restore her voice to its former condition. Next time I heard her, it was sharper, cleaner than of late, with its gleam and lustre back. I was overjoyed because I had *loved* her Luisa Miller here in 1979. It had charm, warmth and that lovely Verdian coloratura was just right. In short it was perfect, and Lorin Maazel who conducted the production was as thrilled as I was. I hope she will now stay with this repertoire and not return to the heavier roles.'

Ricciarelli herself decided the furthest she would go in this direction would be Elisabetta in *Don Carlos*, a role she first sang in Piero Faggioni's famous 1972 production of the complete version at the Teatro La Fenice in Venice, and for which, like most artists who sing it, she has a special affection: 'The music is sublime, especially in that final duet, one of the most noble and beautiful ever written.' She also agrees with all of Elisabetta's other interpreters that the five-act version, including the Fontainebleau act, is infinitely preferable. 'It explains everything about the character and makes it easier to follow its dramatic evolution. On one hand you have these two young people in love, and on the other, the political games. This contrast between the private and the public aspect of their lives, which is something I much enjoy, should be reflected both in the voice and the acting. The Fontainebleau act, where we see Elisabetta and Don Carlos officially engaged, puts everything in perspective, whereas in the four-act version, their Act I encounter comes across as almost incestuous. Another thing I love in this opera is the way the drama evolves gradually towards the end, when it explodes, culminating in that glorious duet, "Un di ci vedremo in un mondo miglior". Although vocally it consists of pianissimo, legato singing, dramatically the duet is a real explosion: Elisabetta and Don Carlos, having confessed their love for each other, know there is nothing to expect in terms of its earthly fulfilment; their only hope is that they may meet again in the spiritual world.'

Contrary to the general consensus, Ricciarelli doesn't consider this role heavy or especially treacherous for young voices, and feels that the classification of roles into neat slots is often mistaken. Micaela, for instance, frequently sung by 'light sopraninos whose high notes sound like screams', is written not for a light-lyric but for a full lyric soprano and remains, incredibly, one of the hardest roles she has ever sung. 'A lot of *bel canto* roles as well – such as Giulietta in *Capuleti* and most of the Donizetti parts – are not light but heavy lyric, veering towards the dramatic. One must be able to sustain long lines. Yet they should be sung in a "lunar" sort of way. But because heavy, dramatic voices cannot produce this "lunar" effect, people have come to the mistaken conclusion that they should be sung by light-lyric sopranos. By the same token, it is wrong to say that Desdemona is a pure lyric role. It's not. Parts of it, especially Act III, are very dramatic.'

As Ricciarelli's haunting portrayal makes obvious, she loves this lady very much. 'Both vocally and dramatically, it's a wonderful role. Desdemona is very feminine but also a woman with a lot of character. Imagine having the courage to marry a black man in those days, in that milieu, against her father's wishes. It's not exactly easy even now. But *then*! Only someone with a very strong character could do it. She is also rather naïve and unimaginative in a way, which is why she cannot see through Otello's behaviour and is so insistent in Act II, when she presses him about Cassio – a bit like a woman today nagging her husband about buying her a new fur coat when he's come home obviously tired and preoccupied. A "clever" woman would immediately sense it's the wrong moment. But Desdemona is not "clever" in that way. She's direct and totally honest. My favourite moment in the whole opera is her prayer in Act IV. It starts off in a very ordinary way, because it's something she does automatically every night, like brushing her teeth, and this particular prayer, "Ave Maria" is a very ordinary prayer for us Catholics. But then she senses something is about to happen, she has a premonition she's going to die, and her prayer really takes off. It becomes very dramatic and poignant, and assumes a dimension that goes far beyond a usual, formal evening prayer.'

Both on stage and screen, Ricciarelli is at her most moving in this scene. In the première of Franco Zeffirelli's film of *Otello*, there wasn't a pair of dry eyes in the Barbican as she sang this prayer. She is happy to have made this film and wouldn't mind making another but, like most artists coming from the stage, she found the technique of filming – the long hours, the short takes, the fact that she had to film the most intimate scenes surrounded by a bevy of light-and-sound technicians – frustrating and exhausting. 'I had never imagined the degree of fatigue that built up at the end of a long day's hanging around. Every evening I was a physical wreck. I wouldn't mind making one more film, but that would be it. It's the stage I'm made for, with its wonderful, immediate contact with the public.'

Ricciarelli has now sung Desdemona in almost every major opera house in the world, always with Placido Domingo, *the* Otello of our day, as her partner. She singles out Elijah Moshinsky's Covent Garden production (which was revived in January 1990, again under Carlos Kleiber), as one of the best. But she and Domingo have built up such a degree of empathy by now that magical things can happen even in repertory evenings. During a performance at the Vienna State Opera in February 1989, both attained such a close fusion with their roles and with each other that Ricciarelli felt she was 'almost in another dimension, afraid of what would happen next. I have never experienced anything like it in my career, not *ever*. The audience sensed it, too, and my husband who was sitting in the stalls told me there was a total hush, as if nobody dared breathe . . . These moments are very rare indeed. The Germans call them "Sternstunden", and they happen maybe twice or three times in an artist's lifetime. We had fifty minutes' applause – something I hadn't experienced since my first Luisa Miller at the San Francisco Opera with Pavarotti.'

Luisa Miller is one of many early Verdi roles in Ricciarelli's repertoire, which includes Medora in *Il corsaro*, Lucrezia in *I due Foscari*, Lida in *La battaglia di Legnano*, Giselda in *Jerusalem*, Amalia in *I masnadieri* and the title role in *Giovanna d'Arco*. 'I *love* early Verdi. Of course, you don't find the maturity of *Otello* or *Falstaff* in his early works. But you *do* find tremendous vitality and oomph. I always compare late Verdi to a vintage champagne label and early Verdi to a classic Lambrusco [a gutsy Italian sparkling wine from Emilia]. The heroines in his later operas like, for example, Elisabetta, are more poised and lyrical and their vocal line is legato, whereas for Amalia in *I masnadieri* and Luisa Miller the vocal writing is more up-and-down, instinctive and visceral.'

But she points out that early Verdi in general, and Luisa Miller in particular, are very difficult to sing. 'It's quite a demanding role. Unlike Violetta in *La traviata* which starts off difficult and becomes progressively easier vocally, Luisa is difficult at the beginning and difficult again at the

end. There is an entry in Act I which is quite high, full of "picchiettati" *
and demands a very light sound. Act II is quite dramatic while Act III has
an almost Wagnerian dimension: you are on stage all the time and the
vocal writing again contains a lot of "picchiettati" ranging from pianissimo
to forte. Dramatically, I'm very fond of this young, simple girl who falls in
love with a young nobleman, and I enjoy the emotional range of the role.
Again, we have a very important Verdi father of a particularly rigorous
kind, and a heroine whose self-sacrifice is reminiscent of Violetta's –
something which I think appeals to us women.

'However liberated or emancipated we might be, we still like to be
dominated by love and, speaking for myself, by the male. Although I'm
quite successful, have a substantial career and spend most of my time
travelling around the world alone, my dream had always been to find a
man to whom I could voluntarily submit and who could dominate me in a
loving, affectionate way.' She found exactly what she wanted in her
husband, Pippo Baudo, a television star whose programme on RAI-TV is
a bit like an Italian version of *Wogan*. 'He is a very strong character, a
Sicilian and very much the opposite of the classic "Diva-husband". He is
famous in his own right and very self-assured because his career is every
bit as big as mine. He is also very intelligent, cultured, exceptionally
sensitive and understanding.'

Ricciarelli had been a frequent guest in Baudo's TV programme over
the years. But their love affair blossomed out of the blue, in September
1985. She was at La Scala singing in *Il viaggio a Rheims* when he rang up
to say hello, and should she find herself in Rome, to get in touch. As it
happened she was off to Rome almost immediately to sing a concert of
Baroque music with the La Scala Strings. She called and they arranged to
meet afterwards for dinner. It was a romantic cold supper and champagne
in her hotel suite, at the end of which they decided this was 'it'; and four
months later they were married in a small village outside Catania in Sicily.
The wedding – in the main village square, with people hanging out of
balconies and carabinieri trying to contain the crowds – was a real beano.
('Very operatic,' I ventured. 'No, pure operetta', she contested.)

No one was more surprised by the whole course of events than
Ricciarelli herself. 'I never believed things like this could happen. When I
met Pippo properly in September 1985 after many years' professional
aquaintance, I was 39 and he 49 – so we knew what we were doing. I had
just come out of a long, intense love affair with a famous colleague [José
Carreras], but I wasn't looking for a new relationship. I was emotionally
weary, exhausted really, by the on/off nature of this thirteen-year
association, and felt like being on my own for a while, concentrating only

*See page 77 for an explanation of this term.

on my career. But timing is everything in life. Of course, one should also be clear-sighted enough to go along with it and have the strength to close certain parentheses, certain doors. Otherwise – unless one is free in heart and spirit – new doors cannot open.'

I cannot think of many people who deserve their new-found happiness as much as this sympatico woman whose life has been far from easy. 'I've lived a lot and I've suffered a lot which, I suppose, is good for artists. I've also had some fabulous times. But behind it all, there was always this insecurity, this question mark about my future. "What will I do, what will become of me, will I grow old alone?"' When I first met her in 1980 she had told me she felt a singer's life is a very difficult life for a woman. Fascinating and exciting, yes, but also very complicated, full of sacrifices and restrictions. 'You give and give, and you never get enough back. When I think about my life I realize I have nothing. My mother, my house, of course, but no time to live. I like staying home at my house in Spoleto in the Umbrian hills, taking time off to read and go on long walks. I also like to dance but there is never time to go to discos. I must always think of the voice. I can't risk catching a cold, overeat or drink too much or stay up too late. Ouf! Ideally I would like to sing only eight, ten more years and then retire, hopefully while I'm still reasonably attractive, and live a little.'

There is no trace of these anxieties in her any longer. 'All this is gone now. I am serene and feel secure both as a human being and as a woman. I hope, in fact I know, this is reflected in my work. It could not be otherwise, because when we artists step out on stage we carry all our personal baggage with us. This is why I would now like to return to my early repertoire – things like *Il corsaro*, *Giovanna d'Arco* and *Luisa Miller* – and see if I can bring something new to them.' (Though her return to La Scala in *Luisa Miller* in 1989–90 was far from a success.)

As well as bringing a 'whole new human equipment' to these roles, the technical approach is also bound to be different. 'I did some beautiful things for my age then, but some of them have disappeared meanwhile,' she told *Opera News*. 'These pianissimi, these legati were natural to me then but now I must consciously *think* about them. Concentration and understanding are everything. Sometimes the best performances happen when you think a lot [a point also expressed by Josephine Barstow]. In one year, 30 per cent of your performances are effortless, whereas in the rest you must really think what you're doing. There's always a problem: tiredness, a little cold, some pressure on you. And gone are the days when, as at the beignning of my career, I felt better and fresher at the end of a performance than before.'

Ricciarelli's international career had taken off with a bang in 1971, two years after her début in Mantua, when she won the Voci Verdiane

Competion on Italian Television. She had already won prizes in Milan and Parma in 1970, when she sang Leonora in *Il trovatore* at the Teatro Reggio, with the late Richard Tucker as Manrico. But it was at the Verdi Voices Contest that she made such an impact that invitations immediately began to pour in from all major theatres. She was hailed in the press as 'the new Callas', 'the new Tebaldi', a major star, whereas 'I was only a young singer with talent and the right to make mistakes'. Within a year, she had made her début in Rome, at the Chicago Lyric (Lucrezia in *I due Foscari*) and the San Francisco Opera (Luisa Miller), followed, in 1973, by her début at the Vienna State Opera as Liù in *Turandot* and, in 1974, by her débuts at Covent Garden, the Paris Opéra and the Met as Mimi.

An exception to her hugely successful string of international débuts was her Amelia in *Un ballo in maschera* at La Scala, when she was massively booed and criticized. 'It was a terrible experience, all organized because in the minds of some people I was too young to sing at La Scala. For an artist to go immediately to the first rank makes people mad. The publicity was terrible. To expect me to sing like Callas at her best or Caballé at her best was stupid. I am not Callas. I have my own personality. It was a very difficult moment. A few friends helped me, but the burden was *here* on my own shoulders. I decided to be strong enough to live through this difficult moment. And I did. Now I have proved myself and everybody expects the most of me,' she told *Ovation*.

Nowhere did Ricciarelli prove her right to be herself as decisively and brilliantly as with her first Anna Bolena, an unqualified success. Unlike many sopranos who claim never to listen to Callas when studying 'a Callas role' – 'whereas I'm sure when they make breakfast they turn on the cassette of Callas along with the blender and drink it *all* up together' – Ricciarelli admits she did 'listen and listen' to a tape of Callas in this role. But after two months she stopped and told herself she must forget all this because 'it was not me, the voice is completely different. I had to create a character different from Maria's Bolena and it was a major breakthrough for me when I realized I could. And you cannot imagine what a success it was. The critics wrote: "She is intelligent because she thought of Callas but did a more intimate character better suited to her own personality!"'

Other major Donizetti roles Ricciarelli has sung with distinction are the title roles in *Maria Stuarda*, *Maria di Rudenz* and Queen Elizabeth in *Roberto Devereux*. She particularly enjoyed singing the latter two because the fact that roles like this are performed so seldom means there are no so-called 'traditions' to bog her down . . . 'You are free to mould your interpretation according to your own responses to the music and the drama. This is what I try to do with all my portrayals, to some extent:

re-create them with my own personality. I think the public senses this and responds to my acting because it is simple and sincere.'

Of all *bel canto* composers the one Ricciarelli is most familiar with is Rossini, whose roles suit her voice perfectly. At the time of our last meeting she was preparing Nanetta in *La gazza ladra* ('The Thieving Magpie') for the 1989 Rossini festival in Pesaro, where she is an annual guest and has already performed several Rossini roles to great acclaim: Madama Cortese in *Il viaggio a Rheims* (which she later also sang at La Scala, the Vienna State Opera and on disc for Deutsche Grammophon), the title role in *Bianca e Faliero*, Amenaide in *Tancredi*, Elena in *La donna del lago*, Pamira in *L'Assedio di Corinto* and *Le Siège de Corinthe*, the title roles in *Armida* and *Semiramide* and Mathilde in *Guglielmo Tell*.

She points out that Rossini makes quite different demands on the voice than the other two, and is 'quite a different exercise physically. It's good to alternate Rossini roles with Bellini and Donizetti because the latter two demand sustained singing and long lines, whereas Rossini demands agility: you have to hit the notes quickly and let them go immediately. You don't have to sustain them. Therefore being *just* a Rossini singer could be very dangerous. You have to use the breathing and the vocal cords differently and this could make it difficult to sing a long, sustained legato phrase. I've seen it happen to numerous Rossini singers. That's why specialization is so limiting. If you want to travel around the world singing only Cenerentola or Cherubino, that's fine. But for a truly international career you need variety. Plus a certain intelligence and discrimination in your choice of roles.'

In recent years, Ricciarelli has sung quite a lot of Baroque and classical repertoire, both on stage and in the concert hall: Cherubini's *Anacreon* in Paris, Piccinni's *Iphigénie*, Paisiello's *Il barbiere di Siviglia*, plus a lot of Handel, Vivaldi and Gluck. She has found the experience enormously refreshing 'like plunging into a stream of the cleanest, purest and most transparent water imaginable, in which all stains and impurities vanish at a stroke. This implies a tremendous discipline, which is why Baroque music, the natural forerunner of *bel canto*, is excruciatingly difficult to sing. But I enjoy the fact that it makes me feel I'm dominating my voice rather than the other way round. The thing that helped most in my understanding and singing of Baroque music is my knowledge of Gregorian Chant [a tradition in Venice because of its connection with Byzantium], which I studied in some depth at the Marcello Conservatoire. Gregorian chant consists of "equilismi"-cyclical patterns. It is those cyclical patterns of Gregorian Chant that I always try to visualize mentally when singing Baroque music.' Indeed, concerts with string ensembles feature prominently in Ricciarelli's future plans – even though she finds concerts more draining than the stage because they demand 'a greater weight of concentration, both physical and mental'. One of her strongest ambitions is to sing the title role in *Adriana Lecouvreur*, for which she feels vocally and dramatically ready, but as yet she has no fixed plans to do so. Singing verismo roles is, for her, much harder than *bel canto*, 'because so much of it is written in the middle voice. Even Mimi, with which I made my professional and three major international débuts, is very hard in places, especially the duet with Marcello. But verismo roles are much easier to *act* than *bel canto*, where you have to concentrate so hard on vocal production – those coloraturas and embellishments – that your mind isn't free to give its all to the drama. One should be careful, though, not to let oneself go over the top in verismo, otherwise it becomes vulgar. I have always tried to sing my verismo roles "belcantistically", without exaggerations or vulgarities.' She proved her point with a moving yet delicate portrayal of Tosca on record and in a concert performance at the Berlin Philharmonie under Karajan in February 1982.

This Tosca was one of the Ricciarelli gambles that paid off. She has never been averse to taking chances. 'No one can have a worthwhile career without taking a few risks, sometimes big risks that will stretch and extend you beyond the confines of what comes to you safely and naturally. You might well end up falling flat on your face once or twice. But if you succeed in eight gambles out of ten, you will be the better artist for it.'

RENATA SCOTTO

THE TITLE OF Renata Scotto's autobiography, *More than a Diva*, is an apt description of this prolific singing actress, whose career spans nearly four decades, whose repertoire includes more than 50 roles and whose aim as a performer has always been 'not to give audiences the impression of a singer enjoying the sound of her own voice – I am not that kind of diva – but of an *interpreter*, an artist who seeks to reveal the dramatic truth in every operatic score'. Like Callas, Scotto is what the Italians call 'un animal di palco' ('a stage cat'), electric on stage and a seeker after 'the word in the music'.

She admits to being allergic to opera as it was before the Callas Revolution: dependent almost entirely on vocal virtuosity and pyrotechnics – 'a circus phenomenon'. But with the advent of Callas 'things began to improve and I, too, have tried to do my bit to promote the idea of opera as believable theatre, the way its composers visualized it'. In the process of revealing the dramatic truth of the characters she interprets, Scotto sometimes goes for an ugly sound when she feels the action demands it. But, in the words of Ubaldo Gardini, one of today's foremost operatic coaches, 'an ugly sound that means so much that you instantly accept it'.

The fierce intensity of Scotto's interpretations and her blunt refusal to go for mere beauty of sound (in any case the voice itself, although capable of great finesse, is not conventionally beautiful), have made her a controversial artist, both with audiences and within the musical profession, where her detractors are as vociferous as her admirers. The latter include famous colleagues like Zinka Milanov – 'I like her vocal message' – and conductors like Riccardo Muti, Lorin Maazel and James Levine, with whom she has enjoyed exciting collaborations.

Scotto is also a passionate believer in textual fidelity, and has played an important part in the 'cleaning up' of verismo we have witnessed in recent years. In her opinion, it was the composers of the verismo school – Puccini, Mascagni, Giordano, Cilea, Leoncavallo, Catalani and Zandonai – who suffered most from arbitrary interpretations based on so-called performing tradition. (For an opposite view, see the chapters on Ghena Dimitrova and Eva Marton.)

'These composers wrote beautiful and very interesting music . . . But it was seldom performed in a way that did it justice. More often than not, one heard it sung in a vulgar, exaggeratedly melodramatic way that bore little resemblance to what was actually written in the score – all chest notes, with scant attention paid to pitch or to "piano" indications. But these composers thought long and hard before writing down their phrases – Puccini wrote five drafts of *Manon Lescaut* and four of *Madama Butterfly* – so why not try to do what they wanted? Why go for an arbitrary interpretation?'

She accepts that in certain music, such as that of the Baroque period, where phrases were deliberately left unfinished so that singers could add their own embellishments, textual fidelity is not an issue. 'But the music of Verdi (especially late Verdi where, in operas such as *Aida*, *Don Carlos*, *Otello* and *Falstaff*, he compresses into a few phrases emotions that, in his earlier operas, would be spread over a whole cabaletta) and of the verismo composers is written in a different style and makes for different theatre: much more dense and concentrated, both musically and dramatically. My aim has been to try and lift verismo to the musical and artistic level it deserves. In fact, to try and do with it something comparable to Callas's revival of *bel canto* which, with the help of Tullio Serafin, she was the first to *really* understand.'

It was as a *bel canto* singer that Scotto herself began her career. Born in 1934 in Savona on the Ligurian coast of Italy, she began studying singing at the age of fourteen. Two years later she moved to Milan to continue her studies while staying at a convent for Canossian nuns. In 1953, aged nineteen, she won a young artists' competition with 'Sempre libera' from *La traviata*, and made her professional début in this opera at Milan's Teatro Nuovo shortly after. At the time, she had 'a beautiful voice with a dark colour and a lyric timbre' and plenty of temperament. On the strength of it, she was engaged by La Scala, where she made her début as Walter in Catalani's *La Wally*, with a cast headed by Tebaldi and Del Monaco under the baton of Carlo Maria Giulini. She admits that it was her temperament, 'definitely not my technique', that helped her get by for a while. But within a couple of years, her lack of sound technical foundations caught up with her and made her feel virtually crippled on stage.

'I just couldn't do what I wanted. There I was, with my temperament, but having difficulty even with my acting, because if you have no technique you spend all your time worrying about vocal problems and are not free to interpret. So I thought the moment had come to look for another teacher.' She had had four up to then, but none had been able to teach her what she needed to learn. Luckily, she happened to be singing *La traviata* with Alfredo Kraus at the time, and he offered to introduce her to his teacher, Mercedes Llopard, a former Spanish soprano to whom, as he never tires of stressing, he owes his superb technique and vocal longevity.

On being introduced to Scotto, Llopard exclaimed: 'My God, you have a beautiful voice but you don't know what to do with it. We will start off by making you sing nothing but E flats for two months.' Scotto replied that, as she didn't even have a high C at the time, this would be impossible! But she decided to give Llopard's method a try and took six months off work, to devote herself entirely to improving her technique. And, sure enough, after two months, she began to hit E flat. So they began working on the coloratura repertoire. 'This was very intelligent on my teacher's part because there is nothing better for young singers than studying Mozart, Bellini and Donizetti, whose music teaches you line, intonation, breath control, all those basic things on which a young singer's technique should be grounded. Temperament can wait until later!'

Llopard concentrated mostly on voice placement rather than breath control, and kept asking Scotto to place her voice high. 'She taught me that the voice doesn't have to come from the throat, that it can come from the head. This way, and through the coloratura repertoire, she helped me focus the voice without pushing the middle register, which would have forced the sound and shortened my career. And, unlike many teachers, especially today, Llopard taught me that the most important thing is not only learning how to sing but how to understand music.'

After seven months' study with Llopard, Scotto was ready to resume her career. In 1956 she made her international début in London, at the Stoll Theatre, as Adina in *L'elisir d'amore* and Elvira in *Don Giovanni*. During the next decade she consolidated her reputation in Italy, singing for ten consecutive seasons at La Scala and many other Italian theatres. In 1957, there was a big international breakthrough when she stood in for Callas in *La sonnambula* during La Scala's visit to the Edinburgh Festival. She made her Metropolitan Opera début in 1965, as Madama Butterfly, returning for Gilda, Violetta, Lucia and Adina. After a triumphant appearance as Elena in *I vespri siciliani* in 1974, she became a resident Diva at the Met, where for many years she appeared almost every season, in all her major roles, many of which have been shown live on PBS Television. She considers this aspect of her work, 'public relations and television', very important for singers nowadays. After gaining weight shortly after the birth of her children, she went on a special diet and lost 45 lbs over a year. 'The camera never lies, so it's important to ensure that my Mimi or Manon Lescaut could *really be* Mimi and Manon Lescaut.'

Scotto has been clever in her choice of repertoire. For over a decade, she concentrated almost entirely on *bel canto* plus some early Verdi roles with coloratura, like Gilda and Violetta. Later, as her voice began to grow darker, she added more Verdi roles like Griselda in *I Lombardi*, Elena in *I vespri siciliani* and eventually Lady Macbeth, as well as verismo parts like Maddalena in *Andrea Chénier* and the title roles in *Manon Lescaut*, *Fedora* and *Adriana Lecouvreur*. In the process, she took some risks that may have contributed to the occasional vocal shrillness her detractors find disagreeable. But, she explains, 'I always had the wish for a wide repertoire and *hated* routine. I could never be a singer who plays safe with a repertoire of half-a-dozen roles. I like challenge. I know sometimes this can be very dangerous. You go on stage and, by challenging yourself, you can risk your whole career. But I like that.'

She stresses that 'the singer in me enjoys singing *bel canto* but the actress prefers verismo because it gives me the opportunity to shape and mould characters into real people. The problem with *bel canto* operas is that, because of their musical construction of recitative-aria-cabaletta, they are very difficult to act. There are places where *musically* there is nothing to do *but* stop and sing and show off the beautiful *bel canto* line. Verismo operas, on the other hand, belong to a different world, the turn of the century, and have a totally different musical construction. The sequence of recitative-aria-cabaletta, as I've already mentioned à propos of late Verdi, has been abandoned in favour of a new brevity and density, and in theatrical terms this is much better because the drama is so tight and focussed that you can really *act*. Late Verdi and verismo operas are really plays set to music. Even the most "show-stopping" kind of arias seem to further the action instead of suspend it, as they tend to do in *bel canto* operas.'

The sole *bel canto* work in which one finds the same sort of density and where the action doesn't stop even for a moment is *Norma*, which Scotto rightly considers 'the perfect *bel canto* opera'. Like most of her colleagues, she also considers the title role one of the most difficult in the soprano repertoire, not only to sing but also, and especially, to *interpret*. 'Norma emerges from the libretto, which is also wonderful, as a very deep, multi-faceted character. Firstly as the High Priestess of a barbarian nation, who not only has to embody the ideal of purity but also has the power to declare war or make peace: a very powerful woman. Secondly, as a woman in love, experiencing all the feelings every woman in love is familiar with; and thirdly, as a mother, a very tender mother indeed. You have to get under the skin of this woman and bring out all the facets and conflicts within her – the melancholy, the nostalgia, the fury, the tenderness, the pain, all of which are so beautifully expressed in Bellini's music.'

Scotto finds it strange that the drama should be so densely packed in a musically typical *bel canto* opera; and even stranger that it should contain hints of early Verdi in its recitatives, which are far more important than *any* recitatives in *any bel canto* opera. 'In fact they are even better than the arias. Despite the fact that Norma's famous prayer to the moon "Casta Diva", is breathtaking in its beauty, this is not the key to Norma. Her character comes across much more in the recitatives, which are far from being a mere transition to the aria. Each of them has a musical and dramatic purpose.

'Take that monumental recitative in Act I, which starts off with Norma talking to her maid. She already knows Pollione is tiring of her and suspects he may have another woman. Then comes her duet with Adalgisa, the young priestess who comes to her High Priestess for help. Norma starts off sympathetic towards this girl who, like herself, has broken her vows of chastity. But when she discovers that Pollione's "other woman" is Adalgisa, she becomes furious and treats her as a rival. Then the two women forge a strong bond of friendship. In the gigantic Act III, Norma gives up everything for his sake. I feel that at this moment she uses her power to say something to him, while all the time *knowing* that she will give up her life and die for him. But she wants to *use* this moment, and to me this shows the greatness inside her. This is when she becomes a great woman, the great tragic figure that is in Bellini's music.

'And if the interpreter fails to understand or bring out this tragic dimension, if she doesn't follow the tension of the drama through every line and every recitative, she will have failed the music. This is why Tullio Serafin, the veteran operatic conductor, told the young Callas when she first turned up at his house to study this opera: "Go home and come back tomorrow, when I shall want you to declaim the whole opera to me, from start to finish. Not the music, just the words. I know you can *sing* the role, that's why we engaged you. But when you can match the words to Bellini's music, you will find the key to Norma." And he was right. Because as far as the music pure and simple is concerned, Norma is not all *that* difficult to sing, provided, of course, that you have a good technique.'

She immediately went on to add that what she means is that it is not difficult in comparison to Verdi, the most demanding of *all* composers. 'It makes no difference whether you happen to be singing a so-called light or a so-called heavy Verdi role. The mere fact that it is a Verdi role makes it more difficult – more "serious" – than anything else you are ever likely to tackle. Because to sing Verdi you need a simply *fabulous* technique. Take the scores of *I vespri siciliani*, *La traviata* and *Rigoletto*, for instance. Elena is usually labelled a dramatic role, while Violetta and Gilda are labelled light-lyric. Yet this is wrong because, vocally, the three roles are written in the same way. In *Rigoletto* you have a *character* who is dramatically, psychologically, softer. But *musically* you have coloratura and you also have some very dramatic writing in "Tutte le feste al tempio" and in the duet that follows it. Ergo, you have the same *kind* of music as in *I vespri siciliani*, because Verdi almost always demands a soprano who can produce the whole gamut of vocal possibilities: high notes, low notes, piano singing, dramatic singing, coloratura, a beautiful legato line. This is why *nobody* can sing Verdi without a perfect technique.'

Scotto singles out Elena in *I vespri siciliani* (which she first sang in Florence and in which she later scored an immense personal triumph at the Metropolitan Opera in 1974), as *the* most difficult of all Verdi roles – indeed of *all* roles in her repertoire. 'It demands just about everything you can do as a singer: power, softness, line, long breath, high notes, low notes, dramatic singing, coloratura singing and, as it is four-and-a-half hours long, the kind of stamina and resilience demanded by Wagnerian roles. And incidentally, most Wagner sopranos are very much afraid of singing Verdi!

'Dramatically, Elena is as multi-faceted as Norma: a fighting-woman for her people and also a rather sad, romantic woman in love. In the prison scene, she sings of her love for Arrigo, to whom she can never be married. This wonderful aria, which comes after a very dramatic duet, starts off with a pianissimo B flat, goes on to low, even softer singing and culminates in a cadenza that is almost impossible to sing. It starts off with C sharp, goes down to F below the stave; in fact, most sopranos transpose it up. But Verdi wrote it this way and expected his sopranos to manage it. So when I sang Elena in Florence and later at the Met I decided to try and do what he wrote. And I was really proud that I managed to because I had to work very, very hard to find that note. But this is what the art of singing boils down to: putting your technique at the service of the composer, to the best of your ability. After this aria, Elena goes back to coloratura singing for her most popular aria, the Sicilienne, at the Wedding Scene. And this particular bit of coloratura singing comes at the end of the opera, at eleven o'clock at night (or two in the morning if you happen to be singing it in Spain, where performances sometimes start at nine-thirty). Which is why, as far as *Vespri* is concerned, I tend to prefer matinées.'

Scotto scored another major success in a Verdi role when she first sang Lady Macbeth at Covent Garden, in a production directed by Elijah Moshinsky and conducted by Riccardo Muti. She especially relished the challenge of tackling a major Shakespearian heroine for the first time in London. She had begun to think of Lady Macbeth as a possibility about two years before, after recording *Nabucco* with Muti, even though she would *never* contemplate singing Abigaille on stage, for both vocal and dramatic reasons. Scotto has always felt 'an antipathy' towards this character whom she considers 'hard, ugly, antipatico and totally one-sided, unlike Lady Macbeth, who has two sides to her and is altogether more interesting. Yes, she is incredibly bloodthirsty and ambitious, but she is also a beautiful, young, sexy woman very much in love with her husband and I was happy that both my directors – Elijah Moshinsky in London and Peter Hall in New York – gave me the chance to put this across.'

Scotto stresses that Lady Macbeth is not a role for inexperienced young sopranos. 'You need plenty of life-experience, both as a woman and as a singer. The music is fiendishly difficult for sopranos of *any* age because Verdi demands every imaginable kind of sound: coloratura, pianissimi with six ppppppp's, hissing sounds, whispering sounds, groans and a number of ugly sounds you have to find for yourself. And the only thing that can help you is the meaning of the words.' The role is even more difficult dramatically because *Macbeth* displays all the usual difficulties found in early Verdi operas. The characters are not as clearly mapped-out as in Shakespeare and musically the work retains the structure of recitative-aria-cabaletta.

'Lady Macbeth comes on stage reading her husband's letter and immediately plunges into the aria "Vieni t'affretta", which is followed by a cabaletta and leaves you no time at all – just three minutes – in which to establish the character. I feel that she needs more time to react to the letter [Grace Bumbry stresses exactly the same point] and create an impression of steely ambition and ruthless lust for power. In the play she has sufficient time, but in the opera she doesn't. This is where experience and maturity come in handy.' Scotto feels she tackled this role at exactly the right time in her career. The proof was that, after singing ten performances preceded by a month's rehearsals, her voice was in the best possible condition. Her performance of Lady Macbeth earned high praise from another famous Lady Macbeth: Grace Bumbry, usually not given to bestowing compliments on colleagues!

As we have mentioned, Scotto's first role was one of Verdi's most famous heroines, Violetta in *La traviata*, which she also recorded in the sixties, with Antonino Votto. The pair worked togther on the role for two months, in his apartment, perfecting every word and every phrase. The disappearance of this old-fashioned breed of conductors who took time to coach and nurture singers and who knew so much about every operatic

role that coaches were superfluous is, she rightly feels, one of the
tragedies in opera today. 'Contemporary conductors are much too busy
to do this sort of thing. They have their own careers and are much more
egocentric. To them, opera is almost like a symphony concert in which
they see their orchestra playing the most important part. Certainly they
have a good technique, certainly they know the symphonic repertoire
very well. But of opera and the art of singing most of them know next to
nothing. They say "this is the tempo and follow me".' So the young
generation has no one to learn from.'

In the fifties and sixties there were, apart from Votto, several great
operatic conductors like Serafin (who helped her a lot and called her 'La
Scottino'), Gui and Gavazzeni, who were 'very paternal, they loved
singers and protected us from harm. Never would they allow – let alone
urge – a singer to sing the wrong role or even the right role too soon. And
when they coached us, they talked about expression, the meaning of the
words, not just tempi and "follow me". Not that I expect conductors to
follow *me*, either. Communication between the two should, ideally, be so
intense and subtle that, during the performance you feel linked to the
conductor by some sort of invisible thread, and both should *sense* what
the other will do. A conductor who *follows* you is already too late. He
should *anticipate* you, he should sense what tempo you are about to take
or when you need a breath. When there is this level of communication,
the singer will reciprocate by doing what *he* wants.' (The late Herbert von
Karajan understood this perfectly, realizing that this made the singers
feel free. 'And when they feel free, they will sing well.')

In a different way, Scotto found the same intensity of communication
in her collaboration with Riccardo Muti with whom she also recorded *La
traviata* again, in 1981. She felt immediately at home with his purist
approach to scores and impatience with all the so called performing
traditions that can result in distorting the composer's original intentions.
Nothing illustrates his approach more clearly than this recording of *La
traviata*, which Scotto calls 'the fulfilment of a dream as far as I was
concerned. When I first sang *La traviata* in Italy in the early fifties, I had
to follow the performing traditions of the work – which included cadenzas
by great singers of the past such as, for example, Toti dal Monte. I was too
young to realize I didn't have to follow other people's performing habits,
that I could be myself, and this weighed on my shoulders. But when I
came to record *La traviata* with Muti, he said: "Why don't we try and do
exactly what Verdi wrote, and nothing more?" And we did. We looked
inside the score and sought to understand and interpret the character with
my personality certainly, but mainly with, and through, Verdi's music.

'Every phrase in that recording is faithful to his score. There are singers

– I have heard several – who use composers to show off their vocal virtuosity. Yet to me, embellishing a phrase like Amina's "a, non credea mirarti", one of the most beautiful in all opera, is a *crime*. Riccardo Muti and I speak the same language as far as these matters are concerned. And apart from him, I have also enjoyed my collaborations with the late Herbert von Karajan and with James Levine, who really understands the voice, enormously. Also with Lorin Maazel, especially in Puccini, whose music he seems to carry inside him and understands better than most.'

Scotto considers Puccini the most human of all composers and has read all his letters, which she found enthralling. 'He had a good many troubles in his life and everything he experienced he poured into his operas. He identifies with all his characters, especially his female characters, one-hundred per cent – I wish he had lived to finish *Turandot* himself – and knows exactly how to reach the audience.' Herself famous for the whole-hearted way she throws herself into the heroines she portrays, Scotto, like all true actresses, tries to become those characters and put them across 'with simplicity instead of melodrama' as believable people. And none more so than Madama Butterfly, one of her greatest portrayals.

As soon as she first sang this intimate, sympathetic heroine it became one of her greatest favourites. 'Every time I sing Butterfly I feel I'm reaching out and talking to each member of the audience personally. This makes a big difference because it renders every performance unique. I don't get the same sensation with other characters such as Manon Lescaut. But with Butterfly I never fail to, and perhaps this is why people everywhere have always responded particularly warmly to my Butterfly. Yet I never *ever* cry when singing her because I feel this would be the wrong way to reach the audience. My aim is to show them the truth about her and leave it up to them whether they wish to cry or not. It would be cheap to *underline* for them that in this or that spot they should cry and this is also true of *Suor Angelica*, an opera in which it is also very easy to cry. I do so myself whenever I go to see it as a member of the audience.' But for similar reasons she refrained from crying when she performed the title role as part of the whole Puccini *Trittico* (in which the other two operas are *Il tabarro* and *Gianni Schicchi*) at the Metropolitan Opera during the 1981–82 season – the first singer ever to perform all three operas in a single evening. Scotto also later directed this *Trittico* at the Verona Arena.

Other famous Puccini portrayals include both Mimi and Musetta in *La Bohème*, 'a masterpiece about young, free people of a certain period. Puccini knew everything about this sort of life, having himself lived very similarly in his early days in Milan, when he was always writing to his mother for money to buy food with. When I first sang this opera, at the

Met in 1977, I thought Mimi was wonderful. But gradually I began to realize Musetta is rather marvellous, too. The two are different and yet so similar in their lifestyles: free to live as they like and be with the men they choose. Except for the fact that one is healthy and the other sick. Apart from this crucial difference, both are full of life, full of fun, and of the need to love and be loved.

'When I sang Mimi, I looked at Musetta through her eyes, and when I sang Musetta in Zeffirelli's production at the Met in 1981–82 I did the reverse. And it was a very special experience to see Mimi this way, desperately trying to cling to life, and to find love. Because it is she who wants to meet Rodolfo and goes and knocks at his door. Even though she is sick, she wants to have a friend, someone to talk to, maybe a new boyfriend. It is she who instigates the meeting, and when one thinks of how girls were supposed to behave in those days this is a daring move. So both she and Musetta are very free spirits. At one point Mimi leaves Rodolfo because she thinks the need to pay for her medicines is ruining him and goes to live with another man. But when she knows she is dying she comes back because she wants to die in Rodolfo's arms.' Like Mirella Freni, Scotto also finds Mimi one of the most human of operatic characters.

The title role in *Manon Lescaut* – which she first sang in 1980 at the Met with Placido Domingo as Des Grieux in a production conducted by James Levine and directed by Giancarlo Menotti – is another of her major achievements; and one of the 1980 Met performances was televised live both in the States and Britain. Scotto has enjoyed happy and fruitful collaborations with several directors, including Elijah Moshinsky, Peter Hall, Luca Ronconi and Raf Vallone, but found this experience of working with Menotti, who as a considerable operatic composer 'understood everything', one of the most rewarding of her career. He in turn was amazed by her eagerness to act and move around while singing – something many singers are still loath to do. 'I had read the book many times and had a very strong vision of Manon as a young, flirtatious girl of sixteen, full of *joie de vivre*, who enjoys being admired by men. And I feel all this must be put across, especially in Act II. So I lay on my back, and jumped and careered about to the point where Menotti said he would never have believed a singer could do all this. Working with a great musician like him was wonderful. Mind you, the directors I've just mentioned, who are not musicians and know nothing about music technically, are nevertheless very musical and never asked me to do anything that went against the music.'

In fact, when asked which director she would pick for her first production of *Adriana Lecouvreur* (which she first sang at the Met in 1983 with Placido Domingo as Maurizio), she named Raf Vallone, the famous

Italian actor and director who had directed her first Norma and 'taught me how to act. It's easy enough to come on stage as a great prima donna. But you have to express this many-faceted character not just through singing but through acting. And it was very hard for me at first. Raf Vallone was always urging me not to use my hands in the usual operatic way but make only one big gesture when I wanted to underline something really crucial. Acting and singing are difficult enough in themselves. But acting while you sing is even more difficult.'

Yet it is particularly crucial in the case of *Adriana Lecouvreur* which is based on a real-life character who was a great actress, revolutionary for her period because she advocated realism and simplicity. 'Therefore it is vital not to behave like an opera singer but like a singing actress. I love and identify with this heroine most especially because she is an artist, and an artist in love. The opera is a beautiful love story between a great actress and a Prince, Maurizio of Saxony, whom she loved as only an actress or a singer can love. I believe we artists love differently, more, than other people. We have this extra dimension of our lives in music and on stage which enlarges our capacity for love and widens our emotional extremes. Adriana was like that, full of love for this Maurizio whom she also helped financially but who also had eyes for other women. In her love for him we see the great actress change and become simply a woman in love, with a great heart to give to this man, and with all the troubles of a woman in love. This is why I find this opera so exceptional and its music so fantastic, one of the best examples of *bel canto* singing in a verismo opera. (Because *bel canto* is not only a certain period in opera. It is a way of singing that can be applied to most roles, with obvious exceptions like Lulu or Marie in *Wozzeck*.) But it could easily be vulgarized, which would be a crime.'

Scotto lavishes a good deal of time and care in the preparation of new roles, during which the text always comes first. 'But on stage, the music comes first. Yet when learning a new piece, I must know *why* a composer wanted the music to be the way it is. So I look for the explanation in the poet, the libretto or the historical background and try to understand the characters this way. This work must be complete before I start working on the music, which I learn with the help of a coach and which, in the last resort, gives me the *real* clues to the characters. Musically, I can learn a role in a fortnight. But I took a whole year to prepare a role like Lady Macbeth.'

On the day of a performance, Scotto likes to relax, concentrate and avoid idle chat with family or friends. She goes for a walk in the morning and eats a large sandwich about one o'clock. Before the performance she likes a cup of tea, followed by another in the interval. After the show, it's straight to bed. She likes to vocalize for an hour every day, and for half-an-hour before a performance, in her dressing room, because 'the vocal cords are muscles, and if they're not exercised every day they grow slack, like dancers' muscles'. Scotto is married to conductor Lorenzo Anselmi and they have a grown-up son and daughter. Home is a big house in Westchester County (where she has gained a reputation as a wily poker player and harmless, if enthusiastic, golfer) and a pied à terre in New York City, a stone's throw from the Met, her artistic home. But she protests that although 'everyone thinks I prefer the Met to other theatres, it's not true. I love singing anywhere, everywhere.'

CHERYL STUDER

AT THE END of the 1987–88 season – which began with a triumphant Covent Garden début as Elisabeth in *Tannhäuser* and ended with acclaimed performances as Elsa in both London and Bayreuth and as the Empress in *Die Frau ohne Schatten* at the Munich Festival – Cheryl Studer was named 'Soprano of the Year' by the opera critic of *The Times*. The accolade was fully justified. For, as Sir Georg Solti was quick to note when Studer auditioned for him in 1986, there hasn't been a soprano voice as exciting as this in over a decade. Peter Katona, Artistic Administrator of the Royal Opera, is equally enthusiastic: 'Studer's is a wonderful, thrilling voice, in fact the *ideal* voice for the lyric Wagner roles.'

Studer's first big international break was her début as Elisabeth in Wolfgang Wagner's 1985 Bayreuth production of *Tannhäuser*, into which she stepped with only three weeks' notice, after Gabriella Benackova withdrew. Studer was in Bayreuth for Freia in *Das Rheingold*. She had never sung, and didn't know, the role of Elisabeth, and managed to sight-read 'Dich teure Halle' impressively enough in a hastily arranged audition for Wolfgang Wagner and conductor Giuseppe Sinopoli. They gave her the role, which meant learning it while rehearsing at the same time. But Studer did not disappoint them. Her performance won standing ovations and critical eulogies: 'Cheryl Studer is the discovery of the evening,' wrote *The Times*. '"Dich teure Halle", Elisabeth's greeting at the start of Act II, had all the impetuousness and youthful onrush of feelings that mark Wagner's early operas. Miss Studer, at the start of her career, has a freshness of tone and the volume to provide exactly what Wagner demanded. And the prayer in Act III was shaped with care, a precise sense of line and no fading of tone.' Here, at last, was the kind of soprano the music world was waiting for, capable of breathing new life into the youthful-lyric Wagnerian repertoire.

Studer, who is highly intelligent, articulate and thinks a great deal about her roles, describes interpretation as 'an art of the obvious, in the sense that it is, or should be, supremely *logical*. Our task as interpreters is to bring out the logic behind the action and the emotions of each character thus clarifying the *reason* why the music is written as it is. The clues usually lie in small nuances and details hidden away in the text and the score; they often go unnoticed; but they can make all the difference to a portrayal. Provided one has the voice for them, broad lines can take care of themselves. But the small notes, the sixteenths, the pauses, the little sighs, are the sort of things that, if overlooked, could mean missing the point of a character altogether. These are the things I pay most attention to and work hardest at. I do this for every role, but especially for Elisabeth. Elisabeth is totally honest and it's vital that this should come across. In fact her honesty, especially vis-à-vis herself, is her downfall.'

Studer had been accustomed to singing Elisabeth in the Dresden version of *Tannhäuser* preferred by most theatres, including Covent Garden and Bayreuth. But when she came to record the work (for Deutsche Grammophon, with Placido Domingo in the title role), she discovered that conductor Sinopoli, like Solti before him, opted for the longer Paris version and she found it fascinating to compare the two. The Paris version is better in her view because it helps clarify this complex work: 'The music for Act I – in which Elisabeth is not involved – is completely different. When I first heard the orchestra rehearsing, I was amazed. It has so much more colour, is so much more sensual and *modern*; it almost amounts to a different Wagner from the one we know in the Dresden version. Venus has a much larger part and dramatically this is important because it further highlights the conflict between the two women – symbolizing the two different sides of Tannhaüser.' Elisabeth's music is not at all different, though, and in both versions she emerges as 'a woman untypical of her times because she is the only one not to recoil or run away when Tannhäuser announces he has been to Venusberg – whatever one takes this to stand for. On the contrary, she is prepared to defend him by pointing out that everybody is a sinner. Obviously, she is hurt by his revelations. But she is willing to face up to them and confront all of society on his behalf. The *real* tragedy is that, in the end, she is not capable of confronting its full implications, either. She dies for him, of her own free will. But she can't live with him. It's a very powerful and rather tragic role.'

Vocally Elisabeth lies very well for Studer's voice and is written in an interesting way. For example, the most difficult things are not, as one might imagine, Elisabeth's two arias, 'Dich teure Halle' and the Prayer to the Virgin, 'but all her small monologues which are very *parlando* and where the text is absolutely crucial. Naturally, the voice must carry above the orchestra. But *how* I'm singing – the vocal aspect – matters less than *what* I'm singing. As far as vocal development is concerned, Elisabeth is written totally differently from Elsa in *Lohengrin*. She takes off immediately with a jubilant, exuberant aria, "Dich teure Halle", and gets more and more solemn, and vocally more lyrical as the opera goes on. Elsa, on the other hand, is written in a more "Italian" way, with long, melodic, cantabile lines. Unlike Elisabeth, she starts off lyrical – pure, simple singing, almost like a Schubert Lied – gets more dramatic in Act II and, by Act III, she's almost hysterical, momentarily insane.'

When Studer first saw *Lohengrin* she didn't like it very much, finding it static and somewhat boring. But as she began to delve deeper in preparation for her 1988 Covent Garden performances, she gradually understood what this piece is all about and decided Elsa has often been misunderstood by singers, who portray her as too soft, far less powerful than she really is. 'I'm convinced she is not a weak sort of person daydreaming about her Knight in Shining Armour. This "saviour" is really an obsession with her. And when he becomes a reality her reaction is to feel she's part of righteousness. She goes on a kind of ego trip of feeling wonderful. Ortrud smashes the delusion.'

Elsa's singing should reflect her obsessional nature. Even her Dream – 'Einsam in trüben Tagen' – which is almost visionary, should not be sung in too soft or dreamlike a manner. 'It should be sung in a *fanatical* way, as if she's obsessed by this vision. In fact Elsa is more of an obsessed person than the milk-and-water-miss she is usually portrayed to be.' The critic of the *Sunday Telegraph*, after lavishing praise on the 'soaring, arrow-like accuracy' of her vocal portrayal, 'radiantly phrased in the classic Wagnerian manner', stressed that 'her characterization was striking, too. Elsa is liable to come across as a rather soppy lady, but this Elsa's passionate, relentless questioning of Lohengrin in Act III as to his true identity reminded one of Judith in Bartók's *Duke Bluebeard's Castle*, with her similarly disastrous inability to let her husband keep his innermost secrets to himself.' (The connection between Elsa and Judith is also noted by Eva Marton.)

Studer rightly believes that the issue of love destroyed not by hate but by doubt and fear is the crux of *Lohengrin*, 'which is about human and superhuman elements. Whether Lohengrin is a holy spirit or a great artist or whatever, he is someone out of the ordinary sent into this world to quicken the vibrations of those he comes into contact with. That is why Elsa feels so inadequate, and this sense of inadequacy lies behind her doubts. She doesn't yet *know* she is inadequate, so she thinks 'who's this person I can't be equal to?' This eats her away inside so that Ortrud's words immediately strike a chord. But she and Lohengrin belong to two worlds that can never come together. They're on different wave-lengths. In the end, she realizes this and sings in Act III that she can never reach his level – "Ach! Könnt'ich deiner vert erscheinen" – regardless of whether he tells his name or not.'

At the time she sang Elsa at Covent Garden Studer had already sung ten other Wagnerian roles: Rhinemaidens and Norns Freia, Sieglinde, Gutrune, Eva, Irene in *Rienzi* and Drolla in *Die Feen*. But, much to her admirers' chagrin, she had decided to change the direction of her career and give up Wagner for the next few years. Her appearances as Elsa and Elizabeth at the 1989 Bayreuth Festival and during Bayreuth's Japanese tour of autumn 1989 were her last for some time. Apart from Elsa and Elisabeth, she finds the tessitura of many Wagnerian roles too low for her at present and cites Eva in *Die Meistersinger von Nürnberg* (which she sang at the San Francisco Opera in 1986), as an example. Despite being written lyrically, with long, arching phrases reminiscent of Elsa's, Eva also contains some rather low *parlando* passages – especially in her duet with Sachs – that required a good deal of physical effort. Studer therefore decided that, despite excellent reviews, this role was out. So is Sieglinde, 'the most wonderful role in the world', which she sang in Munich and recorded for Ariola. But she took the role out of her repertoire because, although she knew it was low, until she sang it she didn't realize *how* low, or what other roles it could safely be combined with. It could, for example, be combined with Elisabeth, but not with Marguerite in *Faust*, which Studer sang at the Metropolitan Opera in 1991, or with Donna Anna, Violetta, Lucia, Norma, Semiramide or Mattilde in *Guglielmo Tell*, which she sang at La Scala in December 1988.

'So you see, although I have sung a lot of Wagner – but with big gaps in between – I have also said "no" many times. But after my successes at Bayreuth and Covent Garden, it was becoming increasingly difficult to say no because all people were asking me to do was Wagner. It isn't that singing Wagner at my age would be dangerous, unless I were to do it too often. But it would mean I couldn't sing a lot of repertoire I'm anxious to explore. So, although I enjoy singing Wagner, love his roles and will certainly come back to them one day, for the time being I have to throw them all away in order to sing everything else I want to sing.'

Studer particularly savours lighter German lyric roles: Mozart parts such as the Countess in *Le nozze di Figaro*, Donna Anna, and Strauss heroines such as Arabella and Chrysothemis in *Elektra* – but not too often as this could be potentially dangerous because 'it is very low and dramatic and consists of pushing and pushing, with no respite'. She would also like to sing the Empress and the title role in *Daphne* again, in new productions. (The latter part fits her like a glove vocally and the whole work fascinates her on account of its modernity and relevance today. 'I believe Daphne is the founder of the ecological movement!')

What is likely to prove more controversial is her expansion into the Italian repertoire, for which at first glance she lacks the necessary 'Italianità. Apart from the two Mozart roles just mentioned, she sang Lucia in Philadelphia in 1989 and opened the 1989–90 season at La Scala as Elena in *I vespri siciliani* under Riccardo Muti. She defends her decision by stressing that although these roles – especially Elena and Semiramide – are not necessarily *lighter* than her Wagnerian parts, they are *higher* and lie where her voice is naturally set: 'I have a very high-set voice and although people find it hard to believe, I also have a very easy coloratura. I have high F's, and have just recorded the Queen of the Night for Philips. But the Wagnerian roles within my reach at present have a lower tessitura and only go up to B natural. The only high C I've ever sung in Wagner was Irene's in *Rienzi*. This means a large part of my voice is not being used. And unless I'm careful, it's bound to be pulled down.'

Peter Katona agrees that Studer shouldn't be pushed into singing *too* much Wagner or tackling his heavier roles, 'otherwise her voice will spread and in two years' time she will be asked to sing Isolde, which she certainly should not do'. He applauds her choice of the Mozart and Strauss roles but laments the fact that they won't be interspersed with the lyric Wagner roles at decent intervals. As far as the Italian repertoire is concerned he feels she should limit herself to roles such as Desdemona, which don't demand a typical Italian timbre or a typically Italian attack. 'I don't think she should go too much in the direction of Lucia, Gilda, Violetta or Semiramide, because even though she may have all the notes, she does not have the presence or temperament of an "Italian" singer.' It is interesting to compare this view with that of Riccardo Muti, who feels Studer's voice is 'tailor-made for Italian opera'. What it basically boils down to is that once a voice as exceptional as Studer's appears on the scene, many conductors are eager to exploit it by diverting it to the repertoire that interests them. It is therefore up to the singer to assess him or herself as accurately as possible and, taking into account their specific vocal, dramatic, physical and temperamental qualities, to decide the course of their career.

When I spoke to Studer after the critically acclaimed premières of *Semiramide* and *Guglielmo Tell*, she said that she felt very comfortable vocally with both roles, especially Semiramide, which she refused to transpose and for which she wrote her own cadenzas. But Studer also admitted that emotionally and intellectually she had not found these roles as fulfilling as her Wagner and Strauss heroines. This very important point is one of the main reasons why so many of her admirers are disappointed that she has abandoned the German in favour of the Italian repertoire. Apart from Desdemona and Elena, which she will probably excel in and which occur in works of much more than mere vocal brilliance, the question must arise: Does anyone insist on seeing works like *Guglielmo Tell* even if this means we are to be deprived of a singer capable of bringing to sublime life the great roles of the German repertoire and especially Wagner? I have a sneaking suspicion that Studer is beginning to ask herself this question, too, even though she protests that singing the Italian repertoire 'boils down to returning to the foundations on which both my training and my career were based'.

Studer was born on 24 October 1955 in Midland, Michigan, the youngest child 'by a long margin' of parents who 'like all good small-town Americans' were active in their local church. Every Sunday, young Cheryl sang in the children's section of the church choir and invariably people complained her voice stood out too much. She was moved to the adults' section, but still stood out too much. So she was given some solos. By the time she was eight, she was participating in local talent contests and taking ballet, piano and viola lessons, the latter invaluable for what they taught her 'about intonation, phrasing, sustaining and supporting a note'.

Soon she clamoured for singing lessons and, by the time she was twelve, persuaded her mother to take her to a singing teacher, who rightly felt the child was still too young. But realizing the child was determined to get her lessons, she accepted her on condition that they would go very gently. They started off with exercises by Vaccai, which Studer still finds invaluable (as does the American bass, Samuel Ramey, who swears by them because 'they are designed to develop both line and agility').

After school Studer studied at various American Conservatoires and the University of Tennessee, before attending a course at the Berkshire Music Centre, Tanglewood for three successive years (1975–77) on full scholarships from Leonard Bernstein. Seiji Ozawa, Music Director of the Boston Symphony, was impressed enough to invite her for a series of concerts in 1979. By then she had won the High Fidelity/Musical America Award (1977) and the Metropolitan Opera Auditions in 1978. Buoyed up by all this encouragement, she decided to come to Europe for further study and, in 1979, headed for Vienna. Then she joined the Franz Schubert Institut, winning the 1979 Prize for Lied interpretation. In 1980 she joined the Hochschule für Musik, and also studied with Hans Hotter.

On completion of her studies she auditioned and was accepted at the Bavarian State Opera in Munich, where she made her début as the First Lady in *Die Zauberflöte*. But although she had auditioned with arias from *Faust* and *Rigoletto* and was still only 25, she immediately began to be cast as a Walküre and a Norn and generally steered towards the German repertoire and especially Wagner. 'I was very naïve and gullible by nature

– I still am, but less so. I hope – and thought "if these people who *know* think these roles are right for me, who am I to say no?" So I didn't even question their choices.' But when the roles got as heavy as Marenka in Smetana's *The Bartered Bride* and backstage rumour had it she would soon be cast as Salome and the Empress, she decided not to renew her contract after two years as a member of the BSO. Perhaps understandably, as it was the Bavarian State Opera who had discovered her, so to speak, her defection caused much hard feeling and, she says, made her many enemies.

Although she was later to realize the move away was a mistake, at the time she was still under 30 and felt she wanted to try out some different repertoire in a small theatre. Thus, in 1982, the Darmstadt State Theatre lured her into a two-year contract with a new production of *Otello* in which she sang Desdemona for the first time. There was also talk of Constanze, which interested her a lot at the time. But the contract didn't specify any other particular roles and, in the event, she found herself making her début as Tatyana in *Eugene Onegin* and singing the title role in *Katya Kabanová*, none of which took her in the direction she wanted to go. On top of everything she sang 90 repertory evenings a season! So, on completion of her contract in 1984, she left and joined the Deutsche Oper in Berlin. But this move was to prove equally frustrating. In two years all she sang was Freia and Gutrune in Götz Friedrich's new production of *The Ring* – which was very interesting – and was *forced* to sing Elisabeth, which she had not wanted to do except in Bayreuth where the acoustic eliminates much of the strain of singing Wagner. There were three staged performances of *Messiah*. 'Then I went and *begged* the administration for some performances of Donna Anna. I got them but only after begging. So I left and have been freelancing ever since.' (One marvels at the shortsightedness of a management that could find no use for a talent of this magnitude!) Still, her time there was useful because it led to the invitation to sing Freia at Bayreuth in 1985, which in turn led to her triumph as Elisabeth that put her on the road to international stardom.

After leaving the Bavarian State Opera Studer continued to appear as a guest artist at the Munich Festival where she sang Irene in *Rienzi* in 1983 and has since appeared every season (Donna Anna, Sieglinde, the title role in Weber's *Euryanthe* and the Empress in *Die Frau ohne Schatten*). She made her American début at the Chicago Lyric Opera in 1984, as Micaela in the Ponnelle production of *Carmen* that featured Placido Domingo as Don José. She considers this début important because it was her observation of Domingo that taught her how to sing piano. 'His ability to fine-hone his sound hit me like a blow. I was used to world-famous tenors screaming and bellowing. Suddenly I realized that, basically, I didn't have to sing louder than I wanted or needed to, either, and asked myself: "I *can* sing piano, so why am I not doing it?" But of course, this is easier said than done because singing piano is much more difficult than singing forte: to maintain an even line in piano singing – like a silk thread that must be stretched smoothly without ever being jolted – takes meticulous breath control and utmost concentration.' (Carlo Bergonzi, another master of this art, explains the technicalities of it in detail in *Bravo*.)

Studer made her Paris début as Donna Anna in 1985 in a performance with Radio France and followed it with her Paris Opéra début as Pamina in 1986 and Chrysothemis in 1987. During this time her first marriage was breaking down. Since then, her constant companion has been one of the former couple's closest friends, Ewald Schwartz, who had been one of her most ardent fans for years, is devoted to her career and encourages her in her decisions. Though after talking to Studer following the premières of *Semiramide* and *Guglielmo Tell*, my clear impression is that she herself is at present monitoring her vocal response to her new repertoire minutely.

Her experience of *Semiramide*, for instance, taught her, and caused her to reflect, a great deal about the nature of vocal technique, which she defines as 'a balance between tension and relaxation'. Every singer has *one* single vocal technique, she stresses, but it has to be adapted to each role, and in turn, to each phrase. The difference between singing Semiramide and singing a Wagnerian role – even if the latter is not much lower – is that in Wagner's music there is more harmonic tension while in Rossini's there is more harmonic relaxation, and consequently less *vocal* tension. This is why his roles are less strenuous and more comfortable to sing. But if she had to pick *the* role in which she feels most comfortable at present, it would have to be Donna Anna.

She first sang the role in concert at the 1985 Munich Festival, and two years later performed it for her La Scala début. She finds it vocally and dramatically ideal: an intriguing character who demands all she can give as a singer. 'There is always this question mark – although there shouldn't be, it's very silly – about whether anything happened between her and Don Giovanni in her bedchamber before the opera begins. I don't think anything did, but that's not important because what really matters is that she *wanted* it to! Whether her physical contact with him was a kiss or a passionate embrace, it awakened her. This is the main, the crucial fact about Don Giovanni: everyone he meets is changed through their contact with him. He is such an overwhelmingly powerful, electrifying personality, almost a laser beam, that nothing he touches can ever be the same again.' Ruggiero Raimondi has expressed a similar view. And their collaboration in the Vienna State Opera's new production of *Don*

Giovanni in spring 1990 by Luc Bondy, under Claudio Abbado, turned out to be a milestone in the history of the work.

Studer also agrees with Raimondi that the protagonist of this, and all the Da Ponte Mozart operas, is social convention, which always comes up trumps at the end. 'I think that if Giovanni had come to Anna's afterwards and formally requested permission to court her, with a view to marrying her some day, she would have leapt at it, because obviously she fancies him like crazy. But the fact that he is beyond the bounds of social convention means that, although she really *wants* to, she cannot accept his attentions. It's hard to fathom her relationship with Ottavio, because he's almost like a father substitute. Full stop. I don't think there is any emotional interest there. So right from the start, Anna is a very divided character – a crazy, crazy woman.

'Vocally, it's wonderful to sing, especially her second aria, "Non mi dir", which I greatly enjoy, and even more so with a conductor like Muti who understands the kind of inner drive there is in this music. In fact he brings out the dramatic, demonic drive in *all* the music he conducts, but particularly in "Non mi dir" because it is not a static aria. It may be floaty, but it has to have a *surging* sort of sound, you have to feel it surging out of the body and the sensuality of it makes it very enjoyable to sing.'

But Studer feels the most *important* moment in this role is Anna's recitative, 'Don Ottavio, son morta' before her first aria. This is not only the most crucial and challenging part of the whole role, but also the most underrated, because 'nobody bothers much with the recitative, though it is the key to the character. It contains the outburst of all the feelings she has recently experienced and those she has kept bottled-up throughout her lifetime. It is both very dramatic, vocally difficult, and so intense it leaves you out of breath. If something *is* intense, I'm not the sort of person to ignore the intensity. I have to give it, I *have* to, I can't stop myself. But now I've found a way to keep the intensity while reducing the *tension* and beginning the aria the way it is written: piano, not forte, yet an *intense* piano. Then it crescendos, but really only towards the end. The second problem has to do with pacing the whole scene, from the beginning of the recitative to the end of the aria, phrasing and developing it so that it comes across not as two items, but as one scene with the recitative leading into the area. It's therefore vital to ensure one isn't "sung out" by the end of the recitative, otherwise the aria won't sound good.'

Despite her affection for and identification with this role (her 1990 Vienna Festival performances were stupendous), Studer has turned down dozens more offers to sing it because they were for routine repertory performances – something she is not interested in either for this or for any other role any longer. She now sings only 40 performances a year, with long gaps in between, and likes to do a string of performances and then let a particular role rest a little, rather than singing two or three here and there every few months and have them become routine. 'I don't want this to happen to any of my roles, *ever*. I'm still in my mid-30s and have now reached a state in my career when I can choose. I have over 50 roles in my repertoire, some of which were wrong for me at the time and still are. So now I'm *going* to choose. Up to now I couldn't. Now I can and I'm going to take this opportunity to do what's best for my artistic development and for my voice – both for its health and its longevity – and to get maximum satisfaction out of my work.'

DAME JOAN SUTHERLAND

As this book was in preparation, Dame Joan Sutherland retired from the operatic stage. Her last full performance was 'Les Huguenots' at the Sydney Opera in October 1990, and her actual farewell appearance was at Covent Garden, in the Party Scene in Act II of 'Die Fledermaus', on New Year's Eve, 1990/91, to vociferous emotional scenes.

'I ENJOY THE physical sensation of singing. But it takes a long time to get it right. Basically it boils down to breathing, supporting and projecting the sound as if on a column of air. But a lot of hoohah goes on about it and one hears singers refer to "the muscles of my throat". *I* say that if I feel *anything* in my throat, it means I'm singing badly – either holding back or forcing the sound, or having something wrong with me.' Characteristic-ally plain speaking from Dame Joan Sutherland, 'La Stupenda', as she was labelled by the Italians and one of the outstanding coloratura sopranos of the century, who, during the course of her 38-year career, made a huge contribution to the revival of *bel canto* begun by Maria Callas.

Sutherland, whose vocal longevity was as remarkable as her artistry, stresses the same point already made by Montserrat Caballé: that the acquisition of a healthy breathing technique at an early age is crucial. 'Without it, I wouldn't have still been singing at the ripe old age of 65. Because the voice is a physical thing, a part of the body. Unlike, other musical instruments which, if destroyed, can be replaced, a voice, once ruined, is gone for ever. Even though, like most bodily ailments, it can be treated, it can never be restored to its previous condition. There will always be a residue of weakness, a lack of lustre.'

Sutherland was lucky in her first voice teacher. Born in 1926 in the Eastern suburbs of Sydney, her father was a Scottish tailor – she adored him but sadly he died when she was only six. Her mother, a trained mezzo, had studied with a pupil of Marchesi from whom she had picked up a first-rate breathing technique. When she noticed that her daughter not only visibly enjoyed the sound of singing from her earliest childhood but could also produce quite an agreeable sound, she felt this was something to be encouraged. 'So she began to sit down at the piano for twenty minutes every morning and twenty in the afternoon and run through some scales and exercises, plus the odd aria and a couple of pretty songs, explaining all about them as she went along. This wasn't teaching in the proper sense of the word, because she wasn't rigid and didn't like the idea of someone as young as I trying to project sound. But a lot of knowledge rubbed off on me in this casual way, especially as I grew older, so that by the time I started to study in Sydney, aged nineteen, I was already quite advanced.'

Her father's early death and the need to earn her living forced her to leave school at sixteen and work as a secretary by day while continuing her music lessons in the evening. While still in Sydney, where her teachers were John and Aida Dickens, she made her professional début, in 1947, as Dido in a concert performance of Purcell's *Dido and Aeneas*. This was soon followed by a chance to sing Delilah and the Israelite Woman in Handel's *Samson* and the title role in *Judith*, an opera by Sir Eugene Goossens, the Director of the Conservatorium.

It was there that she also met a young pianist who was to prove a decisive influence on her life and career: Richard Bonynge, whom she was to marry in 1954, recalled in a television documentary about Dame Joan, *A Life on the Move*, that when he first heard her voice, back in the forties, 'it was a big and very brilliant sound, much colder than it is today. It was very much a technical instrument, without as many overtones or as much warmth as it later acquired.'

Indeed, at this time Sutherland was convinced her voice was more suited to Wagner and her ambition was to become a Wagnerian singer. 'Mind you, I think this was really wishful thinking on my part because I admired Kirsten Flagstad very much and was also entranced by those Gothic tales depicted in Wagner operas. We read them a lot at school and at home there was an enormous collection of Wagnerian recordings featuring Flagstad who, in those days, represented the pinnacle of great singing. So I suppose it was natural for me to want to sing like her. But I have no regrets whatsoever about following a different path. My fascination with Wagner has worn off, although I still greatly enjoy going to Wagner operas. I recently saw a new production of *The Ring* in Sydney with surtitles, which was super, I'm all for them.'

It was after meeting Richard Bonynge again at the Royal College of Music that she decided to 'follow a different path'. She had arrived in London in 1951, after winning the financially substantial First Prize at the Mobil Quest Singing Competition in Australia. That, augmented by a generous cheque from an uncle, enabled both her and her mother to move to London. Bonynge often attended her classes at the RCM, where her Professor of Singing was Clive Carey. He noticed that, in private, she sang with a greater sense of freedom and a higher, different voice from the one she used in class and felt convinced she was a potential coloratura soprano. But she herself was far from sure.

'I had grown up in a household full of mezzo-soprano music: my mother was a mezzo and I, too, was quite used to singing in that register. So, although I could hit the odd top notes, I found it extremely hard to sing at a *consistently* high tessitura. Even Mozart and Handel – the first composers I tackled before moving to the later Italian soprano repertoire which has a more solid middle – sat too high for me. All the time I felt I was trying to do something for which I didn't possess the natural resources and wondered if this was the right thing to do. But Ricky fooled me with some exercises and gradually, as I became conscious of a new voice emerging, I was convinced he was right.'

As Bonynge once confided to *The Telegraph Magazine*, this 'fooling' involved moving her away from the piano so that she could not see the keyboard and – exploiting her lack of perfect pitch – gradually pushing the range higher until she was past her imagined limit of high C and singing E flat! Even so, her transformation into a coloratura soprano was a painful and often stormy process. There were monumental rows with him raging over her failure to measure up to his expectations. But in the end, the emergence of the dazzling coloratura soprano we now know persuaded her to accept both his mentorship and his offer of marriage, out of which grew a remarkably fruitful musical partnership.

'I cannot think of life without Richard, without his constant emotional and artistic support', she declares. 'Going around the world all alone is very lonely, you know, and this can be a terrible problem, especially for female singers. I know what I'm talking about because up to the time of my first big success as Lucia in 1955 we didn't have enough money for Richard to travel with me. That was horribly lonely . . . It made me remember once hearing a famous German soprano complaining: "Why am I here, in this miserable place, always in horrid hotel rooms when I have a beautiful home of my own?" And I, young fool that I was, thought: "You ungrateful so-and-so, you have a great voice, a great career, what have *you* got to complain about?" *Now* I understand her so well, poor woman. I often feel like that myself. What am I doing here, in a borrowed flat in Kensington? I should be home [a large Swiss chalet above Montreux, with spectacular views of Lake Geneva] tending to my garden!

'But at least I have a husband who travels with me and a married son and grandchildren. Being all alone in this nerve-racking profession would be awful. But it's very, *very* hard for a woman with a big career, especially in opera which requires constant travel, to balance the demands of her personal and professional lives. That's why so many of us become neurotic, why a lot of marriages break up and why a great many singers' husbands have pretensions of being managers, often without any qualifications for taking on a singing voice. I have been more than lucky in this way. Richard and I have a relationship where we perfectly understand one another and respect each other's need to be quiet. He does crossword puzzles and I do my gardening, and we have been very happy over the years, even though we still have our differences and plenty of squabbles and huffs!'

According to many who know and work closely with her, Sutherland's stable personal life is largely responsible for her sane, cheerful, down-to-earth disposition – 'I'm a very ordinary, very simple person' – her generosity towards colleagues, her wonderful sense of humour and her knack for poking fun at herself (she could get a job as a stand up comic any time, according to a camera crew who worked with her recently). Franco Zeffirelli stated in his autobiography that 'the main reason why Joan is so sane and steady is her marriage to Ricky who, as a fellow musician, is able to support and inspire her professionally; and even more important is her son Adam. All so different from Callas's passionate yet unfulfilling affair with Onassis.' It could be the other way around, of course: that's to say, Sutherland may have achieved this stability in her personal life *because* she possessed these qualities in the first place.

The crucial importance of a stable relationship to a singer's life can hardly be overstressed according to accompanist Geoffrey Parsons, who has worked with most major singers of the past quarter-century: 'Emotional considerations apart, having a second pair of ears at hand is invaluable. Lucia Popp had it in her first husband, conductor Gyorgy Fischer, Ileana Cotrubas has it in her husband Manfred, also a conductor, Placido Domingo has it in his wife Marta, who was a soprano, and Elisabeth Schwarzkopf had it in the late Walter Legge, who guided and supervised everything she did. I always contrast her with the poor late Rita Streich, who lacked, but longed for, such a pair of ears and used to travel with a tape recorder which she referred to as "my little Walter".'

Yet Bonynge, who has also helped his wife with his extensive knowledge of *bel canto* which extends to writing out embellishments for her, has often been criticized for what some see as his exaggerated role in her career, and especially for conducting nearly all her performances and recordings over the last 25 years. He has also been attacked for transforming what might have been a great dramatic soprano voice into a coloratura, allegedly to satisfy his own obsession with *bel canto*. 'He just decided this was what she was going to be and proceeded to manufacture it,' says accompanist and recording executive Nina Walker. 'It's just brilliant how she has learnt the *bel canto* style and sung all those coloratura roles as dazzlingly as she has. But one can somehow feel the "manufacture" and, however dazzling, her voice fails to grip one, or me at least, by the gut.'

Sutherland's gradual transformation into a coloratura was taking place while she was a full company member of Covent Garden. She had joined the Royal Opera in 1952 (at a salary of £10 a week!) and remained for seven years. 'This was probably the best thing that ever happened to me, a great, solid foundation on which to build my future career. There were coaches helping us all the time and, of course, I was also working at home with Richard. Sadly most younger singers don't often have the benefit of such a solid foundation because they are used to guesting all over the world rather than staying in one theatre for a while, learning their craft and, most important, gradually acquiring the physical stamina for the big roles.'

During those invaluable seven years which, she says, she would not 'exchange with anything in the world', Sutherland sang a variety of roles: Clotilde to Maria Callas's Norma in the historic 1952 production that also featured Ebe Stignani as Adalgisa, the title role in *Aida,* Amelia in *Un ballo in maschera*, Lady Penelope Rich in Britten's *Gloriana*, Helmwige in *Die Walküre*, Agathe in *Der Freischütz*, Countess Almaviva in *Le nozze di Figaro* (also at the Edinburgh Festival) and at Glyndebourne, Donna Anna in *Don Giovanni*, Jennifer in Tippett's *The Midsummer Marriage*, Olympia, Antonia and Giulietta in *Les Contes d'Hoffmann*, Micaela in *Carmen*, Pamina in *Die Zauberflöte*, Madame Lidoine in *Les Dialogues des Carmélites*, Desdemona in *Otello* and, in 1957, a much praised Gilda in *Rigoletto*.

The year 1957 was something of a milestone, during which she scored a triumph that was to prove significant for the future: her performance in the fiendishly difficult title role in Handel's *Alcina* with the Handel Opera Society attracted rave reviews and widespread attention. It was the ideal role in which to show off her brilliant top and outstanding ability for coloratura – the result of Bonynge's long, painstaking coaching. She relished both Alcina and her next Handel part, the title role in *Rodelinda*, in which she scored a comparable success.

'The main characteristics of the Handelian style are the length of the arias and the expressiveness of the recitatives. But his operas tend to be rather static, with a good deal of repetition, and you have to be very, very organized in your singing of embellishments, which require utmost precision. But, like all eighteenth-century music, Handel is always very healthy to sing. Whenever I finish a run of Handel or Mozart roles I feel as if I've just had a cure that's put the voice into good working order. I dare say this is because most eighteenth-century music consists of a constant succession of legato with agility; going up and down the scale in a very regular fashion, almost like a singing exercise alternating line with fioritura. I'm sure this is why, after singing Mozart or Handel, there is always this feeling of vocal well-being.'

A year after her spectacular Alcina, Sutherland scored another major success: Donna Anna in her American début in Vancouver. All this convinced the management at Covent Garden that she was now ready for a major new production: Donizetti's *Lucia di Lammermoor*, conducted by Tullio Serafin and directed by Franco Zeffirelli. Since then, her performance of this role has passed into legend and she has come to think of it as 'an old, comfortable pair of well fitting shoes'. Needless to say, in those early days, it was far from easy; 'I had problems from the physical and the dramatic points of view. But I did have Serafin and I did have Zeffirelli, and all three of us worked together to make a success of it. Serafin was a wonderful old man, sweet and gentle, although he could get cross, on occasion. (I remember him once getting very cross with Zeffirelli for driving me around Palermo in an open car before an important rehearsal!) He wanted what he wanted, but he was never dictatorial or ugly about it. He always said that "tempo is what the singer can cope with comfortably. You have to follow your feeling of what is right for each artist; fast must be fast, but not too fast for the singer at hand." A lesson which, I'm sure you will agree, many contemporary conductors have yet to learn!'

When compared to some of the more arduous roles – like Norma or Anna Bolena – that Sutherland has sung since, Lucia does not seem all that difficult, she explains. 'This is not to say it's easy – I don't think *any* of my roles can be called that – but it's beautifully composed and so well thought out that it seems to carry you along. The key factor is pacing. Until then, my most taxing roles had been Alcina and the three heroines in *Les Contes d'Hoffmann*. But in both these operas, there are places where I could relax and rest a little. In *Lucia*, I'm on stage a great deal and it's crucial not to spill all the beans at once – in Lucia's Act I aria "Regnava nel silenzio" and the big duet with the tenor that immediately follows it, for instance – but save myself for the Mad Scene at the finale. So from the point of view of pacing it was a good lesson, and a good piece to learn this lesson from.'

Lucia remains her most convincing dramatic portrayal – along with Marie in *La Fille du régiment*, which is ideally suited to her comic gift – and she attributes the credit for this entirely to Zeffirelli, who 'tailored and adapted his ideas to me so that I felt wonderfully cushioned and protected.

He was full of suggestions and ideas about the character while at the same time allowing some leeway for my own dramatic instinct, which reassured me I was on the right track. He also gave me such incredible confidence that I could look beautiful that, in this production, I think I did. I learnt a great deal from his flair and sense of "rightness" about costume and what I should and shouldn't wear. He got the décolletage and the line of the bodice and all sorts of details like that right, which made me feel secure and free to concentrate on the character instead of worrying about my shortcomings. This is a very important part of a stage designer's craft. So many have very definite ideas about how they want to dress a certain operatic character but no thought at all about the physique of the artist who will interpret this role – and no plans to adapt their designs to successive casts, either.'

As Zeffirelli recalls in his autobiography, his main aim was to 'make something of her. I could see the main problem was her own fears and frustrations: she knew she lacked grace and was withdrawn and difficult to reach. I moved close to her and put my arm around her shoulder and, to my surprise, she pulled away frightened, almost angry with me. This was making things very difficult, for I'm a tactile animal, I have to touch people, feel the physical presence and warmth of a person. I told her how I felt and, wonderful woman that she is, she took a deep breath and gave me a real hug.'

The première of this production turned Sutherland into an overnight star. As Maria Callas who, after attending the dress rehearsal and calling Sutherland 'a great artist', predicted, both public and critics raved: 'No soprano of our century has sung the great scenes in *Lucia* with so rare and precious a combination of marvellously accomplished singing and dramatic interpretation of the music. Miss Sutherland is now in the company of the most famous Donizetti singers from Pasta to Callas', wrote Andrew Porter in *The Financial Times*; and Sir John Tooley, the former General Director of the Royal Opera House, recalls that 'the leap that took place then was absolutely staggering: from member of the company to stardom. I can't think of any other singer who has become so famous overnight.' Managements from all over the world, already alerted by rumours of 'a new sensational soprano' during rehearsals, were now eager to sign her up. There was now no question of her remaining a company member.

But the problem was that it all happened so suddenly that she was totally unprepared for stardom as far as repertoire was concerned. The only roles she knew in Italian were Lucia, Donna Anna and Desdemona! All her other parts had been sung in English. 'So there I was, an international star with no repertoire with which to sing internationally!

Yet Franco felt it was important to strike while the iron was hot and get me to sing in Italy, and Richard was anxious I should continue working with Serafin who had so much to teach me and would protect and nurture me the way he had Maria [Callas].'

So the three of them together decided to go for *Alcina*, which was little known in Italy and just the sort of opera to show Sutherland off at her best. Zeffirelli designed a spectacular production for the Teatro La Fenice in Venice, conducted by Nicola Rescigno, and the entire operatic world turned up to hear Sutherland's 1960 Italian début. Her display of vocal virtuosity and amazing gift for coloratura drove the audience into a frenzy of enthusiasm. They wouldn't let her go before singing an encore, 'Let the Bright Seraphim' (with Bonynge, dressed in period costume, accompanying her on the harpsichord). On the morning after, the Italian press hailed her as 'La Stupenda' and from then on, the world was her oyster.

The next offer was from the Teatro Massimo in Palermo, which gave carte blanche for a series of new productions spread over a season, beginning with *Lucia* (subsequently also taken to Venice and Paris) and culminating with a production of *I Puritani* that was eventually brought to Venice and Covent Garden. Sutherland's electrifying display of vocal virtuosity in the gruelling coloratura role of Elvira has, like her Lucia, now passed into legend and, along with Amina in *La sonnambula*, it remains one of her favourite parts. Her débuts at the Paris Opera (April 1960) and La Scala (April 1961) reinforced her reputation as the leading *bel canto* singer of the day.

Sutherland stresses that an important thing to remember when interpreting *bel canto* is not to concentrate merely on displays of vocal bravura but to find the *feelings* behind them. '*Bel canto* operas are not just a series of fireworks. They are very expressive music in which you must, nevertheless, maintain an even vocal line. You certainly can't go groaning and grunting, the way you can, up to a point, in verismo.'

She explains that when studying *bel canto* parts her main difficulty lies not in learning the music, which tends to happen reasonably effortlessly, but the words. Although she begins her study of new roles with the libretto, she invariably ends up knowing the music first. 'I have always had an appalling memory,' she confides. 'But one of the main problems about memorizing this repertoire is the similarity of so many standard operatic exclamations and of some of the variants at the end of certain cabalettas. Certain phrases in *La sonnambula* and *I Puritani*, for instance, are quite interchangeable, and the same is true of *Maria Stuarda* and *Lucrezia Borgia*, which I learnt within a short period. In one of Lucrezia's arias I became confused and kept lapsing back into Stuarda!

This is always a problem if you sing several roles by the same composer, I suppose.'

She came up against the problem again when learning the title role in *Anna Bolena*, the final addition to her repertoire, which she disarmingly describes as 'more of the same'. It contains both words and musical phrases that could easily be confused with Lucrezia Borgia's and Stuarda's. As always, she gave herself plenty of time to learn it slowly and thoroughly before singing it first in Toronto during the 1983/4 season and subsequently in San Francisco in October 1984, and Covent Garden in 1988. She considers the role both beautiful to sing and exciting to portray.

'Vocally, Anna Bolena is not quite as comfortable as either Maria Stuarda or Lucrezia Borgia. You need a certain calm and serenity before you can sing it and have to pay a lot of attention to pacing because the cabaletta at the end, like the one at the end of *Lucrezia Borgia*, is a real toughie. The role is also very wide-ranging, from both the vocal and the dramatic points of view: it contains some very important but vocally tricky recitatives and the tessitura is quite low in places. Dramatically, she is rewarding to portray, the poor, maligned thing with that *monster* of a husband. Mind you, in real life he wasn't such a monster to begin with: he started off as quite a good and popular king and only gradually became a monster, silly man. Which goes to show that politics wasn't any better then than it is now!'

Dame Joan enjoys reading about the historical or literary backgrounds to the characters she portrays, even though historical accuracy may have little to do with the way they are depicted in libretti. As an example, she points to a conversation between Mary Queen of Scots and Elizabeth I of England in *Maria Stuarda* which is wonderful theatre, one of the most dramatic moments in the whole work, but which never happened in real life. 'In fact it was Mary's tragedy that she could never get Elizabeth to agree to such a meeting. So, no matter *what* the historical or literary background of an opera might be, we are here to interpret the libretto and, above all, the music.'

Which is why, as far as she is concerned, the greatest challenge in *Lucrezia Borgia*, for instance, is how to equate the heroine's breathtakingly beautiful music with the character of a vicious poisoner. 'This is well nigh impossible! We learn from history that Lucrezia was a pawn in her family's hands and manipulated by evil people like her husband, who really *is* a villain, to suit their ends. Yet what emerges most strongly from the libretto is her overwhelming love for her son and desire to protect him. This is probably why Donizetti gave her such *gorgeous* music to sing. For, hard as I try, I can find nothing evil in her to bring out.'

Sutherland is aware that her preoccupation with the music and the

vocal line, and her comparative lack of concern with dramatic interpretation in the purely scenic sense, is considered a flaw in her artistic make up.
'I have been criticized very severely for relying too much on the vocal line
and not being sufficiently dramatic. But I think the composer has written
the vocal line to the best of his ability to express the feelings he wants. I
think it is primarily for the *sound* of singing that people come to the
opera. If they want a great dramatic performance they should go to a
straight play. Them's my sentiments anyway,' she declared with finality.
Here she echoes the view expressed by Montserrat Caballé, and one
which highlights the perennial controversy about the basic nature of
opera, which has split opera lovers into two opposite camps: the 'canary
fanciers', who are content with superb vocalism (and justly lament its
virtual disappearance among the younger generation of singers); and
those who, in the wake of the Callas revolution that began the
transformation of opera into living theatre, are impatient with
performances that rely mainly on musical values.

In fact, she remained so completely under the spell of those
performances that she shied away from singing Norma for a decade.
Finally, in 1962, she decided to take the plunge, in Vancouver, with
Marilyn Horne as Adalgisa. But she still felt haunted by memories of
Callas and her nervousness was aggravated by the fact that the
performances were badly spaced. 'So, for the first and last time in my life,
I had an awful psycho-somatic reaction: I felt completely nauseous, so
much so that I even wondered if I might be pregnant. I wasn't, so the only
way I can account for this nausea is to put it down to tension about even
attempting to sing this role after You-Know-Who had sung it so divinely. I
feel sure this was a reaction to my tremendous sense of inadequacy,
because normally I'm not this sort of person at all, and anyway the
moment the run was finished the nausea disappeared.' Apart from
teaching her how to overcome her nerves, this Vancouver production

taught her another vital lesson: never to sing this role again without at least two clear days between performances.

She explains that the biggest problem in *Norma*, because of its great length, is learning how to pace it. 'Like most *bel canto* roles, it begins with a "grand entrance" aria. And I tell you, it's quite daunting to get up there and sing that magnificent, dramatic recitative followed by that *gorgeous*, lyrical aria, "Casta Diva", plus that gutsy cabaletta, "A bello a me ritorna" right at the beginning of the opera and *know* there is still a long way to go and that your only real break in the entire evening is Adalgisa's duet with Pollione! I can't help feeling that people who *think* they can sing Norma fail to take this into account. They simply don't realize the range of it, musically, dramatically or from the point of view of sheer physical stamina. They probably think, "Oh, I have this or that note, so I can sing it." But it takes a lot more than that to sing Norma. You really have to know what you are about before you can handle it, because you have to get up there and keep on delivering the goods for *hours*! *And* you have Pollione singing along with you some of the time *and* you have to learn to blend your voice with Adalgisa's. Your duets must come across as a perfectly blended whole: you can't have one voice sticking out like *this* and the other sticking out like *that*. They absolutely have to blend. So you must be able to increase or soft-pedal the sound depending on who your Adalgisa is.' (Hers have included Marilyn Horne, Ebe Stignani, Fiorenza Cossotto, Margreta Elkins, Tatiana Troyanos, the young American Nova Thomas and, on record, Montserrat Caballé.)

Since then the role has, of course, become much easier because her voice has matured. She complains that the fact that it is older and has a different timbre in certain areas makes parts of Norma a lot easier. 'In those early days the voice was much lighter and I was worried about depressing the sound too much in some sections because I had other roles in my repertoire that required me to sing at a consistently high tessitura and I was worried that if I depressed the sound too much, this might affect my top. Now, I find Norma vocally very comfortable, and dramatically riveting. I adore the woman. In fact, along with Violetta in *La traviata* and the title role in *Adriana Lecouvreur*, one of my most recent parts, she is my favourite. I love those three women because they are more human, more "real people" than some of the other heroines I sing.'

Sutherland first sang Violetta during the hectic period that followed her triumph as Lucia in 1959 and she confesses that it was 'absolute panic stations. Mind you, I was neither the first nor the last to underestimate the length and the demands of this role which requires many different kinds of voice: you have the brilliant opening in Act I, "Sempre libera", with plenty of coloratura. But as far as I'm concerned, the role is a real *killer* because it sits a lot in the middle voice. You still need lots of voice, for the low tessitura of Act II Scene I, which is very tricky, culminating in her cry of "Ammami Alfredo". Violetta's music in Act II Scene II is wonderful, especially after Alfredo's denunciation of her. I shall never forget the way Callas sang "Alfredo, Alfredo, di questo core", as if she were on a different plane. It created an incredible effect, as did her heart-breaking way of singing "Dite alla giovine" in Act II Scene I.'

Adriana Lecouvreur, which she first performed in 1983 in San Diego, remains with Puccini's *Suor Angelica* the only other verismo role she has performed on stage. The reason why she loves Adriana so much is that 'she is so very human, with those all too human feelings of jealousy, rivalry in the theatre and so on. Possibly owing to my age, I don't see her as an immature character in the Gilda, Amina or Elvira mould, even though the real Adriana Lecouvreur died quite young. Because she was an actress of note, she automatically comes across as a worldly, sophisticated woman. Of course, the verismo style also has something to do with this.'

She has always enjoyed listening to verismo and relished singing both Adriana and Suor Angelica, even though, she points out, unless the singer is careful and exercises a certain restraint, verismo can be dangerous for the voice. 'Unlike *bel canto*, which is composed with a sense of decorum, verismo is composed with a sense of abandon which creates a problem: you tend to get more carried away by the emotion of verismo than by all those wilting *bel canto* heroines and this makes it easier to fall into the trap of pushing the voice. But it's tremendous fun. At one stage I even considered having a go at *La Gioconda*, but finally decided against it. For one thing, there is Gina Cigna's incredible performance to live up to, and for another, there are plenty of less dangerous things to sing.' Such as, for instance, French opera, an area which Joan Sutherland has explored as deeply as *bel canto*. 'French is a wonderful language to sing, akin to Italian but with even more vowel permutations. My French coaches keep telling me I over-accent the closed sounds but I keep pointing out to them that this is a defence mechanism against slipping into my best Australian accent! But try hard as I can, a nice Australian diphthong always manages to creep in – it really *is* terrible, this twang of ours!' Her French repertoire included the three heroines in Offenbach's *Les Contes d'Hoffmann*, Ophélie in Ambroise Thomas's *Hamlet*, Queen Marguerite de Valois in Meyerbeer's *Les Huguenots*, Sita in Massenet's *Le Roi de Lahore* and the title role in his equally rarely performed opera, *Esclarmonde*, which she sang first at the San Francisco Opera in 1974 and later, in 1983, at Covent Garden.

Richard Bonynge always felt her voice was just right for the title roles in *Thaïs* and *Manon*; but there came a point, she felt, where she could no longer get away with either of these roles: 'Even though they would suit me vocally, portraying a young temple dancer and a girl just out of a convent when you are as long in the tooth as I am really would be going too far! But it's sad Massenet should be known mainly for *Werther* and *Manon* when he wrote so many wonderful operas. *Esclarmonde*, for instance, contains some wonderful and very singable music. But it stayed on the shelf for ages, ever since the death of Sybil Sanderson, for whom it was composed.' The probable reason is that, until Sutherland, nobody could sing this excruciatingly difficult music.

Another genre Sutherland relished singing is operetta, which was well suited to her comic gifts and which she considered 'real-human-being sort of music' when compared to the far-fetched plots of most of the operas in my repertoire. It's also closer to the music of our own day. But it's actually very hard work, hard to do well, and do justice to the dialogue, because it's easy to underestimate the quality and style of voice it requires.

Having sung so much repertoire and made a great number of recordings, she is justifiably proud that she continued singing with such distinction until the age of 65. She doesn't think this would have happened if she had pursued a career as a Wagnerian soprano because 'the Wagnerian orchestra is much heavier and, to surmount it, singers tend to push their voices, even though they shouldn't. After all, the first Wagnerian singers were trained in the *bel canto* tradition and Wagner invented the sunken, covered pit so that singers could be heard above his dense orchestrations without having to shout. But the problem is that, apart from Bayreuth, his operas are not played in theatres with covered pits and his special kind of turgid sound carries most conductors practically off their feet so that, in order to be heard at all, singers have to give that extra projection. But in trying to enlarge their voices, they diminish their skill in coloratura and fioritura, for the *bel canto* repertoire.

'Therefore I had no regrets about turning my back on Wagner and no secret hankerings after any of his heroines, no, not even Isolde.' Dame Joan beamed as she glanced up from her needle point – a mischievous-looking black cat on a small cushion – which was always one of her trademarks and designed to 'keep me quiet at rehearsals and recording sessions'.

DAME KIRI TE KANAWA

WITH HINDSIGHT, IT is easy to understand why Maori-born Kiri Te
Kanawa became an overnight star after delivering a sensational performance of the Countess in *Le nozze di Figaro* at Covent Garden in
December 1971. The author and critic Andrew Porter hailed it in the
Financial Times as 'such a Countess Almaviva as I have never seen
before, not at Covent Garden nor in Salzburg or Vienna . . . . The new
star is Kiri Te Kanawa'.

First and foremost, she possesses one of the most beautiful soprano
voices of our day. Adjectives like 'creamy', 'pearly' and 'voluptuous'
have been used by critics trying to capture its gleaming, shimmering
quality, its capacity to spin long, soaring lines and the ease with which it
opens up at the top 'like a luscious rose'. Second, she has a radiant stage
presence and an innate communicative gift. Audiences love her and her
ardent horde of fans includes such prominent members of the opposite
sex as Bernard Levin – whose rhapsodies in *The Times* are legendary –
and Prince Charles, who invited her to sing Handel's 'Let the Bright
Seraphim' at his wedding. As a 'thank you', he made her a Dame of the
British Empire in the 1982 New Year's Honours.

The only flaw in her artistic make-up is that, occasionally, when she is
not stimulated by the director she's working with, her performances can
come across as dramatically uninvolved. Yet, under Peter Hall, Otto
Schenk and the late Joseph Losey, she has delivered riveting, utterly
convincing portrayals. She is an intuitive rather than an intellectual kind
of artist and shapes her portrayals from her instinctive response to the
music rather than the text. She dislikes long periods of concentration and,
in earlier days, tended to learn her lines pretty much at the last moment.
(This is not all that unusual. Montserrat Caballé is also notorious for not
learning her lines until the eleventh hour.)

James Lockhart, Music Director of the Koblenz State Theatre (and
formerly of the Welsh National Opera), feels this is natural for singers
with exceptionally beautiful voices. 'If singers have technical problems,
obviously they have to work harder. But if they have a fantastic voice,

then their capacity for work doesn't have to be as great. In the end there has to be an instinct that a Professor of Music may not have. He may be able to describe the whole construction of an opera and give you a word-for-word translation of the libretto. But he couldn't make even a nursery rhyme *live*.' Vera Rosza, Te Kanawa's teacher for many years, feels that her tendency to leave things to the last minute in earlier years was partly because 'she hates to be overworked and likes being left in peace, and partly because she rather enjoys a dangerous edge to things'.

This tension between the serious, dedicated artist and the extrovert, fun-loving woman who enjoys life to the hilt lies at the essence of Te Kanawa's nature and curious mystery. She attributes this duality partly to her Piscean sun sign; it is certainly evident in the contrast between the fiery side of her temperament – ideal for roles like Donna Elvira in *Don Giovanni* – and the calm, placid side given to bouts of lethargy (and which those who know these latitudes consider typically Maori) that makes her the perfect interpreter of the more poised Strauss and Mozart heroines.

In fact for a couple of years after her Covent Garden triumph as the Countess, Te Kanawa sang nothing but Mozart. Like Dame Joan Sutherland, who also became an overnight star after a performance of *Lucia di Lammermoor*, she had no repertoire and was as yet unprepared for the stream of international invitations that began pouring in. The only offers she *was* able to accept were from the Lyons (spring 1972), the San Francisco (autumn 1972) and the Glyndebourne Festival Opera (summer 1973), all for the Countess. During this time she was busy learning new roles and, in retrospect, is grateful that her lack of repertoire prevented her from doing too much too soon and forced her to sing so much Mozart, whom she considers a very 'sobering' composer.

'He is a tremendous technician and very demanding, both musically and dramatically. Vocally because his music is so *clean*, so devoid of anything superfluous, that there is nothing for you to hide behind. Dramatically, because you must find a way of expressing passion and emotion within this very clean, classical form. And express them you must because Mozart was a very warm, sensitive and deep-feeling person whose nature is reflected in his music, which most of the time is just *gorgeous*. So you must find a way of expressing all the emotion in it within this classical framework. I'm not sure I can explain quite *how* you set about doing it. You just do it. There are people who can analyse things and there are people who can do them. I never analyse roles too much and I'm not good at talking. It tires me and is best left to politicians, who always seem to get away with it. I'm better at singing!'

It is now so long since she first learnt the Countess that she can't explain exactly how she arrived at her portrayal, it would be like 'asking a camera how it took a certain picture. It would probably reply, I don't know what went through my mind, I just did it, a reflex response to a particular stimulus which, in my case, was the music . . . . But the hardest moment was and remains "Porgi amor" because you have to sing it as soon as you walk on stage, without any chance to warm up. In those days I took Colin Davis's advice and sang it four or five times before, in my dressing-room.'

Her next big role was Desdemona in Verdi's *Otello* with Scottish Opera in April 1972. The following year, at Covent Garden, she sang Micaela in *Carmen* (in a new production featuring Shirley Verrett in the title-role, Placido Domingo as Don José and conducted by Sir Georg Solti), Donna Elvira in *Don Giovanni* (with Cesare Siepi in the title role) and Amelia in Tito Gobbi's production of *Simon Boccanegra*. After the latter, there was high praise from two of Britain's premier critics, both fervent Verdi connoisseurs: Andrew Porter wrote in the *Financial Times*: 'It is a rare pleasure to be able to praise the interpreter of a Verdi heroine without any reservations whatsoever', while the late Harold Rosenthal, Editor of *Opera*, called her portrayal 'the revelation of the evening . . . here was Verdi soprano singing of the highest level'.

When Te Kanawa made an unscheduled début – a month earlier than planned – at the Metropolitan Opera, in February 1974, her Verdi singing took American critics by storm, too. She had been booked to sing Desdemona in Franco Zeffirelli's production of *Otello* on 7 March. But on the morning of 9 February, Teresa Stratas rang the Met to say she was ill and had to cancel that afternoon's matinée performance. With a few hours to go – and a warning on the day before which had been dismissed as a false alarm by night-time – Kiri was asked to come to the rescue. She was in New York all alone. Her husband, her teacher and her agent – 'my life-support system' – were not due to arrive until shortly before the scheduled début. She felt like 'the loneliest person in the world'. She warmed up for an hour at home, took a taxi and spent only a few minutes on Zeffirelli's complicated, multi-level set before the curtain was due to go up.

But because the role suits her, and because Kiri always operates well on adrenalin, her début, alongside Jon Vickers – who went out of his way to 'make a bit of a fuss of me and show me I was among friends' – was a sensation and was greeted with tumultuous applause and rave reviews: 'Miss Te Kanawa won the audience from the very start and did not lose it', wrote the *New York Times*. 'Her voice had a lovely, fresh sound, her vocal production was smooth, her singing was eloquent and her acting touching and invariably believable'; while the *New Yorker* called her 'an outstandingly beautiful and graceful lyric soprano with a pure, well-trained voice which she uses like an artist'. Jon Vickers recalls that Te Kanawa was 'high as a kite' and took two days to unwind. Her 'official' debut, on 7 March, was equally successful – and less fraught.

Her view of Desdemona at the time was simple because she was 'young and fresh and new to the role', which she had as yet sung only in Glasgow. 'I saw her as a childlike character, a girl in an ecstasy of love. Having fought everyone to marry Otello, she is wallowing in married bliss and blind to any undertones of suspicion, to Otello's inner turbulence and to the giant chip on his shoulder. In Act III, when it's obvious something is seriously wrong, she wonders what *she* did wrong to bring about such a change of mood. Vocally it's a very comfortable role which flows effortlessly. Dramatically, it is a bit frustrating because she is too passive a character for me. I'm a very positive person and find it easier to tune *up*, rather than down, to a role.'

Her next role was a heroine that allowed her to do just that: Donna Elvira in *Don Giovanni*, which she sang at Covent Garden in autumn 1973, the Metropolitan Opera in January 1975 and the Paris Opera a month later. Te Kanawa has always enjoyed performing this role because 'it brings me to the brink of madness. She is a very positive person in a very positive situation she cannot control. She is very wild, all fire, and this side of her finds a deep echo in me. So I always have a good time with her. But there is another, a pitiful side, to her, too: in many ways she is a stupid woman because she is trying to change a man, something one can never do. She is also terrifically oversexed but at the same time a one-man woman – the only woman in the opera who really loves Giovanni and does so through thick and thin. [This is why Elvira never fully identifies with Anna and Ottavio.] I try to put her across as nearly insane: there are moments of calm and clarity and then, ooops, she goes over the top again. The terrifying range of extremes between this manic state and those cool moments in between sums up Elvira to me.' She always enjoys portraying hysterical characters because 'the reasons for their hysteria' must be made apparent in her interpretation, especially for first timers. (Nowhere more so than in her highly individual Elvira in the late Joseph Losey's film of *Don Giovanni*.)

Despite her major international triumphs on both sides of the Atlantic throughout the early and mid seventies, Te Kanawa says she didn't begin to believe her career 'was really getting somewhere' until she sang the title-role in Richard Strauss's *Arabella* at Covent Garden in 1977. It was her first Strauss role and she was scared stiff of it because it's a huge, important part and totally different from anything she had sung to date. After agreeing to sing it – two years before the actual production – she

flew off to Cologne without knowing anything about it, neither text nor
music, to see a performance and find out how it would affect her. 'I
think it's important sometimes to approach a piece "raw" and discover
one's spontaneous feelings and responses to it.'

Her reaction was to identify with Arabella immediately because
'there is a lot of me in her. I, too, can detach myself from emotional
situations and crises and look at things fairly coolly.' To her surprise,
she discovered that when she came to study the role at Covent Garden
she kept returning to the things that had made the greatest impression
on her when she first saw the work in Cologne: Arabella's Act I duet
with Zdenka and her Act II duet with Mandryka. And, again, she
experienced the same irritation with Matteo: 'He kept getting on my
nerves now as he had before because, from Arabella's point of view, he
is unsufferably boring and goes about things in a nice, roundabout way,
which is all wrong. When someone has no love for you, you can't go on
showering them with letters and trees-full of flowers and things like that.
You've got to come to the point and say: "Now do you love me or don't
you? And if you don't I'll kill myself and if you do let's get married."'

As always, it was the music that gave her a real clue to the character.
'If you listen to the music as Arabella is walking down that staircase at
the finale, a glass of water in her hand, you can hear the softening of a
woman. And a woman is wonderful when she is softened up and made
to feel feminine and is giving in to a man. You can hear, in the music,
that humility which is all a woman should be . . . from time to time!'
William Mann, a renowned Strauss expert, wrote in *The Times*: 'The
final staircase scene was as radiant and lovingly detailed as I can
remember among all Arabellas in decades of devotion to this work.' By
the end of the run, Te Kanawa herself felt she was 'on the right track
with Strauss, the way I'd always felt about Mozart'.

Arabella proved, beyond doubt, that she was a born Strauss soprano;
and she explains how 'the secret of singing Strauss boils down to
whether you can sing all those millions of notes, and feel comfortable
doing it. His music is very, very specialized and ten times as difficult to
sing as Italian opera – although, for my voice, not as tiring or as taxing
as Puccini – which is why he is less "popular" in the broad sense of the
word. Italian singing is easier because the melodic line carries you
forward and makes the thing work as if by itself, although there are
some spots, like the ends of certain arias where singers kind of stop and
expect applause. (They even say so in rehearsal. But *I* say never expect
applause until it's there.) In Strauss there is no question of pausing for
applause anywhere. You just keep on. There isn't a moment's respite in
which to even *think* about applause.'

Her next big Strauss role was the Marschallin in *Der Rosenkavalier*, which she first sang at the Paris Opéra in December 1981 and later in a new production at Covent Garden (November 1984 and February 1985) directed by John Schlesinger and conducted by Sir Georg Solti. The preparation for this role was longer and more intricate than for Arabella, 'like a puzzle that had to be put together bit by bit'. Dramatically speaking, she finds the first five minutes of Act I the most awkward in any opera. 'Once you get past these first few minutes when you are in bed with another woman, you can get on with the role. It's crucial to pace yourself, and think ahead to the Marschallin's long monologue at the end of this act, if you are to let the action flow. Otherwise you would get stuck in all the confusion of the levée and all its sub-plots and lose the continuity of the character.

'Musically speaking, if you go through Act I bar by bar, there is just so *much* of it that I don't know how the man wrote it all and made it work. Just singing it – trying to memorize all those mood changes, thought changes, all those wonderful little details he devised – seems almost too much for the brain to cope with. Act III flows almost by itself, but Act I doesn't begin to do that until after the levée. While Ochs is still there, it's pandemonium – panic stations – which is where you have to be hyper-alert for all those mood changes. This, in a nutshell, sums up the difficulty of Act I: learning to react to all the different characters' moods and words, and to what they're saying in relation to what I'm saying, and not anticipating their mood and thought patterns before they've actually said the words. This was the hardest thing about the role for someone like me who doesn't speak much German – far, far harder than learning the music.'

By the time she came to sing the role again at Covent Garden, she had gone through 'quite a few bumps in life. Not serious bumps, not tragedies like some people in this world have to endure, but enough, I think, for me to understand the Marschallin a little better. She is a real woman and a contemplative, rather introspective character. Therefore I feel it helps if one has seen one's own first white hairs before one sings her.' While rehearsing for this run, she worked very hard on her German diction with Sir Georg Solti and made it near perfect.

Solti is one of the two people, along with her teacher Vera Rosza, from whom she has learnt most over the years. 'They are both Hungarian Jews, and the sheer energy input that goes into their mere *thinking* about music is quite mind-boggling. I reckon it would take at least twenty people to produce the same energy input and the same amount of original ideas and insights into music as those two. They are so intense about their work that they occasionally manage to turn a lazy, lethargic person like me into a workaholic. Without these two very significant Hungarians in my life, I would never have had the ability, the knowledge or the oomph to go out and do what I'm doing . . . . Some days I turn up at Vera's feeling ghastly, moribund, but, true to her promise to "make you feel wonderful in two minutes", she manages to cheer and invigorate me in no time.'

Vera Rosza has not only taught Te Kanawa most of her superb technique but also advised her on choice of repertoire, always conscious that 'it would be criminal to push this lyric voice – and I cannot think of a voice more quintessentially lyric than Kiri's.' Her relatively small repertoire includes most Mozart roles (Pamina, Elvira, the Countess and Fiordiligi), Mimi in *La Bohème*, Micaela in *Carmen*, Marguerite in *Faust*, Tatyana in *Eugene Onegin*, Rosalinde in *Die Fledermaus*, Violetta in *La traviata* as well as the other Verdi and Strauss roles already mentioned.

By the 1980s, she felt her voice was sufficiently matured and resilient for her to try out two of the heavier Puccini parts – the title-roles in *Tosca* and *Manon Lescaut* – usually sung by lirico-spinto sopranos. Kiri was aware she was taking a risk and entering an area of vocal insecurity in taking on these roles, and especially Tosca which she considers 'a wonderful role but vocally very stretching. I can only sing it with the voice I have and I expect a lyric voice like mine to get some wear and tear in the process. The problem in Puccini lies in his orchestrations which are large and dense, and in his habit of making the orchestra double a vocal tune. There is no way a pure lyric voice can push through when the tune is being doubled by this huge orchestra, especially in the lower register. I recently thought about this when recording some songs with Nelson Riddle. He told me that one of the golden rules of writing orchestral accompaniments for singers is never to double their tunes with the orchestra. *His* were like cushions I could lean on. Give me a cushion like *that* when singing Puccini!' The reviews after the Paris première of *Tosca* picked up the difficulty she mentioned of projecting fully in the lower register. With acute self-knowledge she decided never to sing this role again because it lies beyond her natural vocal possibilities.

Her experience with Manon Lescaut was not happy either. Yet in this case she sang the première while battling against severe influenza and very much against her teacher's advice, which was to cancel. 'It was the only time I have ever advised Kiri to cancel an operatic performance,' confirms Vera Rosza, 'because she had been fighting ill health for some months.' Te Kanawa feels, with hindsight, that she should have stopped working for two months at the time of Manon Lescaut. But people kept telling her she couldn't, because this would mean letting everybody down – colleagues such as Placido Domingo as Des Grieux, Thomas Allen as Lescaut, conductor Giuseppe Sinopoli and director Piero Faggioni – and the opera house itself, because the production was due to be televised and filmed for video. 'With my kind of schedule, you're not allowed to be sick or to cancel. But if you don't, you end up having problems for months and years. As a result of going through with Manon Lescaut I was below par for a year – working certainly, but *struggling*.

'You cannot imagine how many people are always telling me I shouldn't cancel even when I know I should. And I ask, "But what about *me*?" And they shrug their shoulders and reply, "Oh, you'll be all right, you look okay to me." And the result is that you sing feeling unwell and the world judges you unfit for a certain role for ever. And if you do cancel, as you are sometimes forced to, all those people who don't care – like managements, the recording industry etc. – go about saying you cancel all the time and you get the reputation of being unreliable. So you are in a no-win situation . . . The only way to survive in this business is to believe in yourself and follow your own convictions. If you took all the critics and all those people who have opinions seriously and listened to what they have to say about you, you would just get back into your bed and not bother to get out of it: because you're always being told you're too short or too fat, or wrong for a certain role, or the role is wrong for you, or that your voice isn't as fresh as it was, or that your singing isn't stylish enough. My rule is never to listen to anybody except for myself and my teacher, Vera Rosza.'

Te Kanawa has generally been lucky in her teachers: from Vera Rosza back to Sister Mary Leo, a Roman Catholic nun with whom she studied throughout her adolescence in New Zealand. She was born on 6 March 1944 in Gisborne on the east coast of the North Island, of mixed Maori–European parentage, and was adopted as a baby by a couple who duplicated the circumstances of her parentage: a Maori father, whom she adored, and a dynamic, ambitious European mother whose ancestors came from the Isle of Man. She was an extrovert who loved playing the piano and filling her house with people, and singing. Kiri was adored and made to feel extra special, and it is interesting that she never sought out her real parents.

When she was three, her mother taught her some children's songs and noticed that although the child had only four or five notes, they were loud and dark-coloured. By the time she was seven, she began to give her singing lessons. She was quite determined her daughter would one day have a great career and no trouble was spared in order to achieve this goal. She searched the length and breadth of New Zealand for a suitable singing teacher. On being told that the best one was Sister Mary Leo in St Mary's Catholic School for Girls in Auckland, she wrote to her at once. Sister Mary replied that her eleven-year-old daughter was still too young for serious singing lessons and suggested they wait until she was eighteen. But her mother would have none of this. Two years later, they moved the family lock, stock and barrel to Auckland and enrolled Kiri at St Mary's.

By the age of sixteen, Kiri had left school but continued her twice-weekly lessons with Sister Mary. To help pay for them, she took odd jobs like being a salesgirl in a music shop or a receptionist in a local oil company. In the evenings she sang light songs (like 'Maria' from *West Side Story*, 'I Could have Danced All Night' from *My Fair Lady* and 'Climb Every Mountain' from *The Sound of Music*) at various clubs, dine-and-dance restaurants and weddings, and did some radio recordings. This gave her some experience and a chance to demonstrate her innate communicative gift and ability to captivate audiences. Before long, she was quite a celebrity in her native land.

What she seemed to lack was motivation to pursue a serious musical career and the capacity to concentrate and study for long periods. She wasn't really sure whether she wanted a career in opera or in light music. The 'moment of truth' came in 1965 when her parents had a heart-to-heart talk with her and asked her to decide, once and for all, what she wanted to do with her life. They had persuaded the founder of the Maori Trust Foundation to grant their daughter a scholarship to continue her studies, so she had to decide *now*. 'As I didn't want to be a shorthand typist, I decided to give it a go.'

Sister Mary felt the first step was to get her talented pupil known. She entered her for every local singing competition worth the name and, in 1965, also for the prestigious *Sydney and Melbourne Sun* Aria Competition, held in Australia every other year. Te Kanawa's last minute preparation meant she only came runner-up in Sydney. But this cold shower jolted her out of her lethargy and she threw herself into preparing for the Melbourne competition with all the energy and verve she's capable of when she really wants something. She shut herself away in her hotel room with Sister Mary and an accompanist and worked until every phrase in the arias she was to sing was perfect. She won First Prize: £560 plus a scholarship worth £1,300. While in Australia she also won two smaller competitions, each worth about £100. On her return to New Zealand she was greeted at the airport by a crowd of several thousands.

The competition proved what Sister Mary and her mother had felt for a long time: that here was a voice with enough potential to merit serious further study abroad. Sister Mary wrote to James Robertson, Director of the then newly founded London Opera Centre in the East

End of London, an institution affiliated to the Royal Opera House. He had been on the jury of a local competition in which Te Kanawa had come a close second, so he knew her voice, agreed about its potential and accepted her without an audition.

In 1966, Te Kanawa and her mother arrived in Britain. She began her studies at the Opera Centre, where she was to spend an unhappy three years chafing against the discipline of organized courses, and missing her mini-celebrity status from back home. Sister Mary had correctly assessed her voice as a 'heavy lyric soprano', but at the Centre she was classified as a mezzo. During those years she began to attract attention in the Centre's productions of *Dido and Aeneas*, *Die Zauberflöte* and *Dialogues des Carmélites*. After a performance of *Anna Bolena* she was signed up by agent Basil Horsefield. By 1968 she was singing Idamante in the Chelsea Opera Group's concert performances of *Idomeneo* under Colin Davis and, a year later, a small part in Handel's *Alcina* at the Festival Hall with Joan Sutherland in the title role. In 1970 she joined the Royal Opera as a junior member and sang several minor roles for a year, leading up to her triumph as the Countess. It was around this time that she also began studying with Vera Rosza, after trying one or two other teachers.

During her time at the centre Te Kanawa had also met and married Australian mining engineer Desmond Park, who has proved a very supportive and understanding husband. After she suffered a miscarriage they adopted a baby daughter and, a few years later, after a second miscarriage, a baby boy. Te Kanawa is a doting, passionate mother, fully aware of how important her children are and never tiring of telling them so, 'just as my parents did to me'. The need to be with them during the years when they needed her most was a crucial factor behind her decision to slow down her career somewhat, and her unwillingness to be pressurized into learning new roles: Elisabeth de Valois in *Don Carlos* was dropped from her 1989 schedule for Covent Garden and so was the title-role in *Ariadne auf Naxos*.* Both would be ideal parts for her, and it is fervently hoped she will find the time to fit them into her schedule in the future. Of late she seems to concentrate more on concerts, recitals and Television Specials, which are both immensely lucrative and carry less strain and wear and tear on her nerves. They also leave her lots more time for family life.

Her happy home life has gone a long way to alleviate the pressures of her career. 'The children need me a lot so the pressures of work are left out of the front door and are only encountered again the next day.

*She did sing the Countess in *Capriccio* in February 1991, to unjustly negative reviews.

I feel lucky because I know I am one of the few singers to combine a completely satisfying working life with a happy home life. But it means having no social life at all – just a very few close friends. I only have so much energy, so something had to go. This is why, at the end of the day, I've preserved my sanity for the children and also manage to do my best at work.'

ANNA TOMOWA SINTOW

'IT'S NATURAL FOR us singers occasionally to enjoy the sound we make and to savour the odd note or phrase. There is no harm in it as long as we remember we are mere instruments for the realization of a work and that our function is to merge with our colleagues until we are at one with them, the conductor and, through the latter's imagination, with the composer.' Anna Tomowa Sintow adds that, in her experience, this has tended to happen most often when working with Herbert von Karajan.

From 1973 until his death in 1989 Bulgarian-born Tomowa Sintow formed part of a small, select group of 'Karajan singers' who were regular visitors to the Berlin Philharmonic, the Salzburg Easter and Summer festivals and took part in numerous Karajan recordings on both disc and video. The qualities that endeared her to the great Maestro are immediately apparent: a secure, soaring lyric voice capable of handling a wide, versatile repertoire; innate musicality and sensitivity as a performer; a sweet disposition, amiability as a colleague and a calm, soothing presence devoid of either neuroticism or egocentric, prima-donna-ish histrionics.

Tomowa Sintow's career, which began in Eastern Europe in 1967, has taken her to the greatest theatres in the world: apart from her work with Karajan, she has also been a regular visitor to the Metropolitan, the Chicago Lyric, the San Francisco, the Hamburg, the Bavarian and the Vienna State Opera, La Scala and Covent Garden; and her repertoire includes Mozart, Strauss, Wagner, Verdi and verismo: Donna Anna in *Don Giovanni*, Fiordiligi in *Così fan tutte*, the Countess in *Le nozze di Figaro*, Desdemona in Verdi's *Otello*, Amelia in *Un ballo in maschera*, Violetta in *La traviata*, Leonora in *Il trovatore* and *La forza del destino*, Elisabeth de Valois in *Don Carlos* and the title role in *Aida*; Maddalena in Giordano's *Andrea Chénier*, the title roles in Puccini's *Tosca*, *Madama Butterfly* and *Manon Lescaut*; Elsa in Wagner's *Lohengrin* and Elisabeth in *Tannhäuser*; and four major Strauss parts: the Marschallin in *Der Rosenkavalier*, the Countess in *Capriccio* and the title roles in *Arabella* and *Ariadne auf Naxos*.

Indeed, it is as an outstanding interpreter of Strauss that Tomowa Sintow will be best remembered. Although her interpretations of Fiordiligi, Donna Anna, the Countess and Elsa are also memorable, it is her portrayals of Strauss heroines which display the total fusion of vocal, dramatic and temperamental characteristics that distinguishes the greatest interpretations. Vocally, the long lines and arching phrases typical of Strauss are ideal for her; and the profound emotional and spiritual rapport she feels for this composer is reflected in her thoughtful, well-rounded portrayals.

'Strauss is very much a woman's composer. In fact he is to music what Maupassant is to literature. The central characters in his operas are always women and he has the knack of penetrating deeper into a woman's psyche than any other composer with the possible exception of Puccini. But in Puccini things tend to happen upfront: his heroines mature before our eyes, through the dramatic action – Mimi through her illness, Butterfly through Pinkerton's betrayal, Tosca through Cavaradossi's capture – whereas in Strauss they develop more on a psychological level, under the surface.'

Conductor Jeffrey Tate, himself a noted Strauss specialist, agrees with Tomowa Sintow that Strauss has an unusual flair for penetrating the female psyche and depicting his heroines' inner and mundane lives with unusual vividness and realism, largely, he feels, because of the nature of the libretti which are, in most cases, extremely detailed about everyday life and events. 'Wagner doesn't interest himself in whether a heroine's hair looks all right today or in whether she has discovered a few grey hairs! These are not his preoccupations and these are not his sort of people. But Strauss, who himself enjoyed a mundane plane, encouraged this element – the display of normal events and preoccupations – in his librettists.

'Of course, there is very little of that in either *Elektra* or *Salome*, which are usually called his "Wagnerian" operas. But his analysis of the female psyche is particularly strong in what are called his comedies. Of course, it's true that nuances of the human soul are always revealed more in comedy than in more serious drama. In Mozart, we know the women in *Le nozze di Figaro* better than we know those in *Don Giovanni*, who are more mysterious, harder to penetrate and reveal less of themselves than do the Countess or Susanna. By the same token, we understand the Marschallin and Octavian in Strauss's *Der Rosenkavalier* better than we do the Empress or the Dyer's wife in *Die Frau ohne Schatten*. But, given a comedy situation, Strauss does have a unique ability to reveal women.'

This gift is strikingly displayed in *Der Rosenkavalier* in the description of both a young girl, Sophie, and a mature woman, the Marschallin, which Tomowa Sintow first sang at the Metropolitan Opera in 1979, and subsequently in Herbert von Karajan's Salzburg production in 1983. The same production had been filmed in the sixties with Elisabeth Schwarzkopf, and many felt this could prove a hard act indeed for Tomowa Sintow to follow. Yet she succeeded beyond all expectations with a moving, deeply-felt portrayal, totally different yet every bit as valid as Schwarzkopf's: an interpretation that revealed all the layers and facets of this complex character. Instead of the usual ageing society beauty worrying about her first wrinkles and white hairs, we were faced with a thoughtful, profound human being reflecting on the nature of time and the prospect of approaching middle age without having experienced real fulfilment.

It was hardly surprising to discover that this remarkable interpretation – which, along with her portrayals of Ariadne and Elsa, is firmly implanted in one's private archive of most-treasured operatic memories – was the result of an unhurried, in depth preparation stretching over several years. She had first been asked to sing it at the Deutsche Oper in Berlin in 1974 but declined because she felt that, although the role presented no vocal problems, there was something in it she couldn't yet grasp or come to grips with. 'The Marschallin is a woman in the process of developing and maturing and this provides a singer with the sort of opportunities usually reserved for stage or film actresses. She also represents an entire philosophy of life and a wide range of emotions. Therefore the role requires a certain maturity. Not too much maturity, though, because there is also a very fresh, earthy, lively side to her – she is, after all, a Lerchenau, too – evident in her opening scene with Octavian and during his masquerade as the maid, Mariandel. As she later indicates in her monologue, through Octavian she is experiencing something she never knew in her own youth, and confronts the experience with great gusto.

'The Marschallin is jolted out of this playful mood and set on the road to a hard-earned maturity when Ochs tells her about Sophie, the young girl just out of a convent, whom he intends to marry for her fortune. Instinctively – because she is a very intuitive woman – the Marschallin wishes to protect this girl from a fate similar to hers. Clearly, her own marriage of convenience has not been a happy one, and all her life she has been looking for love without ever finding it. Not even with Octavian. He is simply the latest in a long string of lovers, even though, because of his charm and freshness, she probably loves him a bit more than the others. But he is certainly neither the first nor the last, because the Marschallin is a woman born for passion, excitement and abandon – things she has never found in her marriage. But if hearing about Sophie from Ochs represents the first jolt towards the eventual outcome, the real tragedy begins the

moment she is shown Sophie's miniature and proposes Octavian as the
rose-bearer. At that moment, according to Karajan, "something in the
music is crying": her intuition warns her about what is to come and this is
why she begins to feel old and ugly – not because her hairdresser has made
a mistake with her coiffure.'

Tomowa Sintow feels it's significant that the Marschallin does not
appear at all in Act II, and is convinced Strauss and Hofmannsthal
deliberately planned it this way so that she can make the transition to the
great lady of the finale, who has found the strength to look at things
dispassionately, even though it hurts, and the greatness to withdraw with
dignity, without self pity. 'She sings that although she knew the day would
come when she would have to give up Octavian, she never realized it
would be so soon, or the experience so painful. But still, she has the
strength and generosity to rise above her own emotions and to help him,
even though, like him, she doesn't quite understand the world any more.'

Even though Tomowa Sintow first sang the Marschallin at the Met, she
actually began learning the role with Karajan, long before they had even
discussed her singing it in Salzburg. 'When I was singing Donna Anna at
the 1978 Salzburg Festival under Karl Böhm, Karajan asked about my
future plans. He was always interested in his "children", as he called us
singers who worked regularly with him. So I told him I had agreed to sing
the Marschallin at the Met, that I didn't know the part yet and that I was
frightened of it. Next day, he called me to his room, sat down at the piano
and began singing the entire role himself, explaining it as he went along.
He pointed out that from the purely vocal point of view the Marschallin is
"child's play", as he put it, Everything hinges on interpretation.
Therefore I should pay meticulous attention to the text and be so well
prepared musically that I could feel free to interpret, especially in the
monologue, the subsequent duet with Octavian (where she muses about
the hour-glass and the passing of time), and, of course, in the final trio.
He also stressed that, although the role consists of long parlando
passages, my singing should be as pure as possible, especially in the final
trio the first six bars of which should, he insisted, be sung not just
pianissimo but pianis*sissimo*. (He particularly relished this at the
performances we eventually did together. And so did I. But it's
something one could only do with him, because he produced equally
transparent sound in the orchestra.) For the rest of the trio he demanded
absolute evenness of tone, without stressing any one note more than
another.'

After those initial sessions the two returned to *Der Rosenkavalier*
whenever they happened to meet for other performances or recording
sessions. So, her Marschallin emerged, layer by layer, and by the time she

came to perform the role under Karajan's baton at the 1983 Salzburg Festival, the fruits of this long preparation were obvious: 'Tomowa Sintow, once a singer of no great subtlety, has made enormous progress this year and her Marschallin, in its dignity, delicacy and, above all, in the pure, unforced singing, now stands among the great,' wrote *The Times*, while *Opera* remarked that 'Tomowa Sintow's lovely, unaffected Marschallin was one of the finer elements in this production.'

Equally outstanding is her portrayal of the title role in *Ariadne auf Naxos*, which she first sang in 1987 at Covent Garden. Her Ariadne combines vocal beauty with a subtle, refined dramatic interpretation that helps highlight the somewhat nebulous, 'covered' quality of the work. It also happens to be one of her favourite roles, because 'like Arabella but *un*like the Marschallin and the Countess in *Capriccio*, both of which contain long parlando passages, Ariadne is a very "singable" role, full of those marvellous, soaring Strauss phrases that are sheer joy to sing. From the dramatic point of view, its ambiguity makes it particularly interesting and challenging. In this work, Strauss's philosophy is expressed in rather symbolic terms and the ending is ambiguous enough to leave everybody free to draw their own conclusions, through the music, about the real meaning of the work. Indeed this rather mysterious dimension is one of *Ariadne*'s main fascinations. Although I firmly believe that, in opera, music and text are one – though it could be argued than it *some* Strauss operas, like *Arabella*, the text is slightly superior to the music – it is always the music that provides the clues and answers to all questions.

'In *Ariadne*, for instance, it is the purity characteristic of both the Composer's and Ariadne's music that establishes the inner connection between the two. The character of the Composer is, of course, meant to be Strauss himself but the identification is not as clear in *Ariadne* as it is in *Capriccio*, where one senses Strauss's presence and feels he is almost one of the family: his philosophy is written into the role of the Composer and his music, not so much in his actual lines but in those marvellous songs, at once earthy and lofty. But however clear or unclear the connection between Strauss and the fictitious Composer might be in *Ariadne* or *Capriccio*, it should never be underlined or overstressed in one's interpretation which should, both in terms of singing and acting, be as natural and straightforward as possible. It should be left to the music to establish the connection and clarify the mystical, subliminal meaning.'

Tomowa Sintow relishes the vividness with which the characters in Strauss operas are depicted, and one of the things she most admires in this composer is his capacity to see people as they really are. 'His characters display very "human" emotions and Strauss seems to know their inner life, particularly the inner life of his female characters, in great detail. In fact, his only rival as far as penetration of the female psyche is concerned is, as I already mentioned, Puccini. But Strauss and Puccini also have a lot in common *musically*, because they both write wonderful long, melodious lines which one can sing with real abandon, something one cannot do to the same extent in either Mozart or Verdi, both of whom demand utmost purity of line and precision. But in Strauss and Puccini one can almost forget about vocal control and abandon oneself to the music and the drama and, provided one has a good technique and is not grappling with health problems, one can even get away with minor vocal flaws – unthinkable in either Mozart or Verdi! In fact, one sings Strauss and Puccini better if one is not consciously controlling every sound – which is why I never feel any trace of vocal fatigue when singing music by these two composers. I never experience the same sense of freedom in Mozart, who is the most difficult of *all* composers, even though he happens to be the healthiest from the vocal point of view.'

Tomowa Sintow's first Mozart role was Donna Anna, which she first sang in 1968 in East Berlin. It became her calling card for many years and she made all her American débuts – in San Francisco (1974), the Chicago Lyric (1980) and the Metropolitan Opera (1976) – in this role which is, she feels, ideally suited to her, both vocally and temperamentally: 'I love Donna Anna and the contrasts she embodies, possibly because I'm a bit like that myself. There are things in me that are never expressed in real life but only through music and the roles I portray on stage. As a woman, Donna Anna is, of course, totally unfulfilled. She is obviously not in love with Don Ottavio and secretly longing for something she has glimpsed – or tasted, depending on one's view of what happened before the opening of the opera – in Don Giovanni. While she feels affection and friendship for Ottavio, she is a woman born for passion and for abandoning herself to emotional extremes – suggested by her music and her exaggerated, almost unhinged reaction to her father's death.

'She knows full well she can never fulfil those extremes with Ottavio; which is why she keeps postponing their marriage. Of course, she is also a supreme egotist, a totally selfish woman who can only look at things from her own point of view. In all her recitatives one keeps hearing "I, I, I," all the time. All she can think about is her own suffering. The fact that Ottavio is also suffering doesn't seem to cross her mind. It's a case of "me first", full stop. She also comes suspiciously close to wallowing in her grief, as if she were actually enjoying it, so reluctant is she to give up her anguish. I feel there are two reasons for this: her desire to postpone her union with Ottavio, and her guilt at having indirectly caused her father's death. And this, every nuance of her feelings and character, is written into Mozart's music, which is composed in such an inspired way that every interval and every syllable have a reason because Mozart, as Karajan pointed out when I sang the Countess with him in 1978, composed his psychology into his music.'

Vocally, the most difficult of all Donna Anna's music is her first aria, 'Or sai chi l'onore', whereas her second aria, 'Non mi dir', has a clear lyric line with some coloratura. But, she explains – and all artists in this book agree – it is always difficult to go from dramatic to lyric singing. 'If only the sequence were reversed, and one had the lyric aria *before* the dramatic one, Donna Anna would be a much easier role!' she sighs. The only time I saw Tomowa Sintow as Donna Anna, in the 1987 Salzburg Easter Festival, her performance did not display the vocal precision and excitement one had come to expect of her.

Her least favourite Mozart part is the Countess in *Le nozze di Figaro*. It has always been a difficult role for her to understand and penetrate, even when singing it under Karajan, whose interpretation 'goes a long way to reveal the character's womanly nature. But the fact remains that I just don't *like* the Countess very much. She doesn't seem to know what she wants and comes across as rather helpless and slightly masochistic, especially in Karajan's interpretation, which is in perfect accord with the music. But I feel there is a contradiction between the way the Countess is viewed by Beaumarchais and by Mozart. Mozart's music is far too beautiful for this woman who, although saddened by her husband's infidelities, does not exclude the possibility of having a fling with Cherubino – in Beaumarchais she eventually has a child by him! Still, I suppose that however reluctant one might be to admit it, this is a little bit like real life, where one would like to hold on to what one has, but on the other hand, one would not be averse to a bit of excitement on the side . . .' She points out that, as well as being difficult for her to understand as a character, the Countess is also rather difficult to sing. Her first aria, 'Porgi amor', is short but, nevertheless, it is a 'calling card' sort of aria which, unless sung perfectly, ruins the evening by instantly creating a bad rapport with the audience!

Fiordiligi in *Cosi fan tutte*, on the other hand, the role in which she made her Covent Garden début in 1976, is a part she relished from both the vocal and the dramatic standpoint, because 'she is a natural, sunny, girlish and lovable character, trying to find her way in life while sticking to her ideals. Discovering her human weaknesses and learning to live with them is not as easy for her as it is for her sister, Dorabella. Although it's very long, it is so marvellously well written, that I sing it seemingly effortlessly, in one long breath, from start to finish. In Berlin I sang the "da capo" sections twice, and I also invariably include the rondo, because it helps enhance the "girlish", sparkling side of her, and bring out different vocal colours and nuances. I never feel I have to concentrate particularly hard with Fiordiligi. Everything seems to happen naturally, by itself.' This is an unusual view indeed, because Fiordiligi happens to be a very demanding and difficult role. Yet Tomowa Sintow's obvious liking and suitability is certainly reflected in her portrayal, which has won her high critical acclaim throughout her career.

She stresses that singing Mozart demands a perfect technique 'and in this sense I always link Mozart with Verdi, whose style is also very pure and clean and tolerates no departure from the written score. In Verdi one can get away with a little bit more than in Mozart, because one can do little glissandi and portamenti here and there, always provided they are written into the score. Otherwise, he, too, demands very clear articulation. The things I love most about Verdi are the grandeur and nobility with which his works are imbued. There is incredible nobility in all those choruses and ensembles: the singing seems to pour out from the deepest recesses of the heart; I also love singing those exquisite piani and pianissimi that he writes into the more intimate moments . . .'

But although Verdi heroines have 'sublime' music to sing, she finds them dramatically less interesting to portray than Puccini's, because they are usually unfulfilled women. 'Unlike his male heroes, who are immensely virile, flesh-and-blood characters, his heroines tend to be "dream women", symbols, and almost invariably ill-fated in love. All – be they Aida, Elisabeth de Valois, Gilda, or the two Leonoras in *Il trovatore* and *La forza del destino* – conceal some secret that stands in the way and prevents their love from being fulfilled, and all are very sensitive and tremendously religious. In this sense I feel that Verdi is dramatically more akin to Wagner, whose heroines are also, to a large extent, idealized dream women.'

Tomowa Sintow's Wagnerian repertoire consists of Elisabeth in *Tannhäuser* and Elsa in *Lohengrin*, which she first sang at the 1976 Salzburg Easter Festival under Karajan. In December 1977, she repeated the role at Covent Garden, in an unforgettable production conducted by Bernard Haitink and directed by Elijah Moshinsky, which highlighted the ethereal, dreamlike quality of this work. The late Harold Rosenthal, editor of *Opera*, wrote of her performance: 'I like my Elsas to have some body to their voice, and the full, lush sound Miss Tomowa Sintow brought to her music helped her turn the character into a real flesh-and-blood creature rather than the pale milk sop she often is.'

Elijah Moshinsky found her especially rewarding to work with and was surprised by the fact that, although she had performed this role with Karajan in Salzburg, she was very receptive, unspoilt and un-self-centred. 'And because of her real sweetness of disposition, her Elsa was fantastic. She had the very quality so many full-time Wagnerian sopranos lack – of making you aware of the whole character; and her portrayal was very subtle and slightly "covered". Her vocal interpretation was also very soft, subtle, with a gossamer, ethereal quality essential to the role but very un-German in the sense that it wasn't loud or bombastic the way Wagnerian singing often is . . . She *is* a nice, simple, direct and well-centred person and brings something to Wagner operas which others, whose sweetness is phoney, cannot.'

Tomowa Sintow considers this subtle, 'covered' dimension essential not only for Elsa, but for all Wagnerian heroines: 'If one interprets Wagnerian characters "upfront", one entirely misses the point and risks ending up with nothing there at all. Elsa, for instance, often says one thing and means another, and in such cases it is, as I said before, à propos of Ariadne, always crucial to follow the music, which is where the clues for her real feelings are. Wagner was an idealist and his operas all contain a strong spiritual dimension. His characters, both male and female, are usually symbolic rather than fully human. Like Verdi's, Wagner's women are seldom fulfilled in love, and their intense longing for fulfilment is actually written into their music, which is often at loggerheads with the text but which always reveals the truth.'

Although she loves Wagner, she says the only other Wagnerian character she might contemplate singing is Sieglinde. But, much though she enjoys 'delving into the deep' with her Wagner and Strauss roles, after singing too many in a row she feels a strong need to 'surface for air' and sing some of her Italian repertoire. 'Coming from Bulgaria, the Balkans, I *need* those Italian roles, I *need* the Mediterranean world . . .'

Tomowa Sintow was born in Stara Zagora to a father who was a schoolteacher specializing in physics and a mother who was a singer in the chorus of the local opera house, one of the oldest in Bulgaria and the only one to perform a wide repertoire in the original language. The post-war years in which she grew up were difficult times for her country, and her father was forced to work late into the night to supplement their income. Her mother, who sang in the choir and had no one with whom to leave her only daughter, took her along to all the rehearsals. This meant that she grew up with opera in her ears. She started singing at a very young age and by the time she was eight demanded piano lessons. (She is a competent pianist to this day, and much enjoys occasionally sitting down at the piano after dinner and entertaining friends with arias, folk songs or popular melodies.)

In 1960 she auditioned for the National Conservatoire in Sofia, choosing Tchaikovsky's *Romance* as one of her showpieces. The Professor of Singing, Georgi Zlatev Tscherkin, who had also taught Lluba Welitch, decided she should be admitted, but as a mezzo soprano. So she spent her years at the Conservatoire singing the mezzo repertoire, which was easy enough, she says, because her voice has always been wide-ranging. But gradually she discovered that difficult arias or choir solos would leave her feeling quite tired. 'I also had the distinct sensation they were wrong for me, both vocally and temperamentally – because, of course, one's voice and psyche are one, even though it takes a long time for one to realize it and to find oneself in this way.'

Her mother also realized something was wrong and took her along to a retired soprano, Katja Spiridonova, who within a few lessons sensed she was not a mezzo and succeeded in freeing her soprano register and setting it on the right track. 'The moment this happened, I felt a tremendous sense of release. Suddenly, everything began to happen naturally, as if by itself. I felt free to be myself, at last. While singing in the mezzo register, I had had to concentrate very hard on producing the sound. But as soon as I switched, the sound came almost effortlessly.'

She graduated from the Conservatoire after singing Tatyana in *Eugene Onegin* for her state exam, and was lucky enough to be engaged by the Leipzig Opera right away. She made her début in Leipzig in 1966 as the Countess of Ceprano in an opera-studio production of *Rigoletto* and her official début in the theatre during the following season, as Abigaille in *Nabucco*. ('I know this may surprise you, because it is a heavy dramatic role, but one coped with it all with that ease and optimism of youth . . .') She learnt a large part of her repertoire there – including Violetta, Madama Butterfly, Donna Anna and Arabella – before moving to the German State Opera in East Berlin in 1972. Her first appearance with Herbert von Karajan was in 1973, when she sang Karl Orff's *De Temporum Fine Comoedia* in both Berlin and for her début at the Salzburg Festival. After her American and Salzburg Festival débuts in 1974 and 1975, 1976 was a milestone year, during which she made her Salzburg Easter Festival début as Elsa, her Covent Garden début as Fiordiligi and her Metropolitan Opera début as Donna Anna. Her La Scala début followed in 1981, when she sang Elsa under Claudio Abbado.

Tomowa Sintow has managed to combine her successful career with a stable and rewarding personal life: while still a student at Sofia Conservatoire, she met and married her husband Avram Sintow, from whom she has a grown-up daughter, Silvana, now an executive with an international recording company. Soon after Silvana's birth her career was launched and circumstances precluded her having more children. 'I was born for my profession, I felt compelled to follow my calling, and a singing career isn't ideally suited to family life. But I wouldn't be without my one daughter, without the wonderful experience of having a child . . .'

MEZZO-SOPRANOS

AGNES BALTSA

AGNES BALTSA IS a pulse-quickening performer incapable of dullness on stage. 'She has that Callas tension, that terrific Greek fire and visceral energy which, on top of her gorgeous voice, makes her a truly electrifying stage presence', says director John Schlesinger who worked with her in his Covent Garden productions of *Les Contes d'Hoffmann* and *Der Rosenkavalier*, while Herbert von Karajan, instrumental in propelling her career to the top echelons of the profession, called her 'the most important dramatic mezzo of our day'. At its best, Baltsa's richly expressive voice – languorously sensuous in the middle and lower regions and powerfully penetrating at the top – is one of the most exciting mezzo sounds of the past two decades. Below its best it displays a distressing difficulty blending the registers into a seamless whole. Yet her dramatic presence and charisma make it possible for her to mesmerize audiences even on those comparatively rare occasions when she is vocally below par.

In Baltsa's best portrayals – Romeo in *I Capuleti ed i Montecchi*, Princess Eboli in *Don Carlos*, the title role in *Samson et Dalila*, her more controversial Carmen, Elisabetta in *Maria Stuarda* and Santuzza in *Cavalleria rusticana* – one experiences not only musical/dramatic unity but also a spiritual quest for truth and completeness and a fusion between artist and role that borders on the mystical. Yet according to Baltsa such moments, exhilarating though they might be, fill her with 'fear and melancholy' because they are so transient. 'They are over in a flash and after a few minutes they become just memories,' she sighs. 'Sometimes I wish we could hold on to them a little longer, I wish our art were less ephemeral.'

Yet on the whole, Baltsa seems content with her artistic lot. Unlike some famous colleagues, she has never had the unfortunate desire to become a soprano. Indeed several years ago she turned down Riccardo Muti's offer of Lady Macbeth because she is 'quite happy to be, and remain, what I am. I have expressed myself fully through my mezzo repertoire and have never felt second fiddle to anyone.' Her repertoire includes Italian, French and German opera and ranges from classical roles (Gluck's Orfeo and Mozart parts such as Cherubino, Dorabella, Sextus and, on record only, Idamante and Donna Elvira), to *bel canto* (Adalgisa, Romeo, Elisabetta in *Maria Stuarda*, Leonora in *La Favorite* and a cluster of Rossini heroines like Rosina, Isabella in *L'Italiana in Algeri* and the title role in *La Cenerentola*) and Verdi (Eboli and, on record only, Preziosilla and Amneris), and from Strauss (Octavian, Herodias, the Composer in *Ariadne auf Naxos*) to French opera (Didon in *Les Troyens*, Giulietta in *Les Contes d'Hoffmann*, Dalila in *Samson et Dalila*, Carmen and Charlotte in *Werther*) and verismo (Santuzza).

She stresses that because certain roles force singers to make crucial decisions about the basic direction of their careers, if they are to survive they must acquire early on the ability to say 'no' – 'even to the most important conductors. One criterion should always be: "Can I sing such and such a role without damaging my vocal capital?" In 1980, for instance, I had to *force* myself to say "no" to Karajan's offer of Kundry, both on disc and on stage in Salzburg, because although it is a wonderful role, one must accept the fact that one cannot sing everything. So I asked myself: "If I accept Kundry, what other roles in my repertoire would I have to give up?" And the answer to that was all my Rossini parts which are like a vocal elixir to me. After Kundry I could never have gone on with Rossini, because the voice would have been put into a different mould. I felt this would have been wrong for me, both vocally and temperamentally. I am a Southerner, a Mediterranean woman with an Italianate voice and it is in Italian, and to a lesser extent in French, opera that I can give my best.'

Baltsa's keen self-awareness was evident from very early on. Born on 19 November 1944 on the Greek island of Lefkas in the Ionian Sea (to which she often returns to recharge her batteries), she asked for, and received, piano lessons at the age of six. Within two years, she had begun composing 'invariably tragic or melancholy things'. At the same time, she began writing down her thoughts and feelings – a habit she kept throughout her childhood. When her mother produced those copybooks a few years ago, Baltsa was astonished to discover she could have written the same thoughts today. 'This showed me how little I've changed. There was always something inside me pushing, compelling me to stretch, reach out, discover new meanings in everything and keep trying to make myself better and better. Needless to say, the more one matures as an artist, the higher one's aspirations. Having "a name" and a measure of success helps, of course. But only in a very limited way, and only as far as the public is concerned. For us artists, fame only makes everything more difficult because it makes us more and more demanding and less and less satisfied with our work.'

When Agnes was fourteen, the family – parents and older sister to whom she remains extremely close – went to Athens so that she could study at the Conservatoire. She graduated in 1965 with top grades and won the Maria Callas Scholarship, which enabled her to continue her studies in Munich. Although she studied singing privately, with Dr Schöner, she also took drama coaching and studied German language and literature at the University, 'for how could I allow myself to interpret texts like von Hofmannsthal's without understanding the words and thus having even a possibility of doing them justice?'

After three years in Munich she auditioned for Christoph von Dohnányi, recently appointed intendant of the Frankfurt Opera, where she made her professional début in 1968 as Cherubino and remained for two years. In 1970 came her début at the Vienna State Opera, as Octavian (the youngest ever Octavian in the annals of that House), and a year later she joined the Deutsche Oper in Berlin as a company member. At the same time, 1971, she made her American début in Houston as Carmen and returned to the United States four years later for Dorabella under Karl Böhm during the Vienna State Opera's visit to Washington. It was under his baton and in the same role that she also made her début at La Scala in 1976 – a milestone year in which she also made her Covent Garden and Paris Opéra débuts (as Cherubino) and her New York début, in the concert hall, under Herbert von Karajan. She stresses that 'my voice and I' both matured slowly and gradually and believes 'one should never run after things but let them come to you. At the beginning, of course, I had to sing roles like Maddalena in *Rigoletto* but this allowed my voice time to develop in a way harmonious with my emotional and intellectual growth. The only thing I take credit for is knowing exactly what stage I was at all along and using each stage of my mental and emotional development for the good of my voice.'

She explains that taking care of her voice means planning her schedule in a way that ensures roles with a similar tessitura are grouped together. She would never sing *bel canto* parts like Romeo before or after Carmen, firstly because the tessitura is different, and secondly because the roles belong to contrasting worlds, both vocally and stylistically. 'Carmen has nothing to do with *bel canto*. It stretches and extends the voice and, in order to express its very wide and extreme range of emotions, one has to use all sorts of vocal effects such as shrieks and so on. In short, its interpretation does not hinge on vocalism alone. Factors such as magnetism and stage presence play an important part, too. *Bel canto*, on the other hand, depends on vocalism pure and simple. But after singing Carmen my voice would be too tired and extended to cope with the vocal demands of any *bel canto* role. So I try to group my Carmen performances together and then let my voice rest a bit before "changing gear". Because, like any musical instrument, the voice depends on the level at which you are going to tune it. Just as you couldn't sing Romeo before or after Carmen, you also can't sing Gluck's Orfeo at the same time as Rosina. They are musically different and vocally Orfeo is very low-lying. But one could happily combine Romeo and Adalgisa in *Norma*, because they are stylistically similar and their tessitura is the same. Two other roles that can safely be scheduled near each other are Charlotte in *Werther* and Isabella in *L'Italiana in Algeri*.'

On the whole Baltsa tries to schedule all her Rossini roles near each other because then she can work her voice on exactly the level they demand. 'All Rossini parts require brilliance, lustre and tremendous precision. In fact when singing Rossini coloraturas I always visualize a rosary or necklace composed of precious, even-sized pearls. On paper, Rossini coloraturas can fill you with panic because they contain *so many* notes that you think you cannot ever succeed in singing them all! But sing them you must and in such a way that they sound effortless and natural. The audience should feel that yes, this sounds impressive but so natural that it can't be all that difficult. Because coloratura is not just an opportunity for vocal histrionics but a unique form of musical expression. If you approach it in this spirit it can really be sensational. Of course certain sections of the audience are only satisfied if they feel they have witnessed visible signs of physical effort – the arena mentality. But this is an offence to the composer because it means that, instead of losing yourself in the role, you are absorbed in coping with technical problems or showing off.'

Baltsa has no hard-and-fast rules about how often or how long she works on her voice. It might be every day for a week or not at all for ten days. It depends. If she is in the middle of a tight schedule of performing and recording, then she feels the best she can do for her voice is to let it rest and recoup its moisture and elasticity by itself. She accepts that, as the voice is the most individual and personal instrument, different singers have different views and methods. 'Personally I am convinced that if you sing and practise constantly, every day, you take away some of the freshness from the quality of your sound. This is something every singer should guard against, because ideally *all* our notes should be of the same quality, like spreading a deck of cards and having each one fall into place perfectly. This is true of all great instrumentalists be they pianists, cellists or violinists – all their notes are on the same level, one-hundred-per-cent perfect – and it should also be true of us singers. Of course it is much harder for us than for them because *our* instrument is lodged inside our body and subject to every tiny fluctuation of our physical, mental, emotional and spiritual state. I cannot separate my vocal cords from the rest of my body or from my mind or my psyche. My voice and I are one. They are totally interdependent. If I'm in a good physical condition, I produce dramatically and vocally well-rounded portrayals. But if I'm feeling spiritually low or weary, *all* roles, even the easier ones, weigh on me and become increasingly difficult'. At other times, she admits, she might be feeling just plain lazy. Yet especially at such times she tries to force on herself 'the patience and humility' to put all her great roles and successes aside and return to the voice 'as if it were virgin territory, working at it humbly, almost like a beginner, an ignorant pupil. And I do this with great love.'

Yet working extremely hard does not automatically guarantee success for any performing artist, even when coupled with considerable talent. One needs luck as well, and she, having had a good deal of it, feels 'extremely grateful' for the opportunities that came her way. 'I had the good fortune to work with the best conductors such as Karajan, Abbado and Muti who steered me towards the right repertoire and taught me a lot.' The first time she worked with Abbado was for Faggioni's La Scala production of *Carmen* in January 1985, and later at the Vienna State Opera in 1987 and 1988 for Ponnelle's *L'Italiana in Algeri* and in 1989 for Pizzi's *Don Carlos*. She finds him an 'immensely charismatic conductor' whose economy of gesture and tautness of interpretation make her feel 'as if I've been on a good, healthy diet that has eliminated any superfluous flab.'

Muti, who tends to be dictatorial in rehearsal, she finds wonderful in performance because by then he 'lets you fly and reach top form'. She never needs to discuss anything with him, just as she never needed to with Karajan. They understand each other perfectly and he knows he can rely on her to deliver the interpretation they have worked out together but also lets her own instinct take over at times 'and immediately follows if I do something spontaneous, on the spur of the moment, which is exhilarating'. It was with Muti that Baltsa sang her most famous *bel canto* role for many years, Romeo in Bellini's *I Capuleti ed i Montecchi*, first at the Vienna State Opera, and later in Florence and Covent Garden. She considers Romeo one of the most challenging parts she has ever performed, both musically and dramatically, because, 'as in most *bel canto* operas, you can forget about the libretto. Any clues to the character are to be found in the music, because although the story is based on Shakespeare, the libretto has no dramatic structure to help you build the character architecturally. The word may sound strange but I firmly believe that every operatic character has his or her own architecture. You mould them out of specific materials. But in this opera these materials can

be found only in the music. And the Romeo and Giulietta that emerge
from Bellini's music are quite different from Shakespeare's and imbued
with a sort of death wish right from the start. They come across as terribly
in love, terribly romantic, melancholy and almost resigned to the fact that
their love is so impossible that its only outcome can be death. Indeed they
long to die because in death they can be united.'

What makes Bellini's Romeo especially difficult to interpret is the
extreme softness and gentleness suggested by his music. 'His first entry is
so "sotto voce" that it feels as if an ethereal being, rather than a
flesh-and-blood creature, has just entered. So you have to find a way of
expressing his passion, romanticism, state of being overwhelmingly in
love and his profound, yet almost mute, inexpressible pain through a very
still, introspective and understated stage presence.' Baltsa, who says that
such understated moments are her more powerful on stage, succeeded in
doing just that and Romeo remains one of her most moving portrayals.
'Covent Garden will be lucky to get a better individual performance this
season,' wrote *The Times*, while Harold Rosenthal remarked in *Opera*:
'The way Miss Baltsa launched into the cabaletta of the Handel-like first
aria, and her singing of the loveliest page in the score, "Deh tu
bell'anima" in the closing scene, suggested she has few rivals in this kind
of music today, and confirmed that her Adalgisa four years ago was no
flash in the pan.'

One of Herbert von Karajan's few unfulfilled musical dreams was to
stage and record *Norma* with Baltsa as Adalgisa, though as his ideal
Norma proved elusive the project was never realized. Baltsa's first
encounter with Karajan, which was to prove crucial for her future, had
taken place in 1974 at the Berlin Philharmonie. She went to audition for
the mezzo part in the *Missa Solemnis* and remembers singing 'atroci-
ously'. She attempted to excuse herself by saying this was because she felt
so nervous and flustered. 'You are not nervous *or* flustered,' he replied.
'You *wish* to be.' He instantly perceived the potential in this striking
jolie-laide (Baltsa was not yet the glamorous, tousled-haired, always
fashionably dressed creature she was soon to become), gave her the job
and quickly made her one of the leading members of the small, select
group of 'Karajan singers', with whom he worked regularly both in Berlin
and Salzburg. 'He formed and set a seal on me both as an artist and as a
human being', she says, and to this day her conversation is full of deeply
felt reminiscences of Karajan.

The first Karajan production Baltsa sang in was his historic 1977 staging
of *Salome* that also launched Hildegard Behrens's international career.
Left to her own devices, she would probably never have thought of
performing Herodias, often sung by sopranos past their prime. But

Right: LEONTYNE PRICE as Aida, 'my warrior-part, my heart-beat', the role that made me feel even more *beautifully* black, and the only time when, as a black soprano, I got to sing a black heroine. Normally being black is of no artistic significance whatsoever. But in this case it said things about where I was as a woman and a human being, about the life and progress, or lack of, of millions of people at home in the States – things I could not have said as eloquently in other ways.'
(Donald Southern)

Left: KATIA RICCIARELLI as Desdemona in Verdi's *Otello*, a role for which she is vocally and temperamentally ideally suited: 'very feminine, but also a woman with a lot of character. Imagine having the courage to marry a black man in those days, in that milieu, against her father's wishes. Not exactly easy, even now. But *then!*'
(Christina Burton)

RENATA SCOTTO, 'who is not afraid of sometimes producing an ugly sound – but an ugly sound that means so much that you instantly accept it', as Lady Macbeth: (with Renato Bruson as Macbeth) 'A character who has two sides to her. Yes, she is incredibly bloodthirsty and ambitious, but she is also a beautiful, young, sexy woman, very much in love with her husband. You need plenty of life experience, both as a singer and as a woman, to sing her.' *(Donald Cooper)*

Right: CHERYL STUDER as Elisabeth in *Tannhäuser*, in which she scored a major triumph at the 1985 Bayreuth Festival: 'A woman typical of her times because she is the only one not to recoil or run away when Tannhäuser announces he has been to Venusberg – whatever one takes that to stand for. On the contrary, she is prepared to defend him by pointing out that everyone's a sinner . . . But the real tragedy is that, at the end, she is not capable of facing up to its full implications, either. She dies for him, but she can't live with him.' *(Donald Cooper)*

Above: DAME JOAN SUTHERLAND as Lucrezia Borgia, a role in which the greatest challenge is to equate her 'breathtakingly beautiful music with the character of a vicious poisoner. Well nigh impossible! What emerges from the libretto is her overwhelming love for her son and desire to protect him. This is probably why Donizetti gave her such *gorgeous* music to sing. For try hard as I can, I find nothing evil in her to bring out.' *(Courtesy of Christina Burton)*

Left: ANNA TOMOWA SINTOW as the Countess in *Capriccio*, 'an opera in which one senses Strauss's presence and feels he is almost one of the family. His philosophy is written into the role of the composer and his music, especially those marvellous songs, at once so earthy and so lofty.' *(Courtesy of Anna Tomowa Sintow)*

Right: TERESA BERGANZA as Carmen, the role that changed her life and whose 'spirit entered into me with such force that it compelled me to liberate myself from all my own repressions and self-imposed limitations. Suddenly, I, too, felt free, determined that nothing and no one could hold me back or put brakes on me any more.' *(Christina Burton)*

Below: AGNES BALTSA as Princess Eboli in *Don Carlos* with Herbert von Karajan, 'who moulded and formed me both as an artist and a human being . . . he was the greatest musical aesthete of the century and, almost unconsciously, you *had* to sing as he conducted and produce a long, seamless line, like a rainbow – the famous "Karajan line".' *(Siegfried Lauterwasser)*

Left: CHRISTA LUDWIG, a living legend among singers, is satisfied with her brilliant career and is 'what Oriental people call "centred", moderate, non-excessive which, vocally speaking, is true of the mezzo soprano voice. We are in the middle. So I am a woman of the middle, not extreme, either in my voice or my wishes, but content with my lot . . .' *(Siegfried Lauterwasser)*

Below: TATIANA TROYANOS, a compelling singing actress, as Romeo in *I Capuleti ed i Montecchi.* She attaches enormous importance to the text. 'If you think about the words, and then look at the music to see how the *composer* responded to them, then all that's needed is to decide what *you* can do, with your own voice, to bring out those colours.' *(Bill Cooper)*

Opposite top: GRACE BUMBRY as Salome, her first soprano role, after years as one of the world's greatest mezzos. To this day, she insists she would like to be remembered as a singer whose voice defied classification. *(Christina Burton)*

Opposite bottom: BRIGITTE FASSBAENDER as Octavian in *Der Rosenkavalier,* a role she 'had a chance to develop over a period of twenty years, in minutest detail, to the point of feeling completely under his skin, and never found boring.' *(Donald Southern)*

Left: LUCIA VALENTINI TERRANI in one of her most famous Rossini roles, Isabella in *L'Italiana in Algeri*: 'A real prima donna who dominates the stage effortlessly and completely. The whole opera depends on her. Bright, resourceful and cunning, she is the one pulling all the strings, manipulating everyone in sight, including the audience, like a puppeteer.' *(Deutsche Grammophon)*

Below: FREDERICA VON STADE as Charlotte in *Werther* (with José Carreras in the title role), a part which despite its sadness she finds 'fun to do, because after playing so many boys and Cinderellas it is gratifying to play a heroine who by Act III has left her little-girl world and lives a great passion, which is what I think opera is about.' *(Donald Cooper)*

Karajan, who could be amazingly persuasive, had a different, far more attractive view of the role: 'He didn't want the usual "lump of old flesh" ("kein kaputes Fleisch", as he put it), but a still young, beautiful, stunningly dressed woman – a real rival for Salome – hissing out the most venomous thoughts with utmost composure.' Baltsa accepted only because she identified with Karajan's musical and aesthetic perceptions.

'He always opened up new paths for me and showed me new ways of interpreting roles that were miles away from the usual banal, superficial interpretations. You could never bluff your way around with him. Only the purest form of singing and music-making would do. The man was the greatest musical aesthete of the century and, almost unconsciously, you *had* to sing as he conducted and produce a long, seamless line like a rainbow – the famous Karajan line. And if you couldn't manage it you had to ask yourself why not, when three years ago, it had seemed perfectly feasible. So you got down to some really hard work and got your voice back in form. [Leontyne Price makes the same point about never getting away with second best when working with Karajan.] His personal magnetism was so intense that soon enough he hypnotized you into a trance-like state in which you relaxed and let everything happen naturally and, most important, *joyfully*. There was never anything flustered or hectic about the way he made music.

'But this joyous state was reached only after a long, meticulous preparation during which he instilled the musical form he wanted by first putting you into a very tight corset which he then proceeded to squeeze. Which is to say that he took your raw material – for which he presumably hired you in the first place – and moulded it into *his* musical ideal first by removing all the thorns, all the bad habits, you might have acquired elsewhere. And, like a soldier, you had to obey. But the joy came at the performance itself when after all the drilling you had gone through at rehearsals, he suddenly unleashed and set you free to explode and gallop like a wild animal. That is, he set you free to do what *he* wanted, but with *your* personality.*

Two years after *Salome*, Baltsa sang Eboli in Karajan's 1979 Salzburg Festival production of *Don Carlos*, revived in the 1986 Easter Festival, in which she scored one of the greatest triumphs of her career. The role is vocally and temperamentally ideal for her and she loves this 'sublime opera, steeped in the history and the personalities of a specific period.'

* In my book, *Maestro*, Karajan explained à propos of singers that he always warned them not to expect him to cue in their every entry. 'They have to sing as they want, as they have sung in rehearsals. In fact the whole thing is so much a part of them by then that they are not even *able* to do otherwise. And when they know exactly what to do *then* I can accompany them because they have been prepared in such a way that they think they are free. And when they think they are free they sing well.'

(This kind of depth and substance in a libretto is very important to her. She has so far always refused to sing Azucena in *Il trovatore*, for instance, because she finds the story and the libretto 'so nonsensical'.)

Baltsa's third role with Karajan in Salzburg was Octavian in his 1983 production of *Der Rosenkavalier*. (Meanwhile she had also scored another triumph in this Festival as Dorabella in Michael Hampe's production of *Cosi fan tutte* conducted by Riccardo Muti.) The first time she had sung Octavian, in 1970 at the Vienna State Opera, she says she had fallen 'head over heels in love with this young man and all his surprises, sorrows and tender moments with the Marschallin, and used to portray him as a boy in a constant state of feverish youthful enthusiasm and exultation. But Karajan wanted a stiller, more restrained interpretation, possibly because he wanted the music to say it all. I noticed that during the most ecstatic moments in the orchestra he kept us singers particularly still. Left to my own devices, I would have gone for a more intense contact between him and the Marschallin. But maybe my brand of Greek passion didn't exist in eighteenth-century Vienna!'

Like many of her colleagues, Baltsa found Karajan the director much less satisfying or enriching to work with than Karajan the conductor. She recalls that whenever disagreements occurred he tended to resort to 'do it because I say so' – tactics he *never* resorted to as a conductor – whereas in Baltsa's view 'the mark of a great stage director is the ability to tailor his conception to his cast and adapt his ideas to their personalities. This is what Jean-Pierre Ponnelle [who died prematurely of a heart attack in summer 1988] was a genius at doing. When we worked together for *Carmen* in Zurich, for instance, his production was designed to bring out my best qualities, and drew every ounce of blood I possessed out of me. Yet later he created a totally different, equally valid Carmen, *in the same production*, for Teresa Berganza.'

The interpretation of Carmen that Baltsa and Ponnelle developed in Zurich was 'tailor-made for me, for my voice, my brain and body, my strengths and weaknesses, my capacities, perversities and all possibilities. I am a creature of emotional extremes; my whole human make up, my entire range of emotional colours, were there, to the point where I no longer felt I was *performing* Carmen, I was *being* Carmen.' Baltsa's Carmen was a creature of flesh-and-blood, a wilful, devil-may-care sixteen-year-old and, like Berganza's, definitely not a whore. 'It is not she but the people around her who create the atmosphere of unrest and commotion that surrounds her. She herself is quite unselfconscious about the degree of fascination she exerts on other people. But she only has to appear out of the factory for men to flock to her within minutes, like bees to honey. One of her great attractions, of course, is her independence and her unpredictability. No one knows what she might do next and this makes her irresistible. "Now I love you, now I don't, so make yourself scarce" is her attitude, but other people are unable to follow and accept her sudden switches of mood. This unpredictability is the key to her.'

Musically, the key is to be found in those chords, which Baltsa calls the 'Death Chords', that Bizet inserts into the introduction, and which are repeated the moment she first sets eyes on Don José. 'This look implies: "I have seen and noticed you, I want you and mean to have you even if, in so doing, I am signing my death warrant. If it has to be, so be it, I don't care."' In fact the only thing Carmen cares about is being free to live life as she wants. And in Jean-Pierre's production we 'brought out all her capacity for passion, hate, and loneliness. It was, along with Karajan's *Don Carlos*, the greatest *Sternstunde* of my career. I experienced such ecstasy, such human and artistic exultation that if, at the end, I'd been told I could never sing again, I wouldn't have minded.'

Yet when she came to perform the role in Salzburg, she found, to her dismay, that Karajan wanted nothing like this. He rejected everything she had done in Zurich, but without seeming to have a definite alternative interpretation. 'I felt as if someone had amputated both my legs but failed to provide me with crutches, either. He just had no specific conception to suggest. The whole production seemed like a hole, a backdrop for some folkloric scenery (complete with imported flamenco dancers).' In this case, he lacked the 'genius of directors like Ponnelle, who have the knack of bringing out the best qualities, and minimizing the weaknesses of each of their performers.'

But when Karajan and Baltsa had come together to record the work for Deutsche Grammophon, both had been enthusiastic about each other. 'It took me a long time to find a Carmen with obsession in her voice', he commented, while Baltsa was thrilled about the fact that 'he refined my interpretation. While Ponnelle gave me the wildness, the grit in Carmen, Karajan gave me the perfume, the whipped cream, all the delicate filigree work. To have performed Carmen in a production directed by Ponnelle and conducted by Karajan would have been nirvana. Yet I suspect we are not meant to experience nirvana on stage . . .' The 1985 Salzburg production certainly wasn't that. In fact it was the only boring Karajan production I have seen.

Its revival in summer 1986 led to the break-up of the Karajan–Baltsa artistic collaboration. Tensions and disagreements mounted during rehearsals and reached such a point that at the open dress rehearsal Karajan dismissed Baltsa from the production and the Salzburg Festival – a sad loss for both artists and the musical world at large. (Happily, though, the two patched up their differences towards the end of Karajan's life and, in recognition of all she owed him, both in terms of 'career' and artistic growth, Baltsa sang in the Mozart Requiem in his memory at Salzburg Cathedral shortly after his death in summer 1989.)

Although strong-willed, Baltsa is neither hell bent on 'doing her own thing' on stage nor averse to trying new ideas, provided the director convinces her. Elijah Moshinsky, who directed her first production of *Samson et Dalila* in 1985 at Covent Garden and who stimulated her into delivering one of the most riveting portrayals of her career was struck by the extent to which she is prepared to take risks and make demands on her personality. 'We worked through the emotions rather than the text, and relied a great deal on improvisation, trying out things on the spot. Baltsa has an incredible spontaneity – to an extent I have personally never come across in an opera singer although people say that Callas also had it to an amazing degree. It's this fiery thing, not in the sense of general tempestuousness but an ability to make everything she does look fresh as if it were invented that very moment. This is especially fantastic in an opera like *Samson et Dalila* which is about sex and possession. The way I had directed it the first time round it wasn't about sex at all and came across as slightly dull and sanctimonious. I knew the sex was there, but I couldn't get it out of my original cast (John Vickers and Shirley Verrett). This time, with Baltsa and Domingo, it was a whole new thing and the two stimulated and forced each other to work really hard.

'I got the impression Baltsa is well aware of the power exerted by her stage presence and decided the thing to do was to *use* this power, *use* her presence. Another quality, crucial for Dalila, was this Greek side of hers which enables her to do very sudden switches of mood and temperament, much more sudden than most people can manage. She can do a seduction scene absolutely convincingly and then immediately undercut it with a look that straightaway shows the other side of the character. This very exciting quality is particularly good for depicting treachery and in Dalila's case these twists and shifts of mood immediately excited the audience.' ('This is an artist who makes the stage seem livelier every time she appears on it,' wrote *Opera*, 'not just her own corner but those of others as well.')

Baltsa sang Dalila again at Covent Garden in spring 1991 and it is one of the roles she will retain in her repertoire in the foreseeable future. Since *Carmen* her voice has grown bigger and more dramatic and psychologically speaking she yearns for more real, flesh-and-blood characters than some of the sedate, less earthy roles of her earlier years. She is planning to drop some of her Rossini heroines, such as Rosina (the November 1990 performances at Covent Garden were reportedly her last) and La Cenerentola after singing it for the last time in November 1991 at the Théâtre de la Monnaie in Brussels. She will, however, retain Isabella in *L'Italiana in Algeri* which, along with Charlotte in *Werther* she sang in Munich and Brussels during 1991. Two roles that excite her at present and in which she has scored major personal successes are Elisabetta in Donizetti's *Maria Stuarda* (which she first sang in 1989 at the Vienna State Opera and recorded for Philips and plans to sing again in 1992 and spring 1993) and Santuzza in *Cavalleria rusticana* (which she first sang in January 1990 at the Vienna State Opera and recorded for Deutsche Grammophon), which she had been longing to sing for years, but waited until she felt the moment was right.

Santuzza is Baltsa's first verismo role and she stresses that although it demands every ounce of blood from the performer, in pure vocal terms verismo is less exacting than *bel canto*. 'The orchestration is so large and dense that it cushions and protects you by diverting some of the attention away from the singer, whereas in *bel canto* you are totally exposed. This rich orchestration is also a great help in finding the right vocal colours.' When Baltsa first sang the role in Vienna, both public and critics decided the role fitted her to a T. 'That Agnes Baltsa's Santuzza would be a creature of passion, temperament and fire was to be expected,' wrote *Die Presse*.'What came as a surprise was her ability to develop her portrayal from emotional intimacy to the final outburst. Nothing appeared artificial or calculated. Baltsa's Santuzza is not a raging fury and her revenge is not the wild wrath of Nemesis, but the revolt of a woman in love against humiliation and disdain. The "social outcast" theme was central to the production and Santuzza's horrified cry "I am excommunicated" was delivered by Baltsa in a truly heart-rending way.'

Giuseppe Sinopoli, who conducted the Vienna performances and the Deutsche Grammophon recording of *Cavalleria rusticana*, considers Baltsa the ideal interpreter of Santuzza because she is an artist 'who combines frenzy – a Dionysian, manic streak – with control. It is a *theoretical* frenzy, always tempered by the intellect. A fundamental part of the ancient Dionysian rites was to come to the point of consummating the act but never actually doing so, just coming to the hilt of the *possibility* of consummation. Hers is the most interesting Santuzza I have seen because it is a mixture of passion with the deep suffering that comes from her sense of social isolation. She succeeds in encapsulating the two different kinds of pain – the rejected woman and the social outcast – in a most fascinating way.'

Away from the stage, Baltsa is an active, thoroughly contemporary woman, fond of swimming, shopping for clothes and antiques and not averse to letting off steam occasionally in discos. For many years she was married to baritone Günther Missenhart. Most of the time she travels with her elder sister who is her best friend and a vital part of her life-support-system. Intensely Greek in looks and temperament, Baltsa says that contact with anything Greek – be it food, music or landscape – somehow revives and recharges her batteries. She loves living life to the full and she loves her work passionately. Indeed, as Elijah Moshinsky observes, she is 'erotically excited by being on stage', and as she herself once explained to a German magazine, 'I cannot sing without living and I cannot live without singing.'

TERESA BERGANZA

'WHEN TALKING OF Teresa Berganza, I tend to wax lyrical,' says Janine Reiss, the French coach who knows the voice inside out and has worked with singers for decades, 'because to me she is the *ideal* artist, a mixture of wisdom and simplicity. Here is a singer who can play the piano and read music perfectly and who has immense respect for the score and the text. At the same time she is a complete woman who brings to her interpretations things that only a real woman can. For it goes without saying that a singer can bring more to her interpretations by being a complete woman who has lived a full life and Berganza is the perfect expression of this human phenomenon.'

Berganza herself is more modest and attributes her success to her good fortune in finding a great teacher at the very start of her studies: 'There is no such thing as a great singer without a good teacher. Without an Elvira de Hidalgo there might have been no Callas,' declares Teresa Berganza, one of the best lyric mezzos of the past thirty years and one whose voice, in her mid-fifties, is still an instrument to reckon with. 'The bond between myself and my own teacher, Lola Rodriguez de Aragon, a pupil of Elisabeth Schumann's, is stronger and deeper than that between mother and daughter. Surprising though this may sound, my teacher knows more about me than my mother because she knows my *artistic* side, that dark, inner, mysterious side which nobody else knows.'

Berganza believes singing teachers are extremely important people in a young singer's life and should therefore be scrupulously honest and really *know* what they're about. 'Otherwise they risk ruining not only a voice but an artist's whole life. Yet nowadays many people, including pianists, set themselves up as singing teachers without the necessary experience or qualifications. I was lucky enough to find a teacher who understood my voice and personality and prepared me properly. I have learnt all my roles and songs with her and we still work together to this day. Whenever I come across a vocal problem – such as losing the quality of a certain tone – she invariably helps me solve it.'

When Berganza first arrived in Lola Rodriguez's class at the Madrid Conservatoire she was 'a complete virgin' as far as vocal technique was concerned. She had short breath, three different voices that didn't seem to join together and, because 'Spain was still a very closed and isolated country', had never seen an opera in her life. The first aria she had to sing for her teacher was Cherubino's 'Voi che sapete' from *Le nozze di Figaro*. 'which may sound like the simplest of tunes but is one of the most difficult arias in the lyric-mezzo repertoire. Any of Carmen's arias is easy in comparison.' They worked on it for weeks until Rodriguez's clever choice of exercises enabled her pupil to blend her registers into a seamless whole and produce the evenness of tone essential for sustaining a Mozartian line. The moment Berganza felt 'Mozart's music securely lodged in my throat, I became addicted to it for life'.

After she had mastered this aria they began working on the rest of the role, placing great emphasis on the text and on learning what the entire opera is about, something she has come to consider crucial in the training of young singers, if they are to bring *meaning* to their interpretations. 'When I first went to audition for the Director of the Aix en Provence Festival [where she was to make her operatic début as Dorabella in July 1957], I knew *all* of *Cosi fan tutte* and *Le nozze di Figaro* from start to finish, all those recitatives and duets. The arias are sometimes the easiest parts of an opera. Many people can sing a Verdi aria, for instance. But how many can cope with the entire operas, with all the duets, recitatives and quartets? It is only after learning a role in its entirety that one can decide whether or not one is able to sing it.'

Berganza, born in Madrid in 1935, had made her professional début in 1956 at the Madrid Atheneum with Schumann's *Frauenliebe und Leben*. This was a year before her enormously successful operatic début at Aix-en-Provence. A month later, she sang her first Cherubino at Deauville in a star-studded production that included Graziella Sciutti as Susanna. Cherubino soon became a 'mascot' part which she has sung all over the world – over 100 performances in twenty-five years – without ever getting bored with it. 'Unlike some parts which *can* become boring over the years, Cherubino doesn't, probably because there are so many different ways of singing it. You could sing "Non so più cosa son, cosa faccio" in at least a dozen different ways, for example.' In earlier days, she used to pay more attention to the music than the text, so it took a while for her to get under the character's skin. But by the time she sang Cherubino at the Teatro Colon in Buenos Aires with Gundula Janowitz as the Countess, she had come to identify with him so much that, during his recitative with the Countess, she almost felt a man's frisson which 'rather alarmed me at the time. Needless to say this would never have happened if I hadn't mastered the music and the vocal demands of the role and felt free to lose myself in the character.'

In 1977, Berganza sang Zerlina in Joseph Losey's historic film of *Don Giovanni* and in her impersonation this 'special peasant' emerged not as the usual feather-brained soubrette but a mature, sensual woman. 'In her own admittance, she is an expert in love and in those days few young girls were afforded the opportunity to be that! She is an experienced woman with certain instincts, which is why Don Giovanni immediately singles her out from among all the other peasants. There is about her that certain something, that instinctive sensuality a man can sense right away. This has nothing to do with the way one looks or dresses and it can never be learnt. One either has it or not. It is the same something Carmen has in such abundance, and what immediately distinguishes her from all the hundreds of other cigarette factory girls and ensures it is to *her* that all the men flock.'

Berganza considers Mozart's pure, crystalline music the best school for singers, as indeed it is for pianists. (Leonard Bernstein always said that he practised longer and harder for a Mozart sonata or concerto than for any other piano music.) It demands an almost instrumental accuracy and precision and all singers would profit from the discipline of turning their voice into a perfect musical instrument. 'Personally I try to imitate a cello, the most sensual and beautiful of instruments, whose sound I liken to that of a mezzo-soprano. The cello is very special, because one embraces it, one places it between one's legs, like a man or a woman, and because of this its sound is different from that of other instruments. It's more visceral and seems to come almost from inside the body – like the voice. And ideally the human voice should sound as even and seamless, from top to bottom, as a cello.'

Berganza's teacher took great pains to explain that the voice should have one single sonority – even though, depending on the interpretation of what one is singing, it can have a myriad shades and nuances of colour and dynamics – and, of course, no audible change of gear between registers. 'In reality there is no such thing as the "head" or the "chest" voice. There is only one voice, i.e. two vocal cords that function through the vibrations caused by the passage of air, through well-controlled breathing. What creates the *illusion* of a head or a chest voice is the fact that there are several resonating cavities. In the centre of the voice there is a zone where one can sometimes hear the passage from what is called the chest voice – but which, as I've explained, is no such thing – and my teacher worked very hard to ensure one never heard this transition in my voice.'

After her success as Cherubino and Dorabella in summer 1957, Berganza spent the next decade singing mostly Mozart and Rossini, of whose music she soon became a leading exponent. Indeed, her interpretations of Rosina in *Il barbiere di Siviglia*, Isabella in *L'Italiana in Algeri* and the title role in *La Cenerentola*, which she has sung all over the world, can be considered models of Rossini singing. 'A triumphant success, bringing to the part that peculiar Spanish quality of voice and personality which had characterized Conchita Supervia's classic performance of the same part,' wrote Spike Hughes after her Glyndebourne performances of *La Cenerentola* in 1959* (she had been invited back to Glyndebourne after making a triumphant début there as Cherubino the previous year), while Harold Rosenthal remarked enthusiastically in *Opera* after Berganza's first Rosina at Covent Garden that 'her vocalism was sheer joy. She sings as naturally as most of us talk, and her aristocratic phrasing and legato singing will long be treasured.'

Berganza also sang Rosina in Jean-Pierre Ponnelle's famous La Scala production, conducted by Claudio Abbado, which was also filmed. Indeed, she associates Abbado with some of the most rewarding operatic experiences of her career – 'moments when I was no longer conscious of being myself' – which, apart from *Barbiere*, included productions of *Le nozze di Figaro*, *L'Italiana in Algeri* and *Carmen*. Another conductor from whom she learnt a great deal during her formative decade is Carlo Maria Giulini. 'Great conductors are always enormously stimulating because they bring new, and invariably interesting ideas and insights into a role. Even a new idea about a recitative can change the way you look at the whole part, and in those early days Giulini gave me lots of ideas like that about Rossini. Now, I form the characters by myself, often after doing a lot of research, reading and visiting museums where relevant.'

She learns new roles alone, shutting herself in her sitting room and reading the score through, occasionally accompanying herself at the piano. The first thing is to decide whether the tessitura suits her voice. Occasionally she can be mistaken, though, because although in principle the range up to C natural is fine for her there may be passages in the role that she can't negotiate. Examples are Eboli and Violetta. In the former role she could sing the arias but not the trios and in the latter the range is no problem but the tessitura would be. 'In fact La Scala offered me *La traviata* in 1960 but I had the will to refuse, even though this renunciation was deeply frustrating because I had loved Violetta since 1957 when I saw Maria Callas singing it. I shook and trembled with emotion during and after that performance – those eyes, that economy of gesture that made a look suffice where others might have indulged in all manner of histrionics – and it marked me for life as an artist. I decided I'd rather try and do it this way or not at all.'

* Berganza dislikes the comparison of voices: 'One voice has nothing to do with another'.

Berganza had had the chance to work closely with Callas in 1958 when she sang Neris to her Medea in Dallas. She found this an unforgettable and, in some ways, a surprising experience: 'She was the tenderest, in fact the only *real* colleague in my career. I sang the nurse and had to be made up to look like an old woman. But she came up to me and said to the director: "Let her be a young nurse, let me have a young Neris for a change, she looks much prettier this way." And throughout the rehearsal and performance period she treated me like a younger sister, taking me to all the parties, which made me feel like Alice in Wonderland, and never allowing me to be alone in my hotel room. I also remember that when I got a long, tremendous ovation after my aria, which was sung with my back to the audience, leaning on her, she whispered to me: "Turn around and acknowledge the applause", and gently turned me round herself. This is why, often when I hear people talking about her, it doesn't seem as if they're talking about the woman *I* knew. After the Dallas *Medea*, she often suggested I go and visit her in Paris but, stupidly as it turned out, I never did because I felt I might be disturbing her. And the day she died I felt deeply remorseful. Who knows, if more of us, colleagues she liked, had kept in touch, it might have helped her . . .

'As it is, no singer ever *gave* me so much as she did in those early days in Dallas. And I learnt a tremendous amount from her about the art of discipline: for example, how hard she worked, with her bad eyesight, walking up and down those stairs so that it would look natural. This is almost Lesson Number One for all artists: making everything look effortless and natural to the audience even though arriving at this state of naturalness may represent hours, days, *years* of work. Callas was also the first to turn opera into real theatre and show that the more one brings out the drama in opera, the stronger the music emerges. No one since has ever touched her.'

Berganza's repertoire also includes Gluck, Handel and a large concert literature which, superb musician that she is (a former student of the piano and conducting as well), affords her great satisfaction. Indeed she listens to music all the time – 'I need to be *fed* by music' – except when reading. Although she realized that, as a lyric mezzo, some of the great Verdi dramatic mezzo roles such as Eboli, Amneris and Azucena would always be beyond her reach, by the mid 1970s she began to yearn for more dramatic parts, The first was Charlotte in *Werther*; and then she began thinking about Carmen. 'The moment one touches these dramatic roles one feels like singing only this kind of music. Everything else, all the Mozart and Rossini parts, begin to seem lightweight.'

She explains that her journey towards Carmen was long and produced monumental resonances in her own life. Although her father, whom she worshipped, was a liberal-minded, highly cultured man who took his children to museums, concerts and plays all the time and, almost an atheist, her upbringing had nevertheless been very strict and 'very Spanish. Nobody at home ever mentioned sex and I was never allowed to go out with boys. All this had left its marks on me. Although I had married and had my children young, I was a very inhibited person, locked in a very "Spanish" marriage in which my husband's word was law, not only in the home but also in my career. He made all the decisions about what, where and when I sang. I was so held back by my upbringing that I couldn't liberate myself from this rather closed mentality and needless to say, couldn't even contemplate taking on Carmen, that quintessentially free spirit. I was a bit like Rosina in *Barbiere*: imprisoned and waiting for an Almaviva. But as I had a family, I had built walls around myself and refused even to look at another man.'

Then, out of the blue, Peter Diamand, then Director of the Edinburgh Festival, proposed *Carmen* and his proposal was to revolutionize Berganza's life. She immediately threw herself into Merimée's play which she kept by her bedside for weeks. Then she studied sketches of gypsy life in that period and went to Seville to reacquaint herself with Spanish gypsies and the way they live *now*. She found they have the same dignity and are a lot less extrovert than people think. In moments of great feeling and passion they explode, but the rest of the time they tend to be rather contained. The women in particular she found similar to Indian women in the sense that they are certainly exotic but tend to behave with great restraint and decorum in the company of men. 'The concept of the unkempt gypsy is a myth, at least as far as Spanish gypsies are concerned. Reality was closer to an old sketch I had found, of three gypsies combing each other's hair in preparation for meeting their menfolk.

'This was the way I began to enter Carmen's world. And in so doing, at the same time I began to liberate myself from my own repressions and self-imposed brakes, the first and greatest of which was my husband. Because of Carmen, through her honesty and uncompromising refusal to lie, which became part of me, too, I found the courage to separate from my husband. Her spirit entered into me with such force that it frightened me because it seemed to dictate and make it immediately clear that as I no longer loved this man, I should leave him. Before finally giving in to this force, I spent a couple of very difficult years battling against it and trying to continue with life as it was. But this force was stronger than me and kept urging me to be free, to be my own mistress, no longer under my husband's yoke. Carmen liberated me from all this for ever.'

She vividly remembers the moment when she decided to take the plunge. It was August 1977, at the precise moment when she sang 'La liberté, la liberté' in the finale of Act II at the dress rehearsal in Edinburgh. Suddenly she, too, felt free, felt that nothing and no one could hold her back or put brakes on her any more. Her husband was with her, and there and then she told him she could no longer go on with the marriage. She moved herself and her children, whom she loves passionately, into a hotel and was to spend the next three years in hotels. 'My children, who were there, understood what I had been experiencing at the rehearsals, they understood the freedom of the gypsies which is not irresponsible or licentious but the freedom to go where one wants at any time, without being answerable to anyone. Today I am in Paris but tomorrow I might feel like being in Bali and who's to stop me doing that? For this reason Carmen should never be played as a prostitute, but as a woman who is totally honest – much more honest than Donna Anna in *Don Giovanni* who is dying of love for the Don but is too constricted by social convention to do anything about it. This total freedom of the gypsy is what I associate with Carmen, whom I look upon and love as a friend who liberated me from my yoke and restored my *joie de vivre*.' Eventually Berganza found a man, José ('Pepe') Rifa, to whom she feels closer than to anyone since her father and who appears to have 'everything I need and like' in a man. (Teresa and Pepe were married in April 1986. After 'a ten year rehearsal period', it was time for the performance! It was a very special ceremony. Five minutes later, Berganza's elder daughter married her mother's piano accompanist, and has since given Teresa a grand-daughter.)

She considers herself extremely fortunate that for her first *Carmen* she was surrounded by a first-class team who helped her every step of the way: the cast included Domingo as Don José, Mirella Freni as Micaela and Tom Krause as Escamillo. The conductor was Claudio Abbado, about whom she enthused earlier. And the production was directed by Piero Faggioni, whom she considers a genius and who set her free from any remaining traces of inhibition and created one of the most memorable stagings of *Carmen* in living memory. 'He is one of the rare directors who actually have a stage *technique* and are able to teach you a great deal about movement, possibly because he has been an actor.' Crucial, too, was Janine Reiss, eminent French coach and also one of the most inspired teachers of interpretation in our day, 'with an incredible ability to help singers. She worked on every detail of the text and on diction, because French is a difficult language to sing. Unlike Italian, it has no open vowels and unlike German, its consonants are not clearly or strongly articulated.'

'Carmen is one of the most mutilated scores in the operatic repertoire', says Janine Reiss, 'because to begin with, the character is excessive – a free woman who, at the time of the première, shocked the French bourgeois who immediately feared the liberation of their own wives and daughters – and various singers have turned her into something even more excessive and usually vulgar. I tend to know from the moment I set eyes on a singer, what trap she will fall into. Anyway Teresa kept refusing this role for *years* because she detested the usual vulgar, hip-swinging, cigarette-in-mouth, whoreish interpretations. Needless to say, nothing is further from the truth in the score or the text than portraying Carmen as a whore. On the contrary: she is a woman who has never *ever* made love for money, only for the joy of it, and who is honest enough to want to tell a man when it is all over.

'So, when Teresa told me she had refused Peter Diamand's invitation to sing Carmen at the Edinburgh Festival because she hated all that, I replied that "all that" was not in the score and invited her home to my flat in Paris where I played the score through. She was amazed and stupefied and said she had never heard it like this before. After another session, she decided to answer "yes" and asked Peter Diamand to engage me as coach. The result was a *Carmen* brought back to its original truth, and the production became a "reference Carmen". Now we know this is what Carmen is like. But it is to her we owe the fact, and this extreme professional honesty and fidelity to the text is something she has in common with Callas. Amusingly enough, at the dress rehearsal of the first year, she told me the critics would say this was very interesting but it was "not Carmen", which they duly did. But the second year, they praised it sky high!'

Berganza herself stresses that 'everything is so clearly indicated if you follow the score. Yet you often hear Carmen sung differently from the way Bizet intended. In the Card Scene, for example, there isn't a single *forte* in the score, because here Carmen is singing about fate, she is face to face with destiny and feels a premonition of death. She is singing very softly to herself as this is hardly a moment in which to shout. Similarly, if you listen to the music at the finale, it depicts Carmen literally walking to her death, walking straight on to the knife of Don José, whom she had begun to despise from the moment when, in Act II, he interrupts their love-making to answer the regimental call. All in all, there is a deeply Spanish truth about this opera.'

Apart from this historic Edinburgh Festival production, which was later also taken to Hamburg and Paris (but sadly minus Abbado and Freni), Berganza has also sung Carmen at Covent Garden, Chicago, Nice and in Ponnelle's Zurich production. Interestingly enough, though this was the same production in which Agnes Baltsa sang her first Carmen, Ponnelle adapted and created a wholly different staging for Berganza.

And rightly so because the voice is the most personal of all musical instruments, the sum total of the whole artistic personality in whose throat it lodges. As such, it is also subject to every fluctuation of health and mood and it can also become an obsession which, Berganza admits, is what has happened to her.

'I'm the sort of person who loves and enjoys life, food, drink, clothes, art, my family, my friends. But I live in a state of obsession about my voice. The first thing I have to check on opening my eyes in the morning is whether the voice is in place. By trying out various high-pitched sounds, I can find this out within minutes. If it works, the way is clear for a good day; if not, the day is ruined, regardless of whether or not I happen to be working at the time. The frustration will be the same, because the voice is the centre of my life. My husband always says we live in a *ménage-à-trois*: he, myself and the Voice. And as far as priorities go, the Voice wins hands down! It has to be this way with anyone who is a true artist, I'm afraid, because ultimately, nothing can compare with the sensation we experience when singing well – and we don't always. But during those rare near-perfect evenings one almost touches Heaven. The only thing that could compare with the sensation in terms of ecstasy is the actual moment of childbirth or one of those equally rare moments of rapture in love that occur once or twice a lifetime!'

People often think singers are egotistical but, she points out, the true artists among them are not centred around *themselves* but around *the Voice*, this gift they carry inside them for which, because music is holy, they are answerable to God. 'We should therefore treat this gift from God as sacred. If one thinks about it, there are very few singers in the world. Therefore having a voice *is* clearly a gift – a gift to be used only when we feel in a position to give it everything we have and, through it, heal and put other people in touch with Heaven, too. If I don't feel in a position to do this, I don't sing.'

Being able to express oneself in this fashion, through the voice, makes all the sacrifices demanded by a singing career worthwhile. But Berganza stresses that singers should not go as far as sacrificing *everything* because this will not only make for a very sad and empty life after retirement, but also make their singing arid, bereft of the juice, the mellowness that come from living life to the full. She herself is deeply happy to have had her children while still young because this helped her strike the right balance between her public and private life. Her career started early, at twenty-one, and she says that by the age of twenty-five she had, as a pessimist, already begun to worry about retirement and what she would do afterwards! 'I always thought about the dreadful truth that one day the career will be over and therefore I should try and savour every minute of it while I still can.' (Since then she has sung Poulenc's *La Voix humaine* in Madrid in March 1991 and *Rinaldo* the following month, and will sing *Carmen* with Domingo at the Seville Expo in April 1992.) 'But I don't know *what* I'll do afterwards. Maybe something in the straight theatre.'

GRACE BUMBRY

FEW FEMALE SINGERS since Callas have been 'divas' in the real sense of the word – combining an exceptional voice and the highest degree of artistry with star quality, both on and off stage. Grace Bumbry is one of them and also, along with Leontyne Price, one of the first black singers to sweep the international operatic world off its feet. Price was a soprano and Bumbry, to begin with at least, a mezzo; and both had large and lustrous voices, with that deep sensuous colouring and smoky timbre characteristic of black singers. And to this they added a spiritual quality and a visceral passion equally characteristic of black artists.

Bumbry became a star virtually overnight in the summer of 1961 when, at the age of twenty-four, she was the first black singer to appear at the Bayreuth Festival. Her 'Black Venus' in Wieland Wagner's production of *Tannhäuser* aroused considerable controversy and made international headlines. Like Callas, Bumbry was smart enough to realize that, if an artist is vocally and dramatically outstanding, a little controversy, even the occasional scandal, only adds spice to their career and enhances their fame. She was quick to capitalize on her 'Black Venus' fame and to surround herself with all the trappings of success – a fleet of sleek sports cars, *haute couture* clothes, a bevy of furs, a villa on the shores of Lake Lugano in Switzerland and a devoted following of fans not averse to paying for a special décor for her dressing room in certain cities. She became that relatively rare commodity: a star mezzo.

It is hard to imagine that this woman, with her commanding stage presence and imperious will, was once a shy, diffident youngster, so lacking in self-confidence that she never dreamt of being an opera singer, setting her sights on a career as a recitalist. Grace Melzia Bumbry was the youngest of three children and the only daughter born into a religious and musical family in St Louis, Missouri. Her father was a railway clerk, her mother was a teacher. Her father played the piano, and young Grace began taking piano lessons at the age of seven 'to please my mother'. Both parents sang in different church choirs, and her two brothers in a youth chorus, and on certain days when they were all rehearsing for their various choirs, they had no one at home with whom to leave young Grace. So she was taken along, too, and by the time she was eleven she, too, was singing in the Union Memorial Methodist Church.

Two years later, at the age of thirteen, she joined the 'a cappella' summer choir at Sumner High School and began to study singing with Kenneth Billups, who taught her the technique of correct breathing which lies at the base of good singing. 'I was very lucky to get as good a teacher as Mr Billups in my home town. Believe me, it is a matter of luck to fall into the hands of a good teacher. If you get a bad first teacher or teachers, they can wreck your voice for the rest of your life.'

Encouraged by Billups, who was the school choir director, Bumbry entered and won a teenage singing competition run by the local radio station, KMOX. The prize consisted of a $1,000 dollar War Bond, a trip to New York and a $1,000 scholarship to the St Louis Institute of Music. What the radio executives did not realize was that the Institute did not accept black students. As a compromise, it offered segregated private lessons – a proposal proudly rejected by Grace Bumbry, her parents and teachers. 'I was never, until that point in my life, really aware that there was a racial difference. But it didn't make me bitter. And in fact I was rather glad not to have to accept their scholarship because I wanted to go to Boston University, and that is where I went. So I didn't have to be submitted to the humiliation of taking private classes.'

Embarrassed and keen to make amends for this humiliation, the Director of KMOX Radio Station, who believed in this young talent, arranged for her to audition in the national network's well known 'Talent Scouts' programme, hosted by Arthur Godfrey, which she passed and went on to win.

Bumbry sang Princess Eboli's aria 'O don fatale' from *Don Carlos* and her electrifying rendition reduced Arthur Godfrey to tears, and won her a scholarship to Boston University, later transferred to Northwestern University. There she met Lotte Lehmann, who on the spot decided to take her to California to study with her privately at Santa Barbara, while working for a Music Degree at the Musical Academy of the West. 'I've found a star. She's going to be as famous as Marian Anderson and she's my discovery,' wrote Lehmann in a scrapbook, bequeathed to Bumbry on her death. 'She's a natural. It's like turning on electricity.' Lehmann was to prove the most significant formative influence in Bumbry's life, 'the saving grace, a real godsend for me. I always say my mother gave me my first birth and Madame Lehmann gave me my second. She opened me to the world.'

Bumbry's aim at the time was to follow the paths of Marian Anderson (who declared after an audition that Bumbry's was 'a magnificent voice of great beauty'), and Dorothy Maynor as a recitalist. But as she became more deeply involved in her study of interpretation, Lotte Lehmann began to detect more and more of an operatic nature than either of them suspected. 'What is amazing, in retrospect, was that I was such a shy, inhibited person that I couldn't begin to see myself in any of those extroverted operatic roles.' The change happened virtually overnight, after one of the most frustrating days of her life.

'One day, Lotte Lehmann decided I should sing the role of Amneris in class, and sing it as *she* wanted me to. She realized I had the right voice for it, an enormous voice, and that all the colour and all the emotion were there. But I couldn't express them with the right movements. Well, on that particular day, she was determined I should get it right. I tried and tried and tried, but it just wouldn't work. This was the most awful experience I've ever had in my life, the tears were rolling down, because I *wanted* to please her, I wanted to do what she asked, I knew it was the right thing. And I felt an utter fool. I went home that evening, dismally depressed. I shouted at myself that if everyone else in class could do it, so could I, I wasn't stupid. It was just a question of freeing myself from my inhibitions. I can only verbalize what I mean by saying that, in order to perform, you have to leave yourself behind, you have to lose yourself in the character. Which is to say that you must get to the point where you forget about Grace Bumbry, or whoever *you* happen to be. All that matters is the character you are trying to portray. All this occurred to me, in a flash, as I was wallowing in frustration. And, as soon as I realized it, that was it. The next day I just did it. Lotte Lehmann couldn't believe her eyes, and neither could anyone else in class. She asked what had happened and I told her. She replied this was the quickest personality change she had ever witnessed. And it was all attributed to the fact that I realized I was being overly aware of myself. Being conscious of yourself is a sheer waste of energy.'

While studying interpretation with Lotte Lehmann, Bumbry continued perfecting her vocal technique, at her recommendation, with Armando Tokatyan. As he considered her voice was perfectly placed by nature he concentrated on developing her already solid technique by teaching her to do what she was doing *consciously*, to help her through a long career, and through those nights when she might feel physically below par owing to a cold. 'I can sing through a cold, provided it hasn't gone down to my throat. If it's only in the head and nose, I don't mind so much because sometimes it can make the sound that much more beautiful. If it *has* gone to my throat I won't sing, no matter what the circumstances. Mind you, you can still have problems even when it's only in the head, because you can't hear yourself properly. In such cases, the only thing to do is to vocalize and sing *technically*: I place the sound naturally and rely on that certain sensation you get in your head when the sound is correctly placed.'

Bumbry's first professional appearance was at Lotte Lehmann's 70th Birthday Celebration in 1958 at the Little Theatre of the California Palace of the Legion of Honour when, aged twenty-one, she sang the Schubert, Schumann and Brahms songs usually associated with her great teacher. That same year she won the national Marian Anderson Award and the Kimber Award in San Francisco. At the same time, she won a fellowship from the John Hay Whitney Foundation and a $1,000 dollar prize at the Metropolitan Opera Auditions of the Air, all of which enabled her to go abroad. Lehmann took her around the opera houses of Europe – London, Vienna, Salzburg and Bayreuth – for six months to listen and learn, and she spent the rest of 1959 studying French song with Pierre Bernac. She made her Paris début that year at the church of La Madeleine with the Paris Philharmonic Chorus in Bach's cantata *Actus Tragicus* (no. 106) and also scored a big success with the same group in Handel's *Messiah*.

Her operatic début was also in Paris, at the Opéra in March 1960, in the role of Amneris. The fact that she took the place by storm will come as no surprise to anyone who has seen Bumbry's Amneris – which she has performed all over the world including La Scala for her début in 1964-65, and later Covent Garden and the Metropolitan Opera (where she had made her début as Eboli) and which to this day remains the most vocally and dramatically dazzling I have seen. Her portrayal is based on what she had learnt from Lotte Lehmann, who had explained that 'Amneris has a lot in common with Ortrud in the sense that she is not sincere, except in her love for Radames. She starts off very cunningly in Act I, Scene II, trying to trap Aida into revealing her love for Radames and her cajoling, all that "my sister" business displays all the cunning a woman is capable of. After that, it becomes a matter only of revenge. Amneris cannot accept that the man she loves, the greatest hero of her people, is in love with her slave. She is a very imperious, one dimensional character – you know what she is thinking all the time – whereas Aida is more many-sided although, as you say, she, too, is insincere, up to a point.

'This is what Lotte Lehmann had wanted me to understand. More important, she wanted me to understand the connection between the words and the composer's dynamic markings, so that I could see where he was heading and *why* he required the singer to do certain things. She stressed that the dynamic markings are the real guideline to the nature of each character. This is true of anything one sings, be it opera or Lied. To find out what the composer wants, you have to look at his dynamic markings, and also at his basic tempo indications, to find out where the impetus lies within that dynamic marking. Then you have to ask yourself why he put a crescendo rather than a diminuendo at this point, and finally maybe you then begin to understand that this is because he wants this particular passage sung in this and not in any other way. There is always a reason for everything. The composers knew exactly what they wanted and why. You cannot write your own opera. The composer has already written it, and if you really follow the score, you will find every clue is there.

'Works like *Aida* are masterpieces. People say the opera was centred on Amneris. But if, as I do, you sing Aida as well [Bumbry first sang Aida when she was switching from mezzo to soprano in 1972, in Belgrade, and later in Munich, Wiesbaden and in Rossi's mega-spectacle production in Cairo, Paris (Arène de Bercy), London (Earls Court), and the Verona Arena], and sing it as it is written, there is no doubt as to who the real heroine is: it is Aida. Having sung both roles, I know what I'm talking about. The problem is that most singers don't sing Aida the way it is written. They sing it to fit their voices, without paying any attention to dynamics. For instance, in "O patria mia" there are dynamic markings never observed by lyric sopranos. And the section immediately following "O ciel, mio padre" is written so that the crescendo goes up and comes back down, ending in pianissimo. Needless to say, it is never sung that way. But Verdi wrote it like this for a reason and if you *can* do it the way he wrote it, this makes all the difference to the colouring and the excitement. There are scores of details like that: at the end of "O terra addio" there is a high B flat that should be sung pianissimo or dolce but is usually sung mezzo forte. Of course by then most sopranos are tired; it's human. But Verdi didn't write it for tired sopranos, he wrote it this way because in his day presumably there were singers capable of doing what he wanted.

'But back to Amneris; her most taxing moment, both vocally and dramatically, is Act IV, Scene I, the Judgement Scene, especially the last pages of it, and even more important is the build up to that climax. You have to build it up in such a way that your audience is also taken along with you. And then you must let them know *this* is the most important moment, not the ones before. Because in most cases you have more than one, you have two or three high moments. But you must establish in your mind which is *the* moment, the real climax, and work towards that.

'Vocally speaking, the most dramatic moments usually coincide with the highest notes. In Amneris's case, the highest note is an exposed B flat in the Judgement Scene. (She has a C flat in the Triumph Scene but it occurs in an ensemble.) You have to save yourself for these moments, because no matter how many wonderful low notes you may have or how beautiful your middle voice may be, if your high notes are not substantially affirmed, your audience will feel dissatisfied. They will begin to get worried, and you don't want them to get worried. They should feel very, very comfortable with what they are hearing and have the impression that everything is happening naturally and effortlessly. Personally, I have never had problems with the B flat in the Judgement Scene. But again, if you give out too much voice before, you will tire yourself for the top notes. This question of pacing is very much related to athletics: if runners or tennis players don't pace themselves properly, they, too, "soon run out of steam"!'

Pacing is something singers tend to learn through performance experience. Bumbry has always found the performances themselves not nearly as interesting as the preparation: the research into the background of the works and gradual, in-depth musical penetration. (When she was preparing Lady Macbeth, for instance, she took extensive coaching with Dame Judith Anderson, one of the great interpreters of Lady Macbeth in the straight theatre, and when she decided to perform the Dance of the Seven Veils in *Salome* herself she prepared an exciting choreography with Arthur Mitchell of the Dance Theatre of Harlem.) Nowadays she often feels let down by the standards of most directors and conductors and their lack of in-depth preparation: 'You seldom find directors and conductors prepared to delve deeply into a work and its background. I shall never forget working on Amneris with Fausto Cleva at the Met. He had so much knowledge packed into his little finger that I could sit and listen to him for *hours*. During the first rehearsal we went through all of my music, bar by bar, and then he said I could go. But I asked if I could stay on and listen to what he had to say to the other singers as well. He was mildly surprised that a singer should want to hang around a rehearsal longer than necessary. But he had so much to say, *musically* so much to say, that listening to him was riveting. The things you could *hear*, the details he brought out in the orchestra or on the piano during piano rehearsals were simply amazing. We arranged to work together again the following autumn on *Il trovatore*, but sadly he died during the intervening summer. I have never worked with such a conductor before. Nor have I ever come across anyone who touched me so deeply since then. How often do you get this kind of knowledge and preparation these days?'

After Bumbry's immense success at the Paris Opéra as Amneris, she was immediately re-engaged for Carmen, a role which she says she always found unrewarding, right from the start. It is a rare singer who doesn't like Carmen but Bumbry is the exception. 'Like Don Giovanni, Carmen is the sort of character of whom the audience have a very strong ideal image in their minds. In either role, if you don't add up to at least eight points out of ten, they will reject you. Vocally speaking Carmen is quite difficult – not very wide-ranging but very demanding on the middle voice. The orchestration is also rather thick so you have to push the middle voice a lot. This is why a steady diet of Carmens is not very healthy for the voice [as Agnes Baltsa agrees]. I sang it quite a lot for a while – including a production at the 1964 Salzburg festival conducted and directed by Karajan – but gave it up at a certain point because of the strain it placed on the middle voice.'

Yet the main reasons Bumbry found Carmen frustrating were not vocal but dramatic: 'Carmen never has a scene to herself. All her so called arias – the Habanera, the Seguidilla, the Chanson de Bohème and the Card Scene – are no such thing but scenes with other people: the chorus, José, Frasquita and Mercedes, who join in for some of the way. All the other characters have marvellous, show-stopping arias: José has the Flower Song, Escamillo has the Toreador Song and Micaela has one aria and a duet. But Carmen has none. She is basically a character part, a series of close-ups, as Callas used to say. And if the singer is not a strong character, or is feeling vocally below par, then it's going to be Micaela's evening, especially if you have a Micaela like Mirella Freni!'

Shortly after her Paris assignments as Amneris and Carmen in 1960, Bumbry was engaged by the Basle Opera, where she made her début as Ortrud in autumn 1961 and stayed for two years. During the autumn of 1960 she had also gone for an audition in Cologne with Wolfgang Sawallisch, who was to conduct Wieland Wagner's production of *Tannhäuser* at the 1961 Bayreuth Festival. He knew Wieland was still desperately searching for a Venus that would live up to his high requirements and recommended the young Grace Bumbry. Wieland realized that here was someone sensuous yet subtle enough to fulfil his ideal conception, which he described in a newspaper interview at the time. 'Venus must convey eroticism without resorting to the clichés of a Hollywood sex bomb; yet she cannot personify the classic, passive ideal. Venus must find the middle ground between two extremes and no European singer I know has so far succeeded.'

Venus was Bumbry's first Wagnerian role. But her solid background in German singing and in-depth study of Lied with Lotte Lehmann (which included Wagner's *Wesendock Lieder*) proved especially helpful for a role like Venus. (It is noteworthy that all singers in this book who have performed Venus, such as Christa Ludwig and Tatiana Troyanos, immediately associate the role with Lied). Bumbry explains that although her study of the *Wesendock Lieder* had familiarized her with Wagnerian singing 'in a small way', she wasn't conscious of learning a specific style, because 'when you are young you don't think deliberately about that. You just learn the music, it's all there, in the music.

For her success in Venus and other German roles, Bumbry acknowledges a considerable debt to Professor Selter, with whom she coached at the State Theatre during her two-year period in Basle. 'He was very, very strict and taught me not only German singing but also the German way of doing things – the German attitude, discipline and mentality as well as the German way of singing and manner of emphasizing certain words. This is hard to explain, but basically boils down to the fact that you are dealing with a German text.'

By the time she went to Bayreuth to begin rehearsals for Venus, Bumbry felt comfortable about her German singing. Compared with some other Wagnerian roles, she did not find Venus particularly difficult, because 'it is very melodic, truly beautiful. In the Dresden version, which was the one used in Bayreuth, Venus is definitely a soprano role. The tessitura is high, but as soon as I looked at the score I knew I could sing it. In the Paris version, on the other hand [which, after some resistance to the idea, Bumbry eventually sang at the Metropolitan Opera and came to like best], it is more of a mezzo role and, of course, Venus has more to sing in this version including a middle section that dips quite low. This is tricky – and frequently cut since few people can sing it – because it bears little relation to what you have been singing up to then or to what follows immediately afterwards.' But more difficult than the vocal aspect when it came to the Bayreuth production was the fact that she had to sit motionless on the top of Venusberg for approximately an hour – the introduction, the Bacchanale and all of Venus's music – covered in gold paint and draped in yards and yards of gold lamé.

Her sensational performance won glowing reviews and, as already hinted, came in the wake of a huge scandal caused by the decision to use a black singer for the first time in what many perceived as the temple of the Germanic Ideal. The Wagner brothers were bombarded with violent racist reactions from certain quarters and the mouthpiece of the neo-Nazi party called the affair 'a cultural disgrace'. The international press picked up the issue and its implications and the 'Black Venus' became a *cause célèbre* long before the première, causing Wieland Wagner to reply in a newspaper interview: 'I shall bring in black, yellow and brown artists if I feel them appropriate. I require no ideal Nordic specimens. My grandfather wrote for vocal colours, not skin colours.'

Bumbry's triumph led, on the social side, to her being invited by Jacqueline Kennedy to sing at the White House and to her being chosen by *Mademoiselle* magazine as one of its 'Ten Young Women of the Year.' Professionally, it led to a string of important international débuts. Before going on to list them, it is worth dwelling for a moment longer on *Tannhäuser* because just over a decade later, in 1972, Bumbry was to undertake both the roles of Venus and Elisabeth on the same evening at the Bavarian State Opera in Munich. She found the experience wonderful. 'Of course, I have always thought that these two characters represent two different sides of one woman. To me, *Tannhäuser* represents a man's search for complete fulfilment and ideally this should come from the same woman. Venus represents the very sensuous, sultry side of woman while Elisabeth represents the pure, idealistic side. No woman is complete, or can fulfil a man completely, without combining both these opposites in her nature.'

On this occasion the Dresden version was used, in which both roles are soprano parts, even though, as Bumbry points out, they demand totally different vocal colours. Surprisingly enough for a singer who for the first decade of her career sang exclusively mezzo roles, she found Elisabeth easier on the voice than Venus, because the latter 'is the more dramatic and problematic of the two and also the more base of the two characters. Elisabeth is more human and in a way more placid although there comes a point when she defends and protects Tannhäuser and becomes heroic. But she still remains one-dimensional whereas Venus is three-dimensional and you have to colour her more subtly. Elisabeth's singing is more straightforward, beautiful, Leonora-type singing, and from the purely vocal point of view, I enjoy singing her music more. It is gorgeous and noble, like her character, which is full of warmth and understanding. You can *feel* the love for Tannhäuser pouring out of her and even though it is not yet physical it is wonderfully pure and *honest*. I found the contrast of portraying these two widely different characters enormously stimulating. I like and always seek contrasts. I need the contrast between concerts and opera, for instance, because beyond a certain point, opera doesn't fulfil me.'

Indeed, Bumbry's most important international début, shortly after her triumph at Bayreuth, was in a recital at New York's Carnegie Hall in autumn 1962, which won her rave reviews in the New York press: 'A superbly gifted artist . . . a gorgeous, clear, ringing voice . . . a regal bearing and a thoroughly winning stage presence', wrote the *New York Times*, while the *New York Post* hailed her as 'a young Marian Anderson, possessed of a large, ringing mezzo-soprano capable of filling a hall with a churning sea of sound'.

Next came her equally sensational début at Covent Garden in spring 1963 as Princess Eboli in Luchino Visconti's production of *Don Carlos* which, to this day, remains her favourite staging of an opera she considers to be Verdi's greatest, 'the most beautiful, luscious, cohesive piece of music he ever wrote: a real masterpiece without a single superfluous note. And, after King Philip, Eboli is the most important role in it, the pivotal character whose actions trigger off the development of events. She should always emerge as very strong, but if well done she should also emerge as sympathetic because there is a more human side to her, too, and this is the side one should show first.

'Vocally she has two difficult moments: The Veil Song in Act I and "O don fatale" in Act IV, and they are difficult in different ways. The important thing about the Veil Song is virtuosity. It has nothing to do with Eboli as a character. It is simply a song she sings to entertain the court and should be full of vocal pyrotechnics, charm and liveliness of voice. Then comes the exact opposite, the tortured aria "O don fatale", which should be sung with immense visceral power. But the way Verdi wrote this opera and especially Eboli's part, lends itself to wonderful characterization. First he gives you the Veil Song, a nice little aria with which to warm up the voice – because when you come on stage you very seldom are, or should be, fully warmed up. Then gradually you go from the lightness of the Veil Song to something a bit heavier in the Garden Trio and finally, with "O don fatale", you pull out all the stops. It really is a perfectly written role.' Bumbry, who remains one of the unforgettable Ebolis of our day, went on to sing the part at the Vienna State Opera, also in 1963, and the Metropolitan Opera in 1965, everywhere to enthusiastic acclaim. 'The finest Eboli we have heard or indeed could wish to hear – nothing short of a triumph', wrote *The Times*, while after her Metropolitan Opera début Alan Rich hailed her as 'an exciting, magnetic, dynamic singer . . . filling Verdi's lines with musical fire'.

Bumbry stresses that some roles, even some Verdi roles, are not as well written as Eboli and cites Lady Macbeth, which she first sang in Basle in 1963 and later at the 1964 Salzburg Festival and Covent Garden, as an example. 'Lady Macbeth is the complete opposite: rather awkwardly written. The moment she walks on stage she has to sing an aria *and* a cabaletta and ten minutes after she has another aria. I often wonder whether this is due to the fact that, at the time, Verdi was still relatively inexperienced or whether it has to do with the story line. But as Radames in *Aida* – and by the time he composed that Verdi was very experienced indeed – has to sing "Celeste Aida" the moment he walks on stage, I am inclined to think that it has more to do with the story line. In the case of *Macbeth*, one has the feeling that something is lacking from the libretto. One isn't given time to develop the character gradually. The role consists mainly of arias with very little in between, and everything happens rather abruptly. Take the Sleepwalking Scene. It occurs too suddenly, too much out of context. Something seems to be missing. Maybe something is needed between the previous scene [Malcolm and Macduff with the people] and this scene which, by the way, I have seldom seen well staged except once, in Salzburg, in Oskar Fritz Schuhe's staging which made use of the wonderful Felsenreitschule setting. He had Lady Macbeth wandering in and out of each of those arches, candle in hand, throughout the prelude.'

By the early seventies, Bumbry had begun to take on more soprano roles, the first and most successful of which was the title role in *Salome*, first at Covent Garden in 1970 under Sir Georg Solti, and later at the Metropolitan Opera and her débuts at the Toronto (1975) and the Houston (1986) operas. A switch of this kind is always controversial and carries a certain amount of risk: one might damage the middle voice and thus cease to be a top mezzo without becoming a top soprano, either. When that voice happens to be one of the most thrilling mezzos of the post-war era, the question remains: Why? 'Because the offer came! To be sure, I had already had many offers for soprano parts, but turned them down. However, this particular offer came from no less a man than Georg Solti, then Music Director of Covent Garden. So I thought I had better take it seriously.'

As always when confronted with a potential new role, she had a look at the score, and played her vocal line on the piano. In the case of a role such as Salome which was unknown territory, she paid particular attention to 'where the high, extended notes are to be found, and how they are approached [this, as most singers both in this book and its twin volume *Bravo* stress, makes all the difference to the roles' relative difficulty], whether they are loud, mezzo forte or piano, how they should be sung and what sort of orchestration I would have under me. And I must say that my original impressions at first reading turned out to be exactly right. The only problem I could foresee was in the scene with Jokanaan. But I remember thinking that if the conductor does it as it is written, then I would have no problems. As the conductor in this case was Solti, who had conducted this opera many times before with many different singers, I knew he was aware of the problems and bound to help me, as indeed he did. While it is always a joy to have a good conductor, in an opera like *Salome* it is absolutely *vital*. You cannot get by just through your own intelligence and musicality. And I must say, that, having now sung Salome almost everywhere, I can remember only four occasions when the conductors understood, supported and were with me all the time.'

Vocally, Salome is high but not as high as Tosca, the other most famous of Bumbry's soprano roles (which she first sang in 1972 at the Metropolitan Opera, then at Covent Garden, Rio de Janeiro, Berlin, Munich, Vienna, Chicago etc, and in Piero Faggioni's staging at La Scala), and

which is 'very high and very difficult. Less so in Act I, which is
essentially a dialogue, a love duet interrupted by a lover's tiff. But after
Scarpia's entry to the church, the mood changes and the writing
becomes a bit higher and more biting. Act II is very high, full of B flats,
B naturals and high Cs, and it's not just a matter of high notes but of the
overall tessitura which stays high all the time. Most important, it's also a
matter of what the text is about. Take Cherubini's *Medea*, for instance
[which Bumbry sang in 1981 at the New York City Opera, and at the
Barbican in London in late 1983 in memory of Maria Callas], which is
not as high as Tosca, but about as high as Salome. But it feels as high,
even higher than either because of the text, because of the kind of
woman she is. It goes without saying that it must be sung in a different
way. Negative characters always need a different tone and tend to put
greater pressure on you.

'In this sense Salome and Medea are in the same groove, while Tosca
is in a different, more lyrical groove reminiscent of Leonora in *Il
trovatore*. These latter two are about beautiful singing, so you have to
concentrate on beauty of sound, without stretching the dramatic dimensions. I put more drama than most into my Tosca but always within her
emotional limits. So, you see, the quality of sound and the way I
approach the sound and especially the high notes depends overwhelmingly on the nature of the character, whether it is negative or
positive. Abigaille's high notes in *Nabucco*, for instance [which Bumbry
first sang at the Paris Opéra to a noisy reception organized by claques
and later very successfully at the New York City Opera and San
Francisco in 1981], should sound much more strident than Leonora's,
which should be sung more limpidly.'

Although at the end of the day I suspect that it is as a great mezzo that
Bumbry will have earned her place in operatic history, yet the parts that
brought the house down most vociferously in the joint recital she gave
with her colleague and, if one believes sections of the press, arch-rival
Shirley Verrett at Covent Garden in 1983 after New York's Carnegie
Hall, were the soprano roles: Norma and Adriana Lecouvreur. She says
she feels equally comfortable in soprano and mezzo parts. 'It's all a
question of technique,' she explains, and indeed she mastered the
transition to the soprano register better than most colleagues who made
the switch. It was after her success as Salome at Covent Garden in 1970
that she decided to concentrate primarily on the soprano repertoire, but
as she had contracts for mezzo parts for a further three years, it wasn't
until 1974 that she really started working the voice into the soprano way
of singing, with a teacher. She herself would like to be remembered as a
singer whose voice defied classification.

Bumbry is now in her mid-fifties and, as she stated in a newspaper interview a couple of years ago, more than satisfied with her life and career. 'There's nothing in life I haven't had.' Except children. Married for nine years to a German husband – 'seven of which were blissful and then all sorts of jealousies set in' – who had a lot to do with masterminding the beginning of her spectacular rise to international prominence, she somehow never got around to having children. 'I regret that now. Curiously enough, I was discussing that just last night and someone said: "But where would the child have gone to school? It would have had to be a boarding school all the time." So it's just as well,' she says philosophically.

She went on to add that there would have been no question of her sacrificing her career, even temporarily, for motherhood. 'Absolutely not. You see, anybody can have children but it is not everybody who has been given this wonderful gift and I do think that such a gift carries a certain responsibility.' And many sacrifices, great and small. 'Being a singer is like walking on a tightrope. We have to look after our health, watch our diet, get enough rest, avoid talking before performances – personally I don't speak at all for 36 hours before a performance – because the voice is such a hyper-sensitive instrument that it can be affected by the slightest thing like pollen, smoke, excess dryness etc. Nobody understands the problems we have to cope with. They expect us to be note-perfect at every performance, which is impossible. We are not machines, we are not robots, we are human beings. And no matter how great our instrument, or how well prepared we might be, we don't *know* for sure what will come out every time we open our mouth. And once a note is out, it's out, good or bad. You can't recall it. This is why I said that we are walking on a tightrope all the time.'

What makes her love her profession so much then? 'I don't know. You get an incredible high, with singing. It's the most exciting feeling you can possibly experience, well, the second most exciting feeling, an incomparable sensation. I don't think we, ourselves, fully realize how fortunate we are to have been given this gift, and maybe it's best that we shouldn't. But from time to time I am so overcome by a beautiful sound that I just sit back and think "Oh God, how is it possible for *that* to come out of *this* throat?" It gives me goose-flesh at times and as I said I cannot think of any sound that can compare with the human voice. I understand why the Eastern Orthodox churches consider it the only instrument worthy to praise God. I very much love the cello, I love the piano, but I don't think any other instrument is quite as exciting and alive as the human voice.'

BRIGITTE FASSBAENDER

'I NOW FEEL more disciplined and stable vocally and better balanced physically and mentally than I have ever felt in my life,' says the German mezzo Brigitte Fassbaender, explaining she has reached a more serene stage in her life when she feels good about herself, both as an artist and a human being. 'My nerves are steadier and I am generally much healthier. I used to get frequent colds and flus but since becoming a vegetarian about eight years ago, I have felt much better and stronger.'

Fassbaender has equally good reason to feel satisfied with her long and brilliant career, which began thirty years ago in Munich. Her velvety, sensuous mezzo sound has acquired a deeper, more contralto-like colour and nowadays she devotes 70 per cent of her time to concert and Lieder singing and 30 per cent to opera, shedding old parts – such as Octavian, perhaps the role most intimately associated with her – and adding new ones, such as Klytemnestra, the Nurse in *Die Frau ohne Schatten* and Clairon in *Capriccio* as she sees fit. She explains that she has become 'very very careful with my operatic singing because I don't want to lose the flexibility crucial for Lieder singing. If I were to sing a steady diet of Klytemnestras, Nurses or Azucenas [she has sung the latter on a recording conducted by Giulini and featuring Placido Domingo as Manrico, but not yet on stage] I wouldn't be able to sing Lieder as much as I do. In addition, I am very lazy and getting more and more so. I take a long time to prepare a new role.' Instead, she derives profound satisfaction from the introspective, 'philosophical' work involved in learning and putting together a group of songs. She averages about ninety minutes of new songs a year, making for a very wide repertoire of Lieder. 'Many singers go through their careers with a programme and a half! I sing in certain places – London, Vienna, Hohenems – every year, sometimes twice, and I pride myself on giving them a new programme every time, trying not to repeat even a single song. It's a lot of work.'

Like her compatriot Christa Ludwig, Fassbaender has theatre and music in her genes. The daughter of baritone Willi Domgraf-Fassbaender and actress Sabine Peters, she was born in Berlin on 3 July 1939, and learnt her craft from her father, whose recordings of *Cosi fan tutte* and *Le nozze di Figaro*, conducted by Fritz Busch are considered classics. But as a child, Brigitte Fassbaender was far more interested in the straight theatre than in music and opera. 'I was obsessed by the theatre and wanted to be an actress like my mother. A turning point came when I found my father's old make-up case in the attic. I took on new identities. I spent hours disguising myself with beards and noses and inventing costumes from old scraps of cloth and chair covers. I wrote plays for my friends, but as they were too shy to speak, I acted all the parts and of course directed. At the time I was not really interested in music, rebelled against the teachers who expected great things of me because I was the daughter of a "Kammersänger" and only enjoyed sitting under the piano while my father prepared his Lieder programmes, never dreaming I might become a singer.' She says she was only vaguely aware of the great musical personalities such as Erna Berger, Maria Cebotari and Hans Hotter, who came to visit her parents. She spent far more time travelling on the U-Bahn all over Berlin, watching 'the incredible types one sees there, unconsciously retaining images for future roles. I still find people-watching the best acting school.'

Fassbaender didn't see her father on the operatic stage – as Scarpia and Don Giovanni – or acquire a taste for opera until the family moved to Hanover in 1958. It was comparatively late, too, when she was still at school in Berlin, living with her grandmother, that she discovered her own voice. One of her classmates was Isolde Schock, the daughter of tenor Rudolf Schock, and as *she* was studying singing, Fassbaender thought 'Her father is a singer, so is mine, she is taking singing lessons, so why don't I?' She started off by singing a little for herself, to find out if there was anything there. To her surprise, it didn't sound too bad, rather developed and mature in fact. So she learnt a few songs and Agathe's aria from *Der Freischütz*, asked a friend to accompany her on the piano, made a tape and sent it to her father for his appraisal. Willi Domgraf-Fassbaender was then Head of the Opera School at the Nürnberg Conservatoire and Production Director at the local opera house. He was both surprised and pleased at his daughter's new found interest in singing and thought her voice was worth developing. He asked her to come to Nürnberg to study with him. She did, from 1958 to 1961, and the two developed an extremely close artistic and emotional relationship. He remained her only teacher and mentor until his death in 1978.

After three years' study, in late 1960, she was billed to sing a few lines in the Opera School's production of Purcell's *Dido and Aeneas*, and her name on the poster caught the attention of Rudolf Hartmann, Intendant of the Bavarian State Opera in Munich. He asked her father if he, by any chance, happened to have a daughter who was a mezzo and when he replied that he did, Hartmann suggested he should bring her to Munich for an audition, as there happened to be a vacancy for a mezzo in his 'Young Opera' studio. Willi Domgraf-Fassbaender didn't want his daughter to be nervous or self-conscious, or indeed for her to have any great expectations from this audition, so he underplayed the whole thing. To her protestations that, since until then they had only studied technique and Lieder, she had no repertoire to audition *with*, he replied that this wasn't a proper audition anyway, but only for 'informative purposes'. They set out to prepare three arias, including Dalila's 'Mon coeur s'ouvre à ta voix' from *Samson et Dalila* and Olga's from *Eugène Onegin*.

Hartmann and Joseph Keilberth, Music Director of the BSO, engaged her immediately, but urged her to lose her baby fat, as her first part was to be a trouser role: the Page in *Lohengrin*. She was in the ensemble and, at her father's insistence, started off only in very small parts. Her real début came as Nicklaus in *Les Contes d'Hoffmann* but she continued to sing a wide variety of Maids and Pages (such as the one in *Salome* in a production conducted by Karl Böhm, and featuring Lisa della Casa and Dietrich Fischer-Dieskau). On nights when she was not singing herself she would stand in the wings and observe famous colleagues such as Astrid Varnay, Martha Mödl, Birgit Nilsson and Hans Hotter, all of whom were kind to her because, she supposes, they knew, liked and admired her father.

Growing up in an ensemble was an excellent way for a young singer to develop slowly and gradually, learning from observation and, despite occasional bursts of frustration, without putting the voice at risk by taking on the big parts prematurely. 'It is crucial to build up vocal power slowly, with small and mainly lyric parts, and leave the dramatic parts, which are dangerous for vocal flexibility, for later. Otherwise one couldn't sing Mozart.' She started off with Mozart very early, first with the Third Lady in *Die Zauberflöte* and then with Cherubino and Dorabella, both of which she has sung with distinction but for which she feels no deep affinity. 'I enjoyed singing Dorabella, her drolerie and the variety of colour demanded by the role, but found the character rather one-dimensional. The same was true of Cherubino to some extent. My favourite Mozart role was Sextus in *La clemenza di Tito* who is many-sided, torn between conflicting loyalties, develops considerably during the course of the opera, was vocally very comfortable for my voice and wonderful to sing.'

She confirms what most singers in this book have stated regarding Mozartian singing: 'Mozart is the best voice teacher. His music demands crystalline purity and precision, without any mannerisms. Yet this almost instrumental way of singing is also an emotion-packed vehicle for the deepest human feelings, which flow through and out of the sound. This is where Mozart's genius lies.'

In addition to the Mozart roles just mentioned, Fassbaender's repertoire in Munich during the sixties included Clarissa in Rossini's *La pietra del Paragone* (her big breakthrough), Olga, Hänsel, Narcisso in Handel's *Agrippina*, Fatima in Weber's *Oberon*, Zaide in *Il Turco in Italia* and, in 1967, her first Octavian, a part of which she was to become one of the most distinguished exponents of our day. Her portrayal of this role – which is her favourite, along with Sextus and Charlotte in *Werther* – grew not out of these early repertory evenings, but during preparation for the now legendary Otto Schenk production, conducted by Carlos Kleiber, which was first seen in 1973 and went on to be performed annually, to this day (for most of the time with a cast which, apart from Fassbaender as Octavian, also included Gwyneth Jones as the Marschallin, Lucia Popp as Sophie and Kurt Moll as Baron Ochs).

'I love Octavian. I have had a chance to develop my portrayal over a period of twenty years, in minutest detail, to the point of feeling completely under his skin. He himself is in a state of constant development and transformation, of youthful exuberance in the process of discovering life, and although I have performed him for twenty years not only in Munich, but more or less everywhere, I have never found him boring. Vocally the main difficulty is the length. As a famous colleague once pointed out, when Octavian is not on stage he is hurriedly changing his costume. But it is an amusing part, fun to do both vocally and dramatically with the added irony of the "transvestite" element: a woman singer playing a man who in turn must impersonate a woman, the maid Mariandel. And everything happens in such an interesting way: his rapture with the Marschallin giving way to hurt at her dismissal of his protestations of eternal love and to "love at first sight" for Sophie, and the irony of his first love introducing him to his second, and, one hopes, more permanent attachment. Or is it? I doubt it . . . I must say I never got tired of singing him. He certainly has a fascination for the public. We "Octavians" get some very peculiar fan mail!' But in 1988 she decided to 'bid farewell' to him while still in top vocal form rather than risk tarnishing people's memories of her earlier performances.

She considers Schenk's production a model that cannot be changed or improved 'because you cannot try turning *Der Rosenkavalier* upside down or make it into anything but what it is. Different directors might ask you to come in from the left rather than the right, but in essence, the opera remains the same.' (Which must have made Fassbaender's task even harder, when, as she explains later, she came to revive this production, with a new cast, this time as director at the BSO in 1989.)

Musically she learnt everything she knows about Octavian from Carlos Kleiber who, throughout the years they performed it together, approached it like a new piece each season. What had struck her right from the beginning, back in 1973, was that unlike most conductors who only appear at the later orchestra stage rehearsals, Kleiber was present from the very first rehearsal.

'He was there and he had a great deal to say. Sometimes he stopped us after the third word or note and made us repeat, repeat, repeat the same words or phrases for maybe an hour and always with some new idea about each word! He knew not only Strauss's score and von Hoffmannsthal's text by heart, but their mentality as well. And as he is a wonderful actor, he sang our parts and showed us exactly how to do everything. He was almost like a director in this sense, except that *his* ideas and insights always sprang from the score. [Indeed Otto Schenk told me that Kleiber wanted him to be "a translator of the music in terms of staging and acting".] And as you probably know, he is a fanatic. But he never aims solely at aesthetic perfection of sound but allows the works to breathe and unfold in full dramatic essence.'

At the time of this historic production of *Der Rosenkavalier* and throughout the early seventies, Fassbaender began to make a string of major international débuts, starting with *Carmen* in San Francisco in 1970. She had first sung Carmen in 1969 at the Bavarian State Opera after which the Munich critic of *Opera* had written: 'She was a natural, spontaneous, animally-magnetic, sixteen-year-old gypsy girl . . . the finest exponent of the title role heard here in the past decade. Her effortless technique and the glorious quality of her voice made hers one of the most beautifully sung accounts of the role it has been my joy to hear. Also as an actress, this was her finest achievement in Munich so far.' (Fassbaender herself, though, says she only came across a staging of *Carmen* that coincided with her own concept when she sang in Ponnelle's production in Frankfurt in 1979.)

Next came her Covent Garden début, in 1971, as Octavian, and her Salzburg début, in 1973, as Dorabella, which she also sang for her début at the Vienna State Opera in 1975, a few months after her Metropolitan Opera début as Octavian. By the late seventies, she felt ready to expand her hitherto mainly German repertoire to include some major Italian parts – Eboli in *Don Carlos* and Amneris in *Aida*, the latter in a new production directed by Franco Enriquez and conducted by Riccardo Muti in 1979. 'I am not asked to sing Verdi very often, but I greatly enjoyed singing Amneris, which psychologically is a very interesting part – definitely the most multi-faceted of Verdi's mezzo heroines.' She stresses that she learnt a tremendous amount about the character and about Italian singing

from Muti, 'who explained the meaning of each word, was unusually
aware of technical problems and helped me a great deal with the long,
arch-like Verdian phrases by always giving me enough time to breathe. I
had started off by telling him I realized I was not a typical Amneris voice
or type, but he was very nice and sympathetic and told me not to worry,
he had accompanied singers for a long time at the Milan Conservatoire,
was married to a singer and understood our problems. So I ended up
enjoying the experience of singing Amneris immensely.

'Dramatically it is, as I said, a wonderful role and vocally, at least as far
as I'm concerned, not as difficult as Eboli. For a start, it is not as high.
Amneris has only one high B flat (plus an ensemble C flat, but that doesn't
really count because in ensembles you are not exposed), whereas Eboli
has at least five B flats and B naturals. Eboli is shorter than Amneris, but
for me it is far more difficult not only vocally but dramatically. The fact
that she has only two arias and a trio means she has little scope to put
herself across as a character, on top of which the first aria, the Veil Song,
has nothing to do with her as a person; it is merely sung to entertain the
court. Amneris has much more time and scope to develop: she has arias,
recitatives, duets and whole scenes in which she reveals and pours out her
psyche: we see her loving, deceitful, vengeful, repentant, imperious and
humbled. In fact we see her going through the whole gamut of emotions
of a woman in love. Eboli's development, on the other hand, is
spasmodic. There is a big pause between her two arias – the Veil Song and
"O don fatale" in Act IV, interrupted only by the Garden Trio. I found
this long gap uncomfortable and felt acutely nervous throughout its
duration. Amneris has to be on stage more or less continuously, and this
makes life much easier because you are constantly involved in the action.'

She has also sung Mistress Quickly in *Falstaff* spasmodically over her
career. 'The opera is such a dream, it is fun to take part in. I am only now
growing into the role in terms of my age and my voice (the low notes),
although she is not an old crone – rather a sensual woman in fact.'

Fassbaender's repertoire includes several Wagnerian roles. Although
she did not make her Bayreuth début until 1983, as Waltraute, she had
already tackled several Wagner parts with distinction. The first was
Fricka in *Das Rheingold*, which she found a 'bore' because she just stands
about for two-and-a-half hours with very little to sing and most of *that* is
dialogue. Next came Fricka in *Die Walküre*, which on the contrary is 'a
very beautiful, very dramatic and interesting part. One should always
strive to distance her as much as possible from the usual "nagging
Hausfrau" interpretation and project her human/godly tragedy as a
betrayed woman. Her outbreaks are fantastic to sing and full of longing,
and frustration at Wotan's constant need for change and variety. Is it

vocally tiring? That depends on the individual voice. One can sing Wagner in a very concentrated cultured way (Karajan and Kleiber have always fought for this "transparent" way of conducting and singing Wagner) without constantly screaming at the top of one's voice. It's hard in America – with their huge houses they love big voices. We are lucky in Europe – one can be a bit more subtle.'

Fassbaender's most famous Wagnerian role, though, is Brangaene in *Tristan und Isolde*, which she first sang in 1989 at the Vienna State Opera and also on record, for Deutsche Grammophon, conducted by Carlos Kleiber. The part is dramatically absorbing and vocally taxing, 'a heavenly piece of music, but hellish to sing; full of long lines, long arches that have to be sung smoothly and seamlessly, almost like Italian lines. The tessitura, especially in Act I, is very high, the same as Isolde's. But the most difficult moments are undoubtedly Brangaene's famous "calls", her warnings, in Act II. While the part is not as long as Isolde, it is written in a similar way, and is a real singing role for which you need a good top, good substantial high notes.'

She finds the part riveting from the psychological point of view, and is fascinated by the relationship, the deep friendship, between Isolde and Brangaene, whose destinies, she explained at the time of her recording, 'have been conceived and set out so wonderfully by Wagner. There are plenty of opportunities to illustrate the relationship between the two in Act I. Brangaene is the intermediary, the mother substitute who, out of love for Isolde, substitutes the death for a love potion. In doing that she assumes a crucial part in the unfolding of events and her maternal love and anxiety for Isolde find full expression in the finale.' Sadly I have not seen Fassbaender's Brangaene on stage but on disc at least hers is an exemplary interpretation.

Fassbaender enjoys recording and the perfectionist, detailed work it involves. The possibility of getting everything right compensates for the absence of the frisson provided by contact with a live audience. It is sad that an extensive discography of operatic and Lieder literature does not include recordings of two of her three favourite roles: Octavian and Sextus. The third, Charlotte in *Werther*, is available on a Supraphon disc (with tenor Peter Dvorsky), made as the soundtrack for a film of the opera directed by Czech film-maker Petr Weigl. She first sang this part in Munich in 1978, with Placido Domingo in the title role. Fassbaender speaks of her love of French music in general and Massenet, whom she considers underestimated, in particular. 'His music is very expressive. There is tremendous feeling and passion there for a good conductor to bring out. Charlotte is a beautifully written part, with wonderful arias and very interesting dramatically. I was immediately drawn to her as a character and, as a woman, felt strong empathy for her plight: the intense pain caused by her conflicting loyalties, the clash between passion and duty. As you have probably gathered by now, the characters who interest me most are those who develop a great deal through the course of an opera. And I can think of few who develop as dramatically as Charlotte. (Tatiana in *Eugene Onegin* springs to mind, but then she is not a mezzo part.) She starts off as an innocent young girl in Act I, engaged to a man who is more of a friend than a lover, and suddenly with Werther's arrival, she experiences passion for the first time. This plunges her into a headlong clash between her conscience and her heart. Eventually it all leads to tragedy, and by the end, Charlotte has changed beyond recognition. Making a success of the Munich production, by Kurt Horres whom I found stimulating to work with, meant a great deal to me.' (The distinguished German critic, the late K.H. Ruppel, called hers 'an outstandingly intelligent Charlotte'.)

Vocally the part is testing, particularly at the end which is very high, 'but musically it is beautiful to sing'. It is one of her greatest regrets that Puccini never wrote any great mezzo parts because she loves his operas and to her 'something about Charlotte reminds me of Puccini. But of course it isn't and must be sung in the French style. This is inextricably entwined with the language, which sounds very refined, not as open as Italian, which is the ideal language for singing with those open vowels. The quality of sound is directly linked to the emotions it expresses, which are also more restrained and require a certain lightness of touch. French music is difficult to learn, but I love it.'

As already mentioned, other recent parts have included Klytemnestra in *Elektra*, which she first sang in Munich and later in the Vienna Festival of 1989 in a new production by Harry Kupfer conducted by Claudio Abbado. Christa Ludwig who sang the role in the same production loathed its gruesome, overstated visual conception (I tend to agree with her), but Fassbaender found working with Kupfer exciting and stimulating, and the part very interesting from a psychoanalytic point of view. 'It's a very emotional, tortured, psychologically complex character, suffering endless sleepless nights and to be pitied rather than condemned outright. She is a horrible woman, yes (Elektra is no great shakes either), but she became horrible because of circumstances, her marriage to a man she obviously didn't love and who was ready to sacrifice their daughter Iphigenia. That was the beginning of the rot.

'Technically speaking, it is not a "singing role" – it's an acting role, full of emotional sounds such as shrieks, ejaculations, screeches and suchlike. It is rather low, very strongly written and very, very hard to sing, especially the end of the scene where, in this production, Abbado opened up all the customary cuts, which made it virtually unsingable while I was clambering around that set. I was always happy when it was over, and felt utterly physically exhausted afterwards. It's idiotic because it amounts to only twenty-five minutes' singing. But those twenty-five minutes are so packed with stress and emotion that they leave me more exhausted than an entire evening of singing Amneris or Octavian. At least that is so in the Kupfer production. I can't remember feeling like that in Munich, but then that was "down to the footlights and sing out". I know which I prefer!' (Christa Ludwig makes the same point about Klytemnestra having this draining effect on its interpreter.) 'But I'm happy to be seeing this other side of Strauss now. I had sung Herodias for a record which was never released before I sang her on stage – I've recently recorded the role for Sony with Eva Marton and Zubin Mehta conducting the Berlin Philharmonic – so I had my first taste of the "Strauss-Weiber" with the Nurse in *Die Frau ohne Schatten* [which she first sang in Ponnelle's La Scala production in 1986], and found it relatively easy to sing and enjoyable because it lends itself to vivid characterization. My voice has got lower of late and I risked a lot in taking on these parts. But one has to make *some* experiments.'

Fassbaender's operatic repertoire also includes Marie in *Wozzeck* and Countess Geschwitz in *Lulu*. Musically these two Berg roles represent a different world and she sings them with varying degrees of enjoyment. Marie she finds a 'wonderful character part' and not too difficult vocally, whereas Countess Geschwitz she does not particularly enjoy because 'quite simply it is not beautiful to sing. Only a couple of her phrases amount to real singing. She had a bit more to do in the three-act version, but I'm not sure the "Paris" scene is worth sitting through to get to the completed "London" scene. All those characters talking endlessly about stocks and shares – interestingly it is also the only boring scene in the original Wedekind play. I'm sure Berg would have cut it drastically. You tire your voice in the role without deriving any satisfaction from having contributed something. Lieder recitals, on the other hand, are profoundly satisfying and fulfilling. Everything stems from the text and your own understanding of it so that you can be your own director. I find Lieder evenings more interesting than churning out the same operatic roles all the time.'

Directing is an activity Fassbaender is already devoting some time to, and plans to devote even more in the future. In 1989 she directed a re-staged revival of Schenk's production of *Der Rosenkavalier* in Munich, in which she had so often sung Octavian. Then came *La Cenerentola* in 1990 in Coburg and plans include Franz Schreker's *Der ferne Klang* in January 1992 at Opera North, and *Lulu* in Innsbruck in March 1992. There are already offers for 1993/94. The obvious plan seems to be to learn the craft thoroughly, relatively out of the limelight before becoming a fully-fledged director after her retirement from the operatic stage. She finds directing fascinating, and has herself learnt a great deal from the directors with whom she had the strongest rapport: the late Günther Rennert, 'in whose rehearsals one sweated inside and out and after which the days felt empty; Otto Schenk with whom one works as a partner; the late lamented Jean-Pierre Ponnelle who turned every rehearsal into a performance; and Kurt Horres whose lengthy lectures are at first unclear but then reveal brilliant clues to the characters'. She also expresses admiration for Harry Kupfer, Ruth Berghaus and Herbert Wernicke. She herself needed and needs long and profound work with the director, and when she sees that a director has an accurate assessment of her strengths and weaknesses, then 'I trust him, put myself in his hands and let him guide me.' Her own artistic credo as a director is similar to that as a singer, as she recently explained in the *Sunday Times*: 'Be honest, and do not betray the work. Do not betray the composer and the poet.'

It is a creed she tries to instil in her pupils at the Munich Hochschule für Musik, where she taught between 1982 and 1990. (She is taking a sabbatical at the moment, but continuing to give master-class courses regularly around the world.) She insists that she learns a great deal from teaching because 'in order to teach, I have to think about every role and song anew. I think people talk about a singer crisis in our day; they should also talk about a director/conductor/record-company crisis in the same breath. Because it all boils down to the fact that nowadays we have no time to work properly. The greatest enemy of our art, what kills most young singers, is commerce. One needs to be very strong and very well advised in order to resist. If one is smart and can afford to, one should say "no thank you".'

Spacing performances and roles properly and getting adequate rest is also essential. Fassbaender tries to have a pause between heavy weeks of singing to rest but also to 'sleep and live. Because a singer's life is not easy. If you are in it body and soul, then it's a difficult life.' She escapes sometimes by going to the theatre, films and especially exhibitions and by indulging in her great passion: painting. She professes to be 'entirely self-taught and entirely enthusiastic' about it. 'It's a creative art I can enjoy without the dimension of duty that attaches to my singing.' She takes her sketch book on her travels and often wishes she could sit and only paint for six months. 'But then I would probably miss the stage – and I hope I sing better than I paint!'

CHRISTA LUDWIG

CHRISTA LUDWIG, A LIVING legend among contemporary singers and rightly called 'one of the beacon lights of our time: a centre of radiance . . . a durable flame' by John Steane, is still going strong in her sixties. Throughout her forty-five-year career, she has been as active and distinguished on the concert platform as on the operatic stage which, as the scion of two performing artists, she regards as her spiritual home. Her mother was the mezzo Eugenie Besalla who had sung Elektra with Karajan at Aachen before the war, and her father was the tenor Anton Ludwig, who had started life as a baritone, later became leading tenor at the Vienna Volksoper, sang for twenty-one years at the Met in New York and ended up as a stage director and later Intendant at Aachen. He, too, often worked with Karajan, whom Christa Ludwig knew from the age of seven. Being 'a second generation singer', as she puts it, has been enormously helpful both because of the constant training she received at home and because she could 'learn from the first generation's mistakes'. Her mother ruined her voice prematurely, mixing low mezzo and high soprano parts without taking care to schedule or space them properly. It was a lesson her daughter never forgot.

'I was always very careful with the voice. My only teacher was my mother who not only taught me the rudiments of singing but also ensured that I learnt to play the piano, the flute, the cello as well as acquiring a basic knowledge of musical theory. She also took care that I should avoid some of the pitfalls lurking in the path of every young singer: taking on the big roles and singing in large theatres too early. Mine was never a case of overnight fame but one of slow ascent. I developed slowly, allowing the voice time to grow naturally while watching and listening to other people in the singing school my parents ran on the side. And my money also came slowly! Today it comes so quickly and such a lot of it that many singers feel "what if I only manage a ten-year career before my voice is ruined if by that time I have made enough money to last me a lifetime?" But my mother always said she hoped that, unlike herself, I would still have my voice intact when I was mellow enough to *know* what it's all about, what's inside the music. This can only come with age and eludes all those people who make a quick career but ruin their voice before they reach this ripe stage of *knowing*. I am very happy with my slow career because I think that now I know a bit more than I did when I was young.'

Ludwig was born in Berlin on 16 March 1928 and spent most of her childhood at Aachen. Thanks to her parents' singing school and their life in the theatre she knew most operas by heart, so this part was 'easy, easy, easy'. Everyday life, on the other hand, was very hard indeed. The war had brought financial ruin, as it had on most German families. The war years were spent in Giessen, near Frankfurt, where Ludwig made her first public appearances, in 1945, aged seventeen, singing operatic arias in a concert hall and a half-destroyed theatre. She confessed in an interview with Mel Cooper in *Opera Now* that her motive for becoming a professional singer 'was also the drive to have a bed, an apartment, clothes, dishes and ultimately to have a house, because nothing was inherited'.

The following year, 1946, she was engaged by the Frankfurt State Opera where she made her début as Prince Orloffsky in *Die Fledermaus*. Her salary was 400 marks a month at a time when a pound of coffee cost 800 marks. But she remained in Frankfurt for six years and sang all the small roles, including angels in the Christmas play plus some of the 'easier' big roles such as Octavian. Meanwhile her parents had divorced and her mother came to live with her, bringing the advantage that 'I could study with her every day without paying. I could never have afforded to pay for lessons.'

By 1952, her mother felt it was time for her to learn about stagecraft and acting, so she moved to Darmstadt for two years and worked with a good stage director, Gustav Rudolf Sellner, who 'taught me how to concentrate and enter the skin of the various characters. At the time, everything was very stylized. The stage was practically bare so the entire onus fell on us, the performers. We learnt to watch and control our movements minutely, down to our little finger because the barest hint of movement even of a little finger can look very big on an empty stage. Today there is so much clutter on stage that we tend to lose sight of the characters and wonder where they are. But in those days concentration was so intense that the characters really *lived*. Money was very short in post-war Germany. But the ideas were great, whereas today we have lots of money and fewer ideas. Directors love to shock and scandalize. But making a scandal is much easier than revealing the inner truth in the works we interpret. Still, it's important that opera should evolve and develop with the times, that it should be talked about and be in the public eye. So maybe these crazy stage directors are helping to keep it alive and lively.'

After mastering the basics of stagecraft at Darmstadt, Ludwig and her mother felt it was now time to work with a good conductor and open up the voice by singing in a bigger theatre. She went to Hannover, which boasted a good conductor from the Berlin State Opera, Johannes Schüler, with whom she began to sing the big roles for the first time: Eboli, Carmen, Ortrud, Kundry, her first Marie in *Wozzeck* (plus her first *Das Lied von der Erde* in the concert hall) and her first Amneris, an early favourite!

'But I never became known as "an Italian singer" because in foreign countries they prefer to cast Italian or black singers in Italian opera. But I adored Amneris, it was heaven to sing. It's wonderfully written, basically around the middle range with some high notes, so you have this big, solid middle voice to sit on and long, really beautiful *bel canto* phrases. The most challenging moment is Act IV, Scene I which is so dramatic and emotionally charged that the acting also has to be good. It is this very exhausting scene that singers auditioning for the role are always asked to sing.

'But Strauss is relatively easy for mezzos because his mezzo roles such as Octavian or Klytemnestra tend to contain a lot of "Sprechgesang". They also contain some very long notes which I was rightly advised to shorten occasionally. Strauss is much more difficult for sopranos because his soprano roles are very high, but for us mezzos, he is on the easy side. So is Wagner, believe it or not, because so much of it consists of expressing the text. And like Strauss, he has very good texts which you have to communicate in the most expressive way you can. You are dealing with "Gesamtkunstwerke", so the singing alone is not the most important thing. As far as the mezzo is concerned, the same is also true of Strauss.'

In 1955, Ludwig was invited to join the Vienna State Opera by its Music Director, Karl Böhm. Ludwig was nervous about going to Vienna because of her age, still only twenty-six. But Böhm (who was married to a singer and understood the voice), equally anxious to protect this young voice from harm, assured her that 'no, you won't sing Marie, Brangaene and Amneris, you will sing Cherubino, Dorabella and the Composer in *Ariadne auf Naxos*!' This way her voice was spared again for several years, until she started singing the bigger, higher roles with Karajan.

Ludwig made her Vienna début as Cherubino and went on to sing Dorabella and the Composer, hating the two trouser roles 'because I had to starve myself for them' but enjoying singing Dorabella to Irmgard Seefried's Fiordiligi, despite the latter singer's wish to monopolize all the attention. But she got out of singing Mozart, 'the most difficult of all composers because of the purity of line and intonation he demands' early basically because she didn't feel she had a 'Mozart voice' and also because 'the emotion in his music is different, too, more restrained, more Baroque-like, reminiscent in this sense of Bach and Handel, and this is not my feeling. I'm more in tune with romantic music.'

Vienna established Ludwig as a singer of the first division. During the late fifties and throughout the sixties she was in great demand and asked to sing 'anything from Octavian to the Marschallin, from the Nurse to the Dyer's Wife and, had wanted to, Brünnhilde and Isolde, too!' She also landed an important recording contract with EMI, thanks to that legendary figure in classical recording, Walter Legge, Elisabeth Schwarzkopf's husband. Schwarzkopf had sung the Countess to Ludwig's Cherubino at Salzburg in 1957 and liked this new colleague. She asked Legge to listen to her. He, too, liked what he heard and soon became one of the most important mentors in Ludwig's career.

'He taught me to express the meaning of the words I was singing, to concentrate so hard that I made the word "sun" shine and the word "flower" bloom, when I made my first Lieder record with him. He also said I should "listen with long ears" to where the true beauty of my voice was and never pass over an opportunity to stress it. With some singers their most beautiful sound comes out in a fortissimo while others shine in pianissimi. But we should always listen out for this best sound and maximize it.' The result was a string of vintage recordings, some of which, like the historic *Der Rosenkavalier* conducted by Karajan with Elisabeth Schwarzkopf as the Marschallin, have become classics.*

Der Rosenkavalier is one of four Strauss operas that have featured prominently in Ludwig's career. (The others are *Ariadne auf Naxos*, *Die Frau ohne Schatten* and *Elektra*.) Her first role in this opera was Octavian, which she first sang in Frankfurt and later in Vienna, with great success. Yet she always disliked this character because 'he is vapid and always uttering the stupidities of a seventeen-year-old, while all the interesting things are said by the Marschallin.' He also happens to be much less grateful to sing than the Marschallin because he has no line – most of the time he consists of Sprechgesang while *she* does all the singing.'

Yet, left to her own devices, Ludwig would never have thought of taking on the Marschallin, not least because it is a true soprano role, and was intensely surprised when asked to do so by Leonard Bernstein for his first *Rosenkavalier* ever, at the Vienna State Opera in 1968. But she remembered that when her mother had bought her a score of *Der Rosenkavalier* before her first Octavian in Frankfurt, she had inscribed it

---

* Ludwig recently told a Spanish newspaper that she considers today's technically 'advanced' way of recording – with each singer often being recorded alone in a different city and having his voice mixed and integrated with those of the other artists at a later stage – 'soulless and, in a way, dishonest'.

'Now for Octavian, later for the Marschallin!' 'So she always knew it was possible. And I must say the Marschallin proved to be one of the most important roles not only in my career [she has sung it with Böhm and Bernstein], but in my life, because it taught me a great deal that I found very helpful in my personal life: the fact that there is a time for everything (*"jedes Ding hat seine Zeit"*), and that one should never cling but let go of things with a light touch. Whenever I'm tempted to act otherwise, I say to myself, "think of the Marschallin!" I suppose that of all operatic characters she is the one from whom one can learn something relevant to one's own life. I found Kundry in *Parsifal*, one of my favourite roles, also very interesting. She is looking for salvation, which I suppose we all are in a way, and finds it in a sort of religiousness which, as often happens, is deeply mixed with the erotic. A case not unlike that of Mary Magdalene, and a truly wonderful part to perform. Singing those words to that music was always a profound thrill. But I cannot say that I learnt anything from her that I could apply to my own life.'

A part, also by Strauss, in which she finds important resonances for life in our own day is the Dyer's Wife in *Die Frau ohne Schatten*, which she first sang in 1964 in Vienna with Karajan and later in Paris and New York with Böhm. The role is usually sung by dramatic sopranos like Nilsson and Jones, and proved one of the most difficult in her repertoire. She recalls that, at the time, Böhm wanted her to sing the Nurse, which she found too low, and Karajan wanted Barak's Wife, which was too high. Yet she decided to go for the latter and 'I must say I always had a big success with it.* I find the Dyer's Wife very interesting as a character because, like so many women nowadays, she is ready to give up motherhood in pursuit of material things. This was something rare until now, when there is precious little family life because husbands and wives both prefer to go out and work for a new car, ski-ing holidays, or whatever and choose not to have children . . . . At least the Dyer's Wife realizes this is not right and goes back to her husband. The development of this character is a wonderful thing to follow and put across. Vocally it was very difficult, one of the most difficult parts I ever had to cope with, but I did so by forgetting my Amneris voice, the middle voice, and imitating the sound of a high soprano.'

She had to do the same, but with more strain, for another, perhaps the most famous, of her soprano roles, Leonore in *Fidelio*, which she first sang in 1962 in Vienna with Karajan and subsequently all over the world, including Munich, Berlin, Tokyo and the Metropolitan Opera (where she had made her début in 1959). It was one of the greatest successes of her

* A live recording exists of a 1964 Vienna performance of *Die Frau ohne Schatten* with Karajan, by Nuova Era.

career and she is one of the role's greatest interpreters, despite the fact that, vocally, it was far from ideal for her. Indeed, when a laryngologist examined her vocal cords after a performance of *Fidelio* he found them red and swollen (a sure sign that a role is wrong) and advised her not to sing Leonore again. But she did so for several years and loved the humanitarian side of this character 'with so much to say about mankind in chains. But I always felt very nervous before singing it – more so than for any role in my career – because I was doing something unnatural for me. I had to *construct* the kind of voice that was needed and which was not my natural voice. I managed to pull it off by spacing the performances well – at least three days between each one – refraining from speaking as much as possible because speaking tires me almost as much as singing [to this day she avoids having to talk a lot before and between performances], and scheduling it very, very carefully. I never ever *ever* mixed it up with my mezzo roles because, as Callas said, the voice is not an elevator. I also had my mother's example, who had ruined her voice by mixing up her Leonores and Sentas with her Ulricas and Azucenas.'

Making a success of this role was, she says, one of the deepest satisfactions of her operatic career and she is very glad that, in the case of Leonore, the Marschallin and the Dyer's Wife, she threw caution to the winds, slightly. 'You see, I am not a frustrated singer. I did almost everything I wanted to do. But when I reached my borderline, I realized and retreated in time to my mezzo repertoire.' For example in 1968 it was announced that Ludwig would sing Brünnhilde and Isolde with Karajan. Her admirers awaited these events with a mixture of excitement and trepidation. But a year later, Ludwig declared that she had changed her mind. 'You see, when a singer reaches the peak of his or her career, everything suddenly comes on a silver platter, so to speak: money, fame, everything and, of course, you want to take it. But mercifully, at the same time comes also the fear of "God, if I do this today, what happens afterwards?" and sometimes this can be salutary.'

In the middle of the seventies Ludwig went through what she calls a big 'mid-life crisis' both in her professional and in her personal life. She was divorced from her first husband, the distinguished bass Walter Berry, and began to experience severe vocal problems. 'In other words, although still in my mid-forties, I was having the menopause, which can play havoc with the voice. In those days the menopause was taboo so nobody liked to talk about it. But as hormone pills were not as developed as they are now, many singers simply stopped singing at this time. I had no clue that this could affect the voice in a significant way because my mother had retired before she came to that stage. But we women are very closely linked to and dependent on our hormone flow and, as the vocal cords are made of tissue very similar to that of the breasts, at the time of the menopause this tissue thickens and becomes wobbly, in the same way that a woman's breasts do, at the time of her monthly period. At first you are not aware of what this means and think "what *is* this? I'm forty-five and I can't sing any more, I can't hit the high notes, what's the matter?" Because there you were, in full bloom and then something suddenly hit you and you didn't know anything any more. Nowadays Hormone Replacement Treatment is a great help. But the most important thing is to *know* about this, to know that although every woman experiences the menopause differently, it is bound to have some effect on the voice. Singing teachers should warn young singers about this phenomenon.'

Apart from medical treatment, the way around the problem was to change her repertoire. 'I went back to mezzo roles but stopped singing the big ones like Ortrud and Kundry which are very demanding on the vocal cords – and, of course, at forty-five I could hardly sing Octavian any more – and started with all the old ladies such as Klytemnestra in *Elektra*, the Countess in *The Queen of Spades*, the Old Nun in *Les Dialogues des Carmélites* and stayed with my Wagner roles, such as Fricka and Waltraute, which are not too demanding.'

She also began to expand her activities as a Lieder and concert singer. Now she sings a limited number of operatic performances a season and a great number of concerts and Lieder recitals. She would advise all singers to start learning the Lied repertoire early in their career because 'one cannot decide, at forty-five, to become a Lieder-singer, one cannot master the style overnight. It is something one should work at over the years. Again it was my mother who said, and she was not thinking of the menopause at the time, that Lieder are like a youth elixir for the voice and that if I wanted to keep my voice neat, well-focussed and flexible, I should sing Mozart and I should sing Lieder. But for Lied one has to pull another kind of voice out of the drawer. Because needless to say, there is such a thing as the "opera voice" and the "Lied voice". This wise advice proved my salvation. Lied has been a source of as deep a satisfaction and fulfilment as the greatest of my operatic roles.'

To the interpretation of Lied Ludwig brings a unique blend of mellowness, variety of vocal colour, psychological and spiritual insight. Her interpretations of Schubert (including *Die Winterreise*, which is usually sung by male voices, although more recently Brigitte Fassbaender has also tackled the cycle with distinction) and the great Mahler song cycles remain unforgettable. She first learnt to 'feel Mahler and understand the soul of his music' with Bernstein. Before then she had been singing a lot of Mahler with Klemperer but 'I didn't have a great idea of what I was singing. I sang the music but I didn't feel it', she told Mel

Cooper in *Opera Now*. 'But Klemperer was marvellous for the singing because he did nothing against the composer: everything was logical, and he was never too slow. People of his generation knew a lot about opera and the voice and could really help singers. Nowadays – with the exception of Solti and Levine who are very knowledgeable and helpful – conductors tend to come from the orchestra and have only a fleeting knowledge of opera and of singing.'

Apart from this, have conductors changed a great deal over the years? 'No! Conductors are very funny people. They *have* to have a big ego, otherwise they couldn't do their job. They are the only autocrats in the world, they can do whatever they want, they have us singers completely in their hands. Barring Third World dictators, this degree of power doesn't exist in any other profession any more. Coming to think of it, even dictators depend on their army or bodyguards or *something*. But conductors can have it all their own way. They can set the tempo, decide on dynamics, choose their casts, they are like emperors!'

The three conductors Ludwig was most closely associated with and whom she calls 'my three gurus' were Karl Böhm, Herbert von Karajan and Leonard Bernstein. 'They were the three I learnt most from. From Böhm I learnt to be musically accurate, the fact that a sixteenth [semiquaver] is a sixteenth and that the clues to the character you are trying to interpret can be found in those little things.' Indeed, when asked to single out the greatest 'Sternstunden', the most unforgettable moments of her career, she named the Salzburg performances of *Così fan tutte* and the New York performances of *Die Frau ohne Schatten*, both conducted by Böhm. 'For some moments what we were doing then really was Art. Not all of it, because you cannot always get all the singers being at their best at the same time so that the whole thing fits together perfectly. But there were moments when it happened, when these performances really became "Sternstunden", and when this happens it's Heaven. But it's very rare. Equally rare, and nearly as marvellous, are those productions where there is a truly good atmosphere at rehearsals, with everybody liking what they're doing and in accord with what everybody else is doing.' I wondered whether there was any reason why both those ultra-special moments in her operatic life should have happened under Böhm?

'Böhm was the servant of the music. He didn't have a big Ego. He just served the music and he liked, understood and was very helpful to singers, as was Karajan, if he liked you. When Karajan did *Fidelio* with me, for instance, he rushed sometimes because he knew I couldn't make it at a slower tempo. The critics wrote he was too fast, but he did it for me. He worked very, very hard with singers and most of his artists loved working with him. He taught me beauty of phrasing, beauty of tone, how to listen to the orchestra and merge my voice with it in a homogeneous way, until it became like another instrument. There is a spot in *Das Lied von der Erde*, for instance (which Ludwig and Karajan recorded for Deutsche Grammophon, making for interesting comparisons with her earlier EMI recording under Klemperer), where the singer comes in on a cello line and he taught me to colour my voice accordingly. And I always remember his advice when we were doing the Paris version of *Tannhäuser* in Vienna. He said I should sing Venus like a Hugo Wolf Lied!' (A fascinating pirate recording exists of a 1963 Vienna performance of this work, by Nuova Era, with Karajan conducting a cast which also includes Gre Brouwestijn as Elisabeth, Hans Beirer in the title role and Eberhard Wächter as Wolfram.) Böhm and Karajan understood the voice because they had begun their careers as coaches in opera houses where singers were often not of top quality. They knew the works from beginning to end and the spots where singers need help, which is very important because *all* singers tend to have the same difficulties.

'Bernstein, on the other hand, didn't know where to spare the voice. He looked at opera like a symphony with singers. But he was a marvellous teacher, like a Rabbi, he loved to share his knowledge and from him I learnt to go *inside* the music. He was never satisfied with what he did and was forever looking for new insights, new details, new colours and studied the score until the last minute. I was already thirty-eight when I met him and, as well as doing my first Marschallin with him, we also did a tremendous number of concerts together over the years.' Ludwig delighted London audiences in December 1989 when she sang the old lady in an unforgettable concert performance of Bernstein's *Candide*, conducted by the composer and recorded live for Deutsche Grammophon. Her brio, fizz, 'Gallic' lightness of touch and comic timing stole the show and, despite a heavy cold, she seemed to relish every minute. Other 'old ladies' she has enjoyed in her latter years are the Old Nun in Poulenc's *Les Dialogues des Carmélites*, and Klytemnestra, which she first sang in 1973 in Paris, and since then almost all over the world.

'When I first sang it, in 1973, I felt too young for it because this is a character who grows inside you slowly, slowly, slowly. You cannot hurry up the process. It's never good to "jump into" a character. Basically there are two ways of doing Klytemnestra: Astrid Varnay's more extrovert way and Regina Resnik's way, which was more introspective. But she should never *ever* be done as a caricature, as she was in Harry Kupfer's 1990 production for Salzburg and Vienna, [one of the most visually repulsive and cluttered productions imaginable, and one in which Ludwig hated singing], because then one loses sight of the fascinating complexity of the

mother/daughter relationship. Nor should she be portrayed as *too* old and
decrepit. After all, she has a lover for whose sake she conspired to have her
husband murdered. Kupfer dismissed this by saying "there was nothing
physical between them" but I fail to see how this could be. Nor should
Elektra's misery allow one to forget that Klytemnestra is a very unhappy
woman, too. *She* is the one who is having sleepless nights. Altogether a
very Freudian character and it's a shame when this is concealed in an over-
made up caricature. Vocally it's easy – mostly Sprechgesang with a few
wonderful phrases – and hinges on vocal characterization. But it is an
extremely exhausting, emotionally draining part. Although it only
amounts to half-an-hour's singing, when it is finished *I* am finished, too.'

Ludwig is aware that the next few years will be the last of her professional
life. She had just come back from the Metropolitan Opera, where she sang
Fricka and Waltraute in Otto Schenk's production of *The Ring* (which was
also filmed for television), and was soon off to Japan. She confessed she
was tired 'of all that travelling, it's not fun anymore. I may go on this way for
another two or three years and then retire. My son [Marc Berry, a pop
composer whose song was Austria's entry in the Eurovision Song Contest]
tells me I announce I'm about to retire every ten years! But as long as the
timbre and colour of the voice are there, I'll probably continue. I have a
very good adviser in my second husband, Paul Emile Deiber, an actor and
director at the Comédie Française, and I'm relying on him to tell me when
it's time to stop.'

Ludwig is not sure whether she would teach or do master classes as yet.
So far she has done some master classes in Paris but found them tiring
because speaking too much is not good for her at present. 'When the young
people concerned have talent it is wonderful, but when they don't it's awful
and I'm afraid I have no scruples about telling them not to embark on a
singing career . . . . But I think we should pass on what we know, just like
Callas who learnt about *bel canto* from Ponselle and de Hidalgo, and now
the tradition is suddenly gone.'

Her son nearly became the third-generation singer in the family. He had
a good baritone voice and once asked his mother if she was *certain* he could
have a good career. She replied of course not, nobody could *guarantee* that
to anybody. 'So rather than risking a career of Papagenos in second-rate
theatres, he chose to become a pop composer which, of course, is a creative
thing. We singers are only interpreters. We bring something of ourselves to
a performance certainly, but we are not creative.' Does she regret that?

'No. I am stupid enough to be satisfied with what I am. Even in the Bible
it says we should love ourselves. This means we should accept ourselves as
we are and I'm stupid enough to be content. I have a limited amount of
talent and, within those limitations, I think I have done my best. I tend to be

on the lazy side. The profession absorbs so much of my energy that I have none left for diets, exercises and suchlike. I just need rest and peace in order to *think* and replenish the well. I'm also what Eastern people call "centred", moderate, non-excessive and, vocally speaking, this is also true of mezzo-sopranos. We are in the middle. So I am a woman of the middle, not extreme, either in my voice or in my wishes, but happy with my lot. I love my concerts and I love the stage and feel at home in it. Of course, sometimes it hurts a little not to be singing the big roles any more. Because pouring out the full voice and unleashing that torrent of sound over a full orchestra is a nice feeling, almost orgiastic, like making love. When on top of this the part you are singing is full of emotion, it's quite, quite wonderful, in fact it's Heaven.'

TATIANA TROYANOS

SHORTLY BEFORE OUR first meeting, the American mezzo Tatiana Troyanos had been watching *Fame*, the American television series about life in a New York drama school. What had struck and amused her most among goings on in this institution was the attempt by each of the teachers – the professors of music, acting, dance etc – to convince the students that *his* particular art was the greatest, the one they should dedicate themselves to, body and soul. 'No one said anything like this to *me* when I was a student. But I *knew* this was so, that I would have to put everything I have into my art and that it would take a long time to get it right and attain enough insight to do what I wanted to do.'

Commitment of the most intense, obsessional kind is indeed the keynote of Tatiana Troyanos as an artist. She experiences the inner life of the characters she portrays very deeply and her fanatic dedication to artistic truth, coupled with her dark, expressive yet soft-grained mezzo voice, makes her a compelling and moving performer. Her career has taken her to the greatest theatres and festivals in the world and she has worked with the finest conductors: Karajan, Kubelik, Bernstein, Boulez, Solti as well as those of her own generation. The most decisive influence on her career has been James Levine, Music Director of the Metropolitan Opera, where during the past fifteen years Troyanos has done her most important work, adding new roles to her repertoire almost every season, watched by millions in Public Broadcasting Service's *Live From the Met* telecasts.

Her regular presence at the Met, after ten years spent in Germany, has meant a return to her roots for Tatiana Troyanos, who was born on the West Side of New York City in 1938 to parents who were both singers. Her Greek-American father was a tenor and her German-born mother a coloratura soprano. Paradoxically, her own ability for coloratura (brilliantly displayed in her Baroque and classical roles such as Monteverdi's Poppaea, Handel's Ariodante and Giulio Cesare and Mozart's Sextus), which she attributes partly to inherited genes, did not point her towards Rossini. Yet anyone passing by her window on the corner of

Columbus Avenue would, for many years, have heard her practising the aria 'Non più mesta' from *La Cenerentola* as an exercise, singing along to Teresa Berganza's recording which she considers a model of Rossini style. But she always sensed that Rossini ladies were wrong for her and points out that she would have had a very different career if she had gravitated towards such parts 'for which, among other things, I didn't have the confidence. I do now, but I didn't then because of the way I was, both physically and emotionally, as a personality. I was too tall, too dramatic and tempestuous, and didn't feel they suited me at all.' The result was that she never became a 'specialized singer', and her ability to change styles – from Baroque and classical parts to Wagner and contemporary opera – is one of her remarkable artistic assets.

Troyanos's musical formation began early on. She was taught solfège, 'which was the basis of my musical education and extremely useful later on', at the age of eleven by an Italian bassoon-player in the orchestra of the Metropolitan Opera. One day he asked her what instrument she would like to learn and suggested either the piano or the violin. She replied she would sleep on it and decided on the piano, which he taught her for several years. At the same time she sang a great deal in her school choir, where she remembers everyone making fun of her voice which was already very dark and 'this made me feel it was also very ugly'. Nevertheless, although she was a reserved teenager, she felt 'a tremendous *need* to sing'. She didn't talk about it much, but inside she had already made up her mind that, like her parents, she, too, would like to have a career in music, either as a pianist or a singer. The music teacher at school was impressed enough by her work in the choir to arrange for her to study at home with him. 'He gave me a lot of confidence at a time when I had none,' and also personally saw to it that she was admitted to the Juilliard School of Music.

After a traumatic spell with the wrong teacher who was 'a lovely person and totally committed to me' but classified her as a contralto, her throat began to ache every time she left class, a sure sign that she was on the wrong track. 'I *had* top notes but wasn't allowed to use them. A fellow-student used to imitate the way I was made to sound in class and it just didn't sound natural. I complained to my fellow students and we all agreed I probably had the wrong teacher. It was a terrible experience because it's agonizing to change teachers at a school like the Juilliard. Yet you must pay attention to your own instincts.' Finally she was allotted to another teacher, Hans Heinz, who was perfect for her and with whom she continued working even after the onset of her professional career.

'He understood my voice and helped me open it up at the top. He started off by making me *feel* what it was like to have a head voice and gradually I found all my top notes.' He also stressed that, instead of worrying about the notes, she should concentrate on the words, on *what* she was singing. The rest, he said, would come by itself. 'Go home and *speak* the text to yourself, and *think* about what you want to bring out in each particular scene. *Then* decide on the right vocal colour.' To this day, the importance of the words is the key to Troyanos's approach to interpretation: 'Of course, I also think about technique a great deal; I can't help it, it's second nature. But if you really know what you want to do, you can always find a way of doing it provided, of course, that the role is suited to your voice. If you practise the words at home and think about them and then look at the music to see how the *composer* responded to those words, then all that's needed is to decide what you can do, with your own voice, to bring out those colours. It's an endless process with endless possibilities for constant discovery and improvement, and one of the things I like best about our profession. Words are also important from the stylistic point of view. It is the way they are spoken and sung that, partly, brings out the stylistic differences between Italian, French and German opera.'

For this reason she feels that, if she were to start her career all over again, she would go and spend at least two years in France and Italy, instead of an entire decade in Germany, in order to 'get those languages properly in my ear. I would have liked to have put more time especially into Italian and Italian singing, which was the most difficult of all styles for me: that legato, that *bel canto* line, the evenness of sound from top to bottom, going for the vowels, in fact the ability to make the voice do just about everything.' Yet Troyanos has delivered much-acclaimed portrayals of two of the most difficult *bel canto* roles for the mezzo: Adalgisa (to Montserrat Caballé's Norma for her La Scala début in 1977, and later in Houston and the Metropolitan Opera); and Romeo in *I Capuleti ed i Montecchi* at Covent Garden, the Metropolitan, the Chicago and the San Francisco Opera. 'If it had not been for the passionate naturalness of voice and portrayal of Tatiana Troyanos in her La Scala début as Adalgisa, I would have felt, as I often do, that *Norma* should be done as an oratorio,' wrote the Milan critic of *Opera*, while its Texas critic enthused, after the Houston première: 'Tatiana Troyanos was the lovely Adalgisa: her voice was the perfect match for Scotto's, her high Cs brilliant, her recitatives deeply felt.' All the hallmarks of a good *bel canto* singer, in fact. Reviews were equally favourable for her 'Byronic-looking' portrayal of Romeo: 'She showed complete command of its impassioned, lyric writing' and 'sang her exhausting role with great ease and in the grand manner'.

On the other hand, Troyanos has never considered herself a Verdi mezzo. The only Verdi role she feels is right for her and which she can 'do something with' is Eboli in *Don Carlos*, which she first sang in Hamburg during the late sixties. 'I always do it with great joy because I do it well. It lies well for me and I'm proud to have pulled it off because it is a great test for a dramatic mezzo. I remember that afterwards a critic christened me a "mezzo spinto". But I realized early on that I was not the right lady for parts like Amneris, which I sang a couple of times at the Met with James Levine. It didn't come naturally to me, didn't lie well for my voice, and my sound was just not right for it – the grain of it was too soft – nor was my way of communicating.'

After graduation from the Juilliard, Troyanos was engaged by the New York City Opera, where she made her début in 1963 as Hippolyta in Britten's *Midsummer Night's Dream* and stayed for two years.

Rolf Liebermann, who saw her performing there, decided to take a chance on her and invited her to the Hamburg State Opera. 'I want you to arrive with a big truck and that's all. Hamburg will be your home and nowhere else.' It was, for six fulfilling and productive years, from 1965–71, during which time she consolidated her technique and took on some of the big mezzo roles for the first time: Poppea, Dorabella, Eboli, Carmen, Santuzza, Jeanne in the world première of Penderecki's *The Devils of Loudun* (in 1969) and the Composer in *Ariadne auf Naxos*, with which she made her début in 1965.

The Composer immediately became one of her favourite roles and she has since performed it with great success at the Aix-en-Provence Festival where, in 1966, she was hailed as the discovery of the Festival, and at the Metropolitan, the Chicago Lyric and the San Francisco Opera. 'Miss Troyanos offered milky tone and clean, expressive phrasing in her top-class portrayal of the Composer,' wrote *Opera* after her San Francisco performances. She explains that this character, which immediately struck a strong personal chord, is tricky to perform, precisely for this reason: 'It's dangerous to get over-emotional about something you, yourself, feel very emotional *about*: Music and Art and the Theatre. When you're on stage as the Composer, it's tempting to get a bit hysterical, a bit rash, which is what *he* is supposed to be. But *you*, the performer, have to remember that you have more singing to do and therefore you must pace yourself carefully and conserve some of your resources. This is very tricky indeed, because on the one hand you have this rapturous commitment to the beauty of music, this sacred art, which is wonderful to put across, and on the other you have to control and save your voice for the finale, for which you cannot afford to sound exhausted or hoarse. It has to be lyrical, it has to be beautiful and those top notes have to *ring*. They shouldn't be screamed and, boy, is it easy to do just that at this point! But you must find the right balance. You must get the temperament right – and in my case, because our temperaments are similar, this happened naturally – and you must check yourself constantly so that you *sing* the words, instead of screaming them, and sing them well, so that they can be understood.

'Singing, as opposed to screaming, is easy when you are dealing with a Handel melody which is gorgeous, like butter for the voice. But when you pick up a Strauss score and see those millions of notes and how involved the orchestra is with what's going on inside the character, you simply panic [a point also made by Kiri Te Kanawa]. It becomes a big temptation to simply *speak* those parlando passages without producing the right sound, without getting the notes off or the words understood.'

The problem is pacing, and it took her a long time to get it right. 'In the beginning I used to be very impetuous, I wouldn't wait, I would just *go*. I was so totally involved that when I look at old pictures of me as the Composer I am amazed at the intensity they exude. There I am, knocking on the Primadonna's door and *glaring* at the lackey over my shoulder, actually *experiencing* the Composer's anger. Every little feeling mattered, in those days. I desperately needed the right vehicle through which to express myself – a role that matched my own personality – and the Composer was It. To be sure, I *knew* the pitfalls of getting over-involved in a role. But I still found it hard to strike the right balance between involvement and control. But, of course, at twenty-seven or twenty-eight your whole vocal apparatus functions differently. It's always there. I can remember no times when I was not in voice, when it wasn't fresh. That could always be depended on, totally. Later on, your body changes, *you* change, and you have to adjust to that all the time. Experience and professionalism replace youth and freshness. I wouldn't say they make your work easier, but they *are* an asset. You know you've done it before, you know you can rely on certain tricks if things are not going the way you want.'

During the late sixties, while a member of the Hamburg State Opera, Troyanos was allowed considerable freedom for guest appearances elsewhere. She made her début at the Paris Opéra in 1966 and at the Metropolitan Opera as Baba the Turk in Stravinsky's *The Rake's Progress* in 1967 and Covent Garden as Octavian in 1968. The following year she was offered a guest contract at the Bavarian State Opera where she made her début in 1969, as Carmen, in a production directed by the late Intendant of the BSO, Günther Rennert. Vocally the role lies well for her. She had already sung it in 1961 at Louisville, Kentucky, in English, and like most singers who tackle this part she found that Carmen changed her life 'in the sense that it made me realize I really had something in me that was my own and which I could bring to my roles. It was raw, but it was there. My teacher, Hans Heinz, who came along to see it, said: "Tatiana, you've got something there and if you work hard, you can make it." Which is all a good teacher *can* say. They cannot *guarantee* that anyone will have a big career.'

It was Günther Rennert's *Carmen*, though, that taught her all she knows about the character. 'He showed me that everything has to come from inside. You should never try too hard, nor can you resort to external gimmicks without immediately cheapening the role. One of his first remarks was "No hands on the hips, *ever*. Let's see how alluring you can be without your hands on your hips." And he made me use my face, my eyes, every bit of animation I had, and every bit of nuance I could find in the German language.' Troyanos didn't perform Carmen in the original French until 1970, when she sang it at Covent Garden. As far as the singing is concerned, she 'just followed the score and trusted in Bizet. The most difficult part is Act II, where Carmen also has to dance, play the castanets and is constantly on stage, dominating the action but without ever seeming to try too hard.'

It was in the seventies and early eighties that Troyanos reached full artistic maturity. Her repertoire expanded to include more Baroque music on one side, and Wagner on the other. The first new part was the title role in Handel's *Ariodante* for the opening of the Kennedy Centre in Washington in 1971. The only other Baroque part Troyanos had sung so far was Poppea in Hamburg. But when she had tackled her first *bel canto* role, Romeo to Beverly Sills's Juliet, in *I Capuleti ed i Montecchi* at the New York City Opera, Sills had been impressed by her coloratura and suggested she might find Baroque opera a rewarding vehicle: 'You have the ability to sing accurately, rhythmically, with agility and equality and, perhaps most important, you have spontaneity,' she encouraged.

Spontaneity is especially important for a role like Ariodante, who is 'young, noble, poetic, dreamy, mad and first seen wandering in a beautiful garden. The tessitura is comfortable and it felt as if all I had to do was stand there and sing some of the most difficult music ever written for the mezzo, with some very elaborate coloratura, as simply as possible, with enthusiasm and spontaneity but without turning it into a huge emotional number. It just had to be *joyous* because in *Ariodante* everything ends happily, with him getting the girl he's in love with, and this joyousness overtakes you and, hopefully, the audience, too.' Since then Troyanos has sung Ariodante again, with great success in concert at Carnegie Hall and on stage at the Geneva Opera in 1984–85.

The success of her first Ariodante encouraged her to be receptive to an invitation to sing the title role in *Giulio Cesare* at the Geneva Opera in 1982–83, under one of the great Handelians, Sir Charles Mackerras. Initially she approached this role with trepidation, realizing it was more difficult than Ariodante, both vocally and dramatically. 'He is a ruler, imperious, triumphant and at the same time tender, so you have to bring out both extremes.' Again, pacing is of crucial importance. 'You have to get a firm grasp of the intentions of the music and the character at each stage, learn to be patient and *wait* for the really triumphant numbers which are mostly near the end.' Sir Charles wrote some special embellishments for her there, and when she first looked at them on paper she thought she could never manage them. 'But the more I did them, the more they became part of me. I must say I hadn't realized how much time it takes for this style of music to become part of you, or how much work you have to put into it – *tons* of it. You have to practise for hours on end, doing scales, arpeggios, trills, working extra hard on intonation and on hitting not from the top, but the bottom. And the constant repetition that is part of the style requires you to take one single big, long breath which has to hold and be constantly behind you. Of course this is true in all singing. But Baroque music is so exposed that it is all too easy suddenly to find that your breath is gone. One must remember that these operas were written for very, very good singers with seemingly phenomenal techniques. But when you are working with musicians like Sir Charles who know the style backwards, you learn a tremendous amount as you go along, and singing Baroque music becomes a highly enjoyable experience.'

Sir Charles Mackerras confirms that the vocal qualities demanded by Baroque music can indeed be acquired. The essential attributes for singing Baroque as well as classical parts are 'parity of voice, the ability to sing rungs of notes with absolute clarity and perfect intonation, plus the ability to trill clearly. That was one of the great pre-requisites of eighteenth-century singers and something on which the critics of the period invariably commented, referring to a trill as "a shake". Equally important is agility and being able to sing with warmth and feeling but without too much vibrato. In fact vibrato was not used at all in eighteenth- and early-nineteenth-century music. Its use is comparatively recent and first appears in the early singers of Wagner. But in Baroque and classical singing it is important to sing with warmth and expression but without, or almost without, vibrato.'

Five years after singing her first Ariodante, Troyanos had the chance to prove herself a first-rate classical singer as well, when she made her début at the Salzburg Festival in 1976 as Sextus in *La clemenza di Tito*, in a new production directed by Jean-Pierre Ponnelle and conducted by James Levine. She was fully aware of the importance of singing Mozart in Salzburg and of striking the right balance in her portrayal: 'Singing well, singing with meaning and being the character. I was able to identify with Sextus and bring the singing, the acting, the emotions and movements together. This *had* to come from inside, there was no way you could fake it. As always I tended to be very intense, but Jean-Pierre would tell me to take it easy. The scenes in *Clemenza* are so beautifully constructed that if I just followed Mozart, the thing would carry me.

Dramatically, the character presents no problems. 'You just have to put across Sextus's own total commitment in a way that makes the audience sympathize with his plight. He is, after all, the only one apart from Vitellia who knows the whole truth, and he is torn between his passion for her and his loyalty to Titus. His love for *him* should be made very clear as should the warm feeling of friendship between him and Annio. It's a very stylized role, so you don't want to do too much, especially in Act I. But you still have to put across a very warm, very young human being who is in thrall to Vitellia. Why I don't know. Probably because, although he grew up with Titus, he discovered physical passion with her. She is his first youthful infatuation and she uses the power she has over him to crush his love for Titus. But his youth and sincerity make him a very sympathetic character, which also happens to be gratifying vocally, although very demanding. The coloratura in "Parto, parto" is probably the most difficult I have ever had to sing because it is ascending, then descending, then ascending again and at a certain speed. It just doesn't let up and you have to go through it three times, which certainly presents some technical difficulties – one of the few spots in this role that does. Which is why I have written all over my score at this point: "Be calm and take a good, big breath." But if you are too calm and careful, it won't have all the élan you want! Tempi are also terribly important and you have to work at this a lot with the conductor. Fortunately I had Jimmy.'

Troyanos attributes a big slice of her success in this role to Levine and to Ponnelle who cushioned and supported her all the way. Ponnelle had seen her Poppea in San Francisco in 1975, rang her up and came to lunch in her house where he asked point blank if she would like to sing Sextus in Salzburg. 'Terrific,' she replied, and this was the start of their long collaboration. 'He was a genius, a very strong personality. I never had to worry about *anything* when working with him. All I had to do was perform. I always tried to do what he wanted, because I knew that he would let me do it *my* way. [Indeed, as Agnes Baltsa also mentions, this was Ponnelle's greatest quality. He had a unique way of tuning into every artist, honing his or her best qualities and tailoring his productions specifically around those.] He understood me very well, the chemistry was right, and he always made things come alive for me. He adored music and the voice and was musically knowledgeable, which, sadly, is not all that usual among directors.' (Ponnelle could, for instance, read even the most complex scores.) Their collaboration was as important to her as her musical partnership with James Levine, with whom she has 'an incredible rapport'.

The two have known each other since their late teens and came together again in March 1976, when Troyanos made her début at the Metropolitan Opera in a big role: Octavian in *Der Rosenkavalier*. This was soon followed by the Composer and Carmen (the latter in the spring tour) and in subsequent seasons by Eboli, Amneris, Jocasta, Giulietta, Adalgisa, Venus, Kundry, Brangaene, Countess Geschwitz, Santuzza Charlotte, Dido in *Les Troyens* and Prince Orloffsky, many of which were sung for the opening of the season and televised live by PBS. One of the most important telecasts was Venus in 1981–82 in a *Tannhäuser* production conducted by Levine. 'As always it was important to be involved yet at the same time removed enough to know what you're doing and, as in all Wagner operas, to familiarize yourself with the orchestration, so that you know what instruments are playing at any given time and where you might be swamped by the orchestra. Also the spots on the stage where they are most likely to cover you. Of course, the conductor must watch out for that, too, as Jimmy did in my case. He suggested I move to a different part of the stage where I would be heard better. And if you feel confident that the conductor will ensure you won't get drowned by the orchestra, you can bring out a much greater variety of vocal colours and sing Venus like singing a beautiful Lied, but in a big way, unlike Kundry, which has some passages where you could be tempted to scream.

'Venus is a really enjoyable part to sing. You have to give it the most sensuous, intimate singing you're capable of. How you look, and especially how you move, how you get up that first time and how this looks to the audience, are also crucial. Because Venus has to lie on top of Venusberg for a good twenty minutes before she begins to sing and you have to be both vocally warmed up and ready and physically relaxed and able to move languorously. I worked a lot with the choreographer at the Met and he taught me how to sit and position myself gracefully and how to get up. You really have to practise this and learn to use your body in a very sensuous way for this role. Otherwise, she is a very straightforward character, not at all complex, unlike Kundry in *Parsifal* who happens to be among my top favourites.'

Troyanos first sang Kundry at the Metropolitan Opera and it is a part which, despite her affection for it, she approaches with trepidation, because she considers it 'a borderline part'. But she would love to sing it again because of the spiritual nourishment she takes from it. 'It's a gigantic experience and I love being a part of this masterpiece. Either you identify with it or you don't, and if you don't, I fail to see why you should be bothering to do this piece anyway. But Kundry does take me to my limits. I'm getting better at it, I've worked hard on making the lyric parts more lyrical and on getting more focussed. The tessitura is the same as Eboli's and the most difficult parts are undoubtedly the last ten pages of Act II. Régine Crespin, whom I admire enormously, used to say the last ten pages of Kundry are *cruel* and indeed they are. But it's a *wonderful* part, deeply, deeply rewarding.

'In Act I Kundry is her hysterical, wandering-Jew kind of self. She presents the balsam to Gurnemanz and then falls into a deep sleep. But *you* certainly can't – ten years ago, maybe but now, definitely not. It is important to think of yourself as a straight actress at this point and maintain concentration. Otherwise the voice can easily get cold during this long silence. When she wakes up and starts singing again, saying she knows something about Parsifal and so on, the tessitura is tricky – middle-to-low and so much is going on in the orchestra that it's hard to make the words understood. But you shouldn't push, either. Christa [Ludwig], who is a wonderful Kundry, never seems to have any problems here. But her voice lies differently, a bit lower than mine.

'Most of Act II virtually sings itself, apart from the conversation with Klingsor at the beginning. You have to sing beautifully and entice Parsifal with your sound, but you have plenty of time to warm up. I think the seduction scene is one of the most beautiful in all opera and so beautifully written it's just perfect. Then, at the point where Kundry realizes she's not going to get what she wants and sings "Grausame", you get a separation spot that divides the Act into sections One and Two, those famous last ten pages where if you are exhausted, if you have already given too much, too soon, you are in trouble, and risk beginning to scream, especially if you are a mezzo and not a dramatic soprano (Dramatic sopranos wouldn't have this kind of problem because their voice lies naturally on those As, A flats and B naturals.) Yet if you can perform Act II *without* separating the two sections too much so that you don't have to start saving yourself – for sometimes in saving yourself you lose yourself, lose the character – so much the better. It's very difficult to verbalize what I mean. You've got to have the physical, emotional and vocal sensation of what it feels like and go with it. I suppose in this case it doesn't matter *that* much if you do scream a bit because of the dramatic situation; Kundry herself is getting pretty shrill at that point. But you don't want to feel pushed, as if you were up the creek and *just* making it, it's the worse kind of feeling. But it happens to everyone, no matter how gifted.

'I would love a chance to sing Kundry again because you grow with it and the more the part mellows, the more you improve. This way you also get a more objective viewpoint about your portrayals. Of course you can never be *absolutely* objective and know exactly what you are sounding like, what is going wrong and what isn't. You have an instinct for it sometimes, and usually your instinct is right. But there are times when you think something is so bad that you lose your objectivity. In reality, more often than not it's not as bad as you think. And if it is, and you are clever enough to understand it, you can compensate with something else: you use the acting, you use the words, or a different gesture – at any rate you do something to ensure that the part stays alive, even if your voice is leaving you. I've done it on a number of occasions when I haven't been on top vocal form. Ours is not an exact science, you see. Every performance is unique, unrepeatable and full of such ebbs and flows.'

This is where having a good director and conductor helps very much. Troyanos says she *needs* good directors and conductors, otherwise 'I get too general, I don't focus closely enough.' Even if she is working on a revival of a production she has done before, she still needs the director there, re-directing her every time. Apart from Ponnelle, another director she has greatly enjoyed working with is Lofti Mansouri, now General Manager of the San Francisco Opera, who directed her first *Werther* at the Metropolitan Opera, and who she says 'did all the work for me. He just stood there, *being* Charlotte, which was very important for me. To a great extent this was the interpretation that stayed in me, and which I carried inside me when I performed it elsewhere. You never forget your first contact with a role, the first time it becomes your own. It's a revolutionary process.'

Charlotte, however – which she recorded for EMI with Alfredo Kraus as Werther – was a part which she found it hard to empathize with, possibly, she thinks, because she never had the sort of sheltered upbringing Charlotte had. 'Although it's a wonderful part, I found it very hard to get *into* her, although I do feel sympathy for her. She starts off young, sweet, lovely, innocent and inexperienced, wanting, yet not daring to, give in to Werther's passion – all those marvellous emotions so beautifully depicted in Massenet's music. But how to put all of this – plus that poetic, idyllic feeling of Act I – across as an actress? Acts II and III roll on by themselves, they have their own dramatic momentum. But Act IV, especially the Letter Scene, was very difficult, for the same reasons. This time Charlotte is alone, the first time we see her by herself, and it's Christmas. And how, exactly, should this woman react? Clearly she's not an exhibitionist. She is reserved, which I am not. So I had to work very, very hard to get this sort of . . . French composure, which is not in my nature. When I see Janine Reiss [the famous French coach often mentioned in this book] I understand exactly how Charlotte should be played because Janine personifies this very French blend of charm, composure, sense of measure and certain serenity to perfection, whereas I have to *think* about all this because by nature I am more rumbustious and excessive.'

Troyanos explains that although Massenet knew exactly how to write for the voice and to express the poetry of the situation his music nevertheless doesn't 'carry' the singer. A lot of it consists of conversation. There isn't a beautiful melody going on all the time so the singer has to 'carry' herself to a large extent. 'The tessitura lies well for me but I had to be careful in the middle part so that the sound didn't become too thick, otherwise the words wouldn't be understood. I had to try to lighten my sound, so that it matched the words, matched what I was saying. Working with Janine was a great help because she helped me understand why I was saying it and bring colour to everything I was singing. But Act I was difficult for me vocally as well as dramatically – getting that sweetness and innocence across. My voice was too dark, too knowing; it never quite had the colour I wanted it to and I was never completely happy with the first two acts. I was too mature-sounding, whereas I wanted a lighter sound. But the last two acts were fine. I sang Charlotte again in Paris, but after that I decided not to do it any more. There are plenty of people around who can do it far better than I.'

There are very few people around, however, who are as objective and self-critical as Tatiana Troyanos, or as forthright in expressing admiration for colleagues. With her the constant quest for self-improvement – and any accompanying self-doubts – are never indulged in for the purpose of self-glorification or self-promotion, but for the sake of the work at hand: becoming a better channel through which the composer's inspiration can be realized. The sincerity and intensity of her commitment to this end is illustrated by an episode during rehearsals for *Ariodante* in New York with the St Luke's Ensemble, whose musicians she considers among the best Baroque specialists in the world. At one point she stopped and told them: 'I *have* to talk to you about this aria because you're playing one thing and I'm singing another! You've got to know what it's *about*.' So she translated it to them, and although it is unusual for orchestras to take any sort of direction from singers, they registered the fact that she *cared* – not just about the way *she* sounded, but also about the way *they* did. She also asked Janine Reiss to take notes during rehearsals of *Werther* in New York and kept them, along with the notes from all her directors. 'I always try doing what they want. I work really hard at rehearsals, watching myself and thinking, "how does this gesture look to the audience?" If I've had a good day, I can go home and sleep. But if things have been frustrating, I still go home but can't stop thinking about it and can't sleep at night. I tend to sleep as well as the day's rehearsals went!'

On performance days she likes to take a nap in the late afternoon after eating a light meal, and finds this very restful for the voice and for the nerves. Feeling relaxed when she comes to the performance is 'the greatest plus. You feel fresher, you know you're on top of it and your nerves are on top of it. But it doesn't always happen. Sometimes *it*'s on top of you. Again, as I already explained, it rather depends how you approach it . . . But, you see, our profession takes its toll. The audience doesn't, and perhaps shouldn't, know what we artists go through. They come to the theatre for a few hours, to be enriched and/or entertained and don't suspect what really goes into it . . .'

At the time of our meetings Troyanos had no idea what she might like to do after retirement. In any case vocal longevity depends on the type of voice. Hers is 'near the natural speaking-voice category' and she reckons that if she is smart she can go for another ten years or so, 'because of the fact of where my voice lies. Tenors and sopranos take most risks. But they pay the price for it whereas a mezzo does not have that temptation. The only temptation for us, and a very dangerous one it is, too, is taking on soprano parts. *My* only temptation in that direction was Leonore in *Fidelio*, which I would have *loved* to sing. So I weighed the pros and cons and thought "why do it when there are so many good Leonores around anyway?" Perhaps one day I might try it in concert. Otherwise, becoming a soprano is something I would never do anyway. My timbre is unquestionably that of a mezzo and I've never felt the urge to be anything else. It would be terribly wrong of me, both vocally and dramatically. So that temptation is non-existent. What exists is the desire to be the best I can at what I'm doing at any particular time and if I don't succeed, to go along with it and hope I'll be better tomorrow.'

LUCIA VALENTINI TERRANI

'I AM NOT a voice fanatic; I am not in love with the voice or technical virtuosity. What I *am* in love with is music, opera and everything to do with theatre,' declares Italian lyric mezzo Lucia Valentini Terrani, one of the most original and appealing personalities in the profession. 'Like many shy people, I feel liberated by music and savour every minute of my life on stage. The theatre provides opportunities to do things I would never have the courage to do in real life and, through the possibility to be so many different people, gives me the chance to express sides of me that would otherwise never see the light of day.'

As a singer, Valentini Terrani feels she is 'a soloist in an ensemble, a team of people trying to serve the composer. I love the composer – all composers whose music I sing – above all and want all of us in the team to do well for *him*. If I hadn't been born with a voice I think I would have been just as happy playing the violin or the cello in an orchestra, especially the cello, which is beautiful to listen to and beautiful to play. I love its sound and colour and it must be a great experience to hold and feel this big, strong instrument become part of your body.' (Most mezzos, including, in this book, Berganza and Troyanos, wax lyrical about the cello, make the comparison between its sound and that of a mezzo voice and underline the distinctly erotic response it evokes.)

Although in recent years Valentini Terrani has won high praise for her interpretations of several French roles, it is as a Rossini mezzo that she made her name and earned her place in operatic history. She won the International Contest for New Rossini Voices, run by Italian Television in 1972, after making her professional début three years earlier in Brescia in the title role in *La Cenerentola*. It was this role, to which she feels linked by destiny, that launched her international career when she sang it at La Scala in 1973, in Jean-Pierre Ponnelle's famous production, conducted by Claudio Abbado.

As a leading exponent of Rossini and the only contemporary *Italian* mezzo to distinguish herself in his music, Valentini Terrani obviously has very precise ideas about what makes Rossini special, about his style of

composition and the various ways of interpretating his music prevalent
today. 'Rossini has an instantly recognizable identity. You can't mistake
a single bar of his music for anybody else's. His style of composition and
vocal writing grew out of the period he lived in, sandwiched as he was
between Mozart and Verdi. Indeed some of his late works, such as
Tancredi or *Guillaume Tell*, seem to usher in early Verdi. But in his day,
singers were still the Kings and Queens of opera, unlike our own day
when the King of opera is undoubtedly the conductor. *His* importance
grew in Verdi's day, when the orchestra became a bigger and more vital
factor in the conception and construction of the new operas. But in
Rossini's day, singers still reigned supreme and this is directly reflected in
his compositions.'

It goes without saying that, to sing Rossini, singers require certain
qualifications, chief of which is agility. 'If you cannot sing coloratura you
cannot sing Rossini. But apart from that, I always think that the calibre of
singers in Rossini's day was different from today, not only in the technical
but also in the creative sense. They were not only allowed, but expected,
to embellish their own arias which were not fixed, finished products but
conceived in a way that left room for the singers to express their own
creativity and gift for tasteful decoration. (Taste is the keyword when it
comes to embellishing *bel canto* arias, then and now.) Maria Malibran,
for instance, wrote her own cadenzas.'

One of the things that Valentini Terrani most relishes about Rossini is
that he loves risk. And so, she firmly believes, should his interpreters. 'It
is better to do something less than perfect every now and then rather than
something boring. Rossini's genius is very modern, yet difficult to
penetrate because it is so marked by duality and contradiction. He is both
easy and difficult; introverted and cerebral in one sense, extroverted,
manic, mad in another; indeed he is all those things, often at the same
time. When you look at a Rossini phrase or aria on paper, it can seem
very simple. Yet it is anything but. A good example is Isabella's aria
"Cruda sorte" in *L'Italiana in Algeri*. First you get a simple bar, followed
by another two or three simple bars. Then Rossini seems to become
afraid of being boring, so he develops the line in that heady, dizzy way
typical of him. Then perhaps frightened lest he went too far, he returns to
simplicity. You, the interpreter, must capture this unique spirit of his and
penetrate his world. Like a clown, he is a comic with a deep melancholy
and ironic streak. I am a bit like that myself and thus feel a deep, deep
affinity for him. On top of that he is an Italian, who epitomizes Italy, *my*
Italy, everything I conceive of as most intimately and uniquely Italian.'

Valentini Terrani's Rossini repertoire includes the title role
(Angelina) in *La Cenerentola*, the title role (Isabella) in *L'Italiana in*

Algeri, Rosina in *Il barbiere di Siviglia*, Malcolm in *La donna del lago*, Arsace in *Semiramide*, the title role in *Tancredi*, Calbo in *Maometto II*, and the Polish Countess in *Il viaggio a Rheims*, which she is due to sing again in Berlin and Paris. The first, the point of departure, was Angelina which she found instantly congenial, both vocally and dramatically, and easier than the others. 'This is not to say it is easy because, believe me, nothing that has to do with operatic singing is ever easy. But certain music is more congenial and comfortable for our voices. In my case, Angelina came naturally to me whereas Isabella I really had to conquer. It seemed as if destiny itself had a hand in linking me with the former. It was not I who chose Angelina, but the role that chose *me*. First through my professor at the Padua Conservatoire, who realized my natural predisposition and flair for coloratura and made me study Angelina's aria "Nacqui all' affanno". This is the sort of aria that immediately reveals what your voice can do: its extension, agility, capacity for speed and colouration as well as its overall musicality. Vocally, it is suited to my timbre: I can call on the pathetic colours with nebulous overtones. Soon it became my calling card, my means of passing several important auditions.' Far from being daunted by those coloraturas, she loves them. 'While I believe in the vital importance of technique, as I indicated before I don't consider technical virtuosity and pyrotechnics an end in themselves. Coloratura should, above all, be expressive and to me, those Rossini coloraturas both in *La Cenerentola* and all his other works, are like an expression of one's whole body – the feeling that *all* of you is in sync with Rhythm with a capital R. Singing a Rossini cadenza is pure physical joy.'

She finds Angelina as congenial dramatically. 'I feel that I, too, can live through this fairy tale, that somehow it is in harmony with my background, my way of singing, even my complexes if you like.' As already mentioned, she first sang it in Brescia for her professional début in 1969 and later, in 1973, in Ponnelle's production at La Scala, conducted by Claudio Abbado, when she was chosen to replace an indisposed Teresa Berganza. Abbado was in Peking at the time, but due back for the dress rehearsal. Valentini (she had not yet married her actor husband Alberto Terrani whose name she added to her own) was asked to sing the dress rehearsal and told that if Abbado liked her, she would sing the première. 'I knew that if I impressed him, I would have the chance to make my début at La Scala in a big production, at the age of twenty-five. I remember that Claudio arrived at about four in the afternoon, still jet-lagged after his long flight from China. After a few minutes, I could see he was pleased with what he heard and saw, because he started to smile in that special way of his. There and then, he decided to trust me and give me my chance. The public, too, were with me on that night, and this début was the beginning of everything for me.'

Since then, Valentini Terrani has sung Angelina all over the world, deepening her portrayal as she went along. Far from getting bored with it, she still finds it as enchanting as ever. But, she points out, with the passing years she has had to exercise increased technical control, especially over her dramatic presentation, in order to go on evoking extreme youth convincingly. 'As far as the acting side of this part is concerned, the most important thing to remember is that the subtitle of this opera is "*La bontà in trionfo* – "The triumph of goodness". If, as an interpreter you cannot relate to this concept, then you might as well not take on this role. On the other hand, it is vital not to fall into the trap of portraying Angelina as stupidly goody-goody, which she is not. She is a winner because justice will have it that goodness should triumph in the end. This should be put across without lapsing into sugary sentimentalism.'

Valentini Terrani's performances of this role justify fully her claims of special identification and have received critical and public acclaim worldwide. 'Lucia Valentini Terrani proved to be an ideal Cenerentola and portrayed the character as girlishly as possible. She is at her best in this part and sang the final rondo with a technical perfection rarely equalled today,' wrote a Naples critic after a performance at the Teatro San Carlo.

While Valentini Terrani took naturally to Angelina, her second Rossini part, for which she is equally famous – Isabella in *L'Italiana in Algeri* – was a more formidable challenge. Now, having risen to the challenge so successfully, she says she enjoys singing it even more than Angelina, precisely because of the sense of achievement of having passed a hurdle. She would never advise a singer to take on this part until they are at least ten years into their career, because it is the sort of role that will tolerate neither vocal nor dramatic immaturity. 'It needs an artist whose singing is very assured and who has considerable stage presence. As a character Isabella is a real prima donna who dominates the stage effortlessly and completely. The whole opera depends on her. While in *La Cenerentola* the strings are pulled by other characters as well as by the heroine, in *L'Italiana in Algeri* Isabella has to pull all the strings herself. She is very bright, resourceful and cunning and manipulates everyone, including the public, like a puppeteer. Everyone is at her beck and call and everyone does what she wants. In comparison the male characters seem feeble and I suppose this is true to life, because women are more resilient than men in every way!'

Valentini Terrani first sang Isabella in 1974 at the Metropolitan Opera and a few months later at La Scala, where she performed it again in 1979. The intervening years had, she says, given her time to master its fierce technical difficulties. The tessitura is middle-to-low, with some very low alto coloratura passages. "Cruda sorte" is pure alto coloratura and, like most of *Semiramide*, pure fireworks. You are always hovering on the lower passaggio and if you haven't worked on and perfected your coloratura technique in that region, you cannot cope with this role. If you think about it, successful interpretations are the result of maturing, both as an artist and as a woman, and my performances of Isabella at La Scala in 1979 coincided with a period when I felt at the peak of my vitality. I often think it a pity that we singers cannot sing all the things we want at the right time, that golden moment which is usually the decade between thirty-five and forty-five. Instead of theatres thinking, "We have such and such singers in their prime, what shall we plan for them?" they think: "We want to put on this or that" and then fish around for someone who can manage to sing it, in however rudimentary a fashion.'

Valentini Terrani's observation that 'some roles you seem to be born for' can be taken to include Rosina in *Il barbiere di Siviglia*, which she first sang at Genova in 1975 and later on tour in Japan, Covent Garden, Aix en Provence and Hamburg. In her view Rosina is a problem for true mezzos because mezzo voices are by nature dark, sensuous and smoky. 'But while Rosina should be played with a certain sensuality, there is a risk that real mezzos can over-dramatize and invest the part with Azucena-like colours. But I don't believe it should be sung by coloratura sopranos, either, because their limited range of colour is more apt to rather superficial characters. Of course, Rosina is not a title role: everything in this opera does not depend on Rosina alone. Indeed, she faces stiff competition from her male colleagues, Figaro and Count Almaviva, both of whom get off to a head start with show stopping arias such as "Largo al factotum" and "Ecco ridente" before she has a chance to show what she can do with "Una voce poco fa".'

One of the greatest musical joys in Valentini Terrani's life, she confided to *Musica*, is the fact that her career coincided with the great Rossini revival of recent years, and most especially, the revival of his lesser known 'opere serie' such as *Tancredi*, *Semiramide*, *La donna del lago*, 'which really amounted to a Rossini revolution. Not so long ago, during my years at the Padova Conservatoire, the serious Rossini was practically unknown and the comic Rossini was usually performed in heavily truncated versions – Vittorio Gui's famous recording of *La Cenerentola*, for instance, amounts to just over half the complete score. As there was no lack of excellent singers at the time, such as Giulietta Simionato or the young Teresa Berganza, one can only conclude that this was a result of public taste. The public wasn't ready yet to accept uncut editions or respond to the lesser known, serious Rossini operas.'

What changed everything was the 'Marilyn Horne cyclone' which swept away all public preconceptions about Rossini. Nothing was to be the same again. The rapturous response she aroused in audiences paved the way for the receptive mood with which the public has reacted to the recent musicological research at the Centre of Rossini Studies, founded in 1940, at his birthplace, Pesaro, on the Adriatic Sea, now the seat of a renowned annual Rossini Festival.

Scholars such as Alberto Zedda, Philip Gosset and Bruno Cagli have unveiled and produced performing editions of several hitherto unknown Rossini operas – of which *Il viaggio a Rheims*, which was later also performed with great success at La Scala and the Vienna State Opera, and recorded by Deutsche Grammophon, is a prime example. 'This would have been inconceivable twenty years ago, when a production such as Pier Luigi Pizzi's *Semiramide* (in which Valentini Terrani first sang Arsace in Torino in 1983–84), might have been confined to a small elite festival. Now things have changed so much that this production travelled to several major opera houses.'

Valentini Terrani has relished singing the serious Rossini operas, especially trouser roles such as Malcolm, Arsace and Tancredi, because of the opportunity they provided to make the imaginative link with a man's psyche. Tancredi in particular she found 'indescribably poetic, yet virile in a chivalrous, almost "stylized" way. But at the same time, his duet with Amenaide shows him to be so soft, sweet and vulnerable as to be almost disturbing. Singing him was pure joy, spiritual and physical at the same time, because this opera contains, densely synthesized, all the musical world of the past: all of Gluck and Handel are there, condensed and presented with a freshness and immediacy that is so moving as to be almost miraculous,' she told *Musica*.

Musically, what moves her most in those works are the long, arduous and very dramatic accompanied recitatives – such as Arsace's 'Eccomi alfin in Babilonia' or Tancredi's first recitative – into which, as she explained in *Opera International*, 'Rossini seems to have poured all his heart. It's amazing how much emotion he can pack into a few bars! The beauty, tenderness and sort of chaste modesty that permeate the music are quite heart-rending. Having sung these works after performing *La Cenerentola*, *L'Italiana* and *Barbiere* for so long, makes me convinced that Rossini's comic operas are a mere façade. The real Rossini is in his "opere serie" and especially in those recitatives.'

This tremendous revival of interest in Rossini produced two very distinct styles of interpretation: on the one hand, the freer style of Marilyn Horne and on the other, the school devoted to rigorous textual fidelity, epitomized in Abbado's recording of *Barbiere* with Berganza.

The conductor's taste and personality are as important a factor in this as
public taste. Whether, but especially *how*, one embellishes *bel canto* in
general and Rossini in particular depends very largely on them.
Conductors such as Abbado and Muti tend towards a very purist style of
interpretation while singers such as Horne, Sutherland and Beverly Sills
take a much freer view. Valentini Terrani believes in the middle way:
avoiding performances that amount to little more than lectures in
musicology but steering clear of all tasteless excesses that make her feel
'My God, what has this to do with Rossini? It's just an exhibitionist singer
showing off.' Certain traditions are acceptable, though. 'The high note at
the end of the Rondo in *La Cenerentola* is not written, but it crowns a
marvellous expressive moment in a very musical fashion, so if the singer
has the note it would be stupid to reject a universally accepted tradition
out of purist motives. Even Claudio allowed me to do it.'

Valentini Terrani says she owes 'everything', her whole career, to
Claudio Abbado, who trusted her with that première of *La Cenerentola* at
La Scala back in 1973, booked her for Pergolesi's *Stabat Mater*
immediately after that, and has invited her to collaborate with him on a
plethora of operas and concerts ever since. 'Whenever he could propose
me for suitable roles in various theatres he did so and this was invaluable.
Because we opera singers make our careers not only through public
appreciation but also, and mainly, through the support of specific
important conductors. [The careers of Mirella Freni, Agnes Baltsa and
Anna Tomowa Sintow, all of whom made their international name
through the constant support of Herbert von Karajan, prove Valentini
Terrani's point.] If a conductor really likes you, he can ensure you have a
good career, both on stage and disc.'

Apart from professional and commercial considerations, she stresses
that her collaboration with Abbado has afforded her maximum artistic
satisfaction and fulfilment, and has been 'the highest point in my musical
life, almost like a musical love affair. His rapport with singers he likes is
such that you experience a sort of union, a fusion through the music which
is quite mysterious, as if your two souls have known each other for ever.
You feel cradled and carried through the music, to different dimensions
of existence.'

Another important influence in her career has been Georges Prêtre,
who introduced her to French opera for the first time when in 1978 they
did *Werther* together in Florence with Alfredo Kraus in the title role, of
which he is one of the most distinguished interpreters. Through Prêtre,
Valentini Terrani grew to like French opera and yearn to explore its
repertoire. 'I love the very subtle yet very sensuous way you have to
colour the voice in French opera. You use very refined, blended shades

and nuances of colour. Nothing is ever "black-and-white" in French opera, or indeed in French music. The sound makes me visualize subtle shades of pinky grey – like the sky at first light, long before dawn or at twilight. The primal hues that correspond to the vocal colours used in Italian opera are nowhere in sight.'

Her view of Charlotte, which she sang again in Florence in 1982 and also for her Paris Opéra début in 1983–84, was, she says, deeply coloured by the portrayal of Alfredo Kraus, whose Werther is endemically melancholy and almost masochistic. This, in turn, made her Charlotte 'very tender, almost maternal. Many people asked how I, a full-blooded woman, could empathize with Charlotte, who is essentially unfulfilled. But to me she is the epitome of every woman of yesterday, today and tomorrow whose love, because of questions of duty or conflicting loyalties, could not be consummated or fulfilled.' 'Lucia Valentini Terrani brings even greater mellowness and intensity than before to her portrayal of Charlotte. Her singing is passionate yet full of sweetness, and she is impressive in the Letter Scene and the big love duets,' wrote *Opera International*, after the revival in Florence.

Her success as Charlotte whetted her appetite for more French opera (to this day, she yearns for Juliette, Dalila and Didon), and she readily accepted Prêtre's invitation to sing the title role in *Mignon* by Ambroise Thomas in Florence in 1983–84. '*Mignon*, which had not been performed for twenty years, is an opera which offers a lot of rewards to the mezzo. For a start, it is a title role, which means that all the responsibility rests on your shoulders. Vocally it is ideal for mezzos because its tessitura hovers around the middle most of the time, which is always comfortable. As in many French operas, the first two acts are higher, with the tessitura leaning more towards the soprano regions, and then gets lower in Act III, as the action unfolds. The writing is very nuanced; there are some wonderful passages where Prêtre drew some sublime colours out of the orchestra, and there is an aria, "Connais tu le pays", which used to be a famous "showcase" aria for mezzos. Nowadays there is a fashionable tendency to despise Thomas, which I find preposterously arrogant. I won't attempt to defend him because composers defend themselves and don't need anybody else to do it for them.'

She enjoyed performing Mignon, which, she says, was a wonderful opportunity for her to bring to life such a rarely performed but dramatically very interesting part: 'Mignon is a street child, kidnapped and picked up by gypsies, among whom she grows up. The part has a lot of potential from the acting point of view because first you have to portray her as a childlike adolescent who falls in love but without realizing it. She is not conscious of what she is experiencing or of being jealous. In the end, when Wilhelm declares his love, she discovers that the emotion she, too, had felt for so long was love.'

It is an indication of this exciting singer's versatility that the next new role she chose to tackle lay in a completely different, and hitherto equally unexplored direction: Russian opera. The part was Marina in Mussorgsky's *Boris Godunov* for the 1979–80 opening of La Scala in a production directed by Yuri Lliubimov and conducted by Claudio Abbado. Having never sung anything Russian in her life to date, not even the odd song, she wondered if she would be able to do the role justice. But she decided to trust Abbado's instinct and, with her warmly supportive actor husband Alberto Terrani, went to Paris for a month to study the part with a Russian coach who happened to be Nicolai Gedda's first wife. After a fortnight, she rang Alberto Terrani and said: 'It's useless staying on and spending all this money. Your wife is ready to sing at La Scala *now*.'

Much to her amazement, because 'it is culturally so distant from me', her affinity for Russian music and Mussorgsky was instantaneous. 'Strange as it might seem, something about the colours, the melancholy, the longing and emotional abandon in this music struck a very deep chord in me. Dramatically, Lliubimov wanted me to portray Marina as something of a Polish Lady Macbeth and vocally Mussorgsky's long, broad phrases suited my voice. It is "big" singing, highly enjoyable. Believe it or not, I am less frightened of taking on something as big and as alien as Mussorgsky than I am of our own Verdi, who terrifies me like an ogre.' Apart from Mistress Quickly in *Falstaff*, which she sang in 1982 at the Maggio Musicale Fiorentino and later in Los Angeles and Covent Garden with Giulini (which she considers a mistake because it is a really low Verdi contralto part), and Eboli on record in the French version of *Don Carlos* under Abbado, the only other Verdi part she would contemplate was Azucena. Yet when she was due to sing it in Piero Faggioni's 1989 Covent Garden production of *Il trovatore*, she cancelled. She reckons this fear of Verdi is partly induced by others who told her that 'if I sang Verdi I would lose my agility for Rossini and Haydn'.

She has recorded two Haydn operas – *La fedeltà premiata* and *Il mondo della Luna* – and considers him the most difficult composer she has ever sung. 'He is very German, both musically and emotionally. German composers have a strong identity stamped all over their music. You cannot change or add anything to their writing, or try to turn them into something they are not. Their music is much more definite, more fixed than Rossini's – where you feel freer and add something of your own – and has a very exact structure and economy. When you sing it you can be sure you are singing what they wanted you to sing and nothing more.'

The coloratura writing of each composer, such as Bach, Haydn, Handel, Mozart or Rossini, is entirely different. Rossini's is very springy and requires a particular technique: the voice must be perfectly placed on the breath; the breath itself controlled and dosed with minuscule precision; and the resonating cavities used in a way that allows the sound to emerge impeccably. Haydn's coloratura, on the other hand, does not spring out from the line but grows and stays within the arch of the musical phrases. It is more linear and demands the utmost physical concentration. In this case you must do what is written and nothing more. There is great purity about it, of the sort that one finds only in German music and which I always compare to a fresh, yet strong and healthy bird. Again, the adjective that springs to mind is 'substantial': there is nothing light or airy about it.

It took Valentini Terrani a long time to get into this style and learn her Haydn roles, especially Celia in *La fedeltà premiata*, which has four very difficult arias and a very extended tessitura. 'Of course what determines a voice is not its extension but its colour – the reason why in Conservatoires sopranos are often qualified as mezzos or vice versa. It is good to have a good upper and lower extension, and for your high and low notes to be secure, but I don't believe in too much jumping about from mezzo roles to soprano. (Black voices are an exception, because their voices have a totally different colour.) When the colour of a voice is amber, then even if it extends to high notes or lacks some low notes, it is a mezzo voice.

'Celia is definitely a mezzo part. Yet its extension is difficult for me. My voice has a very dark, velvety colour, and I always have to look for the metal in it. Had I been born in Germany, I would probably have been a Lieder singer specializing in Schubert, Schumann, Brahms, Wolf and Mahler. But being Italian, I developed the coloratura in my voice. I had a very good teacher at the Conservatoire in Padova [where Valentini Terrani still lives with her husband] who prevented me from making mistakes. With my strong feeling for drama I could easily have thrown myself into Verdi, which would have been my ruin. As it was, I decided it was better to be a good Rossini than a mediocre Verdi singer!'

FREDERICA VON STADE

'IT WOULD BE senseless to try to describe or analyse charm . . . but you know it when you see it. And you see it in all its magnetic mystery whenever Frederica von Stade steps on a stage,' wrote the *New York Times* after a performance in the title role of Massenet's *Chérubin* at Sante Fè in summer 1989. Charm does indeed figure prominently in this American lyric mezzo's portrayals, be they of trouser roles such as Mozart's Cherubino or Strauss's Octavian (whom she also invests with just the right touch of aristocratic bearing), her magical Mélisande or the part of Cinderella, both in Rossini's *Cenerentola* and Massenet's *Cendrillon*, to which she brings a transparent sincerity that greatly enhances its fairy-tale appeal.

The voice, described in the *New Yorker* as 'a real voice: a precise, supple, responsive instrument' – and dismissed by herself as 'my pipsqueak voice' – is ideal for classical roles and French opera: smooth, even, pleasant to the ear and carefully husbanded. Only a very occasional aberration, such as Adalgisa in her early days at the Met, has marred an otherwise impeccable choice of repertoire. Knowing full well that the dramatic mezzo parts such as Amneris, Eboli, Carmen were strictly out of bounds, von Stade has concentrated on Mozart (Cherubino, Dorabella, Sextus, Idamante); French roles which, besides those already mentioned, also include Charlotte in *Werther*, Iphise in Rameau's *Dardanus*, and the title role in Thomas's *Mignon*; a few Italian roles such as Penelope in Monteverdi's *Il ritorno d'Ulisse in patria*, Elena in Rossini's *La donna del lago* and a couple of contemporary heroines: Nina in Pasatieri's *The Seagull*, of which she sang the world première in Houston, and a part written specially for her by Dominick Argento – Tina in *The Aspern Papers*.

Von Stade's international career took off in 1973, when she inaugurated the Liebermann era at the Paris Opéra as Cherubino in Giorgio Strehler's production of *Le nozze di Figaro*, conducted by Solti, and sang the role in Peter Hall's Glyndebourne production. The impact of this coltish, believably androgynous Cherubino was such that invitations from the highest places immediately began to pour in: most importantly, Karajan asked her to sing Cherubino under his baton in the 1974 Salzburg production, directed by Ponnelle.

Fortunately, von Stade was well prepared for sudden fame. Born in New Jersey on 1 June 1945 a few months after her father was killed in action in Europe, 'Flicka' (her nickname to this day) grew up partly in Greece, partly in Washington and partly in Connecticut with her brother and mother, who remarried and then divorced. (On her mother's side, there is a Governor of Connecticut among her ancestors, and her paternal lineage includes a Burgomeister in Stade, a small town near Hannover.) Although a great aunt of hers was a singer who had performed at the Opéra Comique, von Stade didn't think of becoming a singer or even of studying music until comparatively late.

In 1966, after doing all sorts of odd jobs for several years (au pair in Paris for a year, salesgirl at Tiffany, secretary at the Stratford, Connecticut, Shakespeare Festival, her first stage role as the Beast in a children's production of *Beauty and the Beast* at the Long Wharf Theatre Company, New Haven), she returned to New York and decided to attend the Mannes School of Music on a part-time basis, in order to learn to read music. She had no plans for an operatic career at the time, but was soon encouraged to study full-time, and joined the School's opera workshop.

For a while it felt very strange for 'an ignoramus like me' to be among fellow students who had been playing instruments 'since they were in their playpens', and she never thought she would pass her first-year exams. But pass them she did and, in her second year, began taking singing lessons from a man who was to change her life, become and remain her mentor until his death thirteen years later: Sebastian Engelberg. Until then, as she confided in a profile by Janet Tassel in *Opera News*, she had always sung 'very low, alto stuff. During the first two lessons, I didn't sing a note. He just sort of described what the voice looked like and we talked. I was dying to jump in and sing. In the third lesson I sang a high C and nearly passed out. I can still feel those vibrations in my head. Engelberg eventually had me vocalizing up to C sharp while cultivating the plangency of my low register.'

After four years' study, Engelberg encouraged her to enter the 1969 Metropolitan Opera Auditions. Still unconvinced about whether she possessed the wherewithal for an operatic career, she agreed to try, pretending it was all a lark. She was immediately engaged by Rudolf Bing on a three-year contract and made her début at the Met in 1970 as one of the Three Boys in *Die Zauberflöte*. Bing liked her and was very good to her, giving her one plum part, such as Hansel, Rosina or Cherubino, each season, sandwiched among smaller roles such as Flora, Suzuki, Wowkle in *La fanciulla del West*, Stephano in *Roméo et Juliette*, Siebel, Nicklausse and Adalgisa. Thus, for three years, she had ample time to perfect her technique and learn her craft. Rolf Liebermann saw her Cherubino at the Met while making plans for his new regime in Paris, and signed her up for Cherubino right away. Henceforth she would spend most of her time in Europe, while still appearing at the Met on a regular basis until 1976.

To this day, Cherubino remains her favourite part, the one she rightly regards as her mascot. 'I realize that singing Cherubino at my age is bordering on obscenity, but I love it, as I love all the characters in this opera: Susanna, the Countess even the silliness of the Count. All are figureheads and represent such humour, passion, pathos and human frailty. *Le nozze di Figaro* is a very *truthful* opera, the most truthful of all Mozart's works.' In the Paris production, Strehler had urged her to be 'as beautiful as any beautiful woman and move like a dancer, not a soldier. You must be full of fire, like the overture, which is about you, Cherubino.' As she explained in *Opera News*, although Cherubino acts part of the time like a courtly page and part of the time as a bolting farm boy, he remains an aristocrat: 'Not as *raffiné* as Octavian, a bit more hysterical – just that much younger, of course. I love playing that boy, but it's hard – so pure and exposed. You'd think I could just whip off "Voi che sapete" like in the old days, but now I have to work at it.'

What about the differences, vocal and dramatic, between Mozart's Cherubino and Massenet's Chérubin, which von Stade first sang in a concert performance at Carnegie Hall in 1983? 'The differences are not only stylistic but also have to do with the plot: in Mozart, Cherubino is not the thrust of the team, but part of a *family* of closely related characters comprising the Countess, Susanna, Figaro and the Count. The real importance of this sublime piece, which has a definite point of view, lies in the nature of love, human nature and human relationships. Massenet's *Chérubin*, on the other hand, has no point of view as such, no lesson to teach. Chérubin – an older, more developed but still recognizable Cherubino – is the central figure, but the opera is an entertainment, a piece of fluff. Massenet was very conscious of the public's favour and knew exactly how to employ his talents to retain their attention and entertain them, by pacing his operas accordingly. Like a lot of French opera, *Chérubin* is about charm, chic and how the thing *looks*. There are no in-depth vocal or character studies.'

Vocally, she found Chérubin much easier to sing than Cherubino, which is 'so pure, clean and precise. Chérubin requires a high, rather bright sound, because the character itself is very bright, very much about pleasant words, lightheartedness and frivolity. As always, Massenet is very, very specific in his instructions. He tells you exactly what he wants. In this respect he is one of the most *careful* composers, desperately concerned about speed and tempo. There is an overall sense of measure and a very specific, carefully calculated sense of timing. The pieces are most successful when both conductors and singers observe these instructions and allow them to flow along, with their own momentum. They should never be made to sound "Puccinian".'

The times she most enjoyed singing Massenet were with very strict, precise conductors who didn't allow themselves the luxury of going on a personal 'trip' – something to which the music *can* lend itself. 'But then,' von Stade rightly thinks, 'it loses its charm, and all those very deliberate colours, which are definitely *not* Puccinian! Everything in French opera happens within a context of restraint and a certain reserve. The music is never *extravagant*; it is always controlled. Mind you, up to a point, this is true of all music. Every style, including verismo, has limitations beyond which you shouldn't go. There is no such thing as total abandon in singing. It doesn't exist. Voice production has to be so carefully regulated and controlled at all times that it precludes total abandon. Callas came closest to conveying a sense of what *looked* like abandon, but which in reality was the result of the most rigorous emotional, dramatic and vocal control.'

Von Stade lived in Paris for a long time. Apart from her time as an au pair, she and her first husband, vocal coach Peter Elkus, made it their home for about seven years – from 1976 to her return to the Met in 1982–83, when the couple settled in the countryside around New York. She feels those years in Paris helped enhance her understanding of the French psyche. She professes 'enormous respect and admiration for French values, qualities and standards and for French people who, once won over, make deep and committed friends. And all their qualities are eloquently expressed in French music.'

The year von Stade moved to Europe, she also appeared in the Paris Opéra's 1976 American Bicentennial Tour as Cherubino, and made her début at La Scala as Marguerite in *La damnation de Faust*, soon followed by a production of *La Cenerentola* directed by Ponnelle, conducted by Abbado, filmed for television and also taken on a Bicentennial Tour to the United States. Singing Cinderella both in Rossini's *La Cenerentola* and in Massenet's *Le Cendrillon*, which she first sang in 1979 in Washington and Ottawa (having taken a long sabbatical in 1977–78 after the birth of her first child, Jenny Rebecca), has given her a deep insight into the character of Cinderella and the nature of this fairy tale. *La Cenerentola* she considers a classical Italian and 'a deeply spiritual piece. It is about the nature of goodness and is full of symbolism and universal

truths, all expressed in a very classical form. As always, Rossini's music is
very comfortable to sing – a massage for the voice because you can never
push it in those coloraturas – and so well composed and specific that
singing Rossini well can become a lifelong study. When it is not sung as
precisely and perfectly as it should be, it loses its charm. But when it's
done the right way it becomes a most exciting, electric experience, real
fireworks. I consider myself fortunate to have had the opportunity to
study this role with the best Italian coach in the business, Ubaldo Gardini,
for whom I have a deep, undying affection. Studying Rossini with him
was truly an eye-opening experience. For hours and days we worked on
rhythms, accents, the importance of the words and finding ways to
accomplish the composer's musical intentions.'

Le Cendrillon is a very different kind of piece: a pure fairy-tale and a
feast to the eye. It goes from aria to ensemble to ballet in a positively
enchanting way. Again, it's not very deep. The Massenet of *Chérubin* and
Le Cendrillon (which she has recorded for CBS) was the Andrew Lloyd
Webber of his day. His musical formulae were tried and tested and
usually successful.

Von Stade was to discover a different, more profound side of Massenet
when, a year after singing *Le Cendrillon* in Washington and Ottawa, she
sang her first Charlotte in *Werther* at Covent Garden in 1980, with José
Carreras in the title role. The conductor was Colin Davis, who was also
new to the work and did at times make it sound slightly Puccinian,
occasionally putting his singers under strain. However, Charlotte is a part
von Stade always enjoys singing and, strange though this may sound,
always finds 'fun'. The reason is that, after portraying so many trouser
roles and innocent, Cinderella-types, 'it was wonderful, at last, to play a
heroine who, by Act III, has left her "little-girl world" to experience a
great passion, which is, after all, what opera is all about! In this sense,
Charlotte is quite a departure from my other roles and the closest I've
come to a Tosca, to verismo. Vocally it was difficult because it starts off
quite low, then gets high and very dramatic. The conductor is crucial at
this point because if he doesn't control his orchestra he can really blast
your throat.'

Dramatically, she doesn't find Charlotte all that sympathetic at the
beginning, 'but she becomes more so as well as *musically* more
sympathetic as the piece goes on, when she begins to share some of
Werther's very poetic utterances and romantic lines. In Goethe's play,
she is much cooler than in Massenet, who has actually written a lot of
courage and sincerity into her music. By the end, the music clearly
illustrates the fact that, for her, life is finished after Werther's death . . .
It's awful to think of her spending the rest of her days in that desert

landscape as far as the emotions are concerned. Of course, it's all within
the context of the times they lived in. Nowadays, Charlotte would have
had the choice of other options.'

Von Stade's was a moving and affecting portrayal, justly praised by the
late Harold Rosenthal, editor and founder of *Opera*. 'Although the opera
is called *Werther*,' he wrote, 'the most memorable performances on stage
came from the Charlotte, the delectable Frederica von Stade. Perhaps
ideally one would prefer a slightly larger voice in this role in a house the
size of Covent Garden, or one that has slightly more colour to it; but Miss
von Stade did so much that was moving, because she was so natural and
made the conversational passages so realistic that one was caught up in
Charlotte's problems and shared her feelings.'

One of von Stade's vintage portrayals, again in a French role, is the title
role in Debussy's *Pelléas et Mélisande*, hailed as 'the Mélisande of one's
dreams' and 'the sensation of the season' by *Le Monde*, while *Le Figaro*
devoted front-page coverage to Georges Lavelli's controversial 1977
production at the Paris Opéra, which caused an uproar. (Among other
things, it had a set shaped like an oval mirror, and a chair on which von
Stade had to stand during the scene from the Tower.) The only thing von
Stade remembers being criticized for was her French. Yet she feels
Mélisande *should* be alien, *should* have a slight accent, like the role's first
interpreter, Mary Garden.

'She is one of the most enigmatic characters in the repertoire. Her
ambiguity is actually written into the music, which appears to describe
Mélisande's nature much more than the words, which seem to come from
another world. Indeed, the whole work is full of symbolism. It can take
anyone anywhere they wish to be taken. What, for example, is the
significance of the ring? One doesn't really know. But one goes along with
the music, which alone seems to explain the feelings running through the
piece. But despite its ambiguity, *Pelléas et Mélisande* is a very passionate
opera.' (And nowhere more so than in the EMI recording under Herbert
von Karajan, who makes the work more passionate and overtly romantic
than one had thought possible.)

The scenes von Stade enjoyed most were those with Pelléas, in which
Mélisande is almost 'tangible'. 'Momentarily there is something happy
about her, you get a flash of a confident, playful young woman, almost a
Zerlina. And, after the scene with Golaud, you *need* that. I mean, how
terrorized is she? Again, we don't know. She is certainly narcissistic and
enjoys being Golaud's plaything. Do I feel I know Mélisande? No, not
really. There are moments when I *like* her enormously, and moments
when I'm not so sure I do. Her reactions to life and to her child are very
ambiguous. In this sense, she is the embodiment of the eternal female

psyche that conceals things inside it. Boys and men don't do that, there is no corner of their souls they hold back. There is also that fantasy, that part of the female soul that can construct an entire inner world. Maybe that's the sort of person she is. That's why Golaud is driven to distraction. I mean, you want to *shake* her! And maybe that's why you don't care too much about what happens to Mélisande. You care much more about what happens to Pelléas.

'Someone once said she is far more calculating and acid than that, but I don't feel this at all. Basically I think the role of Mélisande is going to come from the person who sings it – and this, of course, makes it even more elusive and changeable. This is all very well to talk about, but how do you do it? How do you put it across? Of course a lot depends on the director. But however one portrays Mélisande dramatically, it is crucial to remember that you, the artist, have to be terrifically concentrated and specific. Otherwise the audience will get very lost. And as I get older, it's important for me to work on keeping the lightness in the voice. For although Mélisande's line tends to be low, she should never sound heavy, there should always be a lightness about her, because it's in the *music*, which is a colourist's feast. [Von Stade's performance on record was praised in *Gramophone* for precisely this reason: "She well conveys Mélisande's wide-eyed innocence and simplicity by her purity of voice and lightness of tone, and makes credible the transition from the startled gazelle of the opening to the awakening woman of Act IV."] Then there is the problem of how to pronounce the words. And, like the Verlaine poems set to music by Debussy, one wonders what they're *about*. But does it matter? It's the music and, as with so much French poetry, the atmosphere created by the words that says it all.'

Poetry and songs play an important part in von Stade's repertoire. She does a large number of Lieder recitals (in May 1990 she was invited to perform at the White House by President Bush at a Gala Dinner in honour of President Gorbachev during the Summit meeting and, in February 1991 in honour of the Queen of Denmark), and enjoys putting together amusing and unusual programmes. One of her favourite combinations might include Schoenberg's *Cabaret Songs* 'which are a scream', some very attractive Strauss songs discovered in the late fifties by Elizabeth Schwarzkopf 'which sound more like Schumann', a handful of American songs, the famous aria from Rossini's *Otello* and 'lots and lots' of French songs. 'There are so many things you can say in French which you can't in English and I am more comfortable in French than in German', she declares, despite her ancestry.

Von Stade's principal German roles are the Composer in *Ariadne auf Naxos* and Octavian in *Der Rosenkavalier*, which she first sang in 1976 at the Holland Festival, and later during the Met's 1983 spring tour. Again, it's a role that benefits from her pedigree and always draws good reviews. 'Miss von Stade, singing magnificently, was thoroughly convincing both as the adolescent youth and Mariandel. Her walk, her posture, her every gesture were totally integrated in an outstanding performance,' wrote *Opera* after the première at the 1976 Holland Festival. As she explained in *Opera News* during the time of the Met spring tour, 'Aside from having to stand in a certain way because of a costume with big tails and a sword, more than anything Octavian is an aristocrat: he holds his head high, his carriage is impeccable. To me this bearing is what determines the physical approach to Octavian. His posture should say: "Look at me, I'm a Count." He's the absolute product of his lifestyle. I love that age in boys anyway. If they feel good about themselves it comes out – they are not falsely modest. Octavian might be boastful, but he's not offensive. Why shouldn't he be boastful? He moves from palace to beautiful palace. Head to toe in silver, coming in on that crash of music – he's just too gorgeous to be true! And he's also full of his own sexual pride and discovery – the whole Mrs Robinson thing. To go through that initiation with that superb woman, the Marschallin, instead of fumbling around with some kid his own age. He has had the *best*, and it's been done with such taste, finesse and fun.'

For a long time, von Stade's own life was sheer fun: her career was thriving, she was apparently happy in her marriage to Peter Elkus, a vocal coach and former fellow student at Mannes College, whom she had married in Paris in 1973, and a doting mother to her two little girls, taking endless pains to ensure her work left her ample time for real mothering. A devout Catholic, she confided in 1983 that she could 'cry for all my joys: my family, my work, my career'. But in the late eighties, her marriage suddenly broke up. Shattered, she seemed for a while unwilling and unable to cope with career considerations. Gradually, though, she found the strength to cope. Her career is in full swing again and last December she married Californian Michael Gorman, who has 'nothing whatsoever to do with music'. She was preparing to move to just outside San Francisco and busily looking for schools for her daughters. In fact, looking after her girls is a crucial factor in deciding what to sing and where. 'Kids mean your energies change,' she said when Jenny and Lisa, born in 1980, were younger. 'I want to play with my kids and watch them develop, not give them over so someone else can have all the fun. The thing about kids is they give *you* so much, especially when they're little; the blood still seems to be flowing between you.' She went on to confess she needed them as much as they needed her, and her feelings haven't changed.

Now, with plans for Penelope and Cherubino in San Francisco and Mélisande in Los Angeles, von Stade is happy to return to 'old parts, old friends like Cherubino, which I will sing for the last time at the Met in 1991–92. It's lovely, now that the girls are growing up and I'm devoting so much time to them, to walk into parts I'm familiar and comfortable with.' She has always firmly believed an artist has to keep on learning and improving all the time. Certain things become easier with maturity and experience while others become more difficult because she can no longer rely on that instinctive thrust of youth. Suddenly it's no longer important to do more but to do things *better*. Yet, as she explained in a newspaper interview, she doesn't believe music is about perfection. The composers were perfectly aware that each and every one of their interpreters would have human weaknesses. 'It's about humility and, more than that, it's about humanity.'

Index

The more important references are indicated by **bold** figures. '*n*' refers to a footnote; 'q' stands for 'quoted'. Use has been made of the following abbreviations: spr – soprano; mspr – mezzo-soprano; tnr – tenor; bar – baritone; bsbar – bass-baritone; bs – bass; accomp – accompanist; adm – administrator (including opera house intendants and managers); cdr – conductor; dir – director or producer; tchr – teacher.